The Underground Guide to
Excel 5.0 FOR
WINDOWS™

Slightly
    Askew
        Advice
            from
                Two
                    Excel
                        Wizards

Lee Hudspeth
and
Timothy-James Lee

ADDISON-WESLEY PUBLISHING COMPANY

Reading, Massachusetts • Menlo Park, California • New York • Don Mills, Ontario
Wokingham, England • Amsterdam • Bonn • Sydney • Singapore • Tokyo
Madrid • San Juan • Paris • Seoul • Milan • Mexico City • Taipei

Many of the designations used by manufacturers and sellers to distinguish their products are claimed as trademarks. Where those designations appear in this book, and Addison-Wesley was aware of a trademark claim, the designations have been printed in initial capital letters or all capital letters.

The authors and publishers have taken care in preparation of this book, but make no expressed or implied warranty of any kind and assume no responsibility for errors or omissions. No liability is assumed for incidental or consequential damages in connection with or arising out of the use of the information or programs contained herein.

Library of Congress Cataloging-in-Publication Data

Hudspeth, Lee.
    The underground guide to Excel 5.0 for windows : slightly askew advice from two Excel wizards / Lee Hudspeth and Timothy-James Lee.
       p.   cm.
Includes index.
ISBN 0-201-40651-9
    1. Microsoft Excel for Windows.   2. Business--Computer programs.
3. Electronic spreadsheets. I. Lee, Timothy-James. II. Title.
HF5548.4.M523H83   1994
005.369--dc20   94-34330
                                    CIP

Series Hack: Woody Leonhard
Sponsoring Editor: Kathleen Tibbetts
Technical Editor: Donald A. Buchanan
Project Manager: Eleanor McCarthy
Production Coordinator: Lora L. Ryan
Cover design: Jean Seal
Text Design: Kenneth L. Wilson, Wilson Graphics & Design
Set in 10 point Palatino by Rob Mauhar, CIP of Coronado

1 2 3 4 5 6 7 8 9 -MA- 9897969594
First printing, September 1994

Addison-Wesley books are available for bulk purchases by corporations, institutions, and other organizations. For more information please contact the Corporate, Government and Special Sales Department at (800) 238-9682.

Contents

Foreword   v

Acknowledgments   vii

Chapter 1   **Read Me First, Please!**   1

Now Just Why Did You Buy This Book?   1
If You Do Numbers, Then You've Come to the Right Place   2
This Spreadsheet Is Empty!   4
Anybody Got a Map?   6
GoTo(ing) My Way?   9
Lexicon: It'll Get You Every Time   13
New and Improved Standard Toolbar   20
Formatting Bar Surgery   33
Tools Options: A Walk on the Wild Side   37
Zooming   42
TipWizard: Good Job, Redmond (Really)   44
Multidimension Schmultidimension   46
Safe Spreadsheets   47

Chapter 2   **The Playing Field**   51

The Workbook   51
A Sheet by Any Other Name   53
Text, Numbers, and Formulas: A Hat Trick   60

Chapter 3   **The Stage Is Set**   77

Data Entry, Stage Left   77
Data Editing, Stage Right   86
Drag-and-Drop: Center Stage   88

Chapter 4   **Formulas, Functions, and Names, Oh My!—Tools for Building**   93

Range Names: Manna from Heaven   93
Formulas and Functions   110

Chapter 5   **Auditing—It's a Good Thing**   143

DefCon1—The Big Picture   143
DefCon2—The Auditing Toolbar   151
DefCon3—The Many Faces of Excel   157
DefCon4—Edit Go To Special   164

Chapter 6   **The Output—Formatting, Charting, and Printing**   171

Formats—Put on a Happy Face   171
As You Can See by This Chart   178
Printing—The Final Frontier   190

Chapter 7   **Data Analysis—the Quest for Fire**   203

Managing Lists of Stuff   203
Data Analysis   227

Chapter 8   **Supercharging Excel**   235

Templates   235
What Happens When You Start Excel   242
Working With Others   247

Chapter 9   **OLE 2.0 Where Marketing Meets Technology**   257

Information at Your Digital Extremities™   257
Reach Out and Touch Some Objects   264
Objects.Envelope.Stretch WorkIt:=True   273
A Caveat Cornucopia   285

Chapter 10   **VBA, the Programmatic Side of the Coin**   287

XLM Veterans Take Heed   289
Required Reading for Everyone   290
Kick-off: Tools Options Module Settings   291
OLEAuto and the Heart of Gold   292
Welcome to Your New Home, the Visual Basic Module   293
Doing with a Macro What You've Already Done Manually,
  Only Faster   298

Appendix   **Assistance and Augmentation**   311

Where to Get Professional Help (Your Shrink Notwithstanding)   311
Other Nifty Stuff   314

Foreword

Welcome to *The Underground Guide to Excel 5.0 for Windows*, our between-the-eyes excursion into Excel territory. Like the other *Underground Guides*, *TUG/XL* offers a unique look into the dark underbelly of the beast, and clues you in on the best ways to make Excel jump through your hoops. No holds barred. No party line. You get the straight scoop, minus the sugar coating. Excel cinema vertité, as it were, with a healthy dose of off-the-wall fun. If you've been having a tough time with Excel, struggling with the beasts within, this book shows you how to fight back. And win.

We're not talking about the 99th rewrite of the user's manual, or 10,001 obscure tips you'll look at today and forget tomorrow. Lee Hudspeth and T. J. Lee aim for the jugular—the parts of Excel you use every day—and show you how to make Excel work *for* you, not against you, all day, every day. What to use. More importantly, what to avoid. Lee and T. J. live, breathe, eat, and sleep Excel, and it shows.

I hope this book helps save a bit of your sanity, and pulls you out of a tough spot or two or three. That's what the *Underground Guides* are all about: nitty-gritty first-hand advice you won't find anywhere else, told in a way that won't put you to sleep, from the folks who have slugged it out in the trenches and returned to tell the unvarnished truth.

Enjoy!

Woody Leonhard, Series Hack

Acknowledgments

This book is dedicated to our families. Jim's family—Loretta, Andreana, Jason, and Victoria. Lee's family—Liz.

Jim and Lee would like to jointly toast Woody Leonhard, our series editor, mentor, guru's guru, and friend; Claudette Moore, our literary agent; Kathleen Tibbetts (sponsoring editor) and all the fine folks at Addison-Wesley; and Don Buchanan for your support and encouragement throughout this project. We couldn't have done it without you.

Thanks and kudos also to Eric Wells and all the members of the Microsoft Excel development team.

Lee Hudspeth would like to thank the following folks for their direct and indirect contributions to this work. Liz Harsch, companion and soul mate, for supporting me throughout. Eloise and George, for their inexpressibly fine and noble parenting. Gloria for accepting me wholly into her family. Dr. Scott Fraser, a Renaissance Man of the highest caliber, for his mentorship and friendship. Vic Brzezinski, Danny Dunham, Liz Harsch, Jack Jonaitis, Beth Lee, and Michael Lee, surfing compañeros whose adventurous spirits I'll always look up to. Michelle Jacobi for coaching me in German.

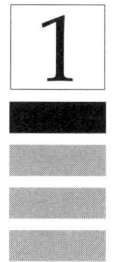

1 Read Me First, Please!

Look to the essence of a thing, whether it be a point of doctrine, of practice, or of interpretation.

Marcus Aurelius Antoninus
Meditations

NOW JUST WHY DID YOU BUY THIS BOOK?

Aaaaalrightie then.

Ace Ventura, Pet Detective

Customizable toolbars…auditing…templates…OLE 2.0…unrepentant bugs. These are some of many quintessential concepts we'll explore with you in *The Underground Guide to Excel 5.0 for Windows*, a place where truth speaks louder than Madison Avenue. And we've got truth by the gleaming, merciless truck load.

Consider us your Excel tour guides, with a twist. The twist is—*we're gonna pay you for the trip*, not vice versa. That's right. In exchange for the nominal price of this book, we're going to roll out the intellectual red carpet and do a full-on Excel brain dump from our heads to yours. So strap on your jet-pack, friend, and *let's ride!*

Maybe you've been working with Excel for a while. Like most users, you **Ask Pareto** probably have taught yourself just what you needed to deal with the crisis of the moment. This has most likely left some gaps in your overall knowledge, and maybe you wonder if you are getting your money's worth (or more importantly, your precious time's worth) out of this amazingly powerful program. Hey, it's a fact that 80% of the users only use 20% of the features. *Maybe it's time to get a handle on things!*

But it's a big jump from plain old spreadsheets to Excel 5. Excel has been around for over nine years and this current version is a powerhouse of really useful features, but it also has a lot of things that smack more of marketing than of meat.

Hacking a clear path

So what are we going to do for you? Well, we're *not* going to describe every feature and function because you can spend years mastering every nuance of this application. Nor are we going to try to rewrite the *User's Guide* (there are plenty of books available that do that already). You've things to do and models to build and can't spend your time trying to separate the wheat from the chaff. Our job is to hack a clear path to the features you need and to give you the know-how to get useful work done. (What a concept!)

We're going to deal with Excel on its own terms. We'll learn to think as Excel thinks. We'll get up close and personal and try to have fun as we go along.

And, because Redmond wants everyone to buy Excel as part of the new Microsoft Office suite, we will try to deal with some of the issues of switching between the more popular components of Office like Excel and WinWord. After all, Microsoft is touting the consistent operation between the Office suite programs. *Heh, heh, heh.*

We'll take a look at where Microsoft did it right and where they, uhm, didn't do it right. Speaking of which, this book is based on Excel version 5.0. It's possible that some of the problems mentioned in this book will be eliminated in later versions of Excel 5 (*we* certainly hope so!). So, if you hear talk of 5.0a or 5.1, you should get it immediately. Call Microsoft at 800-426-9400, or call your local Microsoft office and make sure you have the latest version of Excel.

We hope that a lot of things in here will have you thinking, "Damn, so that's how that works!" So enough of this blather, let's crunch some numbers!

IF YOU DO NUMBERS, THEN YOU'VE COME TO THE RIGHT PLACE

> None of us really understands what's going on with all these numbers.
>
> David Stockman
> on the U.S. budget, 1981

Numbers, anyone?

Let's talk about Excel's raison d'être—numbers. Not pretty 3-D charts, not composing letters, not yellow sticky notes, and (sorry Redmond) not presentation slides. Yeah, you can do that stuff with Excel. Slam dunk. But when it comes right down to it, where the rubber meets the road, Excel's meat and potatoes is numbers, numbers, numbers.

Okay, we admit it. When the only program we knew was Lotus 1.0, we did compose a few business letters inside our spreadsheet application. After all, when all you have is a hammer, the whole world looks like a nail. But that was then, and this is now.

Excel today is a mad scientist's vision of the accountant's 14-column work paper on steroids. Sure, you can build a spiffy front-end in Excel to a back-end database. Hey, sure you can use Excel as a database itself. Fun stuff. But the fundamental reason you use Excel is to pull numbers into an environment where you can easily define relationships between them and manipulate them to your heart's content. There's that key word again—numbers. So if it's numbers you want, you can get them by the truckload with this application.

And what an environment you get! Each worksheet in Excel is 256 columns wide and 16,384 rows from top to bottom. (And the only limit to the number of worksheets in a single workbook is available memory.) Since we're talking numbers, let's see, using Excel's default settings, that's about 11/16 of an inch per column, for a total of 2816/16, which works out to 176 inches, or about 15 feet wide. Each row is about 5/32 of an inch, for a total of 81920/32, or 2560 inches, which is a whopping 213 feet from top to bottom. **Did you say 3195 square feet?**

So an empty worksheet is 15 feet by 213 feet, or 3195 square feet. Hmmm, enough to wallpaper your entire house with some left over for the garage. Sounds impressive, doesn't it? Well, for reasons we'll get to in a minute, that may not be as impressive as it sounds. For now, suffice it to say, Excel gives you all the space you can use.

In Excel you put stuff into cells in the worksheet and establish relationships between the cells. Cells contain numbers, text, or formulas. Formulas can, in turn, return numbers or text. That's it. Sounds simple, and really it is. Oh, you can draw on the worksheet and embed a chart on the worksheet, but these things do not go into the cells, but rather they float above them. This floating area is the graphic layer of the worksheet. It can actually be pretty useful, but the real work in Excel is done inside the cells. You establish relationships between cells and groups of cells, and this is where Excel's power lies.

Back in the halcyon days when spreadsheet applications were just a gleam in somebody's bloodshot eye, spreadsheet applications were viewed as a way to put programming power directly into the supplicant hands of novices. After all, a formula is but a relatively short and sweet program, *n'est-ce pas*?

In the example in Figure 1.1, cell A3 contains a program that assigns a value to a variable (a location in memory), specifically, itself! The value assigned to cell A3 is the sum of two other variables, specifically, the values in cells A1 and A2. (Note **Zen and the art of molecular programming**

	A	B	C
1	2	2	
2	2	2	
3	4	=A1+A2	
4			

Figure 1.1 Two Plus Two Equals Four, Excel Style

that in column B we've provided a view of the contents of each cell to the left in column A. This way, you can see both the cell results and contents at a single glance.)

The clever part of this design is that the source code (represented in Excel as formulas) is embedded inside a predefined two-dimensional table (represented in Excel as a worksheet) of variables (cells). These cells have a split personality—they can display the results of the individual microprograms within them without disrupting the source code that defines them. These microprograms (formulas) can be run across the entire spreadsheet at once by any of a number of simple acts—opening the spreadsheet, changing a value somewhere, adding a value somewhere else, choosing the Calculate Now button, and so on. This Zen-like process of self-actualizing cell values based on internally stored formulas does indeed empower us Common Folk, but it can be our downfall as well. Thus was born *The Underground Guide to Excel*.

THIS SPREADSHEET IS *EMPTY*!

An empty bag cannot stand upright.

Benjamin Franklin
Poor Richard's Almanac, 1740

So you've installed Excel and fired it up and what do you see? Nothing. An empty worksheet. In previous versions of Excel you got a single empty worksheet. In Excel 5 you get several empty sheets, 16 to be exact. Excel 5 is a true multidimensional spreadsheet application and one of the folks up in Redmond decided that 16 sheets (all in a single .XLS file) was just the ticket. We'll talk about this whole multidimensional shtick shortly.

Can we talk?   You see, this is the secret about Excel: it is a development environment. It doesn't do a single blessed thing until you build something! Now, the marketing types don't like to say *development environment* because it is tooooo scary and they don't want to run off any potential customers, but the kids are in bed and we can talk about it like it really is. As we said earlier, you have to program a spreadsheet at the cellular level. Really. Naw, we are not talking here about macros or VBA programming, just the everyday programming that you have already done without knowing it.

Let's look at another example:

```
=SUM(A1:A10)
```

This is programming! Sure it is. You have a function, =SUM(); and you give this function an **argument**, in this case a range of cells, A1:A10; and the function returns to you a result, which is the total of all the values in the range. It's programming plain and simple, and if you have ever added two numbers together in a spreadsheet, you've been doing it. All you need to do is get a handle on the terms. A **function** accepts things (arguments) and returns a **result**. The first step in becoming well versed in anything is learning its special lexicon. We'll throw in more terms as we go along.

The last section revealed that a single worksheet was about 15 by 213 feet. Let's do a quick reality check here. Let's say you start entering the number 100 into each cell in a new worksheet. You start with column A, row 1, and work your way down to the end of the column and start over in the next column. Well, by the time you get about 70 columns or so filled in, your interest will wane and your rip roarin' 486/66 PC with 16 megs of memory will slow to a real crawl. We're talking molasses in January here! Keep it up and you will soon get a nasty "Out of memory" message (or worse) and that will be that.

So why did Microsoft create a worksheet larger than you can really use? It's a holdover from the old spreadsheet wars when the mentality of "my worksheet is larger than your worksheet" ruled the marketing roost. The spreadsheet wars are over (Excel won, by the way), but the legacy is this huge work area that you cannot fill.

Spreadsheet wars

Not only is a single worksheet huge, Excel 5 gives you 16 sheets in a single file (called a **workbook**) to start with by default. This is a far cry from the old Excel 4 paradigm where you had one worksheet per file. Oh, you could *bind* multiple sheets into a *workbook* in Excel 4, but now that feature is gone. In Excel 5 every file is a workbook.

When you start up Excel 5, you get a workbook (which we will oft times refer to as a "book" for simplicity) with the default name of Book1. A book can contain multiple sheets, as in worksheets, charts, modules, dialogs, and macros (this is the old macrosheet provided to maintain backward compatibility with previous versions of Excel). All sheets are in a single file, and Excel gives that file the familiar .XLS extension. No more do you have separate .XLC files for charts or .XLMs for macros. Ah, simplify, simplify.

Okay, you're in Excel and you know that nothing useful happens unless you build something. You know you have this humongous work area to build this something in, but before you start building anything, we should talk about navigating these sheet thingys.

ANYBODY GOT A MAP?

Toto, I have a feeling we're not in Kansas anymore.

Dorothy
The Wizard of Oz

Welcome to the Excel workbook. Let's deal with the keys to successful navigation in both an empty worksheet and a nonempty worksheet (and believe us, there's a big difference).

Waiter, Put This on My Tab

Thanks to Borland's Quattro Pro, all God's spreadsheets now got tabs. Since each book can have multiple sheets, you need a quick way to move from sheet to sheet and tabs fit the bill (pun intended, *<groan>*). See Figure 1.2.

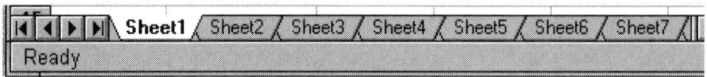

Figure 1.2 Excel's Got Tabs!

You can name each sheet by double-clicking on its tab. You can name a sheet anything you want as long as you keep it under 32 characters, including spaces. You can use any characters you like, too, except for * ? / \ : ' all of which have special meanings in Excel. It's really pretty cool (yea Microsoft!).

Rock and scroll   To move from sheet to sheet, click on the tab of the sheet you want to make active. The active sheet is the one whose tab is not gray and whose name is bolded. But, hey, you got 16 sheets to start with and all their tabs aren't visible. No problem. You can use the VCR-like gizmos to scroll through the tab list. See Figure 1.3.

Figure 1.3 Navigating Your Sheets

The triangles on the buttons shown in Figure 1.3 point in the direction they cause your tabs to scroll. The inner triangles scroll one tab at a time, and the outer triangles take you directly to the first tab or the last tab of all the sheets.

To see a complete list of all sheets in the current book, right-click on any of the triangles shown in Figure 1.3.

You can also grab the tab split box and drag it right or left to make more or fewer tabs visible (at the expense of your horizontal scroll bar, but hey, TANSTAAFL*!) See Figure 1.4.

Figure 1.4 Tab Split Box

Right-clicking on the tab pops up the shortcut menu for manipulating sheets, which is the handiest way to insert or delete a sheet. However, to move a sheet (that is, change its location in the tab order), left-click on the tab and drag it to the left or right. A triangle indicator shows you where the sheet will be inserted.

To copy a sheet, hold down the Control key before you start dragging. Think of the "C" in Control as "copy": CTRL + drag to copy. Piece o' cake. You'll see this Control-drag technique again when copying cells in the sheet.

"C" as in "Ah, I *copy* that Red Leader."

You can select several tabs at a time and perform an action on all selected sheets at once. This works just like making multiple selections in any Windows list box (any list box that allows multiple selections, that is; don't you just love consistency?) You select the first tab you want and SHIFT + click, (hold down the Shift key and left-click) on the last tab you want. When you SHIFT + click you select all the tabs between the first selected and the tab you SHIFT + click on. In other words, you get all the contiguous tabs between the selected tabs. To select noncontiguous tabs, you CTRL + click (hold down the Control key and left-click) on each tab you want to select.

There and Back Again

> I like being able to move around quickly.
>
> · attributed to the Flash
>   *DC Comics*

So you chose the tab of Sheet1. The currently selected cell is the **active cell** and there is no data in sight. Now what? Let's get the different modes of travel down first. Use the arrow keys to move the active cell—nothing new here. Oh, and you can use the scroll bars. You remember scroll bars, right? Standard Windows stuff. Click the left arrow, and the perspective of the sheet is shifted one column to the left. Click the right arrow on the horizontal scroll bar, and the perspective of the sheet is shifted one column to the right. You can drag the scroll boxes. All old stuff. One advantage of the scroll bars is that you can change the perspective on the current sheet *without* changing the active cell.

---

*There Ain't No Such Thing As A Free Lunch.

When in Excel Do as Excel Does

Oh, before we forget, if you are using the Lotus navigation keystrokes, stop it! If you aren't—great, no problem. If you're not sure, run through the following steps:

1. Choose Options from the Tools menu.

2. Click on the Transition tab in the Options dialog box.

3. Make sure the Transition Navigation Keys check box under Settings is *not* checked.

4. Click on OK.

If this setting is not turned off, *nothing* in this entire section will work properly and you'll think we're crazy. Anyway, *this is Excel*, so drop the crutches and do it right.

Da ZAP!

Now since Sheet1 is empty, you can shoot the active cell all the way out to column IV (255 columns to the right of column A) at warp speed with a simple key combination, CTRL + RIGHT ARROW. CTRL + LEFT ARROW **brings you back to column A, zap! Use** CTRL + DOWN ARROW **to zap down to row 16,384. (You didn't think we were kidding about all those rows, didja?) This zap technique is really quite useful for bopping around a sheet.**

If you zap in a direction, up, down, or whatever, the active cell travels in your chosen direction until it hits a cell with contents and it stops with that cell selected or until it can't go any further.

There is a mouse-only version of zapping that requires you to double-click on the edge of the active cell. Not only does this require precise mouse technique, but it *generally* moves one cell *less* than the CTRL + key method. For example, if A1 is empty and C1:D1 have contents, CTRL + RIGHT ARROW moves the active cell to C1, while double-clicking on the right border of A1 moves the active cell to B1. Unlike the CTRL + key zap, if the adjacent cells are all empty, double-clicking the cell border doesn't move the active cell at all. Microsoft calls this Auto Select.

Down, down, down the dark ladder
So what about this zapping stuff, you say? Consider this: you have a spreadsheet with all kinds of data in it. You want to get to the last entry in column D. Easy. If the data in column D is contiguous, click on the first cell in D with contents and zap down (CTRL + DOWN ARROW).

What if the data in D is noncontiguous, you know, a few cells with numbers, a blank cell, some data, some blanks? Even with zapping, you could be old and gray before you reach the last cell in the column with contents. Try this: go to an empty column, zap down to row 16,384, arrow over to column D (or use the Goto technique we will discuss in a minute to get to the bottom of column D), and zap up. Bingo, you're there.

If you are already up on the keyboard navigation key combinations in Excel, you should know that Microsoft changed a couple of the old standards. It used to be that you could shift the active cell one screen left with CTRL + PAGE UP and one screen right with CTRL + PAGE DOWN. Well, no more. These key combinations now change the active sheet one tab left or right. The new and improved way to shift the active cell one screen left is ALT + PAGE UP, and ALT + PAGE DOWN to go right. That's the price of progress.

Home, Home on the Range

Fortunately, the Home key still takes you to column A in the active row, and CTRL + HOME always takes you to column A, row 1. Thank goodness for that because we use these two all the time!

The opposite of CTRL + HOME is CTRL + END, which takes you to the lower rightmost cell that defines the last row and last column that contain data. For example, if you have a sheet with an entry in cell D6 and an entry in A27 and you hit CTRL + END, the active cell will be D27.

> CTRL + END **can be annoying in that it deems whatever cell is originally in the furthest southeast corner to forever be the end. If Z162 is your "end" cell, Z162 it stays. You can delete rows 10 through 163 and columns M through AB, but** CTRL + END **will still take you to Z162.**

Dynamically speaking

If you save the book that contains the sheet and reopen it, Excel will concede that Z162 is no longer the end cell for that sheet. Why can't Excel dynamically change the end cell? Dunno. Bet it has to do with the way Excel recalcs the sheet. Anyway, Excel has behaved this way since Hector was a pup, but it would sure be nice if it was a little smarter and could track the end cell dynamically while you are working in the sheet.

GOTO(ING) MY WAY?

> Remember, wherever you go, there you are.
>
> Buckaroo Banzai
> *Adventures Across the 8th Dimension*

Another way to get from A to B (no pun intended) is with the Go To command (you can choose Go To from the Edit menu if you want to, but everyone around here just presses F5). Hit F5; type in a cell coordinate, like H2001; and click OK. Faster than you can say "engage," poof, you're there!

But the really cool thing is that the Go To dialog box "remembers" the last four cells (or ranges) you visited. Say you're in B237 and want to be in X10000. No problemo, press F5, type in the coordinate X10000, and hit OK. Bam, you are in X10000 without so much as a sonic boom.

Then let's say you are moving around this area of your sheet via a mouse or arrow keys for a while and suddenly you're homesick for wherever the heck you were earlier. Where was that? Dunno. But no matter, just hit F5. There in the Go To dialog Reference box is $B$237. Click OK and time and space seem meaningless as you are magically transported back from whence you came. Each time you make a Go To jump, the place you left is recorded for a quick return. It's like having your own set of wormholes. See Figure 1.5. (Hey, Go To even remembers other sheets and books that you have visited!)

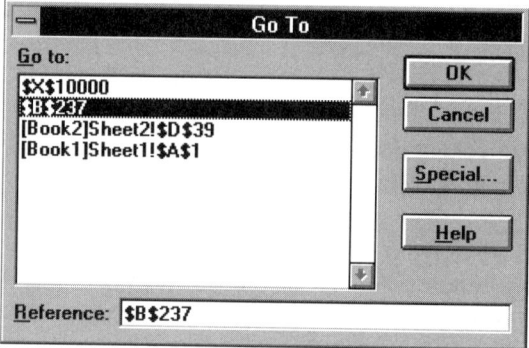

Figure 1.5 Go To, Your Excel Wormhole Generator

Name that box!   In Excel 5, Microsoft provides a formula bar gizmo called the **Name Box** that lets you type in a cell coordinate and do a quick jump. (You can also create and select named ranges using the Name Box, as you will see shortly.) Click in the Name Box, type in the cell (or range) you want, hit Enter, and there you are. See Figure 1.6.

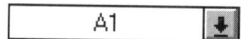

Figure 1.6 Excel's New Name Box

The Name Box is quick and easy and coordinates from jumps made via the Name Box are recorded and displayed in the Go To dialog box in case you want a quick return.

Make My Selection

So now you can move the active cell around like crazy. How about selecting a group of cells? Well, we're glad you asked that question. The easiest way to make reasonably small selections is with the mouse. Simply click and drag over the range of cells you want to select. To select groups of noncontiguous cells, click and drag the first selection, then release the mouse button and CTRL + click and drag the next selection. This technique works fine on single cells as well. Click the first cell, CTRL + click the next cell, and so on.

For larger selections, dragging with the mouse can be slow and unwieldy. Let's consider some quick ways to make a large selection. Select a cell in one corner of the area you want to select. Now, scroll the perspective until you have the cell at the opposite corner of the area visible and SHIFT + click on that cell. Everything in that range is now selected.

You can also select cells using just the keyboard. Hold down the Shift key and use the arrow keys to highlight the range you want. This is a great technique for users new to, or uncomfortable with, the mouse. You can add the Shift key to the zap technique you saw earlier in this section. CTRL + SHIFT + arrow key extends the selection in the direction you choose in the same manner that it moves the active cell. This is really the way to select contiguous cells that contain data.

The Name Game

You saw how the Go To command was gangbusters for jumping around the sheet and selecting single cells, but you can also use Go To for selecting both a contiguous range of cells and noncontiguous ranges. **Fe Fi Fo Fanna**

Hit F5. Type in a range of cells, like A1:D7, click OK, and bam, the range is selected. Type in a range of cells, like A1:D7; a comma; and then another range of cells, like E9:H15. Click OK, and both ranges are selected. But wait, there's more! Click the cell in the upper left corner of the desired range, press F5, type in the lower right cell coordinate, *and hold down the Shift key while clicking the OK key!* Bang! Range selected. The Go To dialog box also displays all the current range names in the active sheet. See Figure 1.7.

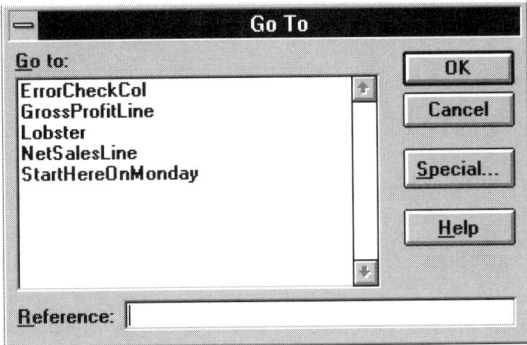

Figure 1.7 Go To, Your Gateway to Range Names

If you wanted to, you could pop up the Go To dialog box, select a range name from the list, click OK, and that range is selected. Or you can use the Name Box that we mentioned earlier. The Name Box is a very cool way to select a named range if you can live with its limitation of displaying only the first 100 named ranges. See Figure 1.8.

Figure 1.8 Name Box Showing Named Ranges

Named ranges are the equivalent of Word's bookmarks if you are of a word processing persuasion. If you are not naming cells and ranges on your worksheets, *start NOW!*

1. In a new sheet, select the range A1:A4.

2. Click on the Name Box drop-down arrow. See Figure 1.9.

3. Type Lobster and press Enter. We use Lobster to show you that you can name a range (or cell) anything you like (but don't use spaces).

4. Click on any cell to change the selection.

5. To get back to the last selection pull down the Name Box list and click on Lobster. *Viola, er violin...uhm...and there you have it!*

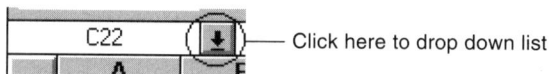

Figure 1.9 Name Box Drop-Down Arrow

Why name things? You can use names in your formulas so you have half a chance to figure out what a particular formula does 10 seconds after you've written it.

Which of the following is easier to figure out?

```
=Sum(H26:H29)-Sum(H31:H38)
```

or

```
=SUM(Revenue)-SUM(Expenses)
```

Sure, if you are auditing the formula, you have to make sure that the names refer to the proper cells, but you have to do that even if you are dealing with the actual coordinates. And, by using Go To, it is easy to jump to the named range and then jump back.

LEXICON: IT'LL GET YOU EVERY TIME

> Linguistics becomes an ever eerier area, like I feel like I'm in Oz, Just trying to tell it like it was.
>
> Ogden Nash
> *The Old Dog Barks Backwards*, 1972

Excel's power can be downright overwhelming—made even more daunting by the apparent lack of a consistent vocabulary. For example, a mere 15 separate mouse pointers are used in Excel, all under a variety of circumstances, most of which are referred to as simply "mouse pointer." You're often left to wonder, "Gee, the *User's Guide* says point the mouse pointer over yonder, but the dad-blasted thing just changed shape on me and I've nary a clue as to why!" Then, somewhere else, the *User's Guide* may encourage you to grab the fill handle and AutoFill until Monday spawns Tuesday through Sunday. "Sure," you think to yourself, "now if only I knew what in tarnation the @#$% fill handle *was*." So send a raspberry right now on up towards the Pacific Northwest, where the Redmondians roost. That's right, feel better? We do too. Because if you thought searching Excel's help file for something so useful as "fill handle" would get you anywhere, *guess again!*

We'd give our, well, uhm, some sensitive part of our anatomies, if only there were a thoroughly consistent, sensible, and rational Excel vocabulary. So we'll cover the high points for you, right here and now.

Mus Musculus **Meets Hydra**

> The Hydra had a prodigious dog-like body, and eight or nine snaky heads, one of them immortal; but some credit it with fifty, or one hundred, or even ten thousand heads. At all events, it was so venomous that its very breath, or the smell of its tracks, could destroy life.
>
> Robert Graves
> *Greek Myths*

The *User's Guide* has no official name for the special mouse pointer we use several million times a day to select cells and ranges of cells, and its fifteen or so other derivative forms that change on a moment's notice depending on exactly where

Pointers ad mouseam

the "mouse pointer" is inside your Excel display space. Maybe we're obsessive-compulsive, or maybe we like having consistent names for this stuff we use all day long. For argument's sake, let's say your significant other asks you, "Honey-pie, would you please go get the *transportation device* 'cause I'd like to grab a banana split down at Baskin-Robbins?" Does that mean the skateboard, the snowmobile under wraps out behind the woodshed, the Honda Gold Wing, or the Bentley?

We rest our case with the generic "mouse pointer." So we're going to come up with context-relevant names for this little bugger so you (and we) will always know what we're talking about. And then we'll get our attorney to notify the Library of Congress. *Heh, heh, heh.* Table 1.1 lists our names alongside the various mouse pointers you're bound to see on your screen. The sections that follow describe each of the doodads.

Table 1.1 The Mysterious Mouse Pointer Defined

What It Looks Like	What We Call It
⍺	The Traditional Northwest Mouse Pointer™
✛	The Selection Crosshair™
I	The I-Beam™
Arial	The Insertion Point™
✛	The Fill Handle Grabber™
⟻⟼	The Horizontal Sizing Grabber™
⇳	The Vertical Sizing Grabber™
⊢⊣	The Horizontal Split Bar Grabber™
⊥⊤	The Vertical Split Bar Grabber™
✛	The Bi-directional Split Bar Grabber™
☝	The Pointing Index Finger™
⍺?	The Help Button Pointer™ (a.k.a. The Traditional Northwest Mouse Pointer with a Question Mark Tote Bag™)

Table 1.1 The Mysterious Mouse Pointer Defined (continued)

What It Looks Like	What We Call It
Q	The Zoom Pointer™
⬚	The Drag-Copy Pointer™
⊘	The No-Drop Zone Pointer™

The Traditional Northwest Mouse Pointer™

This ubiquitous little guy appears whenever you move the mouse over a title bar, menu bar, toolbar, scroll bar, status bar, or sheet tab zone.

The Selection Crosshair™

The mouse pointer is a Selection Crosshair™ whenever it's floating around on top of a cell, a column heading, or a row heading. At this point in its dynamic incarnation, if you click the Selection Crosshair™ once, you select a single cell, column, or row; if you click and drag, you select a range of cells, columns, or rows. Variations on selection involving the Shift or Control keys we've already discussed. If you right-click, a handy shortcut menu appears, complete with the primary commands that can be performed on or by the selected object or objects.

The I-Beam™

The I-Beam™ crops up whenever you drag the mouse over a toolbar control that can accept text directly, like the Font Box or the Font Size Box. It's a clue that if you click here and then type something, that something will appear right where the I-Beam was. As soon as you click the I-Beam, the text control is activated—you see its original contents in reverse video along with a flashing insertion point (see next section). It's a bit tricky, however, because now the keyboard is "looking at" the text control, even though you can still spin the mouse all over hell and back without disrupting what's going on inside the text control—*unless you click somewhere outside it, then the game's up and you're back at ground zero*. Kaboom. So keep a steady click finger, pilgrim.

The Insertion Point™

This indefatigable flashing vertical bar shows you where your keystrokes go. You can move it around with your keyboard's arrow, Home, and End keys, or you can reposition it with the I-Beam™ mouse pointer. See Figure 1.10.

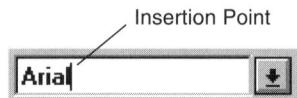

Figure 1.10 The Insertion Point at Work

The Fill Handle Grabber™

+   The fill handle is the humble haft of the AutoFill feature. Aptly named (but, *damn*, it's a tiny little thing), it is the solid black square nestled in the right bottom corner of the active cell border. See Figure 1.11. Aptly named "handle" because you can indeed grab it with the mouse and take off to perform an AutoFill. Guess how you know you've got it? When you see the mouse pointer transmogrify from a Traditional Northwest Mouse Pointer™ to a Fill Handle Grabber™. Now drag and AutoFill to your heart's content.

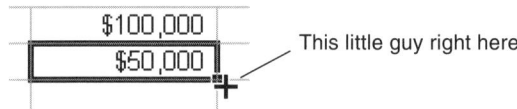

Figure 1.11 The Fill Handle Grabber

Note that when a row or column (or group thereof) is selected, the fill handle appears not at the absolute right bottom corner of the selection, but at the right bottom corner of the selection's heading zone. See Figure 1.12

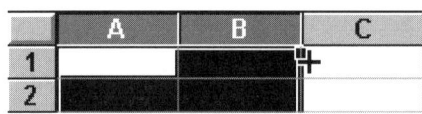

Figure 1.12 Fill Handle Grabber in a Group Setting

The Sizing Grabbers™

┿ ╪   The two species of Sizing Grabbers™ are horizontal and vertical. You'll know the direction in which you're about to resize the object(s) by observing which way the grabbers are pointing. The grabbers rear their pointed little heads only when the mouse touches the border of an object that can be resized. Once you've got 'em in your sights, drag and resize, baby, drag and resize.

In the special case of hidden rows and columns, if you have a brain surgeon's steady hand and land the mouse juuuuuuust right on the object border, you'll see a Split Bar Grabber™, indicating that you can now resize the *hidden* object.

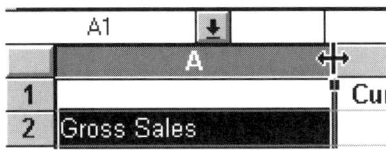

Figure 1.13 The Horizontal Sizing Grabber at Work Resizing a Column

The Split Bar Grabbers™

The three species of Split Bar Grabbers™ are horizontal, vertical, and bi-directional. These critters manifest themselves when you call upon the services of window panes and pass the mouse over any of the pane borders (referred to by the *User's Guide* as "split bars"). The grabbers then dutifully point in the direction in which you can move the split bar.

In the special case of a four-pane window, when you pass through the intersection, the Split Bar Grabber™ points in all cardinal directions, indicating that you can move the split bar intersection in two directions at once. Cool!

The Pointing Index Finger™

When you pass the mouse over a graphic object that is assigned to a macro, it transforms into a right hand with a pointing index finger. Similar to, but not exactly the same as, the mouse pointer inside a help file, when you point to a jump topic (green solid-underlined text). Click and voilà, the macro's off and running.

The Help Button Pointer™

Press the Help button and the Traditional Northwest Mouse Pointer™ gets a sidekick in the form of a solid question mark. C'est magnifique! Instant Help Button Pointer™.

> **Point the Help Button Pointer™ to an object and click—for example, the status bar—and Excel's help file automatically fires up with the Status Bar help topic loaded for your instant edification. Excellent!**

It's the little touches like this that make us weep for joy when we use this product. Really.

The Zoom Pointer™

The Zoom Pointer™ comes to life when you are in Print Preview mode. Clicking in a region with the Zoom Pointer™ magnifies that region.

The Drag-Copy Pointer™

 This pointer looks like the Traditional Northwest Mouse Pointer™ with a little plus sign on its shoulder. The plus sign signals that the selection is being copied as opposed to being moved. (Drag-move looks like the Traditional Northwest Mouse Pointer™ without a little plus sign on its shoulder.)

The No-Drop Zone Pointer™

 When you attempt to perform a drag-and-drop operation and take the source object into an area that doesn't support drag-and-drop (for whatever reason), the classic "No Smoking" image that we call the No-Drop Zone Pointer™ appears.

Graphic Object Potpourri

Excel houses an extended family of graphic object grabbers. These grabbers allow you to select, copy, move, and resize graphic objects (as opposed to cells) like lines, rectangles, text boxes, buttons, and so on. If you're interested in learning more about these objects, see the *User's Guide* Chapter 13, Creating Graphic Objects on Worksheets and Charts. Suffice it to say that if you're comfortable with the 15 pointers we've just enumerated, you'll do fine with Chapter 13's myriad grabbers, all variants on what you've seen thus far.

Selection Marquee™

When you select cells and then choose Edit Cut or Edit Copy, Excel puts a flashing marquee around the current selection. (If you use mouse drag-and-drop techniques to move cells around in a document, you don't see the marquee.) We call this feature the Selection Marquee™. It also surrounds cells you select while building a formula, indicating the range that's about to be injected into your formula.

This Round of Help Is on Us: Bars Aplenty

> Don't get me started.
>
> Billy Crystal
> *Mr. Saturday Night*

Another pet peeve of ours is the inconsistent help provided for super-critical terms like the names of the six "bar" objects in Excel.

All these bar terms should be easy to find (and adequately explained) in the help file. You should be able to perform a simple search for the term itself and… presto! Alas. It's time to let the Lexical Police loose in Redmond with a stack of search warrants.

One could argue—vehemently—on either side of this fence. Should a Windows application assume the user is familiar with such fundamental concepts as menu bar and title bar? Yes? No? Maybe? Admittedly, the developers have to draw the line somewhere. We vote in favor of providing as comprehensive a glossary as possible. More is better than less. Since vocabulary is so crucial in the acquisition of any new skill, let's have pity on the kind and gentle soul who went out and ran the ol' Platinum card through the slot, carried the box home, and fired Excel up, only to find there's no help topic for menu bar. 'Nuf said.

Point, counterpoint

The following list pinpoints what you need to search for to get help on these terms:

- Formula Bar—Search for "formula bar" and then Go To the "Formula Bar" topic. Good job.

- Menu Bar—Even though there's a topic called "menu bars," it doesn't really explain what a menu bar is. However, the What's on the Screen topic in Chapter 1 of the *User's Guide* does graphically point to the menu bar. Partial credit, right? Wrong, because Excel's sibling, WinWord 6, contains *exactly* the kind of succinct description we expect from applications of this caliber, complete with glossary items for "application window" and "title bar." See Figure 1.14.

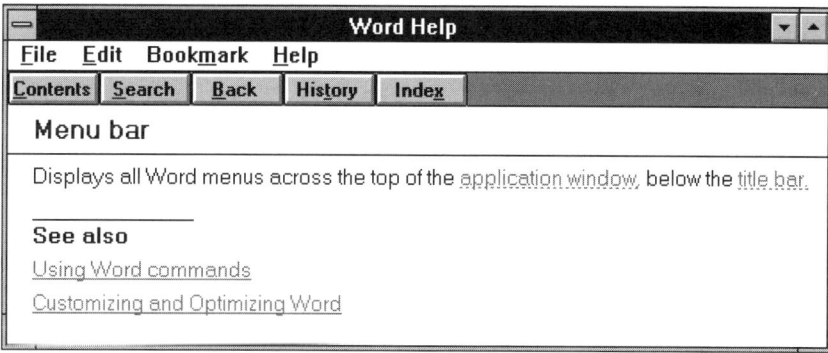

Figure 1.14 WinWord Knows What a Menu Bar Is

- Split Bar—Search for "split box," Go To the "Split and Remove Split Commands (Window menu)" topic, and then select "Splitting a windows into panes." Uhm, quarter credit for this 'n.

- Status Bar—Search for "status bar" and then Go To the "Status Bar" topic. Nice and easy. The way it should be.

- Title Bar—This essential term appears nowhere in either the help file nor the *User's Guide*. You can, however, find it early on in the *Windows User's Guide* (try page 8) or by selecting Help Windows Tutorial from Program Manager and cycling through the first couple of panels.

- Toolbar—Search for "toolbars, customizing," Go To the "Creating and deleting a custom toolbar" How To topic, and then choose the Overview button. Whew. Finally. Too bad the resulting "Overview of Customizing Toolbars" topic can't be searched directly because it contains some very helpful material. An alternate search route is to search for "customizing Microsoft Excel," Go To the "New Features for Customizing Microsoft Excel" topic, and then choose the "Overview of Customizing Toolbars" topic. Why is it so difficult to find an overview of a feature as eminently useful as toolbars? *Don't get us started!*

Display options help   To see a useful summary of numerous Excel display options, search for "display options" and then Go To the "Changing what Microsoft Excel displays" topic. Hang out there or, for more information, click the Overview button.

NEW AND IMPROVED STANDARD TOOLBAR

A stubborn and rebellious generation.

Psalms 78:8

Hold on to your hats campers, Excel's got toolbars! And how. See Figure 1.15.

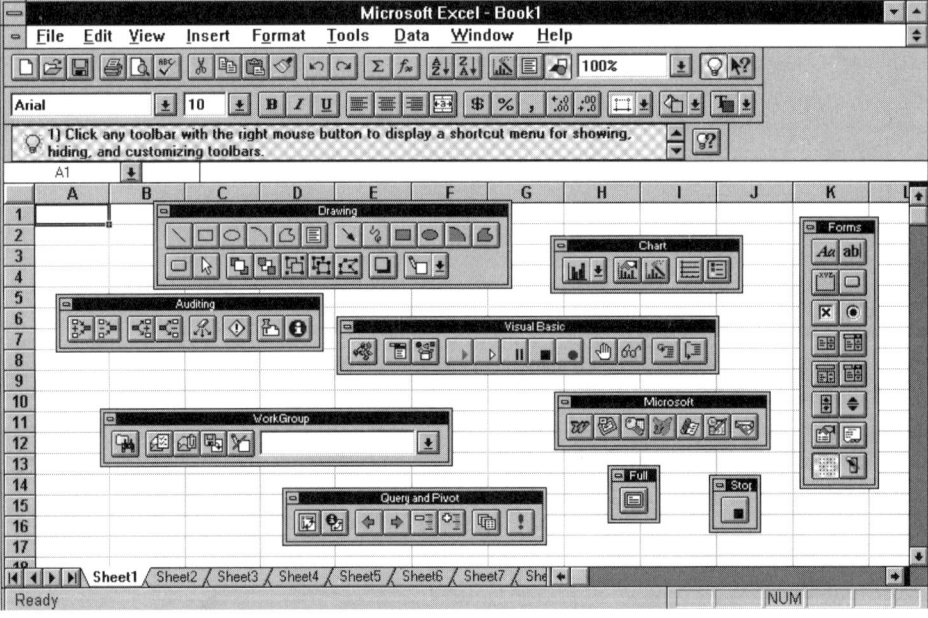

Figure 1.15 Excel with All Bars Displayed

Excel has a passel of "ship with" toolbars. Thirteen in all. To those you can add your own custom toolbars. You can have so many toolbars visible that you can hardly see any spreadsheet!

You can turn these critters on and off either by going to the View menu and clicking on Toolbars, or by right-clicking on a toolbar edge. Anyway, this is way too many buttons for everyday use.

Excel 5 starts you off with two toolbars visible, the Standard bar on top just under the menus and the Formatting bar beneath that. The first thing you want to do is turn on the TipWizard toolbar by clicking on the lightbulb (second from the right on the Standard toolbar). That's better. Okay, as far as it goes, but what if you want to mix and match buttons from the different toolbars into a single modified toolbar set? Not to worry, you can customize toolbars like there was no tomorrow. In fact, we highly recommend that you do so.

This application is where many of you live for several hours a day, and you should have the tools you need at your digital extremities (we would have said "fingertips," but somebody already has that trademarked *<grin>*). Microsoft chose the buttons for the Standard and Formatting bars based on advice from their pet usability lab rats and a predisposition for whizbang wowie-pow-zowie "this will demo real good" buttons. None of their selection process may have the slightest in common with what works for you. **Tools at your digital extremities**

So fix it! We'll get you started with the way in which we have modified our toolbars. But don't you blindly accept our way as gospel anymore than Microsoft's. This stuff is subjective! The important thing is to lay out the tools you need to get your work done. Let's get to it. **One man's ceiling is another man's floor**

Be aware that Microsoft did not put all the available tools on the toolbars, nor did they think of everything. In fact, some of the omissions are downright criminal. No matter, you can fix that, too. And, if you don't like how it turns out, you can always have the default Excel toolbars back.

File Buttons

> You press the button and we'll do the rest.
>
> Kodak advertisment, 1988

The first three buttons on the Standard toolbar deal with files, creating books, opening existing books, and saving files to disk. See Figure 1.16.

Figure 1.16 New, Open, Save Buttons

Open and Save work fine, but we had best deal with the way the first button, New, behaves. This button gives you a new book, bang! "What's wrong with this," you ask? Well, you should be using templates, and you should be able to click on this button and choose what template to use when creating a new book instead of being forced to accept the default book template.

What's a template? Hmmm, we'll get to that in a later chapter, but trust us, you should be using them. For now just humor us, and even though we don't have any custom templates (yet), let's change this button to display the available workbook templates.

Boy, if you have used WinWord, you are not going to believe this, but you cannot just point to a list of commands and drag one to the toolbar to create a custom button. This is one area where WinWord is head and shoulders above Excel. Every command in WinWord is provided in the customize toolbars list, which makes what we're about to do *a whole lot easier!* Are you listening, Redmond? Anyway, you have to write some code.

No wait, come back. It won't be that bad. Like anything in life, it's only easy *after* you know how.

Your first macro! First you need to create a book called PERSONAL.XLS. This book will contain the macros you will create and will be loaded automatically as a hidden workbook whenever you start Excel. Don't worry, you will let Excel do almost all the work. Here we go.

1. From the Tools menu, choose Record Macro and from the flyout menu, choose Record New Macro (yes, we agree, it does seem a bit redundant).

2. For the Macro Name in the Record New Macro dialog box enter FILENEW.

3. Click on the Options button. In the "Store in" group box, check the option button for Personal Macro Workbook. In the "Language" check box, check the option button for Visual Basic.

4. Click on OK. A little floating toolbar with a single button on it appears as if by magic. This is the Stop Recording button.

5. Click on the Stop Recording button to stop recording.

Stop Recording button What you just did was a little sleight of hand. You made Excel think you really wanted to record a macro to get it to create a book using the special name PERSONAL.XLS. This book was created with a single module sheet. You can't see this book because Excel has hidden it, so let's unhide it:

6. From the Window menu, choose Unhide. PERSONAL.XLS appears in the Unhide dialog box.

7. Click on OK to unhide PERSONAL.XLS.

Not so bad, was it. Of course, we're just getting started, *heh, heh, heh*. Module1 contains the beginnings of a VBA macro. Type in the module sheet as though it's a word processor. Make the macro look like this:

```
Sub FileNew()
Application.Dialogs(xlDialogNew).Show
End Sub
```

Click on Window, then Hide. Ya done good, pilgrim. All that remains is to tie this macro to the New toolbar button:

8. Click on View, then Toolbars.

9. Hit the Customize button. The Customize dialog box appears. (See Figure 1.17.) We're going to work with this dialog box quite a bit.

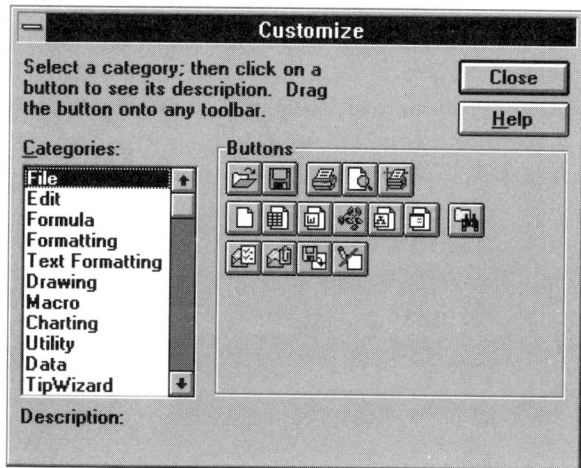

Figure 1.17 The Customize Dialog Box

10. *Right-click* on the New button on the Standard toolbar, *not on the buttons palette on the dialog box*. Cool, huh? You get a little tear-off menu that, among other things, lets you assign a macro to this button. (See Figure 1.18.) You can only

Figure 1.18 Tear-off Menu from New Button

right-click on a toolbar button to get this menu when the Customize dialog box is displayed.

11. Click on Assign Macro and up pops a dialog box with your macro, PERSONAL.XLS!FILENEW.

12. Select the macro in the list by clicking on it.

13. Click on OK.

14. Click on Close in the Customize dialog box, and you are done!

Whew, you've written a macro and reassigned a button on the Standard toolbar to do your bidding. Not too shabby. Now, when you click on the New button on the toolbar, you will not be tossed a workbook based on the default, but you'll be able to choose from your impressive list of custom templates. Yeah, yeah, you don't have any custom templates yet, but you will, you will.

Meanwhile, back on the toolbar   Did you notice anything odd about these first three buttons (shown back in Figure 1.16). What's missing from this group? Well, if you're like us, you will probably close every file you open at some point, so how about a FileClose button? Microsoft left it out of Excel. They put one in WinWord, but they left it off the toolbar; you have to put it on yourself. In Excel they left it out, period, as in there ain't no such animal. Well, that will only take a minute to fix.

First, another macro. Let's unhide that PERSONAL.XLS book. Window menu, then Unhide, then OK. Go to the end of Module1 (CTRL + END), and press Enter to start a new line. Familiar ground by now, right?

Type in the following macro code:

```
Sub FileClose()
On Error Goto EndMacro
ActiveWorkbook.Close
EndMacro:
End Sub
```

The line ActiveWorkbook.Close does all the work. The line above it and the one below it deal with error handling. Not very elegant perhaps, but it will do the job. What error you ask? Say you close all open books and then click on the FileClose button. There's no book to close and that generates an error condition. With this simple On Error statement, your macro keeps going by jumping to the EndMacro label. No sweat.

Now, let's add some text to be displayed in the status bar for this button:

1. Click on Tools, then Macro.

2. Select the FileClose macro name.

3. Click the Options button.

4. In the Macro Options dialog box, click the third text box from the bottom, the one labeled "Status Bar Text," and type in:

```
Close the active book
```

5. Click on OK.

6. In the Macro dialog box click on Close.

Hide the book by pulling down the Window menu and clicking on Hide. Now, you just have to create a new button on the toolbar to hook this macro to. Okay, you need the Customize dialog box again.

1. Click on View, then Toolbars.

2. Hit the Customize button.

3. Scroll down the Categories list and select Custom. (See Figure 1.19.)

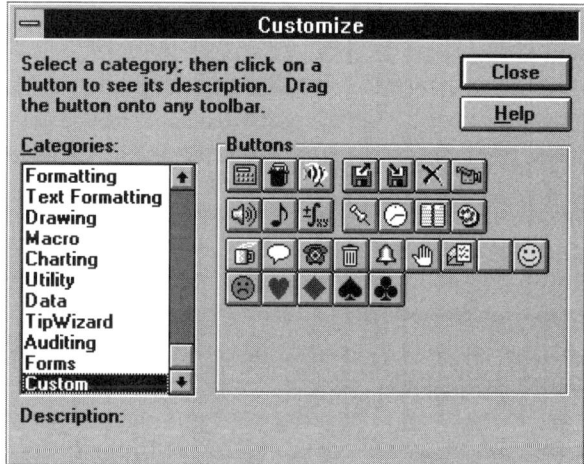

Figure 1.19 Customize Dialog Showing Custom Button Palette

Unless you have an artistic talent, this is it as far as it goes for button designs that are not already associated with some function. Oh, as was demonstrated with the New button, you can reassign buttons and can, therefore, use any button you want for the new FileClose you are creating. But that can get pretty confusing, so use some discretion. We suggest that you use one of these custom buttons, draw your own (that button tear-off menu had a choice for Edit Button Image), or you can snatch a button from WinWord 6.

If you don't have WinWord 6, pick a button you like from the custom palette and click and drag it up to the toolbar to the right of the Save button and drop it.

If you do have WinWord 6, drag any button from the Custom palette (like the blank button, third row, second from the right) up to the right of the Save button and steal, er, borrow a button face from WinWord for it.

Now, select FileClose in the macro list and click OK.

WinWord's Close button

Leave Excel right where it is and fire up WinWord, pull down the Tools menu, and click on Customize. Select the tab on the Toolbars filecard if it is not already selected. That first set of buttons from the File Categories contains precisely the button you want, it's the fourth from the left in the top row. That little button, sort of a puke-yellow closed file folder with the arrow curving upward. Yeah, that one. Drag it up to the Standard toolbar and drop it next to the Save button (unless you have already installed it on your toolbar in WinWord). Whether it was on your toolbar already or you dropped it on the toolbar, you should now *right-click* on it.

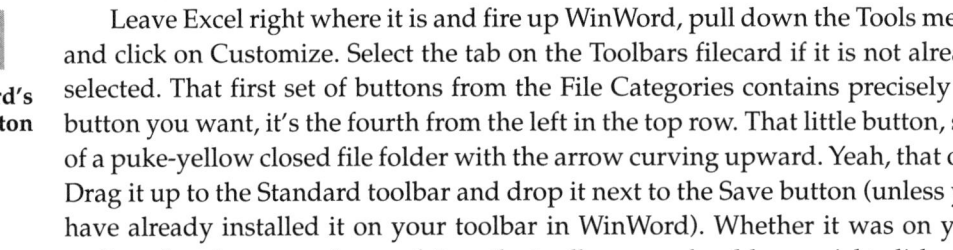

Figure 1.20 Tear Off Menu from Close Button

Click on Copy Button Image. If you want the full story on customizing WinWord, you should get *The Underground Guide to Word for Windows* by Woody Leonhard (Addison-Wesley). For now you can drag the button off the WinWord toolbar since you have what you came for. Click on Close in WinWord's Customize dialog box. Now switch back to Excel.

Right-click on the button you put on Excel's Standard toolbar (remember that the Customize dialog box must be open), and click on Paste Button Image. So far, so good. Click Close in the Customize box, and that's that.

At this point you should save everything. To save the hidden PERSONAL.XLS, exit Excel and respond Yes when asked if you want to save changes to the Personal Macro Workbook. Restart Excel. Your new macros and buttons (as in Figure 1.21) are ready to go!

Figure 1.21 Revised File Operation Buttons

Oops! If you put the Traditional Northwest Mouse Pointer™ on the new File Close button, the ToolTip appears.

A ToolTip is the text that appears when you point to a toolbar button. If you don't see ToolTips, time to turn 'em on. To activate ToolTips, select View Toolbars, check the Show ToolTips check box, and click OK.

But the ToolTip says "Custom." Yuk! Let's round this rough corner. Ah, it seems that to do this you need another macro. No problem! Unhide the PERSONAL.XLS (Window, Unhide, OK).

You'll put this macro in a separate module sheet, so right-click on the Module1 sheet tab and click on Insert. Excel assumes that you want another module and it highlights that sheet type in the list, so click on OK. Now you have a Module2 sheet.

In Module2, type in the following macro code:

```
Sub ToolTipSetter()
Toolbars("Standard").ToolbarButtons(4).Name = "Close"
End Sub
```

"Standard" is the name of the standard toolbar where you added the FileClose button. The (4) indicates the position of the button on the toolbar. If you put the button in a different position, change the number accordingly. The narrow spaces between button groups count the same as a button, so count *carefully*.

Pull down the Run menu and click on Start. The macro runs, but nothing seems to happen—until you put the mouse pointer on the Close button. Notice that the ToolTip now says "Close" instead of "Custom." Cool.

We'll be using this macro again from time to time, so go ahead and hide the PERSONAL.XLS book via Window Hide.

The Chinese Wall

Excel 5's and WinWord 6's toolbar customization features behave just differently enough to be maddening. Comrades, it's the little things that count.

In WinWord, if you want to move a toolbar button around on its parent toolbar, or move it to another toolbar, you simply press and hold the Alt key, and then drag the button as needed. Deleting a button in WinWord is as simple as dragging a button off the toolbar into never-never land, that is, any screen region other than a toolbar. QED. *You don't have to start up Word's Customize dialog to do this!* Whether this is good or bad is up for debate, but it does work. Interestingly, this expeditious technique does *not* support CTRL + dragging (for copying); for that you must have the Customize dialog box up.

In Excel, *first you have to start up the Customize dialog*—View, Toolbars, Customize—then you can copy and move toolbar buttons. Here in Excel's Customize-dialog-is-running mode, traditional drag-and-drop rules also reign— plain ol' dragging moves buttons, ALT + dragging moves buttons, and CTRL + dragging copies buttons. Still, we're left wondering…if the WinWord developers got drag-and-drop to work—halfway, anyway—minus the Customize dialog requirement, why didn't they (and the Excel developers, too) go all the way and save us all some mouse strokes? Dunno.

Print, Preview, and Spell Buttons

Standard printing   The next three buttons deal with printing. See Figure 1.22.

Figure 1.22 Print, Preview, and Spell Buttons

The first button prints one copy of the current sheet, no problem there.

Then comes print preview, which is also very useful for seeing how your finished worksheet will appear, given that Excel does not have a Page Layout view. Sure, you can zoom out and see your sheet from 3 miles up, but you cannot see the margins, headers, or footers. So print preview stays.

Next is Spelling, which, personally, one of us couldn't live without. We won't say who, will we Jim? Anyway, this one makes the cut.

What's missing from this set of buttons has to deal with the new design of Excel 5 and the way you set the print area.

You know how to define the area of your worksheet that you want to print, right? Sure, you click on Set Print Area on the Options menu. What's that? No more Options menu in Excel 5. Hmmm. Well, they must have put Set Print Area on another menu, after all we use it a lot. No? Let's take a look at the *User's Guide* to see how you define the print area.

What! You have to pull down the File menu, select Page Setup, click the Sheet filecard tab, *then* click in the Print Area box, and *then* enter the cell coordinates of the range. What if you don't know the range? Oh, you can highlight the range with the mouse. Uh huh, while the Page Setup dialog box covers 45% of the screen. You can't highlight it first, either. This *violates* the Windows convention of "select then do"! *You can't be serious!* But we are, we are.

What the hell, let's fix it. Open the Customize dialog box. There in the File category palette, the last button in the top row is the Set Print Area button. This button, with the printer and the cross hairs in the upper left corner, sets the print area to whatever the current selection is. Anyway, drag this button up to the right of the spell check button. Click Close. That fixes the print buttons.

Set Print Area button

Portage Buttons

Let's see, what's next? Oh, the Cut, Copy, Paste, and Format Painter buttons. See Figure 1.23.

Cut, Copy, Paste, Format Painter

Figure 1.23 Cut, Copy, Paste, and Format Painter Buttons

We'll leave this set of buttons alone, even though we could probably make a good case against the Format Painter button. It is difficult to determine exactly what the Format Painter is going to paint. For instance, say you have this text string in cell A1: "The quick brown fox" and this in cell A3: "jumps over the lazy dog."

Format the word "brown" in cell A1 as bold. Select A1, click on the Format Painter button, and then click on A3. Hmmm. Now, in A3 format the entire cell as underlined. Click Format Painter, and click on A1. Hmmm, again. Anyway, if you ever need some free space on the Standard toolbar, this button is a good candidate for oblivion.

Undo and Repeat Buttons

Here we have the Undo and Repeat buttons. See Figure 1.24.

Figure 1.24 Undo, Repeat Buttons

The ability of WinWord 6 to perform multilevel undo's is wonderful! And, when they added that feature to Excel, we were really thrilled...oh, they didn't add multilevel Undo to Excel? Just to WinWord. Oh. So these buttons Undo the last action or Repeat the last action. Guess it's better than nothing. They can stay.

But, guess we had all better be pretty damn careful if we have been using WinWord 6, which has very similar buttons on its button bar, so we don't rely on Excel being able to undo several levels of actions. Bad design. They should have used a button face that more clearly communicated that these functions in Excel were crippled when compared with WinWord.

Auto This and Wizard That Buttons

AutoSum and Function Wizard
Next are two buttons generally related to creating formulas: the AutoSum button and the Function Wizard. See Figure 1.25.

Figure 1.25 AutoSum and Function Wizard Buttons

The AutoSum button is one of the best ideas Microsoft has ever had. This is one time where we violently agree with those lab rats!

The Function Wizard is a nice idea. Except (bet you saw that coming) for one thing. You use the Function Wizard to enter functions into formulas. We always begin formulas by hitting the equal sign key. It's a habit, muscle memory, just do it without thinking. And, when you hit the equal sign, the formula bar is activated and lo and behold there is another Function Wizard button on the formula bar. Are we seeing double or what?

So with the Function Wizard button on the formula bar duplicating the one on the toolbar (and the formula bar being where you will most likely need to use it), we think you should nuke the one on the toolbar. Don't worry though, you'll replace it with something we think is just as useful.

So click View Toolbars Customize and then drag that little Function Wizard off into space. It's outta there! Right in the old bit bucket.

Now, what would really be useful is a button that pastes range names into formulas. Well, as long as the Customize dialog box is open, click on Formula in the Categories list.

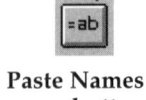

Paste Names button
Paste Names is the button you want (second from the right, bottom row). Drag this button up to the toolbar and drop it to the left of the AutoSum button. There, that is much better. See Figure 1.26.

Figure 1.26 Paste Names and AutoSum Buttons

Sorta Gotta Go!

The burden of lean and wasteful learning.

William Shakespeare
As You Like It, ca. 1600

Now you have to deal with the Sort buttons. We're going to dump them because they are *sorta* dangerous (bad joke, but we couldn't resist). See Figure 1.27.

Figure 1.27 The Diabolical Sort Buttons

Have you ever screwed up a sort in Excel? We have. You know, you select a range and miss the last column and scramble your data. Makes you real careful when it comes to sorting. Well, these buttons make sorting real easy. Too easy. If you hit one of these buttons by accident, you will not be a happy camper. For example, say you have the worksheet shown in Figure 1.28.

	A	B	C	D	E
1					
2		Part #	Qtr 1	Qtr 2	Qtr 3
3	Cats	99222	465	58	22
4	Rats	99223	404	117	421
5	Bats	99224	175	314	301
6	Dogs	99225	88	261	38
7	Frogs	99226	500	191	302
8	Trogs	99227	272	454	284
9					

Figure 1.28 Before the Accidental Click

Notice that A1 is the active cell. Pretend that your intent is to pull down the Window menu, but you accidentally click on one of the Sort buttons. Say it's the Descending button for the sake of this example.

Without so much as a "by your leave," your spreadsheet is *instantly* transformed into the sheet in Figure 1.29.

	A	B	C	D	E
1					
2		Part #	Qtr 1	Qtr 2	Qtr 3
3	Trogs	99227	272	454	284
4	Rats	99223	404	117	421
5	Frogs	99226	500	191	302
6	Dogs	99225	88	261	38
7	Cats	99222	465	58	22
8	Bats	99224	175	314	301
9					

Figure 1.29 The Dismal "After" Sheet

Not too good, and it only gets worse. Let's say your model is a P&L that has hidden columns for budget vs. actual calculations, and your data covers 12 periods (24 columns) and the last six months of actuals have not been entered into the model. One slip of the mouse with the active cell in close proximity to the data and, not only will a sort take place, it will not get all the columns. Bummer.

Drag the two Sort buttons to their doom. Onward and upward.

Graphics Buttons

ChartWizard,
Text Box, and
Drawing

The next set are related in that that they all allow you to put graphics right on top of your sheet. See Figure 1.30.

Figure 1.30 ChartWizard, Text Box, and Drawing Buttons

The Chart Wizard is cool, and the Text Box is indispensable. The Drawing button—hmmm, this one calls up the Drawing toolbar. That's okay, but what we really would like is the most often used drawing tools right there on the Standard toolbar. Of course, that might be way too many buttons. How about a compromise?

Shape button

First, nuke the Drawing button. Drag that little Drawing button right off the toolbar. Eeeeeieee! Now, in the Categories list select Drawing. From the palette, choose the button in the very last row, last button on the right—the Shape button.

This button provides a drop-down list of drawing shapes and tools. Drag this sucker up to where the Drawing button used to live. Click Close. This button is just the ticket. When you click on it, you get a drop-down list of tools for drawing cool stuff on your sheet. See Figure 1.31.

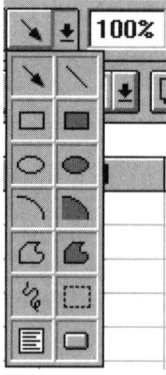

Figure 1.31 The Shape Button Drop-down List

You can select from an assortment of drawing tools, like the arrow, the line, circles, squares. It even has a Text Box tool. If you ever need some space on your Standard toolbar, you can nuke the Text Box button and use the tool on this drop-down palette.

Fit and Finish

That is about it for the Standard toolbar. If you are running standard VGA, it probably looks a little crowded. The Help button may be a bit too far to the right. No problem. You'll notice that the Zoom Control is a little wider than it really needs to be. Let's tighten that up a bit.

Click View, Toolbars, Customize, and then click on the Zoom Control. Put the Horizontal Sizing Grabber™ on the left end of the Zoom Control and drag it a little to the right. That's about right.

Zoom control button

Figure 1.32 shows our revised Standard toolbar.

Figure 1.32 New and Improved Standard Toolbar

FORMATTING BAR SURGERY

> Th' incurable cut off, the rest reform.
>
> Ben Jonson
> *Cynthia's Revels*, 1601

The Formatting bar has some flashy buttons on it, but it also has some glaring omissions in our opinion. Well, it's all subjective, but here's how we redesigned the default Formatting bar.

Once Again, with Style

First we have a question for Microsoft about the new Excel 5's Formatting bar. Ahem, "*For crying out loud, where's the Style drop-down list box?*" Don't tell us, the usability lab rats ate it, right? If users don't grok styles, *educate* them, don't desert them.

Oh, well, the first thing you have to do is put the Style list back on the Formatting bar. You know the drill. View, Toolbars, Customize. Click on Text Formatting in the Categories list. Drag the text box with the word "Style" in it up the left side of the Formatting toolbar. There, that's better.

Here in Figure 1.33 you can see the Style list where it should be, just before the Font and Font Size drop-down lists. So far so good.

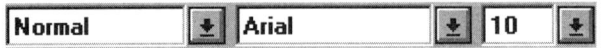

Figure 1.33 Style List Back Where It Belongs

To Boldly Go

...where no electron has gone before.

Pensées Pinecliffius

The next two sets of buttons (seven in all) deal with formatting and aligning cell contents.

Bold it, italicize it, underline it—all very straightforward and very useful when creating styles by example. They can stay. Yeah, we know, we keep harping on styles. We'll get into an in-depth discussion of styles in Chapter 6. See Figure 1.34.

Figure 1.34 Bold, Italic, and Underline Buttons

The next set of buttons deals with aligning text in cells, left, center, and right. They're the same icons that you see in WinWord. See Figure 1.35.

Figure 1.35 Left, Right, Center, and Center Across Columns Buttons

The fourth button is the Center Across Columns button. This critter is slick. It's used to center text entered in one cell across several columns and has probably saved corporate America several man-decades in time that would have been frittered away trying to center text by adding spaces to a label. Yea Microsoft!

Nuke 'Em

The next five buttons need some discussion. Then they need to be nuked. They are the buttons shown in Figure 1.36.

Figure 1.36 Currency, Percent, and Comma Style;
Increase and Decrease Decimal Buttons

The first three, Currency Style, Percent Style, and Comma Style, are Microsoft's attempt to get users to use styles. Not good. First, these are the same default styles as those found in the Styles list that you just added. And the Styles list has *more* default styles—two for currency and two for commas. These buttons gotta go!

The increase/decrease decimal buttons must have come right out of the usability lab. Maybe they escaped. Never mind, they go.

View, Toolbars, Customize, and drag all five of the buttons to their destruction. We'll replace them with several of our own favorites.

Miscellaneous Formatting Critters

Formatting by and large should be controlled via the use of styles. There are, we concede, some types of formatting that you will want to add "on the fly." The last three drop-down list buttons fall roughly into this format-as-you-go category. See Figure 1.37.

Borders and color

Figure 1.37 Borders and the Bogus Color, Font Color Buttons

We have no beef with the Borders button. Bordering regions of the sheet is best done outside of the style paradigm. You can make a similar case for the middle button, Color, and the button on the right, Font Color. We could, but we won't.

The Color button changes the color of the selected cell, whereas the Font Color button changes the color of the text. Notice that the Color button has a gray box even though the default background is white. Hmmm. And the Font Color has a red box even though the default font is black. Too confusing, and it goes against Excel's usually excellent talent to be selection sensitive.

Use of color is one of those Zen things where less is more. You know, where a little is good and a lot is blecccch. We're not sure that making it easier to colorize your sheets is good to begin with (no offense to Ted Turner). Nuke 'em. Drag them off the Formatting bar. You need the space for some more interesting stuff anyway.

One of our ad hoc formatting needs is bordering cells or objects with a drop shadow border. So let's add a button for doing drop shadows on the current selection:

Drop Shadow button

1. Select Drawing from the Categories list.

2. From the button palette, drag the Drop Shadow button (fourth row, second from the right) to the Formatting bar.

3. Drop this button to the right of the Borders button.

Light Shade button

Another type of cell formatting that we use all the time to mark sections of sheets is a light shading. This button is also in the Drawing palette on the Customize dialog to the left of the Drop Shadow button:

1. Drag the Light Shading button to the Formatting bar.

2. Drop this button to the left of the Drop Shadow button.

Make some space

If you are getting cramped for space, and this will depend on your screen resolution, you can tighten up the Font and Font Size boxes by clicking on them while the Customize dialog box is displayed, and dragging the left edge of each one a little to the right.

Toggle Grid button

The next two buttons we have added to our Formatting bar are more general utility-type tools. We like to be able to turn the sheet gridlines on and off, so we add a button to do this. This button is on the Forms category button palette:

1. Scroll the Categories list down and click on Forms. The Toggle Grid button is in the second row, second from the right.

2. Drag the Toggle Grid button up to the Formatting bar and drop it to the right of the Light Shading button. Leave a skosh of space between the Shading and the Toggle Grid button.

Full Screen button

The last button to add is the Full Screen button. The full screen view is pretty cool. When you are crunching data into your sheet, you don't need to see toolbars, you need to see your sheet. This view removes everything from your display except the menu bar, the column and row headers, and the scroll bars. This button is on the Utility category button palette:

1. Click on Utility and the Full Screen button is in the last row, last button on the right.

2. Drag the Full Screen button up the Formatting bar and drop it to the right of the Toggle Grid button. Leave a little space between them.

Click on Close to be rid of the Customize dialog box and you are done! Here is your supercharged Formatting toolbar. See Figure 1.38.

Figure 1.38 Revised Formatting Toolbar

Now you know how to take control of the tool set that Excel provides. Empowerment to the user! Now we repeat, this is what works for us. If it doesn't work for you *change it!* But, do not just take what you're given and live with it. Those Redmond Rangers have provided the ability to customize Excel to suit *your* very personal needs. Seize the day, er, program!

Play around with this configuration. Look at the buttons provided in the Customize dialog box for the various Categories. You can find out what each does by clicking on it. A short description appears at the bottom of the dialog box. Experiment! The TipWizard will help you by showing you different buttons that you should consider using for the things you do repeatedly.

Back to the Beginning

If you decide that you really want to go back to the Excel default Standard and Formatting bars, no problem. In your Windows directory is a file called EXCEL5.XLB. This file stores your custom toolbar settings and, to get back to the default configuration, rename this file. But be forewarned, your custom AutoFill settings are also stored in this file (AutoFills are discussed in detail in Chapter 3). You can restore your default settings like this:

1. Exit Excel.
2. Go to File Manager.
3. Log onto the Windows directory and select the EXCEL5.XLB file.
4. From the File menu, choose Rename.
5. Rename the file EXCEL5.CUS (for "custom") and click on OK.
6. Restart Excel and you are back where you started with Excel's default toolbar settings.

Renaming EXCEL5.XLB lets you restore it again later if you wish. If you simply want to wipe out any changes you made to a toolbar just open the Toolbars dialog box (View, Toolbars), select the toolbar to restore, and click on the Reset button. Hey, this method is permanent, so be careful!

TOOLS OPTIONS: A WALK ON THE WILD SIDE

As long as we're customizing Excel, we should walk through the various default options that you might want to look at and consider changing. Not that this is a comprehensive review of the zillions of settings you can tweak in Excel 5. These are some that you might want to think about right out of the box. We will talk about other settings in later chapters, where appropriate.

To access these option settings, pull down the Tools menu and click on Options. See Figure 1.39. This tabbed dialog box is where all the default settings hang out.

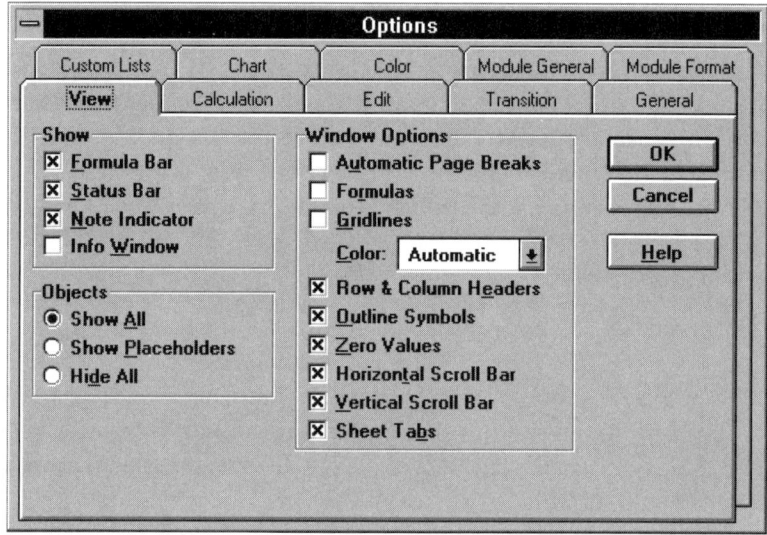

Figure 1.39 Tools Options Dialog Box

Room with a View

Let's take a look at the View filecard. It should be selected, but if it isn't, click on its tab to bring it to the front. See Figure 1.39.

If you never look at the Status Bar in Excel, you can turn it off in the Show group box. We don't turn it off, but if you do, another row of your sheet will be visible on screen.

In the Windows Options section we like to check the Automatic Page Breaks check box. This displays the default page breaks for your sheets, meaning it shows you where the breaks will appear *if* you enter data out to that point. For example, turn this setting on and open a new book. You get a page break line every 9 columns and each 51 rows (assuming default font and point size). But, if you enter a single number in cell A1 and hit the Print button, your printout will have only one cell on it. It will not print the empty cells out to column I and down to row 51 unless you enter data in that area or define that range as a print area.

Now you see it, and now you don't.

Anyway, we turn Automatic Page Breaks on so we can see what part of the sheet we have to work with on any given page. Once you actually define a print area, the page breaks conform to that defined area unless you define a noncontiguous range as the print area, in which case you *will not see any page breaks* on your sheet.

Another option on this filecard that you should be aware of is the Formulas check box. If you think of the formulas in your sheet as the questions and the results of those formulas as the answers, this setting lets you swap the sheet display between them. If you check this box, instead of seeing something like 100.00 in cell B10 you might see =SUM(B1:B9). Don't check it now, just remember where to find it when you need it. This view is invaluable for auditing, as we will discuss in depth later in Chapter 5.

If you do *not* want your sheets to have gridlines on them when they first appear, you can clear the Gridlines check box. Remember, you can easily toggle gridlines on and off using the handy dandy Toggle Grid button you hung on the Formatting bar earlier.

General Settings

Click on the General tab to bring the General filecard to the top of the deck.

Note the Reference Style group box with the A1 and the R1C1 buttons. We'll be talking about the relative merits of each of these settings in Chapter 5. R1C1 is how spreadsheets think, where every column is numbered instead of lettered. Working in a R1C1 style sheet takes some getting used to, unless you are an old Multiplan user, because it affects the way relative and absolute referencing are done. Leave it set at A1 for now, and note where you go to change it. As we said, it will come up again later.

A column by any other name

In the Menus section, make sure the Recently Used File List is checked. This turns on the MRU (Most Recently Used) list, which contains the last four files, or books, if you will, that you closed in Excel. Each time you close a book, its filename is added to the list. Unlike WinWord, however, you only get four filenames in the list with no way to change the number. Bummer. You can turn the MRU list off, but it is really convenient when you want to pop open the book you were just working on without having to go looking for it. Way convenient.

The MRU list

Everything else in the General filecard is dumped willy nilly into the rest of the dialog box.

The Ignore Other Applications box *should not* be checked unless you have a very, very, good reason to check it. Checking this box makes Excel ignore other applications that may be trying to get its attention. It'd be sorta like unplugging your phone while you take a bath. Don't check it.

Your call did not go through

The Prompt for Summary Info box is checked by default. This adding of summary information to your Excel files is a new feature for Excel 5. With this box checked, you are prompted to fill out the Summary Info form whenever you initially save a book. See Figure 1.40.

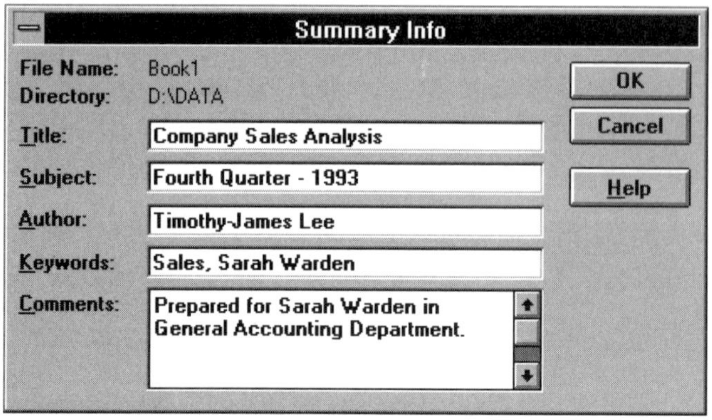

Figure 1.40 Summary Info Dialog Box

Why would you want to take the time to enter this information (up to 256 characters in each field)? Well, you can search for files based on this information. It's pretty cool, at least until Microsoft builds true document management into Windows itself.

To find a file based on this summary information stuff, pull down the file menu and click on File Find. You get the Search dialog box (unless you already have performed a search, in which case you get the results from the previous search). See Figure 1.41.

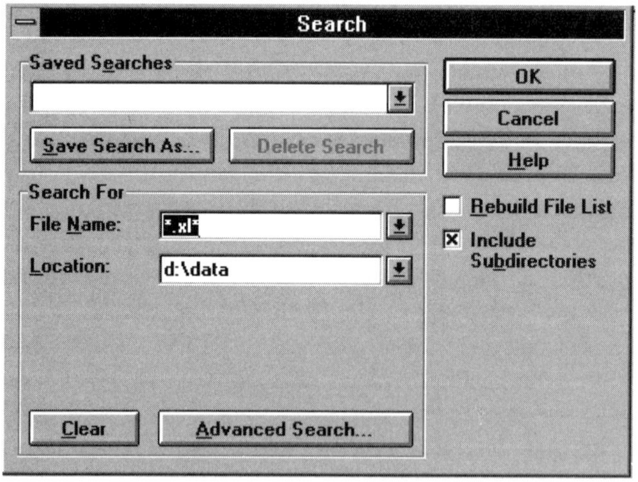

Figure 1.41 Find File Search Dialog Box

You have to give Excel the directory and/or drive to be searched. To enter Summary Info criteria, you click on the Advanced Search command button. Click on the Summary tab to bring that filecard to the top. You would enter the criteria for your search here and then send Excel off looking for files. Pretty cool indeed. See Figure 1.42.

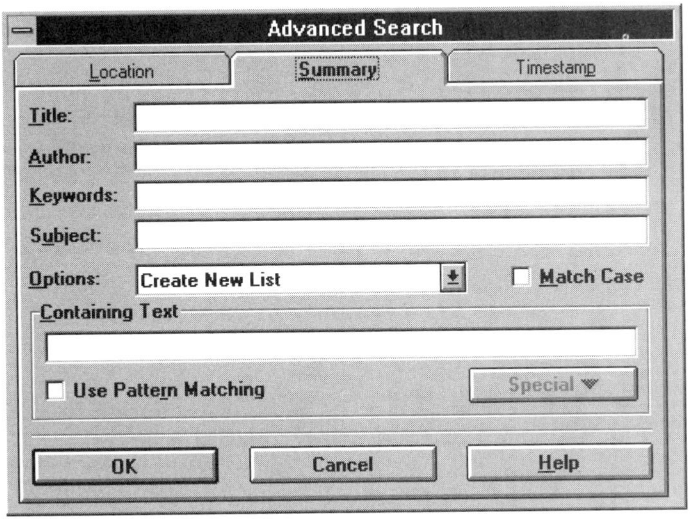

Figure 1.42 Advanced Search Dialog Box

If you've never had a problem finding your files and think this is all a big waste of time, by all means clear this Prompt for Summary Info box. But we *like* it.

If you've been ignoring the cool advice that the TipWizard has been giving you, you might want to check the Reset TipWizard check box. When you check this box, the TipWizard, which has been real careful to not nag at you about the same things over and over, will start from scratch giving you advice.

A tip on tips

This is an odd implementation of the check box control. You check the Reset TipWizard check box and click on OK and the TipWizard is immediately reset. But if you go back to the Tools/Options/General dialog box, you will see that the check box is not checked. Resetting the TipWizard also clears the check box that reset it. Guess it makes sense in a twisted sort of way.

Hey, do you really need 16 blank sheets every time you create a new book? No? Well, you know what? We don't either. The Sheets in New Workbook control is where you stop that nonsense. Set it to uno, single, singular, solo, solitary, *just one stupid sheet!* If you need more sheets in your book, you can, oh my gosh, *insert* them as needed. What a concept.

Sheets in New Workbook

An empty book (no entries) with 16 sheets consumes 11,776 bytes if saved to disk. An empty book with 1 sheet eats up only 7680 bytes, so save some disk space. That's 4K on every single-sheet book versus the bloated 16-sheet book.

Set standard font and point size

Next, you can change the standard font and point size. If Arial 10 doesn't do it for you, here's where you change it.

Default File Location

The Default File Location takes a fully qualified path and sets the directory that Excel will log onto when you first fire it up. This setting overrides the similar setting in Program Manager.

You must type in a correct path (no trailing backslash, please!) or Excel will complain with a "Cannot access directory 'd:\badpath'." type of message. No, you cannot browse the disk, and if you type in a nonexistent directory, Excel will not ask if you want to create it. Why? Dunno.

Alternate Startup File Location

The Alternate Startup File Location is a cool idea. You see, when Excel 5 is installed, it creates a directory called XLSTART right beneath the directory where you installed Excel. If you create a template, (yeah, we know, we still haven't talked about templates yet; they come later, trust us), you put it in the XLSTART directory and Excel can find it later.

Well, a lot of people running Excel are on networks and their companies usually have some templates that they encourage everyone to use. They keep those templates on a network server somewhere. Users, however, like to feel that they have a modicum of control over their lives, and so *they* like to create their own templates. The ability to specify an Alternate Startup File Location reconciles both groups. You can effectively have two XLSTART directories: the XLSTART directory that was created when Excel was installed, and the Alternate directory that you define here. Excel can then use templates (and other things) from either location.

If you want a second XLSTART directory, enter the path here. Sorry, no browse, you've got to enter it correctly or no brass ring *<sigh>*. And you have to exit Excel and restart it in order for changes to this setting to take effect.

User Name Box

Last, but not least, make sure that your name is entered properly in the User Name box. Excel associates you as the author of books and macros and related stuff by getting your name from here, so make sure it's spelled right!

ZOOMING

It is better to take the high ground.

Amok Shing, Mongol
My Years in the Horde (from the modern translation by K. Tibet, 1972)

Zoom, sometimes it's hot...

From a high place you can see better. This is the idea behind zooming the view of your sheet. And a good idea it is, too. If you want to see how your model is shaping up, or see what the heck is going on with someone else's model, zoom waaaay out to about 25% and take the bird's eye view.

Excel provides the Zoom Control on the Standard toolbar for precisely this purpose. You drop down the list of settings, and you can choose from any of the preset choices: 200, 100, 75, 50, 25, or Selection. The problem with the preset choices is that they are always too much or too little. Go figure. The Selection setting is cool. Highlight the range you want to fit on screen and click Selection in the Zoom Control. The sheet is zoomed out or in to fill the display with your highlighted cells.

You can also enter a percentage figure (from 10 through 400) and hit Enter. It all boils down to trial and error to get it zoomed just right, and it can really be quite tedious.

What Excel needs is a slider like Microsoft has in WinWord. What? You say you missed that feature in WinWord. Well, Microsoft is not too proud of it, and you have to manually add it to the toolbar (so new?).

If you pull down the View menu, you will find a Zoom option. This gives you a dialog box to change your zoom setting. See Figure 1.43.

Sometimes it's not...

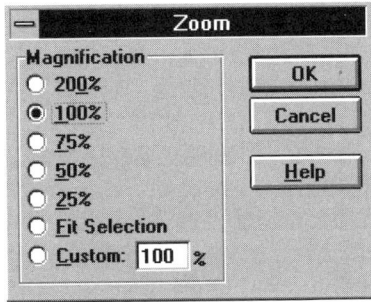

Figure 1.43 Excel's Barely Adequate Zoom Dialog Box

These are the same settings as the toolbar Zoom Control. You get a custom button with a text box (but no spin buttons, so you can forget about using the mouse to change the numbers). There's no preview box. Overall, it's barely functional.

Say you enter a custom setting of 135% and click OK. Now you want to go back to 100%. You can use the Zoom Control, but for now let's stick with the Zoom dialog box. View, Zoom, and click on 100%. Odd, it entered the 100% figure in the custom setting box, too. Click OK. Now you want to change it back to 135%. View, Zoom, and holy moley, Batman, where is the custom 135% setting you entered earlier?

Well, Robin, it's gone! The custom setting is *not sticky*. It does not hang around. It's bye-bye, hasta la vista, baby. What was Microsoft thinking? Dumb, really dumb. Yeah, it was broken in Excel 4, too, but we were hoping they would fix it in Excel 5.

One step
forward, two
back

In case you were wondering, WinWord 2 did keep the custom setting, separate from the other zoom settings, so you could easily switch between, say, 100% and 115%. And if you exited and restarted, WinWord remembered any custom settings. And WinWord 6? Oh, WinWord 6 is slowly going the way of Excel 5. It will remember the last zoom setting in effect when it is shut down, but you cannot switch between a built-in setting and a custom setting. Somewhere in the back of our mind we can hear our Mom yelling, "And if your friends jumped off the roof, I suppose you'd jump off too?" Apparently Microsoft would've answered, "sure, Mom."

Anyway, you will find yourself addicted to zooming once you start using it no matter that they made it real unfriendly to use. Combined with the Full Screen view zooming can't be beat.

TIPWIZARD: GOOD JOB, REDMOND (REALLY)

> The magician Merlin had a strange laugh, and it was heard when nobody else was laughing....He laughed because he knew what was coming next.
>
> Robertson Davies
> *World of Wonders*, 1976

TipWizard is an "over the shoulder" companion, there only when you want it (you can always turn it off). A veritable on-demand back-seat worksheet driver. This mini-expert system really pays off if you give it half a chance. For novice Excelites, it's a great way to learn faster ways to do things. Ditto for power users because you'll be amazed at the number of black holes in your personal Excel knowledge base! Just turn on TipWizard and let it determine how flush your Excel shtick is.

A TipWizard Magical Mystery Tour

This baby has a number of features worth exploring. Take, for example, the simple act of copying from one location to another:

**TipWizard
button**

1. If the TipWizard toolbar isn't visible, click the TipWizard button.

2. Create a new workbook, and then type some data, any data, into cell A1.

3. Select the cell A1.

4. Select Edit from the menu bar, and then choose Copy. TipWizard immediately chimes in with "To copy cells or graphic objects, click the Copy button on the Standard toolbar. ➜." See Figure 1.44.

5. Select the destination range by clicking in cell B1, and then press Enter.

Related tool

Tip Help button

Figure 1.44 The TipWizard Toolbar

In the preceding example, when TipWizard displays its tip, it also displays the Copy button right there on the TipWizard toolbar. TipWizard gives you the tip and the tool all in one fell swoop! If you want to move the button revealed by TipWizard to one of your current toolbars, you can do that as well. Select View, choose Toolbars, drag the tool to the desired toolbar, and click Cancel in the Toolbars dialog box.

Furthermore, if you click the convenient Tip Help button, Excel takes you directly to the "Copying cells" How To help topic. Neat.

Making a List and Checking It Thrice

TipWizard actually has a memory, and a very polite one at that. If you continue to insist on copying the selected cells to the clipboard via the laborious "select Edit from the menu bar then choose Copy" technique, it shuts up. In fact, you could repeat that technique a jillion times during the current Excel session, and TipWizard would be sound asleep in the back seat. Not a peep. But as soon as you quit and restart Excel, TipWizard takes a fresh outlook on your wearisome copying technique, *waiting until you stubbornly repeat the operation for the third time* to prompt you with . the original message, "To copy cells or graphic objects, click the Copy button on the Standard toolbar. ➜." It's so charmingly chivalrous.

Who said chivalry was dead?

The really interesting part is that TipWizard keeps track of all the outstanding operations and counts the occurrences for each one—*independently*. So when we said in the earlier paragraph that TipWizard is catching some zzz's while you doggedly trudge through the long way of copying cells over and over again, that's true. But if in the meantime you decide to interrupt your tiresome toiling with a different, new operation—say, formatting a cell blue—TipWizard's back on point for that operation and lets you have it right between the eyes, "Yo, user, instead of the five mouse strokes you just plunked down, why not click the Color button on the Formatting toolbar?" Oh, yeah *<sheepish grin>*.

You can even reset TipWizard's memory. This sets all of TipWizard's parallel process counters back to zero. The fastest way to do this is hold down the Control key, and then click the TipWizard button. Alternately, select Tools Options General, select the Reset TipWizard check box, and press OK.

They thought of everything!

If you didn't notice the up and down arrows inside TipWizard's suggestion box, then welcome to yet another TipWizard nicety. These up and down controls let you scroll through the history of all the tips TipWizard has proffered during your current Excel session.

TipWizard is keen and well implemented. Microsoft at its best. So, Redmond, why isn't there a TipWizard in WinWord 6? Go figure.

MULTIDIMENSION SCHMULTIDIMENSION

> Don't touch that.
>
> Buckaroo Banzai
> *Adventures Across the 8th Dimension*

When was the last time you fired up Excel to balance your household budget, to project your firm's sales, or to track soybean futures and had cause to use more than one worksheet to do so? Come on, tell the truth.

Ah ha, we thought so, and that is why we had you set the default number of sheets for a workbook to 1 in the last section. Now don't get us wrong, multidimensional models can be very useful, at the right time and place. Multidimensional models are primarily useful when crunching numbers down and across just doesn't cut it.

Say you have two divisions (oh, yes, the classic example) in your company and each prepares an essentially identical spreadsheet. See Figure 1.45.

	A	B	C	D	E	F	C
1							
2		Southwest Divison					
3			1st Qtr	2nd Qtr	3rd Qtr	4th Qtr	
4		Widgets	100	98	101	65	
5		Doohickeys	125	77	108	75	
6		Thingys	117	100	99	87	
7		Total	342	275	308	227	
8							

Figure 1.45 Sample Divisional Recap Sheet

Each division sends you their recap sheets, and it is your job to consolidate this into a grand total. Ta da, a multidimensional model to the rescue. You copy each sheet into a new book and create a sheet therein to do the consolidation. See Figure 1.46.

Here you can see the syntax of the "drill through" sum formula that picks up the contents of the other two sheets, using both cell references and the preferred method of named ranges. We will visit the hows and whys of range names in Chapter 4.

	A	B	C	D	E	F
1						
2		Company Totals				
3			1st Qtr	2nd Qtr	3rd Qtr	4th Qtr
4		Widgets	=SUM(Sheet2:Sheet3!C4)	199	213	140
5		Doohickeys	=SUM(Doohickeys)	169	206	150
6		Thingys	226	186	203	166
7		Total	226	554	622	456
8						

Figure 1.46 Consolidated Recap Sheet

SAFE SPREADSHEETS

> For what appears truth to the one may appear to be error to the other.
>
> Mahatma Gandhi, 1922

Okay. We're down on our knees, supplicant, eyes searching the heavens, hands clasped together palms inward, see, see? Like, *we're not kidding:* **Audit...**

Please, please, please audit your Excel models. **...audit...**

Why? Even the simplest model can contain dozens of formulas. Sure, you've been careful building your latest earnings projection model. But Excel doesn't *automatically* wander past your desk from time to time, lean in over your shoulder and huskily inquire, "Yo, what's that formula doin' right there, yeah, that one pointing off into the gamma quadrant where even Dr. Crusher can't help you?" At least it doesn't do this *automatically* in version 5 … maybe the "automatically" part will come in version 6!? (That would be unbelievably excellent.) But Excel 5 does come very, very, very, very close because you can *voluntarily* use Excel's Auditing tools to get the same effect. See Figure 1.47. **...and audit some more**

Figure 1.47 The Fabulous Auditing Toolbar

The caveat is: it's up to you to proactively do the auditing. We wish we could reach right out through these pages, right here and now, grab you by the lapels and impress upon you how important auditing is. In Chapter 5 we provide a macro that forces the Auditing toolbar to show itself every time you start Excel, even if you turned it off during your last session. *That's how strongly we feel.* Gee, could you tell?

The Auditing toolbar and its associated features may well be the single most welcome, useful, oh-thank-you-God feature of Excel 5. The Troubleshooting and Documenting a Worksheet chapter of the *User's Guide* is required reading. Eat it, breathe it, sleep it. These features will save your bacon some dark and stormy night when you're tangled up in a rat's nest of circular references or just some plain ol' formula that's pointing to the wrong blasted cell.

Savings galore   In fact, the one piece of advice our humble little tome has to offer that will repay your purchase most handsomely is this: *turn on the Auditing toolbar right now and use it.* (You know, Jim, I'd *swear* there's an echo in here.) Call us presumptuous, prescient, omniscient, whatever, but we guarantee that if you use Excel 5's auditing features regularly, you'll save yourself lots of embarrassment and probably some seriously good money. Thank you.

An Auditing Teaser

In Chapter 5 we'll show you how to audit your models, and it's all G-rated! But for now how 'bout a little foreplay? Let's look at Figure 1.48.

B5	⬇	=B3*C2			
	A	**B**	**C**	**D**	**E**	**F**
1		Current Year				
2	Revenue		40%	of Contract complete as of this date		
3	Gross Sales	$500,000				
4	Gross Margin (%)	30%				
5	Gross Profit	$200,000				
6	**Expenses**					
7	General	$25,000				
8	Selling	$25,000				
9	Administrative	$50,000				
10	Total Expenses	$75,000				
11	**Pre-tax Earnings**	$125,000				
12						

Figure 1.48 Covering Your Assets

Trace Precedents button

You select cell B5. Click on the Trace Precedents button. You can instantly see that instead of basing the calculation on Gross Margin, B5's using the contract completion percentage. This overstates Gross Profit, which in turn overstates Pre-tax Earnings. (Maybe that's good for stockholders and Wall Street analysts, but it's bad when your company's tax bill comes due.)

Then you select cell B10 (see Figure 1.49). Click on Trace Precedents again. Now you see tangible evidence, right there on your worksheet, that you've fallen victim to another common spreadsheet error—the summation formula range omits the topmost cell in the range to be added. When you next get near a color monitor, try this on for size yourself 'cuz these precedence tracing arrows are an electrifying, elucidating bright blue. Very snazzy.

B10	⬇		=SUM(B8:B9)				
	A	**B**	**C**	**D**	**E**	**F**
1		Current Year				
2	Revenue			40% of Contract complete as of this date		
3	Gross Sales	$500,000				
4	Gross Margin (%)	30%				
5	Gross Profit	$200,000				
6	**Expenses**					
7	General	$25,000				
8	Selling	$25,000				
9	Administrative	$50,000				
10	Total Expenses	$75,000				
11	**Pre-tax Earnings**	$125,000				
12						

Figure 1.49 The Hits Just Keep on Comin'

Vanishing Formula Syndrome

Another common problem is what we call the "vanishing formula" syndrome. It happens when a formula gets overwritten with a value at some point in the worksheet's life. In Figure 1.50 you see a traditional cell display.

J1	⬇		Expenses		
	J	**K**	**L**	**M**
1	**Expenses**	**Jan**	**Feb**	**Mar**
2	Rent	$6,000	$6,000	$6,000
3	Insurance	$720	$0	$0
4	Supplies	$225	$250	$287
5	Payroll	$22,187	$22,187	$37,500
6	Total Expenses	$29,132	$22,187	$43,787
7				

Figure 1.50 Cell Display View

Press CTRL + ` (back apostrophe) to switch to a formula display, as in Figure 1.51.

J1	⬇		Expenses		

	J	**K**	**L**	**M**
1	**Expenses**	Jan	Feb	Mar
2	Rent	6000	6000	6000
3	Insurance	720	0	0
4	Supplies	225	250	287
5	Payroll	22187	22187	37500
6	Total Expenses	=SUM(K2:K5)	22187	=SUM(M2:M5)
7				

Figure 1.51 Formula Display View

Notice anything odd about good ol' L6? It's not a formula, just a value, and therefore it understates February's expenses. Once again an auditing feature saves the day. We like CTRL + ` so much that in Chapter 5 we show you how to add a button to your Auditing toolbar so you don't have to remember that awkward hot-key sequence. Nonetheless, we rest our case. Excel 5's auditing features will pay you back lavishly, so use them.

2 The Playing Field

To understand the way of a thing, be it a sword, a woman, or an army…
that is what gives one an advantage in any venture.

Amok Shing, Mongol
My Years in the Horde (from the modern translation by K. Tibet, 1972)

Let's start off with a relatively large chunk of Excel, the workbook, and chew it finer and finer as we digest some Excel fundamentals. Ah, the mighty "book." You tamed it somewhat when you limited a new book to only a single sheet to start off its existence. So what's the scoop?

THE WORKBOOK

Would you like to make a little book on that?

Nathan Detroit
Guys and Dolls

Startup switches notwithstanding, when Excel fires up its warp engines, it presents you with a brand new workbook called Book1. Create another new book and Excel calls it Book2. There's a sort of symmetry to it, don't you think?

The "book" is the primary unit of a spreadsheet model. Throughout this text we use the term "model" in the sense of "a hypothetical or stylized representation, as of an atom."* Your profit and loss statement, for example, isn't the actual cash flowing in and out of your pockets over time, but rather a representation thereof.

The book, and all within it, is stored as a binary file, which is written to disk when you save it.

Webster's New World Dictionary, 1988

51

The book is the outermost container into which you put your sheets. Sheets are the layers upon which you build your model. And a fine assortment of sheet types you have to choose from:

- The Worksheet (This is the standard worksheet that you all know and love.)
- The Chart Sheet (You can also embed a chart on a worksheet if you don't want it on a sheet of its own.)
- The Visual Basic Module (This is where you program your macros as you did in Chapter 1.)
- The Dialog Sheet (This is where you build dialog boxes for your VBA macros.)
- The MS Excel 4.0 Macro Sheet (Oh yeah, you can still have good old macro sheets 'cuz Excel's XLM programming language is alive and well and fully supported under Excel 5.)

How many sheets can you have in a book? You're limited only by the amount of memory installed in your computer. And each sheet is *bound* into the book.

Bound and unbound sheets are terms used in Excel 4. If you were used to having a central worksheet as an unbound worksheet in several Excel 4 workbooks, forget it! In Excel 5 all sheets are bound in that they have no independent existence outside of the Excel 5 workbook. If you want to share information across books, you do it via linking. This can really wreak havoc with Excel 4 models being transferred to Excel 5, as you can imagine.

Saving the Book

> It would be bad.
>
> Dr. Egon Spengler
> *Ghostbusters*

You could save a book under its default name such as Book1. It's easy. *Too* easy. Start Excel, hit the Save button, and hit Enter. Your book is saved as `BOOK1.XLS`. Saving an Excel book under its default name is bad. Major bad. *Don't say we didn't warn you...*

Anyone who gets in the habit of saving files under default names is an accident waiting to happen. Why? Because, when you shut down Excel and then restart it, you get a new book, again named Book1, that's why.

 Excel has a long and glorious history of this bizarre behavior. Since day one, it has provided default names for its files. Oh, it's not a bug, it's a *feature*. Some feature! Say you get lazy and name a book `BOOK1.XLS`. The next time you use Excel, you go to save your book and Excel cheerfully offers to save it for you

under the name Book1. You try to save it to the same directory that has the Book1 that you saved in the previous session. Excel warns you, sorta, by asking you if you want to "Replace existing 'BOOK1.XLS'?". So now what? Do you replace it because you're sure that this book is the book you want to save and the other is some old scratch book that you don't need, or do you decide you'd better pick another name. And how much time do you spend pondering this little puzzle.

There is a law of physics, er, spreadsheets that says that if you ever, ever, save a file under its default name and overwrite an existing file with the same default name, the file you overwrite will be the file you desperately need. And the more you need it, the less likely it is that you have a backup copy handy, if at all. This is not a pleasant sensation.

You can't change the laws of physics, Jim

A Word of Warning

So why in the name of three-corner bank shots does Microsoft make it so amazingly easy to foul up like this? Dunno. We've trained a passle of users in the ways of Excel and have always had to issue the warning about default filenames. Like your mother warned you about strangers with candy. Sheesh.

WinWord 2 had this problem licked. It gave you a default document name of DOCUMENT1, which was great. Each new document was incremented, and you couldn't save a document under the default name. In WinWord 6 the first new document is still DOCUMENT1, but that name *is the window name only*. When you go to save it, WinWord defaults the file name to DOC1.DOC. Like laying Astroturf over quicksand, a disaster waiting to happen.

Remember, *don't take any rides from…oh…sorry, don't save any files using the default name!* Always, always, always give each file you save a unique name.

Use unique filenames.

A SHEET BY ANY OTHER NAME

> Somewhere, what with all these clouds, and all this air,
> There must be a rare name, somewhere…
> How do you like "Cloud-Cuckoo-Land"?
>
> Aristophanes
> *Birds*, 414 BC

If you've been humoring us, er, we mean taking our sage advice from the beginning, your Book1 should only have a single sheet—worksheet. What if you decide you want another worksheet, or some other type of sheet for that matter. How do you insert sheet thingys into your book?

You have to be left to be right. Easy. New sheets are inserted *to the left of the active* sheet. So right-click on the sheet tab to the right of where you want the new sheet to appear. Excel displays the shortcut menu. See Figure 2.1.

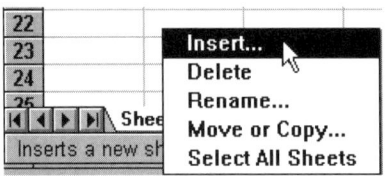

Figure 2.1 Sheet Tab Shortcut Menu

Click on Insert and you can select the type of sheet you want to add (see Figure 2.2). The selected sheet type in the Insert dialog box defaults to the "type" of the current active sheet. This is another rounded corner that makes Excel a pleasure to work in. You cannot add a sheet to the right of the active sheet. You can, however, left-click and drag a sheet tab to reorder the tabs displayed along the bottom of the book.

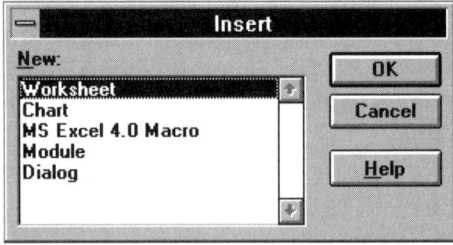

Figure 2.2 Sheet Selection Dialog Box

The Worksheet

As sudden as a slammed door, I'm a Booth Tarkington character in a Mickey Spillane situation.

Oscar Gordon
Robert Heinkin, *Glory Road*

The worksheet is that empty spreadsheet we talked about in Chapter 1. Lots of empty cells in every direction. Lots. This is where you build whatever it is that you're gonna build with this program.

It's an Array, It's a Matrix, It's a Really Large Table

> Space is big. Really big. You just won't believe how vastly hugely mind-bogglingly big it is.
>
> Douglas Adams
> *The Hitchhiker's Guide to the Galaxy*

A worksheet is a colossal two-dimensional table made up of rows and columns. Where each row intersects with a column you have a cell. You put stuff in the cells and define the relationships between them.

Basically, building a worksheet goes something like this: you enter headings, type in some labels, add your numbers, write some formulas, maybe format it so it's pretty, audit the hell out of it, and print out the results. Well, maybe there's a little more to it than that, but you get the idea.

It Shrinks, It Grows, It's Alive

Columns and rows are elastic in that you can widen, narrow, shorten, and stretch them. The easiest way to deal with resizing rows and columns is with the mouse. For example, you put the Sizing Grabber™ on the line between two column headings and you can click and drag, changing the width of the column on the left. See Figure 2.3.

One size fits all

Figure 2.3 Column Sizing Grabber™

If you double-click on this line, the column snaps to fit (called AutoFit, natch) the widest entry in the column. You can limit what snaps to fit by selecting only the cells you want to adjust for, but to do this you are forced to use the main menu and go through the whole Format Column AutoFit Selection routine. Microsoft should have put this option on the shortcut menu (where are those lab rats when you need 'em?). You can AutoFit rows as well. AutoFit applies to the entire row and cannot be limited to a selection.

To change more than one column, select all the columns you want to change and drag the right edge of any one of them. You can multiselect columns by clicking and dragging across the column headings or by using the SHIFT + click or CTRL + click methods shown earlier. The columns need *not* be contiguous.

While you're dragging the edge of a row or column with the mouse, you can take a gander at the Name Box, which displays the exact height or width figure for the row or column you are changing. It takes a steady hand, but you can get very precise in nailing an exact figure using the mouse. But what do the numbers mean?

Row height   Well, row height is measured in points. There are 72 points per inch, so if you want a ½-inch row, you set it to 36 points. No sweat. A standard row starts off at 12.75 points. Why? Why not? That's like asking who built Stonehenge.

Column width   A column starts with a default setting of 8.43. Ah, but 8.43 what, you may ask. We vaguely remember asking someone that very same question. Seems that it's 8.43 monospaced characters per inch, dependent on the font that is used for Normal style, that can fit into a single cell width. If the Normal style font is a proportional font, 8.43 represents the number of zeros that can fit into a single cell width.

A row or column can be reduced to a zero height or width (they cannot go below zero), at which point they disappear and are said to be "hidden." Let's all say this together: *just because you can't see it doesn't mean it isn't there!* A hidden row or column is not visible on screen and doesn't print, but you can bet your sweet bippy that it's there. If you have formulas in a hidden row or column, they formulate as if they were visible. (Column width units must be in the range from 0 through 255 and row height units must be from 0 through 409.)

It used to be a real pain to unhide hidden rows or columns, but no longer. The Redmond Rangers done real good on this 'un. Say you have hidden columns C, D, and E. Now you want to display them. No problem. Place the mouse pointer between columns B and F (you'll note that the line between these two column letters is a tad thicker than usual). As the mouse pointer touches the dividing line, you'll see the familiar Horizontal Sizing Grabber™. Move the pointer a skosh to the right and you get the Split Bar Grabber™. See Figure 2.4.

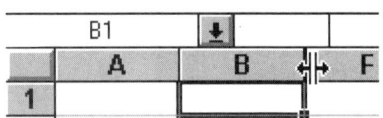

Figure 2.4 Resizing a Column That You Can't Even See

Drag to the right to resize first column E, then D, and then C (one at a time and in that order).

You can also change the standard width for every column that has not been manually resized. Pull down the Format menu and select Column. From the flyout menu, select Standard Width. Type in the new standard width setting. Every column that has not been manually resized changes width to the new setting. Note that any column that is part of the current active selection is resized, whether it was manually resized or not. There is no similar provision for changing the standard row height. Then again we have never wanted to change the standard row height. Maybe those lab rats aren't as wacko as we thought. Nahhhh.

Spreadsheet Modeling on the Worksheet

The worksheet is where you build your model, so we had best discuss what a model is or should be.

Spreadsheet models are often built using a diagonal diamond pattern. A typical model might look like the one shown in Figure 2.5. General descriptions, constants, error checking calculations all go into the top left shaded area. Down and to the right go raw data and general calculations. Down and to the right of that goes the report area. You keep adding sections, as needed, down and right as far as needed until you either finish your model or run out of memory. What this type of model construction allows you to do is insert rows and columns or change column widths or row heights in any one section without disturbing the layout of any other section.

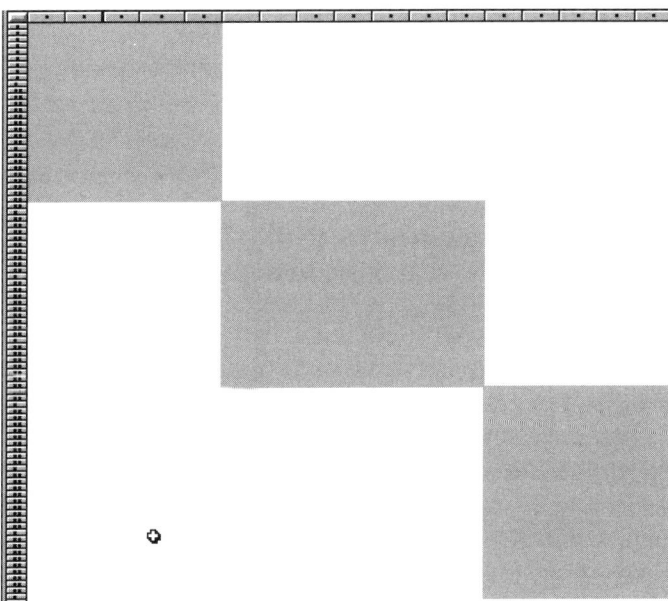

Figure 2.5 Classic Diamond Pattern

There are some minor problems, however, with this approach. Excel calculates each cell from left to right and top to bottom, so the optimal way to construct a worksheet is narrow and tall to maximize performance.

Oh, what a tangled web…

An alternative practice is to place each section of a model in its own worksheet and link the key data where needed from one sheet to another. Ah, but linking presents its own special problems. You do not want to link helter-skelter from this sheet to that, hither and thither. This type of construction is to be avoided. See Figure 2.6.

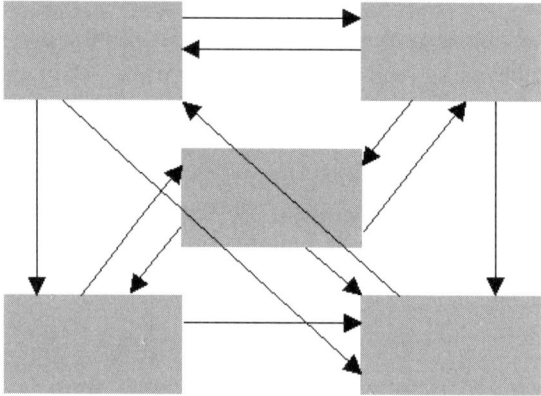

Figure 2.6 Not Like This, Please!

Neatness counts

A better design keeps the number of links minimized and flowing from sheet to sheet only where needed. Figure 2.7 shows a better linking model. Try to limit your links between sheets (or books, for that matter) to a one-to-many relationship (the dash arrows) *or* a many-to-one (solid arrows) relationship. This saves on recalculation performance and gives you some hope of deciphering the model's data flow after it has been built.

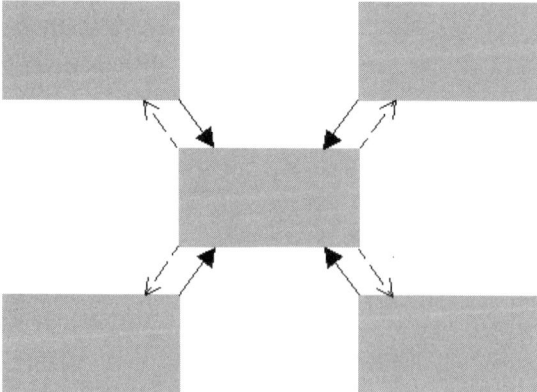

Figure 2.7 Either One-to-Many or Many-to-One

The Chart Sheet

> ...essentially statistical graphics are instruments to help people reason about quantitative information.
>
> Edward R. Tufte
> *The Visual Display of Quantitative Information*

Excel does charts. You can embed a chart on the graphic drawing layer of a sheet or a chart can be created by itself in its own sheet.

One picture is worth 1000 words and all that.

Which way is better? Sorry, pilgrim, that is a subjective question and our mothers didn't raise any foolish children. We respond with the standard hedge: "It depends on what you want to do." The pat answer is that you embed when you want to show the chart on the same printed page as some other data. There. How's that for going out on a limb?

For example, you might embed a chart on a worksheet when you want to show the chart next to the table of data that the chart is based on. Or you might want to embed a chart of one type on a chart sheet showing the same data charted as a different type. Ah, the possibilities are endless.

The way to do a chart is first select the data (that sounds simple, but *oh, brother!*) and insert a chart sheet. This kicks in Excel's wondrous ChartWizard. ChartWizard is very cool and walks you through the steps necessary to create a chart. Walk through the steps or hit the Finish button and you have got your chart sheet complete with chart. We'll talk more about charts in Chapter 6. *Oh, brother!*

The Visual Basic Module

> The word-coining genius, as if thought plunged into a sea of words and came up dripping.
>
> Virginia Woolf
> *An Elizabethan Play*, 1925

The module sheet (as you saw in Chapter 1) is where you write your Visual Basic for Applications (VBA) code. VBA is the Wunderkind universal macro language soon to appear in a Microsoft program near you!

In case you've been living in a cave for the last year, those mighty morphin' Microsofties have this plan to conquer the world, er, no, well *yes*, they do have *that* plan, but they *also* plan to implement a single macro language across all their applications, like WinWord, Excel, PowerPoint, Project, Access...hmmm, a regular *Office* full of products! The point is that you learn one language and then you can program in any application. A lofty goal and one we heartily support. It needs a little work but they're on the right track. We'll talk more about VBA in Chapter 10.

The Dialog Sheet

Prior to Excel 5 you could run a separate program called `EXCELDE.EXE` to create **custom** (also referred to as **user-defined**) dialog boxes for use in your macros to avoid having to enter the dialog box coordinates manually. You then copied the dialog box into your macro sheet or worksheet, where it appeared as the XLM coordinates required to display the dialog box.

In Excel 5 you get an integrated dialog box builder. You create your custom dialog box on the dialog sheet using the Visual Basic type drawing tools. In your module sheet, you add the code to your procedure (a **procedure** is a fancy way to say macro) to display the dialog box at the appropriate time. Ta da!

Dialog sheets are usually hidden (that's Format Sheet Hide, *not* Window Hide, which hides the entire book).

The MS Excel 4.0 Macro Sheet

> Microsoft has promised that Excel 6 also will be able to run Excel [XLM] macros.
>
> Ron Person
> *Using Excel Version 5 for Windows*

Here's an old friend. The good old macro sheet is still around as those of you who cut your teeth on XLM, Excel's older programming language, will be relieved to hear.

We recommend the VBA language, we really do. But it is nice to know that if you need to knock out a macro using the XLM language, you still have the option. And most of your old macros will work unmodified in Excel 5.

TEXT, NUMBERS, AND FORMULAS: A HAT TRICK

> Meanwhile, back at the ranch...
>
> Radio drama cliché

Meanwhile, back at the worksheet, the topic of discussion turns once again to the lowly cell—that intersection point of row and column. A meeting place, as it were, in the matrix. There's the sign post up ahead...oops, got carried away.

Let's talk about what you can put inside cells. Excel provides several cell content "types" as follows:

- Text
- Numbers
- Formulas

- Blanks

- Booleans (a.k.a. logicals)

- Errors

String 'em Up Boys

> Reason, in itself confounded,
> Saw division grow together.
>
> William Shakespeare
> *The Phoenix and the Turtle*, 1601

Since you now know that when you work in Excel you're actually programming, you can probably cope with our calling a piece of text a **text string**. We are talking about plain old text as in you type something like SALES REVENUE in a cell and hit ENTER. Text is also known as a **label**. Text is limited to 255 characters in a cell. Text is left aligned in a cell, numbers are right aligned, and Booleans and errors are centered, unless you override the general alignment settings. You can change the alignment of the results of a cell, and you can format a number so it *appears* to be text.

Text strings

Basic text strings behave pretty well. Remember that you are in a programming environment and should use the tools available to you. For example, you should never have to type in a label twice. Consider Figure 2.8.

	A	B
1	Sales Income	
2	West Coast	
3	East Coast	
4	Total Sales Income	

Figure 2.8 Text Strings (Labels by Another Name)

Say you change your mind and decide to use the word "Revenue" instead of "Income" in your model. You could edit every cell with the string "Income". Excel even provides great search and replace tools that you could use. But, if you learn to manipulate text strings like you do numbers, changes are a snap. Instead of entering the string "Total Sales Income" in cell A4, you use a string concatenation formula like ="Total "&A1 then any changes to the string in cell A1 would be reflected in cell A4. Note the space between the "l" in the word "Total" and the closing quotation mark in the formula. You've got to watch your spacing when you concatenate strings.

The ampersand (&) is the concatenation operator and is used to join text strings together. The text strings can be located in other cells or entered in the formula itself inside double quotation marks or both as in this example. You can concatenate cells with numbers in them as well as text strings.

Excel 5's help file says you can format numbers as text and gives you two ways to do it, implying that both methods are the same. Uh, they left something out. You can, they say, format a cell containing a number as text by selecting Format Cells Text OK. Or you can precede the number in the cell with an apostrophe ('). To see what we mean, try this:

1. Enter the values 1, 2, and 3 in column A rows 1, 2, and 3, respectively. Do the same in columns B and C.

2. Select cell B1.

3. Pull down the Format menu.

4. Select the Cells option.

5. Click on the Number tab in the Cells dialog box.

6. Choose Text in the Category list and click on OK.

Then format C1 by editing the cell contents. Precede the number 1 with an apostrophe or change the entry to either ="1" or =TEXT(1,0). All have the effect of entering the number as text. Leave column A alone as the control (it shows us how columns B and C started out). The 1 in B1 and the 1 in C1 become left aligned as you would expect.

Ah, but if you sort B1:B3 in ascending order and then sort C1:C3 the same way, you get some very interesting results. See Figure 2.9.

	A	B	C	D	E
1	1	1	2	4	=SUM(A1:C1)
2	2	2	3		
3	3	3	1		6	=SUM(A3:C3)
4	6	6	6		
5	=A1+A2+A3	=B1+B2+B3	=C1+C2+C3		
6		B1 as text	C3 as '1		

Figure 2.9 Numbers as Text

To sort the cells as we have in this example, select the first range, B1:B3, and choose Sort from the Data menu. Check the "Continue with the current selection" option button in the Sort Warning dialog box and click on Sort. Next check the "No Header Row" option button in the My List Has section of the Sort dialog box and click on OK. Do the same for C1:C3.

Hold on tight to your reasoning facilities, pilgrim, because we are sailing into uncharted waters where the maps just say "Thyr be Monsters."

The 1 in cell B1 sorts as if it is still a number, for the very good reason that Excel's sort function *sees it as a number*. The numeric value is displayed as text, but it sorts as a number nevertheless.

The 1 in cell C1 sorts as you would expect text to sort and winds up in cell C3 (values precede text in an ascending sort). So the apostrophe method (or the `="1"` or the `=TEXT(1,0)` methods) actually makes the number text *as far as the sort is concerned!*

Let's add the cells A1:C1 using a fairly standard `=SUM()` function in column D (the formulas are displayed in column E). The value formatted as text in B1 is included in the formula. Okay, so the sort and the `=SUM()` function see the 1 as a number. So far so good. Let's try adding A3:C3. Hmmm, the apostrophe keeps the number in C3 from being seen by `=SUM()` as a number. It's treated as text. So sort and `=SUM()` are consistent. And, we might add, you get the same results with other functions like `=MAX()`, `=MIN()`, and so on.

Clang, clang, unidentified sea creature sighted off the port bow! Let's try adding the columns down. In A4 we add the range A1:A3 using a simple formula (*not a function*) and copy it to B4 and C4 (formulas shown on row 5). The result in A4 is fine, no worries, mate. But B4 and C4, oh, the mind boggles. We'll take them on one at a time.

Notice in B4 that even though the formula returns the expected result, 6, it picks up the text formatting from B1. And it's not because B1 is the first referenced cell in the formula. You could have entered the formula as `=B2+B3+B1` and gotten the same result. It's because B1 is the first cell in the range. Okay, follow along closely on this one. If you had *not* formatted B1 as text, entered the formula, *and then formatted* `B1` *as text*, the formula would *not* take on the text format. Oh, man, It's like having your head pushed through a bucket of oatmeal. But wait! There's more.

The formula in good old C4 sees C3 *as a number!* It is more than happy to add it to C1 and C2. So Excel operators see numbers-entered-as-text as numbers and act upon them accordingly, whereas the Excel functions do not.

There are four ways that we know of to make a number appear as text:

- Enter `500` and format it via Format Cells Number Text.
- Enter `'500`.
- Enter `=TEXT(500,0)`. The format code following the comma determines the displayed format of the number, that is, decimal, currency, and so on.
- Enter `="500"`.

Sometimes Excel treats the number as text and, as you have seen in this section; other times Excel treats the number as a number. Watch out for this one, pilgrim. It bites.

Wrap it up   You can wrap your strings within a cell. This was new back in Excel 4 and was (and is) *very popular*. You set your column width and then turn on the wrap attribute. Under Format Cells Alignment, check the Wrap Text check box. You can also force a line break in a text string by hitting ALT + ENTER as you're typing in the string. This breaks the string and turns on the wrap attribute for the current cell.

ALT + ENTER
for a line feed   You may be concerned that Excel uses ALT + ENTER for a line feed (which some of you may think of as a "soft return") and every other program in the free world uses SHIFT + ENTER for it. It concerns us, too, but we have to cut Excel some slack on this one because SHIFT + ENTER has been used in Excel for years for something else. We'll talk about that something else in Chapter 3.

Numbers, Strictly Numbers

Numbers never lie.

Someone who is probably lying

You add your
numbers.   Excel tracks numbers to a precision of 15 places no matter how they are displayed. That's pretty accurate. But this "no matter how they are displayed" can jump up and bite you right where it hurts if you don't understand it. Consider this example (see Figure 2.10).

	C2	↓	=A2/B2	
	A	**B**	**C**	**D**
1	Weasels	Aardvarks	Weasels/Aardvarks	
2	98	13	7.54	7.54
3			C2 does not equal D2	
4				

Figure 2.10 Appearances Can Be Deceiving

The value in C2 is the result of dividing 98 by 13. Push some lead graphite technology through this problem and you find out that the answer is 7.538461538461538461…, where 538461 is repeated over and over forever. So Excel does the best it can do and stores 7.53846153846154, which is 15 digits of accuracy. (Excel rounds the last digit.)

In cell D2 we entered the number 7.54. Both C2 and D2 are *formatted* to two decimal places and they *appear* to be the same. Looking the same and being equal are not always the same thing. Formatting deals only with how a number is displayed, not the number itself. You cannot construct a formula to evaluate C2 as equal to D2 without either rounding the value in C2 or changing the way in which Excel stores numbers.

Precision

Yes, that's right campers, you can change the way in which Excel stores numbers internally. But only for an entire book, not for individual sheets or cells. If you go into Tools Options Calculation, you will see a check box under Workbook Options that says Precision as Displayed. If you check this box, Excel drops the 15-digit stuff and stores only the formatted result. If, as in this example, you have a cell formatted to two decimal places, Excel calculates the formula and displays *and stores* the formatted result.

We recommend that you not check this setting. No, no, no. You never know when you might need a little accuracy. You can always round within your formulas if precision is not giving you the results you want or expect.

It's a Date

> Thus the whirligig of time brings in his revenges.
>
> William Shakespeare
> *Twelfth-Night*, 1601–1602

Numbers are generally right aligned. So why, when you type in 4/1/94 and hit ENTER does the date appear right aligned in the cell, but in the formula bar it appears as 4/1/1994? Good question.

Well, dates are numbers. Simple as that. Way back when, they (ever wonder who "they" are and where you can lay your hands on them?) decided that it would be peachy if you could do math with dates. Stuff like take 4/1/95 and subtract 4/1/94 and get 365 days as the answer.

To accomplish this feat, dates had to be dealt with as numbers. So some bright soul tossed the I Ching sticks and exclaimed, "Eureka, we'll make January 1, 1900, equal to 1" and that was that. January 1, 1900, has a value of 1 and each day thereafter is incremented by 1. Oh, the Macintosh guys decided to start with January 2, 1904 for a difference of 4 years and a day, which plays hell if you develop models for use on both platforms.

That makes May 17, 1994 (Jim's birthday, BTW*, in case you want to send a card or present), has a value of 34471, which is referred to as a **serial date value**. To see this underlying value when dealing with dates, "flip" the worksheet by pressing CTRL + ` (back apostrophe).

*By The Way

When you type anything remotely resembling a date, Excel calculates the numeric value and looks to see if it has any date formats that it can apply to the cell to make the number "look" like a date. To make sure you realize that you're dealing with a date, the formula bar displays the year in four digits. That way you shouldn't confuse 1/1/1900 with 1/1/2000.

Excel does not always come up with a format that matches what you typed in the cell. For example, type July 7 and hit ENTER. Excel displays 7-Jul in the cell and 7/7/1994 in the formula bar. If you want an exact match, you'll have to make a custom format.

Formulas, the Crux of It All

> Nam et ipsa scientia potestas est.*
>
> Francis Bacon
> *Meditationes Sacrae*, 1597

Ah, finally, where it all comes together. Formulas. With formulas you program your worksheet. You establish the relationships between the numbers and text in the various cells, and this is really the point of the entire model.

Formatting makes it pretty, but the formulas make it right. Or wrong if you zig in a formula where you shoulda zagged. Remember those old movies where everything hinged on finding the secret formula? By thunder, Holmes, he's stolen the professor's formula! Ah, now that was drama.

Formulas must begin with an equal sign (=). Microsoft made it as easy as they could and, if you type a plus sign or a minus sign followed by a number and an operator, Excel decides that this is going to be a formula and it tosses in the equal sign for you. But an equal sign you must have to start a formula.

"=+-@" is not a four-letter word

Operators are symbols like +, -, * (multiply), / (divide). There's a bunch of operators available in Excel for math, text (like the concatenation operator you saw earlier), and logical expressions. For a complete list, see the "Understanding Operators" section in the *User's Guide*.

Formulas are important enough to warrant their own section, so we'll break off the discussion here and pick it up again after we have covered some additional topics that let you do some interesting and practical things within your formulas.

---

*Knowledge is more than equivalent to force.

Cell Results = Contents + Cell Formatting + Row/Column Formatting

> Appearances often are deceiving.
>
> Aesop
> *The Wolf in Sheep's Clothing*

Converting Contents to Results

When Excel displays a cell's results on your screen or printer, it marches along a sensible but not-so-obvious-until-you-head-scratch-it-awhile logic path you should be aware of. The payoff comes when you begin formatting in earnest—*ahem, of course, well after you've entered, validated, and audited your model, right?*—and need to understand why a particular cell looks the way it does. Or doesn't look the way you expected it should.

First Excel converts a cell's contents to a result. If the cell contains text only (no formula), up pops the text. The appearance of the text depends on several formatting parameters. More on that in a moment. If the cell contains a number only (no formula), up pops the number. Here again, the number's appearance hinges on formatting rules to be discussed shortly.

If the cell contains a formula, Excel's calculation engine takes its cue from your Tools Options Calculation settings. If, under the current calculation settings, the formula in this cell returns a result different from its last calculated result, Excel displays the updated result. If the formula returns the same result, the appearance of the cell doesn't change. The format of the formula result depends on...you guessed it...some formatting rules. More about that just ahead. "Geez," you're mumbling, "they've said that three times already." Patience, friend. Besides, we're fond of the number three. Humor us (somebody has to).

Formatting the Results

> Whate'er is well conceived is clearly said,
> And the words to say it flow with ease.
>
> Nicolas Boileau-Despréaux
> *The Art of Poetry*, 1674

A vocabulary, a vocabulary, our kingdom for a vocabulary. Heard that before, eh? Well, get used to it! We sure have. 'Cuz here comes another black hole in the documentation. The docs never open up the hood and flip on the mechanic's light so you can understand why stuff looks the way it does. Goodness gracious, what a concept.

Character formatting

The appearance of text-only results depends first on any formatting you have applied manually to characters in the cell. If you've used Excel 5's nifty new in-cell editing feature to change individual characters (or groups thereof), those are the formatting parameters that get evaluated now. We call this **character formatting**. Character formatting settings that you can tweak are located in the Format Cells dialog's Font filecard (some of these are also found on the Formatting toolbar). See Figure 2.11.

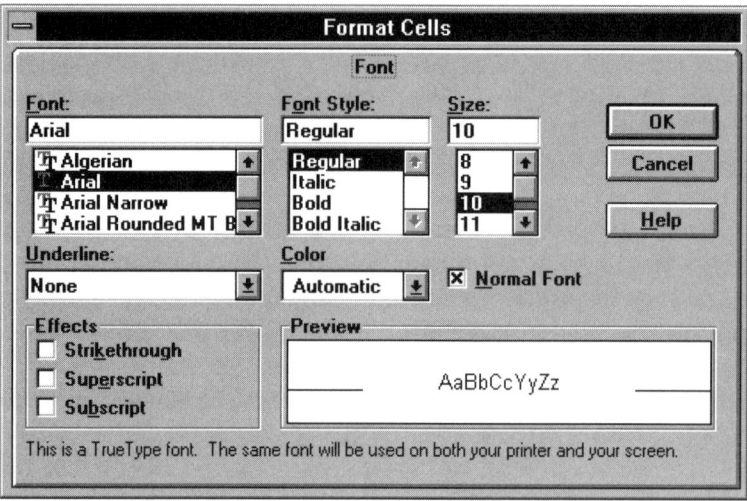

Figure 2.11 Your Friend, the Format Cells Dialog

Notice in Figure 2.12 that the while you're editing a cell, character formatting effects only appear inside the cell, *not* inside the formula bar. Interestingly (and it's jarring until you get used to it), while you're in the formula bar, you can select characters and observe the state of various Formatting tools (like the font name box) or simply fire up the Format Cells dialog box and check settings there.

Figure 2.12 A Character Formatting Sampler

Any characters not manually formatted via in-cell editing take on the appearance dictated by what we call **cell-level manual formatting**. Hang on, friend. Cell-level manual formatting applies to text when you select a cell—not individual characters but the *entire cell*—and manipulate *any* of the Format Cells, Font parameters mentioned earlier. Plus, at this point in the formatting labyrinth, cell-level manual formatting kicks in for nontext contents as well, meaning numbers and formulas.

At the cell level, all of the Format Cells parameters apply equally to text, numbers, and formulas. They are:

- Number
- Alignment
- Font
- Border
- Patterns
- Protection

Remember that for numbers and formulas, you *cannot* apply Font attributes to *individual* characters or numbers in the displayed result. No way, no how.

Keep in mind also that Border, Patterns, and Protection settings affect the cell itself independently of what's inside the cell. After all, you could be sitting inside your cherry red '57 Chevy while your kids gleefully spray paint it sunburst yellow, but you (the vehicle's contents) won't change color…well, as long as you keep the windows rolled up.

Style formatting sits at the top of the formatting dog pile. The final appearance of a cell is really a survivalist exercise. This is because Excel uses the cell's style as the starting point for each possible formatting parameter. By the time Dr. Excel has completed its rounds and examined any character formatting and manual cell formatting you've applied in a fit of creative vim, any remaining, unsullied setting is there staring back at you *because it started out that way with the cell's initial style!*

Ever hear of the LIFO inventory rule in cost accounting? LIFO stands for "Last In, First Out." (Don't be intimidated by this industry jargon. We use it 'cuz we like to laugh at ourselves and our industry where obfuscation runs rampant like some Andromeda Strain virus.) Picture yourself piling into an already chock-full elevator. Whether you like it or not, at the next stop you're gonna spill out of that elevator …the last few souls in are the first ones out. Similarly, the last level of formatting applied to a character or a cell, moving "up" the formatting hierarchy (individual character, manual cell, cell style), determines the cell result's appearance.

**Cell-level
manual
formatting**

**Formatting
with styles**

So, traveler, you made it! The final push! Take off your alpine parka and day pack. Sit a spell. And have a cold one on us, to boot. You deserve it.

Here's a carrot on a stick…We spend plenty of time on the concepts behind all-powerful styles in Chapter 6. At this point just be aware that styles exist and are applied at the cell level. A style is simply a name you give (or Excel provides for you, in the case of several freebie "built-in" styles) to a collection of cell-level formatting settings.

Table 2.1 shows the relationships between a cell's data type (contents) and formatting levels. As far as this table and the other two tables later in this section go, to quote Woody in *The Underground Guide to Word for Windows*, "I hope you find this categorizing useful; far as I know, nobody has ever looked at them in quite this way."

Table 2.1 Formatting Levels Permitted by Data Type

	Formatting Level		
	Individual Character	**Manual Cell**	**Cell Style**
Text	Yes	Yes	Yes
Number(s)	No	Yes	Yes
Formula(s)	No	Yes	Yes

Table 2.2 shows the relationships between all possible formatting parameters (via the Format Cells dialog) and formatting levels.

Table 2.2 Formatting Parameters Permitted by Data Type

	Formatting Level		
	Individual Character	**Manual Cell**	**Cell Style**
Number	Yes	Yes	Yes
Alignment	No	Yes	Yes
Font			
Font	Yes	Yes	Yes
Font Style	Yes	Yes	Yes
Size	Yes	Yes	Yes
Underline	Yes	Yes	Yes
Color	Yes	Yes	Yes

Table 2.2 Formatting Parameters Permitted by Data Type (continued)

	Formatting Level		
	Individual Character	**Manual Cell**	**Cell Style**
Normal Font	Yes	Yes	*
Strikethrough	Yes	Yes	Yes
Superscript	Yes	Yes	Yes
Subscript	Yes	Yes	Yes
Border	No	Yes	Yes
Patterns	No	Yes	Yes
Protection	No	Yes	Yes

*Not meaningful

The IFCIF Rule (Pronounced if 'kiff)

> When copying the formats of a cell to another cell with the Format Painter button or the Paste Special command on the Edit menu, the formatting of the first character in the copied cell is pasted into the destination cells.
>
> *Microsoft Excel Version 5.0 User's Guide*, page 207

With those innocent forty words ringing in our ears, let's embark on a trek through Character Formatting Hell. Gird up your asbestos underwear, friend, 'cuz it's gonna get hot. Real hot.

BTW, if you're following along with us in Excel on your PC while on this journey, *don't touch that Format Painter tool* 'cuz that's a brush of an entirely different color <*groan*>.

What happens if you apply character formatting to a cell (call this the **source cell**), the character formatting happens to affect the first character, and you then clear the cell contents (Edit Clear Contents) and copy the cell to another cell (call this the **destination cell**)? Any text you enter in the destination cell takes on the character formatting of the source cell's *first character*. Surprised? You shouldn't be because so far this is in keeping with the minimalist counsel offered in the *User's Guide*. At least this if-first-character-is-formatted rule (the "IFCIF rule," if we do say so ourselves) is consistent. (We can make up cute but obfuscatory acronyms too, ya know! *Heh, heh, heh*.)

A subtle variation is to copy not the entire source cell (that would be a plain ol' Edit Paste) but only its formatting (Edit Paste Special Formats) to a destination cell. Watch in amazement as all characters in the destination cell take on the formatting of the source cell's *first character*! So far so good.

Wait, there's more! (And you thought otherwise?) If the source and destination cells have different styles, after the Paste Special, Formats operation, the destination cell does take on the source cell's style name. However, the characters inside the destination cell all take on the character formatting of the source cell's first character.

And, of course, if the source and destination cells have the same styles but the destination cell's first character is formatted, well, lay on down 'cuz the swift kick's a-comin'. The trouble starts when attempting to unravel exactly what happens when the destination cell contains one or more formatted characters. This is a likely scenario, of course, but one not explained in the least by the 'Softies' Sacred Forty Words.

A Formatting Test Drive for Lab Rats in Absentia

Let no one be willing to speak ill of the absent.

Sextus Propertius
Elegies, ca. 54 BC–AD 2

Table 2.3 is a log of a little formatting experiment we conducted. Did someone say "little"!? Damn project turned out to have a life of its own. We had to go buy lab smocks, safety glasses, latex gloves, get a government grant, the whole nine yards. Sheesh. The following abbreviations are used in Table 2.3:

- CF = character formatting
- FCF = first character formatting
- SAS = second and subsequent (characters)
- SASCF = second and subsequent character formatting (where first character is decidedly not formatted)
- Normal = Normal style (Font Arial, Font Style Regular, Size 10, Underline None, Color Automatic, no Effects)
- JustCourier = JustCourier style (Font Courier New, Font Style Regular, Size 10, Underline None, Color Automatic, no Effects)

Table 2.3 IFCIF Three-Level Hierarchy

Source Cell Formatting	Destination Cell Original Formatting	Destination Cell Results after Paste Special
Normal + No FCF	Normal + No FCF	No changes
Normal + FCF	Normal + No FCF	Normal style; all text changes to source's FCF
Normal + SASCF	Normal + No FCF	No changes

Table 2.3 IFCIF Three-Level Hierarchy (continued)

Source Cell Formatting	Destination Cell Original Formatting	Destination Cell Results after Paste Special
Normal + No FCF	JustCourier + No FCF	Normal style; no CF
Normal + FCF	JustCourier + No FCF	Normal style; all text changes to source's FCF
Normal + SASCF	JustCourier + No FCF	Normal style; no CF
Normal + No FCF	Normal + FCF (single underline)	Normal style; FCF goes away
Normal + FCF	Normal + FCF (single underline)	Normal style; FC takes on source's FCF and loses underline; SAS chars do not change
Normal + SASCF	Normal + FCF (single underline)	Normal style; FCF goes away

In Figure 2.13 you see destination cell A17 with only the fifth character manually formatted.

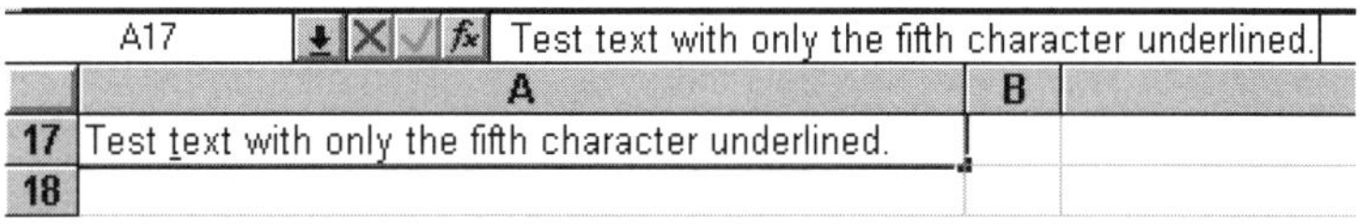

Figure 2.13 A17 Before the Edit Paste Special Formats

Figure 2.14 shows what happens to A17 when you Edit Paste Special Formats from A1 (the manually formatted cell pictured in Figure 2.12).

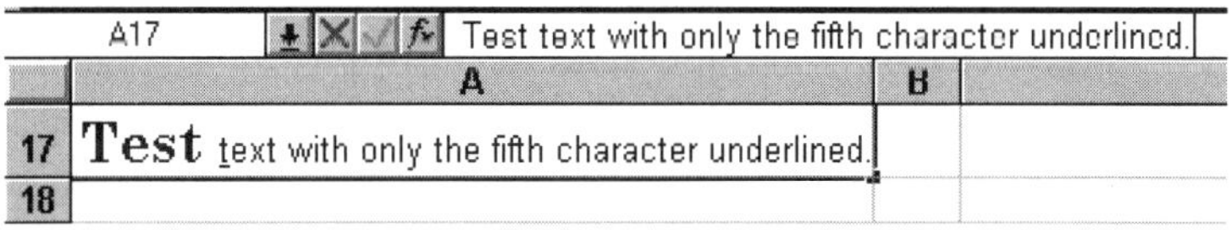

Figure 2.14 A17 After the Edit Paste Special Formats

Our conclusions after studying the results of our experiment are as follows. (You might want to take two valium first, then pick back up here in the morning.)

1. If the destination cell contains absolutely no character formatting of any kind, period, the source cell's first character formatting wins throughout the destination cell. QED.

2. If the destination cell contains any character formatting, the formatting of the source cell's first character is applied only to unformatted destination characters left-to-right one character at a time, beginning with position 1 (the leftmost character), *stopping altogether as soon as a manually formatted character is encountered*. Or maybe the rule is: stopping as soon as a change is detected in any of the nine possible character formatting attributes. Trouble is, with no guidance from the ExcelGods, there's absolutely no way to reverse-engineer this mess and tell what's really happening down at the molecular level.

So this is where we give up. Hang it. Shine it. Flip it. Flog it. And other declaratives that are too, uhm, off-color to sneak by our erudite, watchful editors. Throughout this exercise, a voice in the back of our collective minds was chanting "declining marginal utility" so we applied our cardinal rule when in such a situation—TMT*.

Best thing for you to do when you're copying character formatting around is this—when you're done pasting, if it looks good, great, otherwise, fix it. This way, you can use the Format Painter or brute-force Paste Special Formats. Carpe diem. Go fer it. If you use the preceding rule, you'll get a lot more work done. Nuff said.

Row and Column Formatting…Beyond the Cellular Level

You didn't *really* think we were done yet, did you? *Heh, heh, heh.*

Once a cell's contents have been formatted, and the cell itself formatted, Excel has to deal with two final masters—column width and row height.

If the column width of a text cell is too narrow to accommodate the results and the cell has a nonempty right neighbor then the results text is immediately truncated. On the other hand, if this same cell has an empty right neighbor, then its contents spill over beyond its own right border. The contents continue to spill across cells in an easterly direction until reaching a nonempty cell, at which point the results text is truncated. If the results text fits within the current column width, it's a slam-dunk. Right-aligned cells spill to the west, and those wily center-aligned cells spill in both directions.

Ever wonder what the dreaded "#####" cell display means? The fix is easy—AutoFit the column width. When a number or formula cell's value cannot be displayed within the column width, Excel displays as many # symbols as will fit. Unless you have a formula like `=TEXT(G14,0)`, where G14 contains the value one billion, in which case, your zeros get truncated so fast it'll make your portfolio swim. Base a buy/sell decision on that cell's results and you could be in a world of hurt, pilgrim.

*Too Much Trouble.

Column width, row height, and a cell's Alignment Wrap Text settings work together, if you know the rules. If a cell contains more text than will fit given its current column width and row height, and you turn on Wrap Text, Excel changes the row height to accommodate the request *but leaves the column width unchanged*. See Figure 2.15.

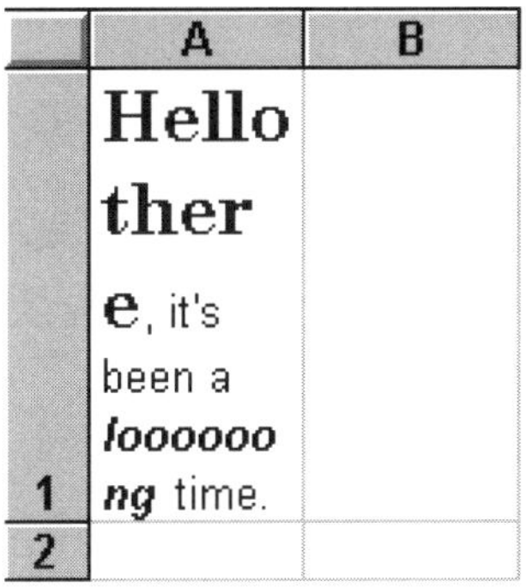

Figure 2.15 Wrapped Text in a Standard Width Column

Here's a fun little experiment that actually produces some useful results. No federal grant money required, we promise.

1. Create a new sheet.

2. Type a long sentence into A1, "long" meaning one that's too long to display completely inside A1 (whatever column A's column width is).

3. Format Cells Alignment and check the Wrap Text check box. Click on OK. The row height adjusts to whatever height is required—given the current column width (it's fixed during this row adjustment time slice, remember?)—to display your long sentence. So far so good.

4. Change row 1's height to 12.75 (standard height when your Normal font is set to Arial 10).

Not surprisingly, the row compresses back down. But lean on in until your nose touches that hummin' VDT screen, pilgrim, and notice that *A1's contents don't spill over into the blank neighbor B1*. This is different! This is cool! "Why," you ask? Fair question.

If you dislike the way text automatically spills into nonblank neighbors, particularly when you've forgotten to go back and reapply AutoFit to the current column, now you can do something about it! Simply set the cell's Wrap Text property and then *explicitly set the row height back to whatever it was initially*. Hangdog cool and somebody pass us two mint juleps, pul-eeze.

Blanks, Booleans, and Errors

> It's a living.
>
> Daffy Duck

To Excel's way of thinking, a blank cell is either an empty cell or a cell containing a formula that returns an empty string, for example, `=" "`. A formula that refers to a blank cell returns a value of zero. You can go to blank cells via Edit Go To Special Blanks. The `COUNTBLANKS()` function counts the number of blank cells in a range.

Excel supports the Boolean values (a.k.a. logical values) `TRUE` and `FALSE`. The number zero is `FALSE`, and any other number is `TRUE`. You can go to logicals by Edit Go To Special Formulas Logicals.

When errors occur, Excel formulas produce a variety of error values: `#DIV/0`, `#N/A`, `#NAME?`, `#NULL!`, `#NUM!`, `#REF!`, `#VALUE!`, and `#####`. We cover error tracing in Chapter 5. You can go to logicals via Edit Go To Special Formulas Errors.

3 The Stage Is Set

All the spreadsheet's a stage…

With apologies to William S.

Now that you've got the general lay of the land under your belt, it's time to look at the methods available to get stuff into the worksheet. What? Did you think that you simply type and press ENTER? *Heh, heh, heh.*

DATA ENTRY, STAGE LEFT

Where were you when the page was blank?

A common writer's lament

In Excel 5 you can enter text, numbers, or formulas directly into a cell. The docs call this feature **in-cell editing**, even if you're just entering.

In-cell editing

Prior to Excel 5 your entry appeared only in the formula bar until you hit ENTER. In Excel 5 your entry appears in both the formula bar and the cell (stereo!) as you type it, although the cursor is only visible in the cell. It's a little distracting until you get used to it, especially if you are used to focusing on the formula bar. If it bothers you, you can turn in-cell editing off. Do a Tools Options Edit and clear

---

fx This is text typed directly into F3. This is a long text entry and the text appears to drop down to the next row. It doesn't actually. This pseudo "expanding" cell is for display only. When you hit Enter the text is dumped into the single cell.

This is text typed directly into F3. This is a long text entry and the text appears to drop down to the next row. It doesn't actually. This pseudo "expanding" cell is for display only. When you hit Enter the text is dumped into the single cell.

Figure 3.1 In-Cell Entry

the check box for "Edit Directly in Cell." We like it, though, and suggest that you give it a chance.

As you can see in Figure 3.1 the cell area appears to "expand" as your entry fills the display. This is only so you can see the entire entry as you type it. Once you hit ENTER, the entire entry is dumped into the active cell.

When the formula bar expands to show two lines of your entry, all but the lower 18.75% (bottom three pixels) of the vertical scroll bar's up button is obscured. This can be really maddening if you like to scroll around the screen display while editing a cell in order to find something. (There we go again, thinking you might actually might want to be doing two things at once. Oh, well.) All the ExcelGods have to do is reduce the formula bar's width by 16 pixels to avoid obscuring the upper 80% of the vertical scroll bar up button. "Head's up," as they say on campus. And, yes, we counted the pixels, after all, this is The Underground…*heh, heh, heh.*

When the formula bar expands to show three or more lines, you can kiss the vertical scroll bar's up button good-bye. If you look *real* close at the top of the scroll bar in Figure 3.1, you can see what looks like the bottom of the scroll bar's up arrow, but it's not. That's the bottom three pixels of the scroll box.

A related problem (you mean *another one*?) is the cell area's expansion as you type in a long entry. It obscures the nearby cells to the right and below. If you are entering a long formula and want to click on a nearby cell to enter its reference, you are out of luck. You have to either enter the reference manually or use the keyboard to select the obscured cell.

Also new in Excel 5 is the ability to apply text formatting to less than the entire cell.

AutoEntry™

With all the hype over "Auto" this and "Auto" that from the Redmond PR machine, we can't understand why they didn't rename this old feature in Excel and tout it as something "new and improved."

If you go to Tools Options Edit, you can turn on "Move Selection after Enter" by checking the appropriate check box. This makes the active cell selection move down one cell every time you hit ENTER. If you're into tricky keyboard techniques, you can turn this setting on and not only will pressing ENTER move the active cell selection down one cell, you can amaze and mystify your friends by pressing SHIFT + ENTER and making the active cell selection jump *up* one cell.

Now whether or not you have the "Move Selection after Enter" setting on, you can also control which way the active cell selection jumps by pressing TAB to enter the data into the current cell and make the active cell selection jump one cell to the right. Pressing SHIFT + TAB causes the active cell selection to jump one cell left.

SuperAutoEntry™

Actually, the four keystroke/shift keystroke combinations (ENTER, SHIFT + ENTER, TAB, **and** SHIFT + TAB**) are quite useful. Here's the power data entry technique that we use to get the numbers crunched into the spreadsheet (at least when we have to manually enter them, bleccch), and it doesn't matter if "Move Selection after Enter" is on or off (we leave this setting turned off, by the way).**

Let's say you have to enter numbers into a table. Select the table area as shown in Figure 3.2.

	A	B	C	D	E	F	G
1							
2		Southwest Divison					
3			1st Qtr	2nd Qtr	3rd Qtr	4th Qtr	
4		Widgets					
5		Doohickeys					
6		Thingys					
7		Total	0	0	0	0	
8							

Figure 3.2 Select the Data Area

This method is designed for hard-core power data crunching. If you want to enter the data by column, key in a number and hit ENTER**. The active cell selection moves down one cell. Type in a number and hit** ENTER**. Boom. Down to the next cell. Type in a number and hit** ENTER **again. This time the active cell selection jumps to the top of the second column. The active cell selection moves through the selected range, down through each column, each time you hit** ENTER**.**

When you reach the end of the selected range, the active cell selection jumps back to the first cell (upper left) in the selection. To skip a cell, hit ENTER. To go back after you make a mistake, hit SHIFT + ENTER. To move by row instead of by column, hit TAB instead of ENTER. To move right to left, hit SHIFT + TAB.

A little practice and you can *blaze* through the drudgery of keyboard input. Table 3.1 is a handy reference.

Table 3.1 Moving Through Selections

To Move Through a Selection	Press This
Down by columns	ENTER
Up by columns	SHIFT + ENTER
Across (left to right) by rows	TAB
Across (right to left) by rows	SHIFT + TAB

AutoFill 'er Up

> Badness you can get easily, in quantity: the road is smooth, and it lies close by. But in front of excellence the immortal gods have put sweat, and long and steep is the way to it, and rough at first. But when you come to the top, then it is easy, even though it is hard.
>
> Hesiod
> *Works and Days,* ca. 700 BC

Three cheers for Microsoft! *AutoFill is absolutely brilliant.* **('Twas brilliant in Excel 4, and it shines even brighter in version 5.) Well conceived and well implemented. Like, killer, dude. And in Excel 5 you can create your own custom fills.**

If you've always used the old Data Series command to fill data into ranges, you may be dismayed to find that there is no Series command on the Data menu. Worry not. They moved it to the Edit menu. If you want to use the old Series dialog box to do your fills, you can get to it with Edit Fill and choose Series from the flyout menu. See Figure 3.3.

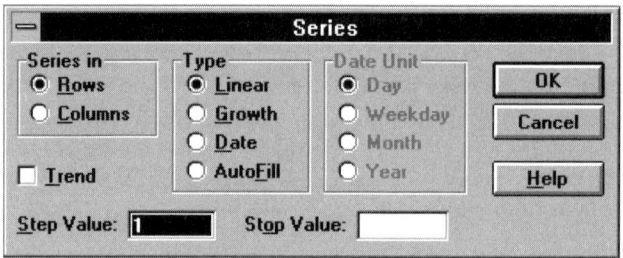

Figure 3.3 The Good Old Series Dialog Box

There will be times when you need the fine tuning provided in the Series dialog box to do what you want. For example, the Series dialog box lets you enter stop values, and that is what you need to do when your fills involve a large range. But for the smaller fills that most of us do day in and day out, use the fill handle. Way cool.

That Handy Haft, the Fill Handle

> To fill something is good, whether it be your belly with food, your pocket
> with gold, or your enemy with arrows.
>
> Amok Shing, Mongol
> *My Years in the Horde* (from the modern translation by K.Tibet, 1972)

Say you want to dump some numbers into a table. Any numbers will do. You
might type the value 100 into cell A1 and then start copying and pasting. But
much better is to enter the value and drag the fill handle across the range of cells
you want to enter the value into.

If you don't have a little black box in the lower right corner of the current cell
or selected range, you had best make sure you have cell drag-and-drop turned on.
Do a Tools Options Edit and check the "Allow Cell Drag and Drop" check box.

So there's the fill handle. Grab it with the Fill Handle Grabber™ and drag it
across the range you want (down or across, but not both at once) and release the
mouse. See Figure 3.4.

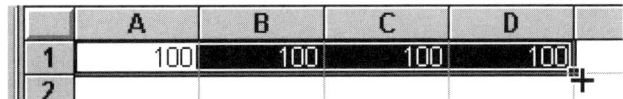

Figure 3.4 Drag Fill Handle Across

Swell, but how often do you want to put the same figure in each cell? Besides,
you can do the same thing by selecting the range, typing in the figure, and hitting
CTRL + ENTER. And you can use CTRL + ENTER to dump a value into a range
extending across rows and columns. So there.

But there's more to the fill stuff than first meets the eye. To increment the
value of the starting number by 1, hold down the Control key and then drag the
fill handle. See Figure 3.5.

	A	B	C	D
1	100	101	102	103
2				

Figure 3.5 Fill and Increment!

You'll notice that when you are incrementing a fill via the Control key, the Fill
Handle Grabber™ mutates and grows a little plus sign over its right shoulder.
Format the first cell however you want, and the formatting extends with the fill.
Cool! What's even more frigid is that as each cell is filled, you see the current cell

contents displayed in the Name Box. This is very useful when doing an incremental or decremental fill.

Step values   What about step values and all the things you grew to love about the old Series dialog box? No problem, pilgrim. Say you want to step the fill by 10. Enter the first value and, in the adjacent cell, enter that value plus 10. Highlight both cells and drag the fill handle.

It gets better. You can repeat a series. For example, type in 125 in A1, type 150 in B1, and leave C1 blank. Highlight A1:C1 and drag the fill handle to F1. Figure 3.6 shows what you get.

	A	B	C	D	E	F
1	125	150		175	200	
2						

Figure 3.6 Step Including Blank in Series

If you mix text and numbers in your fills, Excel 5 automatically increments the number. So when you want to label some columns as Year 1, Year 2, Year 3, and so on. type Year 1 in the first cell and drag the fill handle. The text is static and the number increments. See Figure 3.7.

	A	B	C	D
1	Year 1	Year 2	Year 3	Year 4
2	Qtr 1	Qtr 2	Qtr 3	Qtr 4
3	1st Qtr	2nd Qtr	3rd Qtr	4th Qtr
4	6 Lobsters	7 Lobsters	8 Lobsters	9 Lobsters
5				

Figure 3.7 Text and Number Fills

Microsoft made this fill handle feature very smart. Notice in row 3 that Excel not only incremented the number, but it also changed the text appropriately to denote first, second, third, and fourth. And, because Excel knows that there are only four quarters, if you dragged and filled another column, row 3 would start its series over with 1st Qtr, while rows 1, 2, and 4 would increment.

 Here comes the gonzo confusing part. If you hold down the Control key, Excel does *not*, repeat *not*, increment the number when you have a number and text combination in the starting cell. With Year 1 in the first cell, holding down the Control key and doing an AutoFill would get you Year 1, Year 1, Year 1, and so on. So, if you have a number only, CTRL + AutoFill increments the number, but if you have text and a number, CTRL + AutoFill *prevents* it from incrementing. Hoo, boy! This behavior is opposite to what happens when you are doing an AutoFill with a number alone in the first cell.

Everything else generally works the same between numbers and text with numbers. If you enter Year 1994 in the first cell and Year 1996 in the adjacent cell, select them both, and then do AutoFill, you would get a series with a two-year step.

If you want a decrementing fill, you can enter your values in the rightmost column or at the bottom of your range and then drag right to left (or from down, up) through your range. It would be easier, perhaps, to do the traditional drag across or down and set up your step value to force a decrement. You could enter 100 in A1 and 90 in B1 and then select and drag to the right and get a 10-unit decrementing step result.

Do not get lax and hold down the Shift key by mistake instead of the Control key when trying to do an AutoFill because *nothing* will be filled.

Things that don't work

Another thing that won't work is if you were to enter 100 in cell A1, AutoFill down through A5, then with A1:A5 selected try to AutoFill across to column C while trying to increment the values. You can copy them, but they won't increment.

You cannot increment values in multiple rows across columns or multiple columns down rows without entering the step values in the adjacent row or column and selecting both the value and the step value before dragging.

Custom AutoFill

You've seen how numbers can be automatically filled through a selection. What about text? Glad you asked. This can be done by creating custom AutoFill lists.

Excel 5 comes with several custom lists already set up as examples to get you started creating your own. To get at them, do this:

1. Pull down Tools and select Options.
2. Click the Custom Lists tab. See Figure 3.8.

You already have the days of the week and the months of the year, both abbreviated and spelled out in the Custom Lists list box. You can type in Wed in cell A1, AutoFill down to A3, and you get Thu and Fri in A2 and A3, respectively. The entire list sequence repeats itself if your drag area extends far enough.

Custom lists increment through their entries automatically. Holding down the Control key before dragging prevents the list from incrementing, even though you get the little plus sign over the shoulder of the grabber. Just think of it as the Wacky Effect.

To create your own lists, click on NEW LIST and type in your list items in the List Entries list box. Put each item on its own line. If the focus is on the List Entries box, hitting ENTER does *not* trigger the OK button, rather it starts a new line in the list box.

You're limited to 80 characters, including spaces and punctuation, per item, and each custom list is limited to 2000 characters overall. The total number of

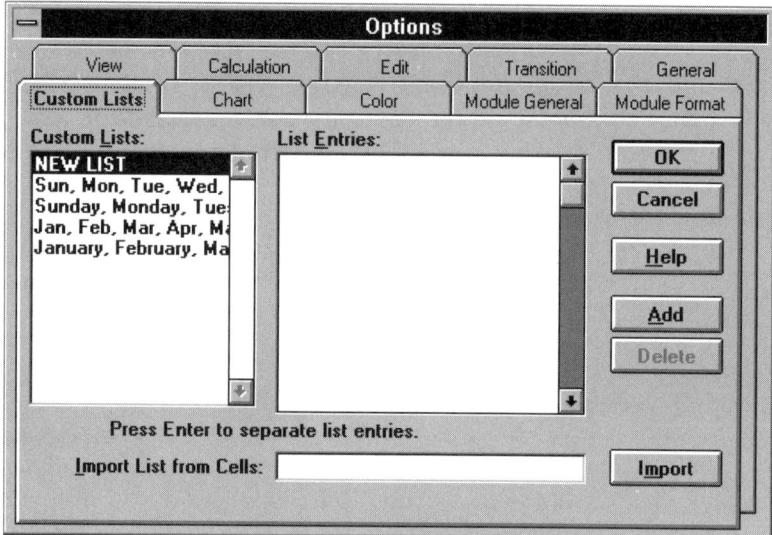

Figure 3.8 Custom Lists

custom lists is limited by available system resources. Custom lists are stored in EXCEL5.XLB, along with changes to the toolbar settings.

Da Fill Handle Double-Click

If you are building a table and you have one column with data in it, you can use the double-click-on-the-fill-handle trick to fill down the current column within the same row bounds as the adjacent column. Hmmm, an example should help. Consider yonder Figure 3.9.

	A	B	C
1	Item 1	100	Jan
2	Item 2		Feb
3	Item 3		Mar
4			Apr
5			May
6			Jun

Figure 3.9 The Old Double-Click-on-the-Fill-Handle Trick

If you double-clicked the fill handle in this example, the value in B1 would be filled down column B automatically to row 3 or to match the row bounds to the column on the left. *But if column A was empty, it would fill down through row 6!* That's right, Excel matches the bounds to the column on the left unless that

column is empty, in which case it democratically looks to the column on the right. Like the way you look both ways when you cross the street. This is way cool stuff, yea Redmond!

The Right Mouse Button, Finally Some Respect

> A dark horse, which had never been thought of, and which the careless
> St. James had never even observed in the list, rushed past the grandstand
> to sweeping triumph.
>
> Benjamin Disraeli, Earl of Beaconsfield
> *The Young Duke*, 1831

These AutoFill techniques work great for simple stuff, but what if you need to do a heavy-duty fill like an exponential curve, for pity's sake? What if you enter a date and want to fill by weekdays only? Happens all the time, right? Well, you're in luck. Microsoft has hooked the prodigal rodent's right digit to a very useful shortcut menu tailored to AutoFills.

Instead of dragging the fill handle with the normally overbearing left mouse button, drag it with its shy retiring sibling, the *right mouse button!* Bingo, when you release the button, you get the fill shortcut menu. See Figure 3.10.

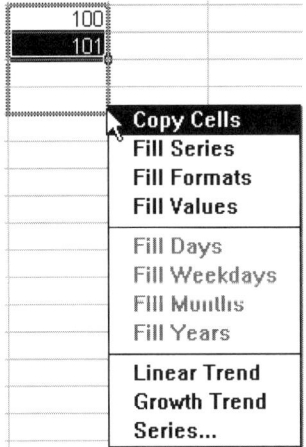

Figure 3.10 The Fill Shortcut Menu

Here you can decide to copy, fill, do special things with dates, do straight linear regression or the kinkier exponential regression, or pop up the good old Series dialog box.

Now You See It, Now You Don't

Finally, we present the disappearing cell contents trick. Profoundly useful prestidigitation. With a range of cells selected, grab the fill handle and drag back up and/or left through the range-obliterating cells as you go. Better than a particle beam, zzzzzzzzfffttt. All gone. Also way cool.

DATA EDITING, STAGE RIGHT

> In times of great change the situation is excellent.
>
> Chinese proverb

After you enter some information what do you want to do? Change it, of course! Your wish is our command.

Delete vs. Clear

> Ships are only hulls, high walls are nothing,
> When no life moves in the empty passageways.
>
> Sophocles
> *Oedipus Rex*

When you delete a cell (via the Edit Delete menu or the cell editing shortcut menu), you are obliterating the physical cell itself. Like dip to a 'toon we're talking a hole in your worksheet. Deleting cells is not to be confused with using the Delete key on the keyboard to *clear* a cell.

Of course, Excel doesn't actually leave a big hole in your sheet. Nahhh, wouldn't look nice. It'd be hard to print as well. So what happens? Well, you delete a cell and Excel asks you if you want to shift all cells over from the left. Perhaps you want to shift all cells up to fill in the hole that you are about to make. Or maybe you really meant that you wanted to delete the entire row or column based on your selection. See Figure 3.11.

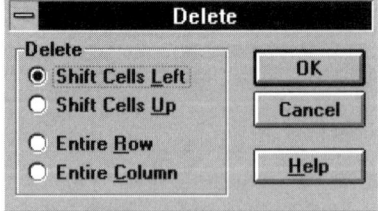

Figure 3.11 Delete That Cell!

Hmmm, you delete cell A1, for example, and up pops this dialog box. You tell it to Shift Cells Left and hit OK. Every cell in the worksheet, starting with B1, shifts one cell left. What happened to the cell at the end of row 1, good ol' IV1? It shifted one cell left and became IU1, that's what. And, since nature and Redmond abhor a vacuum, a new cell, IV1, was magically manufactured from the ether. Cool, huh? Same principle as when you insert a new row 1 and the bottom row 16128 falls off the edge of the worksheet into the great void. Something from nothing and nothing from something. Way metaphysical.

So what about clearing a cell? You hit DELETE, which automatically does a "clear contents," or you choose Clear Contents from the cell-editing shortcut menu. This used to be called "clear formula" in Excel 4, whether you had a formula in a cell or not. We applaud the change in lexicon. Yea! This new Clear Contents does what you expect (*and it is about time, too!*) and zaps the contents of the cell, be it text or number or formula.

If you want a little more control over what you are clearing, select Clear from the Edit menu and choose exactly what you want to clear from the flyout menu. You can clear:

- All—as in all of the above, the formats, the contents, and any note attached to the selected cell(s).
- Formats—all your cell formatting. If your cell is formatted with a style called Lobster and you clear formats, you get a cell with the Normal style and format attributes.
- Contents—just that.
- Notes—you can delete the note attached to a cell without changing any other aspect of the cell's contents or formatting.

South of the Shift + Border-Double-Click

In Chapter 1 we explored the CTRL + SHIFT + arrow key zap, multicell selection technique. There's a spiffy mouse technique you might dig, too. Picture the active cell as the first cell in a 12-cell series of month column heading labels, labeled "January" through…you guessed it…"December." Here are the ingredients to the SHIFT + border-double-click trick. (Of course, you used AutoFill to fill in February through December, right? *Riiiiight!*)

1. Press and hold the Shift key.
2. Point the Selection Crosshair™ at the active cell's border that represents the direction you want to select in. In this example, it's the right border. This requires a brain-surgeon's steady hand, pilgrim, and you know you've got it when the Selection Crosshair™ turns into a Traditional Northwest Mouse Pointer™.

3. Double-click. (If instead of an extended selection you find yourself staring at an in-cell editing session, you must have double-clicked when the mouse pointer wasn't a Traditional Northwest Mouse Pointer™. Sharpen up the ol' scalpel and try it again, doc.

4. Release the Shift key.

Editing a Nonblank Cell

> Empty barrels make the most noise.
>
> John Lyly
> *Eupues*, 1579

You can initiate an edit of a nonblank cell in myriad ways:

1. Double-click on the cell for in-cell editing.

2. Click the I-Beam™ inside the formula bar.

3. Press the F2 function key.

4. To replace a cell's contents entirely, select it and start typing.

5. Use our AutoEntry™ or SuperAutoEntry™ techniques to create a multicell selection and iterate the active cell selection through the selection, merrily editing as you go.

Note that, while in SuperAutoEntry™ mode, you can use all of the preceding techniques to edit the active cell *except* double-clicking on the cell. Doing this would have the rather, uhm, disruptive effect of undoing your selection, leaving only the current cell selected.

DRAG-AND-DROP: CENTER STAGE

Drag-and-drop (not to be confused with drop and roll, which is what you should do if you catch on fire; or dragon drops, which is the preferred fertilizer in mythological locales) is a feature that the marketing types *love* big time. It shows really *well*. Flash, sizzle. Look at the ads for Microsoft Office and you see objects being dragged and dropped all over the place. But is it any good?

Yup. It's one of those features where you look past the sizzle and actually find a great steak. Of course, the hype machine touts drag-and-drop as something that is intuitive and easy for new users. Wrong. But with some practice and pointers it is very useful.

Within the Sheets

You can drag-and-drop a single cell or a contiguous range of cells. This feature makes new users crazy and probably causes them to give up on the feature altogether. The trick is to watch the mouse pointer. See Figure 3.12.

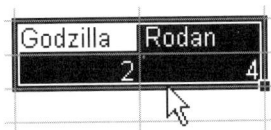

Figure 3.12 Drag-and-Drop with the Traditional Northwest Mouse Pointer™

When you touch the mouse pointer to the edge of the active cell or a selected range (as shown in Figure 3.12), the pointer mutates faster than Young Radioactive Kung-Fu Reptiles. It changes from the Selection Crosshair™ to the Traditional Northwest Mouse Pointer™.

Touching the pointer to the exact edge is like riding a bicycle, it's ridiculously easy once you're able to do it. Until then it's the pits. One pixel one way or the other is the difference between success and failure. But, with a little practice you can master it.

Once you have the mouse pointer in the proper state, which tells you that you can go ahead with the drag-and-drop, you hold down the left mouse button and *drag* the selected cell or cells to some new location on the sheet where you *drop* it or them, depending. It works the same way as dragging a graphic object like an embedded chart or text box. Point, click, and drag.

Lots of folks discover this feature by accident when they try to select a different range and suddenly move a bunch of cells to who-knows-where. They hate it when that happens.

While dragging, you'll see a gray outline of the selection as you move the mouse, and this outline snaps to the cell grid. What you are actually doing is the equivalent of cut and paste. When you release the mouse button (the drop), the cells are pasted into the new location. If you try to drop on cells that already have contents, you're asked if you want to replace the contents of the destination cells with whatever you're dropping.

Cut, Copy, and Paste—Excel's Way

Excel does not deal with cut and paste in the same way that some other Windows applications do. In most Windows apps, once you copy or cut something, that something goes "up" to the clipboard. And there it stays until you send something else to the clipboard or shut down Windows.

Excel is much more fussy about leaving evidence of its passage than other applications. When you select a cell and perform an Edit Cut (or Copy), for example, the cell contents are placed on the clipboard. But once you complete a Paste operation, Excel clears the contents of the clipboard. Very tidy program our Excel.

When you do the drag-and-drop, you are performing the same steps of cut and paste only you're using just the mouse. But Excel is still running the selected cell contents through the clipboard. In WinWord you can select text and drag-and-drop it to a new location as well, *but WinWord bypasses the clipboard!*

If you've been using drag-and-drop in WinWord and have come to trust drag-and-drop not to disturb the contents of the clipboard, you've got to be aware that Excel does not behave in the same manner. *Drag-and-drop in Excel clears the clipboard.* Bam! Just like that.

Cut and paste, so you can move stuff with the mouse? Big deal, you say? But wait there's more!

With the Shift Key

What if you want to do a cut, but instead of a straight paste you want to do an insert paste? No problem, hold down the Shift key and then drag-and-drop.

Oh, what's an **insert paste**? That's when you insert from the clipboard but instead of overwriting the destination cells you push them down or to the right. When you hold down the Shift key and perform a drag-and-drop, you see a gray indicator the height or width of the cut range. This indicator, when on a horizontal row edge, allows you to do an insert paste "shift cells down." On a vertical column edge, you can "shift cells right." See Figure 3.13.

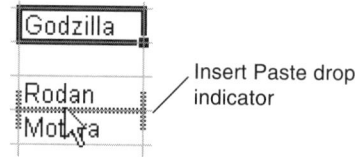

Figure 3.13 Shift + Drag-and-Drop

With the Control Key

You can copy instead of cut by simply holding down the Control key before starting the drag. You'll know you are doing a copy instead of a cut by the little plus sign that automagically appears over the right shoulder of the Northwest Mouse Pointer. It makes sense if you think of the plus as adding another copy, *n'est-ce pas?*

With Both Keys

If SHIFT + drag-and-drop is to cut and insert paste and CTRL + drag-and-drop is copy, what the heck is CTRL + SHIFT + drag-and-drop? We're glad you asked.

With both keys held down before beginning the drag-and-drop, you get a copy action combined with the insert paste. Easy as pie.

Look Ma, No Keys

What if you would rather not remember what keys you have to hold down to do what, thank you very much? Okay, we can deal with that. In fact, this next technique is the preferred way to do cell moving and copying.

Select your cells and, instead of doing your drag-and-drop with the left mouse button, use the *right mouse button.* Select the destination and drop. You get a shortcut menu that lets you choose what you kind of a drag-and-drop you want to do after the fact! See Figure 3.14.

Figure 3.14 Shortcut Menu with Right Mouse Button

This method gives you the added benefit of being able to do a paste special for just formats or values. This right mouse method gives you the most flexibility and is the hot tip. So there.

Between the Sheets

> The difficult we do immediately. The impossible takes a little longer.
>
> Slogan of the United States Army Service Forces

On the flip side, some stuff you can't you do with drag-and-drop in Excel:

- You can't drag-and-drop between sheets in different books.
- You can't drag-and-drop between the same sheet displayed in different windows.
- You can't drag-and-drop between different sheets in the same book.

To accomplish these cellular maneuvers, you have to do the traditional cut, copy, paste thing using the menus, buttons, or shortcut keys. And, speaking of the shortcut keys, if you haven't committed the keys for cut, copy, paste to muscle memory *do it now*!

Cut: CTRL + X
Copy: CTRL + C
Paste: CTRL + V

These keystrokes are important to know because:

1. They work in most all Windows applications.
2. We're guessing that the old shortcut keys (CTRL + INSERT, and so on) won't be supported forever.
3. These keystrokes work in dialog box text fields where there is no other way to cut, copy, or paste.

When we were knee-high to a deuce of grasshoppers, we really loved to climb walls and fences to see what was on the other side. Oh, the halcyon days… Anyway, here we are, some, uh, unspecified number of decades later, looking over Microsoft's Chinese wall. Basically, what Excel 5 doesn't do, WinWord 6 does. That's right, WinWord 6 *does* drag-and-drop between windowed documents, and WinWord 6 *does* drag-and-drop between a split document. Go figure.

Across Applications: How Do You Spell OLE?

You can drag-and-drop across applications, but that is a horse of a different color. See Chapter 9 for the naked truth on OLE.

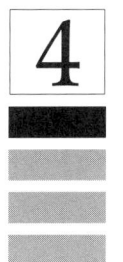

4 Formulas, Functions, and Names, Oh My!— Tools for Building

> If we are to perceive all the implications of the new, we must risk, at least temporarily, ambiguity and disorder.
>
> J. J. Gordon
> *Creative Computing*, October, 1983

Welcome, pilgrim. By now, you've whetted your appetite in Chapter 1, looked around Excel's vast environment in Chapter 2, and sharpened your data manipulation skills in Chapter 3.

Now it's time to dig into some real meat and potatoes. Putting information into cells and establishing relationships between same. This means writing formulas, dealing with functions, all kinds of interesting stuff. But first a word about range names, something no formula should be without. And away we gooooo!

RANGE NAMES: MANNA FROM HEAVEN

> I'm telling you. Who's on first, What's on second, I Don't Know is on third.
>
> Bud Abbott
> *Who's On First*

Ah, names. If ever there was an underutilized feature, this is it. If you are not currently using range names, it's time to start.

If you use WinWord 6's bookmark feature, think of an Excel range name as a bookmark that contains a cell or range of cells—at least as far as Excel absolute range names are concerned. Even if you use bookmarks in WinWord 6, you'll find that Excel does some tricks with named ranges that WinWord 6 only can dream about. So, pull up a chair and check this out.

You've seen how you can reference cells using the cryptic absolute addressing scheme in A1 notation style, as in $A$10. In the more straightforward R1C1 notation style, you would refer to the same cell as R10C1. But you are not limited to this coordinate referencing methodology, no, no, no. You can *name* a cell (or range of cells) and refer to it by that name.

Creating Names

Omnis cellual e cellual.*

Rudolf Virchow
Cellular-Pathologie, 1858

You can name a cell, a group of cells (contiguous or noncontiguous), a row, a column, a group of rows and/or columns, or the entire bloody worksheet. *A name is usually referred to as a range name even if it references a single cell.*

You can name graphic objects floating on the sheet, too, but that's another story. We'll get into that in a minute.

You can use alphanumeric characters in your names, so long as you do not try to use a name that Excel might mistake for a cell reference. For example, you cannot name a cell A1, $A$1, $A1, or R1C5, no matter what notation style you are currently using. You're limited to 255 characters. Spaces are verboten. You can't start a name with a number, period, or question mark. You can't partake of most nonalphanumeric characters, although you can use:

- The underscore character _
- The backslash character \
- The period . (but not as the first character)
- The question mark ? (but not as the first character)

You should use proper case for your range names. For example, you could use a name like MyCoolCell. This has several benefits. It makes the name easier to read, does not require you to type separator characters like those just mentioned, and if you type the name in lowercase in a formula and Excel recognizes it, Excel switches it to proper case.

By Example—The Name Box

The **Name Box** is a drop-down list box that displays the first 100 range names in the current sheet and/or book. This list is sorted alphabetically.

You have to watch the 100-name limitation because once you get used to always using the Name Box, you may think a name is missing in action when in reality you exceeded the list limit.

*Every cell comes from a cell.

If you type in something in the Name Box that Excel chokes on, you get an error message telling you to enter a valid reference to go to, or to type a valid name. If you hit the Help button, you get advice like

```
"The name contains invalid characters. Numbers, letters,
and underscores (_) are valid characters for cell and
range names."
```

which is actually wrong by omission in that the question mark, period, and backslash characters are not mentioned.

The Name Box is a first-class, multifunctional spreadsheet control. Yep, not only can you use it to jump instantly to a named range (this topic was thoroughly beaten to death in Chapter 1), you can use it to create range names.

Select a cell or range, click on the Name Box, type in a valid range name (Excel barfs with an error message if you try to slip in a bogus name), and press ENTER. That's it. Done. Name created. You know you did it because the Name Box proudly displays the new name—unless you already had 100 names in the list. The Name Box displays names alphabetically, so if the name you entered falls alphabetically within the first 100 names, it goes in the Name Box and the previous 100th entry (or last in the list) goes a-missing. If the name you created falls alphabetically outside the list, it goes a-missing. To confuse things even more (if that's possible) even if the Name Box is maxed out at 100 names and you select a range whose name is not on the Name Box list, that name *still* appears in the Name Box rectangle on the formula bar. Go figure.

The ability to define names *and* jump to a range location is a double-edged sword. Here's a case in point: you can't redefine a range name using the Name Box because if you try to type in an existing name, you zap to that range name's coordinates.

You can use the Name Box to name graphic objects on the sheet by selecting the object and typing the name in the Name Box. You can jump to the named object by typing in that name. *But, object names do not appear in the drop-down list.* If you use the Define Name method to create a range name on the worksheet identical to the object name, both range and object will have the same name. The range name now appears in the drop-down Name Box list and clicking on it takes you to the range. The object still has the same name, but it can no longer be selected via the Name Box or the Go To method discussed earlier.

Using Define Name

The Name Box is swell for jumping to a given name or for defining a name, but as we've discussed, it has limitations. But don't despair because there's the good old Define Name dialog box (didn't think we painted ourselves in a corner, did you?).

To access the Define Name box, pull down the Insert menu, click on Name, and choose Define from the flyout menu. See Figure 4.1.

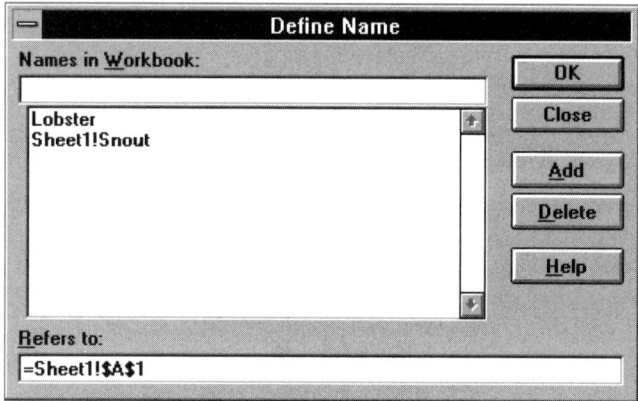

Figure 4.1 The Define Name Dialog Box

The current selection in the current sheet is shown in the Refers to box, and you can type in the desired name in the Names in Workbook box. Click OK if you're done or Add if you want to add your range name and leave the dialog box displayed. Be careful with that Delete button, pilgrim, there is no confirmation and no safety net. Not even Undo will save you.

If you try to add a bogus name using Define Name, you'll get an error message telling you "That name is not valid." But hit the Help button and you get these tips:

"The first character must be a letter or an underline character. Other characters can be letters, numbers, periods or underlines."

"The name cannot look like a cell reference ("A1" or "R1C1")."

"Use an underline character or a period, not a space, to separate words."

"The name must be less than 256 characters long."

Again Excel makes no mention of the backslash key or the question mark. At least they mention the period character.

The Define Name dialog box suffers from the limitation of all dialog boxes in that a text box (like Refers to) can't contain more than 255 characters. A complex reference including numerous rows, columns, or ranges could easily

exceed this limitation. When this happens, Excel lops off the extra characters (backing up to the nearest complete range in the complex reference) and truncates the named range—*without telling you.* Nuts!

The Name Box by example method is slightly more flexible in that it avoids having to stuff a reference into a dialog box control. But it is not without limitation. In a purely empirical test in our lab, the Name Box lopped a reference after the 843rd character—*without any indication.* Go figure.

Name Box by example

Do It Yourself

> Let every vat stand on its own bottom.
>
> William Bullein
> *Dialogue Against the Fever Pestilence*, 1564

It's simple. To name a single cell, you select it and enter the range name using either the Name Box or the Define Name dialog box. A range is just as easy, highlight the range and name it. Remember the cells in the range need not be contiguous but are limited to a single sheet, that is, a single range name cannot span sheets.

No problem to name an entire row or column. Select the row or column and name it. You can give a single name to several rows and columns. This is how Excel keeps track of print titles. You tell Excel what rows and columns to use as titles on a worksheet and Excel names those rows and columns Print_Titles. More on these special names that Excel itself uses shortly.

The Relative and Absolute Shuffle

> Dreadful indeed are the feuds of relatives, and difficult the reconciliation.
>
> Euripides
> *The Phoenissae*, ca. 410 BC

You'll notice that Excel defaults to using absolute cell references in the Refers to box (the dollar signs are a dead giveaway). In the next section, we'll wax philosophical about formulas and functions and talk at some length about relative and absolute referencing. Suffice it say for now that you do not want to monkey around with relative referencing until you understand exactly how relative and absolute referencing work and differ from each other. You'll see how a relative name would work in the Absolute and Relative Cell Addresses section.

Let Excel Do It

Now here is another one of those exemplary features of Excel that really makes your life easier. Say you have a table of data in your worksheet and you want to name the rows and columns. What'll you use for names? How about the row and column labels that you already have in the table?

Select the table of data. See Figure 4.2.

	A	B	C	D	E	F
1						
2		Northwest Divison				
3			1st Qtr	2nd Qtr	3rd Qtr	4th Qtr
4		Widgets	98	101	112	75
5		Doohickeys	110	92	98	75
6		Thingys	109	86	104	79
7		Total	317	279	314	229

Figure 4.2 Use Existing Labels as Range Names

Pull down the Insert menu, click on Names, and choose Create from the flyout menu. You get this very handy dialog box that lets you choose to use the labels on the perimeter of your selection. If you include the labels in the selection, the dialog box guesses which rows and columns you will most likely want to use and checks the appropriate boxes for you. See Figure 4.3.

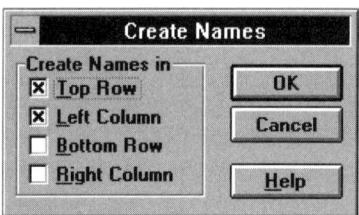

Figure 4.3 Let Excel Name It

If Excel guesses correctly, hit OK. If not, you check the appropriate boxes and hit OK. Done. This is a very neat feature.

In this example, you would wind up with the named ranges listed in Table 4.1.

The range names come from the row and column labels as we said, but they have been tweaked slightly to conform with Excel's naming requirements. Since a range name cannot start with a number, Excel automatically inserts an underscore for you. Ditto for spaces. Note that the actual row and column label cells are *not* part of the resulting named range *even if the initial range selected is composed of the labels plus the data.*

Table 4.1 Range Names and Their Coordinates

Range Name	Cell Range
_1st_Qtr	$C$4:$C$6
_2nd_Qtr	$D$4:$D$6
_3rd_Qtr	$E$4:$E$6
_4th_Qtr	$F$4:$F$6
Widgets	$C$4:$F$4
Doohickeys	$C$5:$F$5
Thingys	$C$6:$F$6

Book-Level Names

So far you have been working with book-level names. A **book-level name** is a defined range that means the same range on the same sheet no matter which sheet in the book you refer to it from. Well, that's clear as mud. Let's try another tack.

It works like this. You select cell A1 on Sheet1 and name it "Lobster." Say you add several sheets to this book. You are working in Sheet3 and want to reference the total in cell A1 on Sheet1. No problem, just a quick =Lobster and you've got it. Pull down the Name Box (or pop up the Go To box), select Lobster, and there you are. Sheet1 cell A1. Every time. From any sheet in the book.

Sheet-Level Names

A **sheet-level name** is local to the sheet that owns it. Hmmm, more mud. Stay with us, pilgrim, we'll try to deal with this slippery terminology with some examples.

First, how do you create a sheet-level name? You define a sheet-level name the same way you do a book-level name, only you preface the name with the sheet name. It works like this: if you select cell B2 on Sheet2 and you want to make it local (sheet level) to that sheet, you might name it Sheet2!Snout* instead of just Snout. The name of the sheet precedes the range name and is separated from the name by an exclamation point. Which, by the way, is pronounced "bang" in case you didn't know. Really, we're not pulling your leg. The (!) is pronounced "bang" like the (.) in a file name is pronounced "dot." Ah, but we digress.

The name is Snout, but it is local (sheet level) to Sheet2. If you go to Sheet1 and pull down the Name Box, Snout does not appear. It doesn't exist on Sheet1 nor is it a book-level name available across the entire book. You can refer to it if you include the sheet name in the reference. A formula on Sheet 1 like =Sheet2!Snout returns the contents of B2 from Sheet2.

---

*Excel 5 sheet names can include spaces, so to use a spacey sheet name in a reference, surround the name with single quotes, like this, 'Misc Stuff'!Snout.

When dealing with sheet-level names, be aware that they take precedence over identical book names. Consider Figure 4.4.

	A	B	C	D
1	100	< A1 is global "Spiff"		
2				
3		200	< B3 is local "Spiff"	

Figure 4.4 An Abundance of Spiffs

In the figure we have a book-level name on Sheet1 cell A1 of "Spiff" and a sheet-level name of "Spiff" referring to Sheet1 cell B3. If Sheet1 is the active sheet and you pull down the Name Box and click on Spiff, cell B3 becomes the active cell. Change to another worksheet and you still find Spiff in the Name Box. Click on it and this time Sheet1 cell A1 becomes the active cell. Anywhere in this book (Book1), outside of Sheet1, when you refer to Spiff, you are talking about Sheet1 cell A1. But on Sheet1, if you say Spiff, you mean cell B3.

To continue with the example, a formula on Sheet3 of =Spiff returns 100 (book-level Spiff), but the same formula on Sheet1 returns 200 (sheet-level Spiff).

According to Microsoft, you can refer specifically to the book-level Spiff even on Sheet1 if you preface the name with the workbook name. In a formula on Sheet1, =MYBOOK1!Spiff is supposed to return 100 (book-level Spiff) even when there is a sheet-level range with the same name.

 But, to make this technique (and we use the word loosely) work you have to jump through some, er, hoops. First, the book must have been saved to disk, and you have to be working with a valid filename. The .XLS extension is not needed. In fact, if you use the extension, you'll not get the book-level name at all. If you type =MYBOOK.XLS!Spiff and hit ENTER, you'll wind up with =Sheet1!Spiff, which is the local reference to Spiff. The joys of external references. Read on, it gets worse.

You have to enter =MYBOOK!Spiff and hit ENTER. Excel immediately displays the File Not Found dialog box (looking suspiciously like the File Open dialog box), which prompts you to pick the file you want for your external reference. Say what? No, we're serious. Pick the filename from the dialog box. *That's right, the same file that is currently the active book in Excel.* Click on OK. There, finally. Except it doesn't update. Try it by changing the entry in A1 (book-level Spiff). See. You have to save the file and then update the link, which involves another visit to the File Not Found dialog box in order for the formulas to update properly. As the saying goes, "let's not and say we did."

Here's the hot tip, save wear and tear and do not use a name to be both book level and sheet level in the same book. Deal? They are gonzo confusing. If you pop up the Go To dialog box, all the book-level names are listed along with the sheet-level names local to the active sheet. And the sheet-level names take precedence over any book-level names that share the same name. But there is no visible clue that some of the names are sheet level and some are book level.

Here's another hot tip (two for the price of one!), adopt a naming convention where sheet-level names begin with a lowercase "s" and book-level names have a lowercase "b". This automatically removes the temptation of having identical book-level and sheet-level range names. Then, when you see a list of range names, you'll have some clue as to which are book level and which are local (sheet level) to some sheet.

Oh, and you might watch out for this. You can select the same range in several **Gotcha!** worksheets simultaneously by selecting the range in one worksheet of a book and then CTRL + clicking on the other worksheet tabs for that book. Whatever you do at this point happens in the same range in all the sheets. If you have several worksheets that are identically configured (row and column labels identical in text and cell location) and you want to create sheet-level names using the row and column labels across all the worksheets, you might be tempted to use this shortcut.

So you select the range in one sheet, CTRL + click on the other worksheet tabs, and then do an Insert Name Create. If you do, this here's what happens. The range names based on the row and column labels are created as *sheet-level* names in all the selected sheets except the active one. In the active sheet, the names are *book level*. Be careful out there.

3-D Names

You can create 3-D names, but they are not as useful as they might be. You can create a 3-D name only through the Define Name dialog box. You type in a name and, in the Refers to text box, you type in the 3-D range using this syntax: =Sheet1:Sheet3!A1, which is the same syntax as a 3-D reference that you might use in a formula.

If you create this 3-D name and call it "Sales," you could enter a formula like =SUM(Sales) anywhere in a worksheet in this book and get the sum of cells A1 in sheets 1, 2, and 3.

3-D names only appear in the Define Name dialog box. You won't find them in the Go To dialog box or the Name Box.

Consider this formula on Sheet4:

```
=SUM(Sheet1:Sheet3!$A$1)
```

This is a typical 3-D reference, and you get the total of Sheet1!A1 + Sheet2!A1 + Sheet3!A1, as you would expect. But suppose you gave each cell A1 in sheets

1, 2, and 3 the *sheet-level* name "Wonka." We think you should be able to modify the Sheet4 formula to be:

```
=SUM(Sheet1:Sheet3!Wonka)
```

replacing the absolute cell reference, $A$1, with the range name Wonka. Doesn't work. Bummer. It would make 3-D modeling a lot easier.

Sort, Cut, Copy, and Names

Here's something that you should be aware of regarding range names. You name a cell or group of cells, *not* the contents of the cell. If you name B7 "Daisy" and then delete row 5, guess what? Row 7 becomes row 6 and Daisy is now B6. And that makes sense. But consider if you sort a range of cells, some of which are named. The contents of the cells may change with the sort, but the range names remain firmly affixed to the cells.

If you copy a cell, you are copying the contents only, not the range name. But if you cut the cell, you are moving the cell—lock, stock, and range name. Paste it somewhere else, and the range name goes with it. Still pretty straightforward, no?

But wait! It gets more complicated. Hmmm, we need another example. Take a two-sheet book. On Sheet1 you name cell B3 Duck. You make it a *sheet-level* name as in Sheet1!Duck. Now select that cell and cut it to the clipboard. Switch sheets to Sheet2. Select cell D4, hit Paste, and while you're there, enter 225 into D4. Pull down the Name Box. No Duck. Odd, don't you think? Switch back to Sheet1 and check out the Name Box. There's Duck. Click on it and faster than a speeding bullet you find yourself back in D4 on Sheet2. Oh boy!

Back to Sheet1. Take a look at the Define Name dialog box (Insert Name Define). See Figure 4.5.

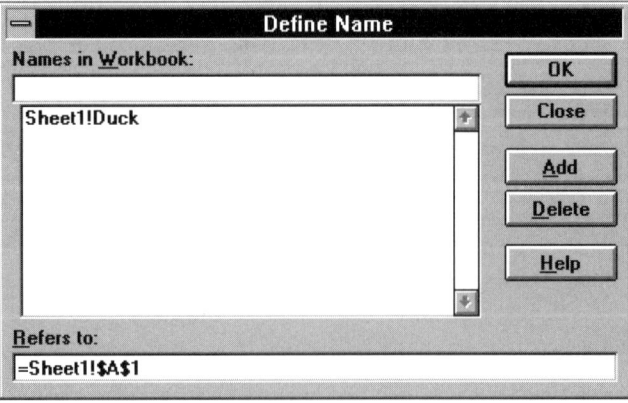

Figure 4.5 A Conundrum

Very odd indeed. In Sheet1 you have a sheet-level range name that refers to a cell *on another sheet!* If you go to Sheet1 and enter the formula =Duck you get the 225 from D4 on Sheet2. But if you go over to Sheet2 and enter the same formula, you get a #NAME? error because Sheet2 has no idea what Duck is all about. The moral of this story is to pay attention when cutting and pasting cells between sheets. Cut and Paste between books and you wind up with a sheet level-name that refers to an external reference (another book). Be very careful out there.

Using Names

> As handy as a pocket on a shirt.
>
> Anonymous

You've seen how to create names and a little about how names can be used. Very useful critters names are. We use them whenever we can, they can be much easier to read than the more cryptic cell coordinates and they're great for moving around the worksheet using the Name Box or the Go To dialog box.

Way back in Chapter 1 when you redesigned the Standard toolbar, we had you add a button specifically designed to make using names easier—the Paste Names button. You'd be surprised how handy this little gizmo is. And, if you're into keyboard shortcuts, note that F3 does the same thing as the Paste Names button.

Paste Names button

Names in Formulas

As you have seen in this section, you can use range names in place of cell references within formulas. It makes your formulas much easier to read, and with the Paste Names button, you can insert names into your formulas without worrying about typos or forgetting the name.

Let's say you want to sum a range of cells and you named the range in question. You type =SUM(and click on the Paste Names button. Up pops the Paste Name dialog box. See Figure 4.6.

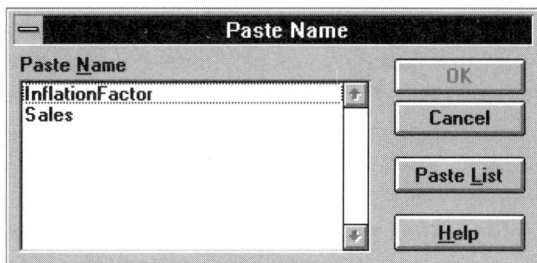

Figure 4.6 Paste Name Dialog Box

Select the name you want to insert in your formula and click on OK. Bam! The name is in your formula. The names that appear in the list are either book level or are local (sheet level) to the current sheet. If you are entering a formula and want to paste a name that is local (sheet level) to another sheet, start the formula, make the other sheet the active sheet by clicking its tab, and then hit the Paste Name button. You get a list of book-level names and the names local (sheet level) to that sheet.

If you want to get a list of range names and their coordinates, pick an empty spot on your worksheet, pop up the Paste Name box, and click the Paste List button. It drops a two-column list (starting with the active cell), where the first column shows the names and the column to the right shows the cell coordinates for each range name. But again you're only going to get all the book-level names and only the sheet-level names for the current worksheet. (We suggest that you pick an empty spot for the Paste List results for a reason. This feature pastes over whatever cell contents lie in its path, *without warning*.)

There doesn't seem to be any way with Excel's user interface to get a list of all names in the book and their related ranges. Go figure.

You can also use the Name Box to insert names into a formula. This has the added benefit of highlighting the named range with the marquee when you select it in the Name Box list. The problem with getting in the habit of using the Name Box is that it is not available in other situations where you might want to access a range name. The Paste Button works in all situations where accessing a range name is appropriate.

You should always use named references in formulas that link cells from a sheet in one book to a sheet in another book. If you use cell references instead of named ranges, you can get some unpleasant surprises. If the book with the dependent worksheet is closed and you decide to rearrange the layout of the source worksheet by moving groups of cells around, the next time you open the book with the dependent worksheet, those links refer to the old cell locations. If you use range names and then move cells around, the names move with the cells.

Applying Names

If you create your formulas in a worksheet using cell references and then later decide to create some range names, you can have Excel substitute the range names for the cell references in your formulas. If you have a formula like this:

```
=SUM(F6:F27)
```

and later you name the F6:F27 range as _1stQtrSales, you need only select Insert Names Apply. You get the Apply Names dialog box. Click on OK, and Excel replaces any cell coordinate that matches the coordinates of a named range with the name of that range. The formula in this example would become:

```
=SUM(_1stQtrSales)
```

The Apply Names dialog box comes up with the relevant names selected for the formulas you have highlighted. This list is multiselectable, so you can choose only the names you want to inject into your formulas. If you highlight a range of cells, only those cells have range names applied to them. In Figure 4.7, you see the Apply Names dialog box. If you click on the options button, you see all the choices displayed here.

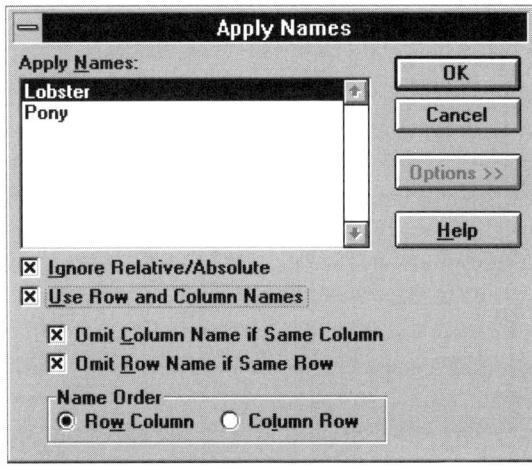

Figure 4.7 Apply Names Dialog Box with Options Displayed

All the check boxes are checked by default and you rarely have to change the settings. The Use Row and Column Names lets Excel use implied intersection (discussed later in this chapter), where an explicit name for a given cell is not available. The Omit options also let Excel use implied intersection instead of having to include a column name where the formula cell is in the same column as the cell being referenced. The Name order tells Excel which should come first, the row name or the column name. It is strictly cosmetic and does not impact the results of a formula.

Formulas in Names

We've discussed using names in formulas, and now we'll talk about using formulas in names. Huh? Wazzat? Glad you asked. This is another one of those underutilized features of Excel. Underutilized because folks lose track of the fact that Excel is a programming environment.

You can create a variable, that is, a range name, and set the name equal to a constant* or a formula. Say you want to use a percentage in different calculations scattered throughout your sheet. The usual way is to stick the percentage in a cell and either name it and use the name or use the cell reference wherever you need to reference that percentage. But what if you don't want the percentage on the worksheet?

No problem, pop up the Define Name dialog box, enter a name like OverHead, and type =3% in the Refers to box. The 3% is not entered anywhere on the sheet. A formula can use the name, as in:

```
=14000*(1+OverHead)
```

This formula returns 14420. The name OverHead does not appear in the Name Box nor in the Go To dialog box, but it does appear in the Paste Names dialog box.

You can define a name to refer to a formula that does not exist on any sheet. You create a name, and in the Refers to box you type in the formula. You can reference other existing names in this formula. Consider a case where cell C4 on Sheet1 has the number 100 in it and is named Sam. You can create a name like FormulaA, and in the Refers to box you type =Sam+200. You could then use the name FormulaA in formulas on your sheets. For example,

```
=FormulaA
```

would return 300.

```
=FormulaA+B27
```

would return 1300 if B27 contains the number 1000.

Miscellaneous Uses for Names

> No, Groucho is not my real name. I'm breaking it in for a friend.
>
> Groucho Marx

What else can you use these versatile name critters for? Excel uses names in places other than in formulas. If you select a range of cells and click the Set Print Area button that you added to the Standard toolbar back in Chapter 1, Excel drops a range name of Print_Area on your selection. When you print, Excel looks for a defined name of Print_Area and, if it finds one, it prints it.

---

*The term "constant" as used here means a number entered directly into a cell as opposed to a formula. A formula may return different results, depending on many things, but a number entered directly into a cell remains the same. It's *constant*.

If you're manually setting up a print area in the Page Setup dialog box, you can switch to the Sheet tab and in the Print Area text box you can type in a range name. Or you can put the cursor in this text box, click the Paste Names button, and pick the name off the list (sorry, the Name Box is not available in this circumstance). Excel creates a range called Print_Area with the same coordinates as the range name you pasted in, and you're ready to print.

The same technique works with the "Rows to repeat" and "Columns to repeat" settings a.k.a. print titles. Excel creates a name called Print_Titles based on your input, be it row and column references or named ranges.

Most anywhere that Excel expects you to enter a cell range reference you can probably pop up the Paste Names list and use a name instead.

Built-in Names

You've seen that certain names have special meaning to Excel, like "Print_Area" and "Print_Titles" discussed in the last section. While they're not reserved words in the programming sense, several other names have special meanings in Excel. Don't use the names described in the following subsections yourself unless you're sure you know what you're doing.

Print_Area

Print_Area is the range of cells on a worksheet that Excel sends to the printer when that sheet is the active sheet.

Print_Titles

Print_Titles defines the rows to print at the top, and the columns to print on the left, of every page. Print_Titles should be defined as entire rows and columns. If you try to trick Excel by defining less than entire rows and columns as Print_Titles, Excel doesn't complain until you try to print or do a print preview, at which point Excel barfs an error message telling you nice try, but no dice.

Database

Excel uses the Database range name to recognize a database on a sheet. Excel 5 has a whole passel of new tricks for working with database tables on a sheet and does not create this name itself. It does allow you to force a given range to be the database range for some of Excel's new wowie-pow-zowie data management features. We'll get into database stuff big time in Chapter 7.

In any event, if the name Database is found on a worksheet, that range is used as the default for Advanced Filter and Pivot tables as well as for the built-in data form.

Data_form

Speaking of the name Data_form, as you'll see in Chapter 7, Excel has a nifty built-in data form for entering records into a worksheet-based database. But you still might want to create your own custom data form.

VBA is the way Microsoft wants us all to do this in Excel 5, but if you want to use the old Excel 4 method of putting a dialog definition right on a worksheet or macrosheet, you can. Defining the range as Data_form overrides the built-in data form dialog box. It's not a bad way to go either if you have a copy of the old Excel 4 EXCELDE.EXE dialog editor. You build the dialog box and Excel itself does most of the complicated work managing the database

Criteria

Criteria is a special range name that Excel uses with the Advanced Filter feature in Excel 5.

Extract

Extract is a special range name that Excel uses with the Advanced Filter feature in Excel 5. We'll revisit both "criteria" and "extract" when we talk about managing lists of stuff in Chapter 7.

Consolidate_Area

Consolidate_Area is a special range name that Excel uses with the Consolidate feature.

Sheet_Title

Sheet_Title is a built-in range name used in Consolidating sheets. It's really a nifty feature, and if you do much Data Consoldating, you're gonna need it big time! Check it out in the *User's Guide*.

Auto_Open, Auto_Close, Auto_Activate, Auto_Deactivate

These Auto_ names are usually used on macrosheets to designate programs that should be executed under specific conditions, that is, when a sheet is opened, closed, activated, deactivated (kind of obvious, huh?). On a worksheet you'll use these names for named formulas, where the formula is a qualified path to the program to be run.

For example, open a new book and save it as TEST1.XLS. Insert a module sheet, create a VBA macro called Lobster() on Module1 like this:

```
Sub Lobster()
  MsgBox "Sheet1's Auto_Open was just executed by Module1.Lobster"
End Sub
```

Pop over to Sheet1 and do an Insert Name Define. For the name, use Auto_Open, and in the Refers to box, type:

```
=TEST1.XLS!Module1.Lobster
```

Now close the `TEST1.XLS` book and reopen it. The message box is displayed as the macro is executed upon the book's opening.

You can use these Auto_ names on XLM macrosheets by naming the macro range, using any of the special Auto_name names.

In VBA modules, you can achieve the same effect by using the Auto_ name as the macro name. For example, the previous macro could simply be rewritten as:

```
Sub Auto_Open()
  MsgBox "Sheet1 Auto_Open was just executed by Module1.Auto_Open"
End Sub
```

It is not necessary to have the named formula to get the macro to execute upon opening.

If you have both a worksheet "named formula" called Auto_Open and a VBA macro called Auto_Open in the same book, the Auto_Open named formula is run first, then the VBA macro.

Auto_Activate and Auto_Deactivate are holdovers from the old XLM language and are used primarily on macrosheets. In VBA modules, you want to use OnSheetActivate and OnSheetDeactivate. More on this in Chapter 10, where we scratch the surface on VBA, so stay tuned!

Recorder

This built-in range name is used on macrosheets to mark where the next recorded XLM macro inserts its code. Excel supports recording and position marking in VBA modules also, but it does so without using a range name.

So, *for a macrosheet only*, the name Recorder is set by Tools Record Macro and either the Mark Position for Recording or the Record at Mark options. If you do not explicitly set a position, by default Excel records a new macro in the next available column of the macrosheet.

FORMULAS AND FUNCTIONS

Eureka!

California state motto

Standing at the crossroads This is where it all comes together, the crossroads of spreadsheet modeling, if you will. Here you program that sucker to do what needs doing. Grab that sheet and over the top!

Absolute and Relative Cell Addresses

You simply cannot ever get out of the bush leagues of spreadsheet modeling without having a firm understanding of absolute and relative cell addresses. And you'd be surprised how many times the seemingly subtle difference between these addressing schemes has dealt a fatal blow to someone's painstakingly crafted model.

Okay, here's a test. What's the difference between these two formulas (see Figure 4.8)?

```
=A1
=$A$1
```

Figure 4.8 Absolutely Relative?

- *Answer 1*—They both refer to the intersection of the first column and the first row. Buzzzzzzz. Wrong.

- *Answer 2*—The first one refers to column A, row 1; but the second one absolutely positively refers to column A, row 1? Buzzzzzzz. Wrong again (no partial credit).

- *Answer 3*—The first one refers to some cell, some number of rows and columns distant from this cell, and the second one refers to the intersection of the first column and the first row. Ding. Give that contestant a cigar!

Confused? You should be. How intuitive is it to use dollar signs to indicate absolute column and row coordinates? *Not very.* This is a legacy from good old Lotus 1-2-3. The propeller heads at Lotus decided to shield users from what they considered scary cell references and so developed the fiction that columns are designated by letters. What? Heresy you say. Columns are always letters, as in column A, column B. Not!

Columns are numbered.

Columns Unmasked!

Who was that masked man?

The Lone Ranger

That's right. Column A is really column 1 as far as Excel is concerned. Oh, if you want to kid yourself that it's really column A, Excel is happy to go along with it (in most cases). Let's take another look at those two formulas, but this time we'll switch Excel's display to its native notation style called R1C1.

1. Pull down the Tools menu and select Options.

2. Click the General filecard to make it active.

3. In the Reference Style group box, click the button marked R1C1.

4. Click on OK.

That's better. Notice anything different? The column letters have been replaced with column *numbers*. Figure 4.9 shows those formulas again.

```
=R[-1]C[-1]
=R1C1
```

Figure 4.9 What Excel Really Thinks of A1

Some difference eh? Okay, so it is pretty scary, but stay with us and see if it makes sense. When you type in something like A1, Excel sees that as a relative reference, that is, a reference to some cell position *relative* to the current cell. In this case, A1 is one row up, R[-1], and one column left, C[-1]. This tells you, by the way, that this formula, =R[-1]C[-1], is in cell row 2, column 2, which is also known as good old B2.

Current cell position is denoted by R for row and C for column. Changes from the relative position of the current cell position are indicated by numbers in square brackets; positive numbers for down and right, and negative numbers for up and left.

The Relative Facts

What does relative referencing do for you? Well, it allows you to copy a formula from one cell to another and have the references *appear* to automatically adjust to new positions. That last sentence sounds confusing even to us, so perhaps another example is in order. Consider the following example in A1 notation style. See Figure 4.10.

=B6+B7	=C6+C7	=D6+D7

Figure 4.10 Simple 'Add Two Cells Down' Formula in A1 Style

This first formula (=B6+B7) was entered into a cell and then copied to the two cells on the right. You've probably done something similar to this a thousand times. Guess what? All three formulas are identical. No, we haven't flipped out (hard to tell sometimes though) and we're not kidding. They really are identical, and we can prove it. Change back to the R1C1 style and observe. Here are the same formulas (see Figure 4.11).

=R[-2]C+R[-1]C	=R[-2]C+R[-1]C	=R[-2]C+R[-1]C

Figure 4.11 Relative Referencing Revealed!

This is what is confusing about the A1 notation style when dealing with relative references: *The formulas look different when in A1 style, but in reality they are all the same formula.* When you copy something like =B6+B7 one cell to the right, the column letters appear to change as if by magic. There's no magic about it. You copy the identical formula, but when in the A1 notation style, Excel tweaks the reference's *appearance*.

Each formula in Figure 4.11 says to take the contents of the cell two rows up, same column, and add to that the contents of the cell one row up, same column. This formula gives different results, depending on where it is placed. Its results are *relative* to the location of the cell containing the formula.

Oh, Absolutely!

An absolute reference in R1C1 notation style is very straightforward. You simply type in the row and column reference without any brackets.

```
=R1C1
```

points to the cell where row 1 intersects with column 1. No matter where you copy this formula, you are going to get row 1, column 1. That's as absolute as you can get.

A reference can be mixed, that is, contain both relative and absolute references.

```
=R1C[3]
```

points to the cell on row 1 (absolute) and three columns to the right of the current cell (relative). Copy this formula where you will, and it always refers to row 1. The column reference is three right from whatever cell you copy this formula into.

In A1 notation style you've got little dollar signs ($) to denote absolute. So instead of:

```
=R1C[3]
```

you would get something like:

```
=H$1
```

Sure the A1 formula is fewer characters, but when you think about it, which is easier to read?

We think R1C1 makes more sense than A1 style for a lot of things. If you want to really understand what your worksheet and formulas are all about, we recommend that you turn on R1C1 notation style and leave it on for a month or so. Give it a whirl. 'Nuff said.

Range Names Revisited

> I have returned.
>
> Douglas MacArthur
> Following the US landing on Leyte, October 20, 1944

Ha! Thought you were off scott free when it came to range names, did you? Not a chance! Break out that bucket of oatmeal and take a deep breath. (If you are missing the oatmeal reference, you probably skipped the Text, Numbers, and Formulas section back in Chapter 2. Shame on you!)

No, we're kidding. It won't be bad at all because you now are up on relative and absolute cell references. Apply that knowledge to range names and you're home free. Won't take but a minute.

The Absolute Range Name

> It was always thus; and even if 'twere not, 'twould inevitably have been always thus.
>
> Dean Lattimer

Absolute range names is what you get by default (it's not your fault, it's de-fault, <*groan*>) when you create a range name. Look at the range name you just created in the Define Name dialog box. The dollar signs in the Refers to box are a dead giveaway…absolutely.

Generally this is exactly what you want in a range name—an absolute reference to some cell or range of cells. All you have to worry about is whether the name is book level or sheet level. You don't have to worry about copying formulas that contain references because you know that the range name always refers to the same cell or group of cells.

The Relative Range Name

> To whom related, or by whom begot…
>
> Alexander Pope
> *Elegy to the Memory of an Unfortunate Lady*, 1717

An absolute range name refers to a physical location on a worksheet that does not depend on the location of the cell that uses the name. A relative range name is a horse of an entirely different color. Relative cell addressing is all about the reference changing, indicating a different location, depending on where the current cell is. This carries over to range names as well.

Try the following example, which creates a relative range name.

1. Select cell A4.

2. Then Insert, Name, Define. For a range name, use ThreeCellsUp.

3. Tab down to the Refers to box so that the sheet reference it selected. Click on cell A1 and drag down to A3.

4. Edit the reference by removing the dollar signs.

By the way, the Refers to box is an edit box that reads references from the sheet. This means if you Tab down to the box (or ALT + R, or click in it) and then try to use the left and right arrow keys to move the cursor through the entry with editing in mind, you'll be sorely disappointed. The arrow keys change the active cell or range on the sheet, and the new sheet reference appears in the edit box. If you want to use the arrow keys in this type of edit box, hit F2 first to get into Edit mode. The arrow keys move the cursor and do not change the sheet reference.

You remove the dollar signs and the reference should look like this (the sheet name may be different depending on what sheet you are in when you start this little experiment):

```
=Sheet1!A1:A3
```

Click on OK. You have now created a *relative range name*. This range name does not refer to cells A1 through A3. That's right, it's a relative reference, *you're getting the hang of this stuff, pilgrim!* This is best seen when using the R1C1 notation style. Switch to R1C1 via Tools Options General and click on the R1C1 option button, then on OK.

Now call up the Define Name dialog box and click on ThreeCellsUp. Look at the Refers to box. You should see something like this:

```
=Sheet1!R[-3]C:R[-1]C
```

ThreeCellsUp refers to three cells above the current cell through one cell above the current row. Now that you've built this thing, how do you use it? Consider yonder worksheet (see Figure 4.12).

	A	B	C	D	E	F	G
1							
2		Northwest Divison					
3			1st Qtr	2nd Qtr	3rd Qtr	4th Qtr	
4		Widgets	98	101	112	75	
5		Doohickeys	110	92	98	75	
6		Thingys	109	86	104	79	
7		Total	=SUM(ThreeCellsUp)				
8							

Figure 4.12 Using a Relative Range Name

You can use the ThreeCellsUp range name in a formula (as shown in Figure 4.12) to refer to the three cells immediately above the current cell. Copy this formula across the range shown in this example, D7:F7, and you sum the proper cells. This lets you build a name reference that adjusts relative to the current cell using the name. Very neat.

Building Formulas

> Have you heard of the wonderful one-hoss shay,
> That was built in such a logical way
> It ran a hundred years to a day?
>
> Oliver Wendell Holmes
> *The Autocrat of the Break-fast Table*, 1858

You've seen numerous examples of formulas throughout this book. Reading this far, you may have picked up by osmosis the basic techniques for entering (a.k.a. building) a formula. This section, however, explores the mechanics of building a formula from the ground up. Consider this section to be like an introductory course in auto mechanics. You may already know how to drive a car, and well, but sometimes it's worth exploring how the parts fit together under the hood.

There are several different ways to build a formula. You can mix and match 'em, too. Here are some of your options:

- You can type in a formula character by character with the keyboard alone. Peck, peck, peck...*hunt*...peck, peck...*gasp*...there must be an easier way! There is. Read on, pilgrim.

- You can type in a formula partly by hand (with the keyboard) and use the mouse to point to cell references.

- You can use Paste Name to pick available range names or named formulas from a list, rather than typing in the names manually.

- You can use Excel's awe-inspiring Function Wizard to build a formula from scratch, or use the Function Wizard in combination with the manual typing, mouse reference-selection, and Paste Name techniques.

With Your Bare Hands

> Work your hands from day to day, the winds will blow the profit.
>
> Louis MacNeice
> *Bagpipe Music*

Building a formula manually is a sure-fire way to build up those guitar-pickin' fingertip calluses, pilgrim. Nothing wrong with it. Sometimes it's the fastest way 'round the mulberry bush (even though most of the time, you'll be able to work faster with a combination of the mouse, Paste Name, and Function Wizard). Now roll up your shirt sleeves and let's do it the manual way.

1. Select a cell.

2. Press the = key. (Excel immediately activates the formula bar.)

3. Type in your formula.

4. Press ENTER or click the Enter box.

Parentheses are to formulas as drawers are to a chef's kitchen. They're absolutely vital to keep everything organized in its proper place. Parentheses are *mandatory* for all functions because they're used to encapsulate function arguments, like this:

```
SUM(NUMBER1, NUMBER2, ...)
```

where `NUMBER1` and `NUMBER2` represent two of up to 30 (in the case of `SUM`) arguments that `SUM` uses as the source material to be added together, ultimately producing the total of all the arguments' values. More on functions and arguments shortly.

You can also use parentheses to override mathematical operator precedence rules. For example, since multiplication always wins (gets performed first) in a scuffle with addition, the formula

`=500*2+1`

returns `1001`. But if you want Excel to multiply 500 by 2+1, you'd better enter

`=500*(2+1)`

to return the desired value of `1500`. Big difference algebraically, not to mention if that's your bonus check being calculated!

When your formulas start getting as convoluted as King Gordius's knot, *parentheses can save the day by explicitly revealing what the darned mathematical operator precedence rules are in the first place!* Even such a simple formula as

`=500*2+1`

if you feel so inclined, can be entered as

`=(500*2)+1`

which returns `1001`.

Optimization freaks might argue that the parentheses surrounding `(500*2)` are superfluous. Pshaw. We vote vehemently for readability and clarity over efficiency. So be kind to yourself, your co-workers, spouse, children, and Excel-loving house pets, any of whom may some day have to read your formulas.

For simple formulas, Excel supplies default parentheses where needed. For example, if you enter

`=SUM(A1:A5`

and omit the closing parenthesis, when you press ENTER**, Excel appends the closing parenthesis for you with aplomb.** *Chivalry lives!*

Errors Do Happen

> It's a working principle of the Head Bureau that the very possibility of error must be ruled out of account. The ground principle is justified by the consummate organization of the whole authority.

Franz Kafka
Das Schloss, 1926

If Excel detects a syntax error in your formula, it gracefully provides an appropriate message box. By far the most common error involves a misplaced, one too many, or one too few parentheses. Try entering the formula

```
=SUM(1,2,3))
```

and press ENTER. Clang, clang, clang. See Figure 4.13.

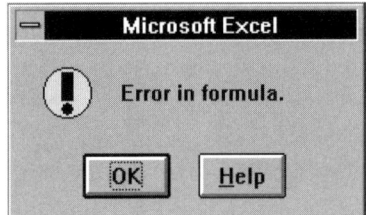

Figure 4.13 Get Used to This One

99.9 percent of the time when you see the message in Figure 4.13, if you take a deep breath and scan the offending formula left-to-right matching open and close parentheses as you go, you'll spot the cause lickety-split.

To verify that all open parentheses have a proper corresponding closing parentheses, Excel has a cool built-in parenthesis matcher. While editing a formula, use the arrow keys to move the cursor through the formula. As it passes through a parenthesis, that parentheses is momentarily bolded along with its matching parenthesis. This lets you visually review how Excel is matching your parenthesis within a formula.

Don't overlook the humbly heroic Help button on this (and other) formula-related error message boxes. Clicking on it often provides precisely the hint you need. Our favorite help topic for formula entry errors is the one linked to the Figure 4.13 message box. This topic presents a treasure-trove of common formula entry errors. The last section of the "Error in Formula" help topic enumerates thirteen—count 'em—excellent tips, presented in order from most common to decidedly esoteric. See Figure 4.14.

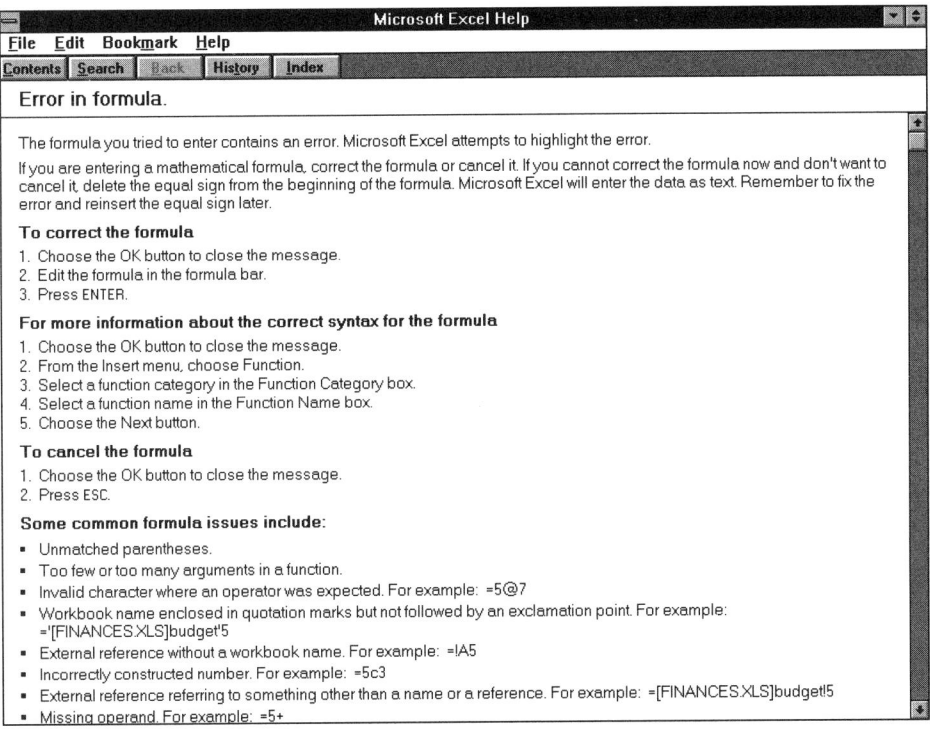

Figure 4.14 When the Formula's Broke, Start Here

Unfortunately *there's no way to locate this topic with a manual search.* (We tried, we really did. Should we take the wand away for this hiccup? Nah. We're feeling kinda magnanimous today. *Heh, heh, heh.*) Instead, you'll have to enter

```
=SUM(1,2,3))
```

press ENTER, and then click Help. Or, if you're really counting keystrokes (and who isn't?), the fewest strokes to generate this help topic would be to enter `=SUM()`, press ENTER, and then click Help.

A word of caution for those of you migrating from Lotus 1-2-3. Although Excel gladly accepts + and - as the leading characters in a manually entered formula, we advise against it. Break the Lotus 1-2-3 habit! You know, when in Rome, etc. Use the = key to spawn your formulas. Thank you.

Formula Error Houdini Tricks

> I am escaped with the skin of my teeth.
>
> Job 19:20

If you find yourself completely bamboozled by a formula and can't get past an error message for love nor money, try this:

1. Enter an apostrophe as the leftmost character in the cell. This tells Excel to treat the cell contents as text instead of as a formula.

2. Press ENTER or click the Enter box.

Now you're jammin'. This allows you to disassemble the wayward formula at your leisure. *Heh, heh, heh.* However,...

The maximum size of a formula is 1024 characters. The maximum length of text in a cell is 255 characters. Hmmm. Something's gonna hit the fan here in a second. So, if you have an erroneous 1024 character formula, you can't insert an apostrophe prefix (Excel tells you "Formula is too long"). "No problem," you say to yourself, "I'll eliminate one character, make a mental or pencil note of what that character was, and insert the apostrophe prefix." Good idea, we'll grant you that, but this results in a "Text is too long" error message because of the 255-character maximum rule. Trapped! Ah, but not for long. *Heh, heh, heh.*

If your erroneous formula exceeds 255 characters in length, here's the Underground bomb-proof escape hatch:

1. Select the entire formula.

2. Cut it to the clipboard (Edit Cut or click the cut tool).

3. Add a text box anywhere you fancy on the current sheet (click on the Shape button, choose the text box button, draw it, bingo).

4. Paste the errant formula into the text box.

5. Return to Excel and press ESC or click the Cancel Box to remove the formula from the cell and end the edit. If you need to print the text box contents, enlarge it as needed and print.

ExcelGods, take note. When you click the Help button in reaction to the "Formula is too long" message, the help text states, and we quote, "The formula you are entering is too long or complex. Try breaking the formula into two or more parts and entering each into a different cell." Fine and dandy, *but how's about mentioning the ultra-critical fact that a formula can contain a maximum of 1024 characters?*

Cannot Quit Microsoft Excel

> Begin at the beginning…and go on till you come to the end: then stop.

Lewis Carroll
Alice's Adventures in Wonderland, 1865

Many Excel neophytes get bitten by the following scenario. It's easy to panic when it happens. *Hell, we still panic when it happens to us!* Many a time we've had to whip out the brown paper bag (every instructor's favorite tool), hand it to a trainee caught in this situation, and instruct her or him to breathe deeply until they calm down.

Excel lets you activate some menu controls—like File Exit, the Control menu box, or the Minimize button—while the formula bar is active. (However, note that most menu commands are grayed out while the formula bar is active, in keeping with the Windows standard of graying out actions that are not currently available. It just so happens that File Exit *remains* available even when the formula bar is active.) If the content of the formula bar is kosher, this can be good. If the content is bogus, this can be scary.

If the formula bar is active and contains valid stuff you can—repeat, you *can*—exit Excel right then and there. Excel actually presses ENTER for ya! Then it asks if you want to save changes to the book in question. Top notch!

If, on the other hand, the formula bar is active *and contains a bogus formula*, you'll never be able to close, exit, quit, shut down, exorcise, or otherwise get rid of Excel. Say you have the formula bar active and then you File Exit. Excel first displays a traditional error message box. You probably take the easy way out and click on OK. After all, you're trying to quit. *This doesn't deactivate the formula bar.* So Excel immediately puts up an "Excel-level" error (in ProgrammerSpeak this means "untrappable") that's so low level that you can't ALT + TAB or CTRL + ESC to another application. (Shucks, we couldn't even get a screen shot of the bugger for you using our best-of-breed screen capture program.) It contains the message "Microsoft Excel … Cannot quit Microsoft Excel" and an OK button. All you can do at this point is click on OK. Then you'll have to either ESC from the formula bar or correct the formula.

The real neverending story

Admittedly, this low-level message is not destructive (unless you're new to Excel and have a weak constitution), but we suggest that the Redmondians trap this particular circumstance and put up a friendlier, more explanatory message. Thanks.

Where's Miss Manners when you need her?

How to Build in Two Places at the Same Time

Who splits his own wood warms himself twice.

Saying

Excel has an extraordinary feature that many of us have grown so accustomed to we take it completely for granted. And the feature is...drum roll, please...the modeless formula bar. Ta da!

When you're building a formula and need to enter a range reference, all you have to do is click and drag the mouse. Piece o' cake. Excel gallantly converts this mouse action into the appropriate range address inside the formula bar. Since you saw earlier that you can manipulate (with the scroll bars) the view of your sheet without disrupting the current selection, you can now appreciate the power of this feature when you're using the mouse to select a range while you're in the process of building a formula. In WindowsSpeak's Elder Tongue, this type of two-things-can-have-the-focus behavior is referred to as "modeless." (The opposite of "modeless" is "modal.") The best way to describe these enigmatic terms is by example.

System modal

Remember the recalcitrant "Microsoft Excel...Cannot quit Microsoft Excel" message described earlier? It was the message that *brought everything in your entire Windows session to a grinding halt until you dealt with it*? That's a very modal message box; specifically, it's **system modal**. Modal does come in less severe flavors. A message box like Excel's "Error in formula," which allows you to switch to another application before you respond to it, is called **application modal**. A dialog box like Page Setup behaves modelessly when, from its Print Area text box, it allows you to click the mouse inside the worksheet and select the desired print range while the dialog box is still displayed. But we digress...

Application modal

The technique for selecting a range address while in the formula bar is so simple, you'll cry. See Figure 4.15.

B2		↕ ✕ ✓ *fx*	=sum(B2:B6	
	A	**B**	**C**	**D**
1		*Sam*		
2	Year 1989	200		
3	Year 1990	165		
4	Year 1991	160		
5	Year 1992	120		
6	Year 1993	105		
7		=sum(B2:B6		
8				

Figure 4.15 Modeless is a Good Thing

Picture the fictional, down-trodden Spreadsheet Sam. He's having one of those soul-wrenching, sweat-dripping, somebody-pinch-me variety nightmares. It goes like this. Spreadsheet Sam's MENSA sponsor has been hounding him about an alleged precipitous decline in his IQ since his initiation. He rushes to Excel, frantically types in his annual IQ test scores, and is horrified to discover what does indeed appear to be a declining trend.

Sam's desperate, so he figures maybe, just maybe, he can fight back with a report on his average IQ. (Like Hunter Thompson sez, "When the going gets weird, the weird turn pro.") Here's how he'd build that formula with mouse in one hand and keyboard in the other:

1. Select B7.

2. Press the = key. Excel immediately activates the formula bar.

3. Type in SUM and then type an open parenthesis (. *The open parenthesis is required.* (We know that Spreadsheet Sam is trying to calculate an average and is using the wrong function but, after all, it *is* a nightmare, *heh, heh, heh.*)

4. Click on B2 and drag down to B6. Excel puts a marquee (a.k.a. the marching ants—look closely and you can see the little suckers in Figure 4.15) around the selected range, B2:B6, and pokes the range address into the formula bar. Voilà!

5. Type a close parenthesis).

6. Press ENTER or click the Enter box. (Actually, you can press ENTER after dragging the mouse because, for such a simple formula, Excel supplies the close parenthesis. OTOH,* typing the close parenthesis is a good muscle-memory habit so you'll avoid pesky error messages when building more complex formulas.) Although Spreadsheet Sam used the wrong function, he did use the mouse effectively to select the range used by the function.

Help, Mr. Wizard, Help!

> In doing we learn.
>
> George Herbert

"A wizard, a true star," as Todd Rundgren crooned. That's Function Wizard all right. If you're in a function kind of mood, let Function Wizard roll out the red carpet.

Modelessness is put to very good use here in Function Wizard. Back in the heat of the MENSA-expulsion nightmare, driven into a panic-ridden frenzy, Spreadsheet Sam suddenly realizes he's using the wrong function, but he can't

**Function
Wizard button**

*On The Other Hand.

remember the correct spelling for Excel's averaging function. Is it AVG? Is it AVERAGE? AVE? Hell, maybe it's AVRG? *He has no #@$%!&* idea, and the MENSA auditors are snapping at his heels!* Soooooo…Function Wizard to the rescue.

1. Select B7.

2. Here you have a choice:

   a. Press the = key. Excel immediately activates the formula bar. Now go to step 3.

   b. Alternately, you can bypass the = key step altogether and select Insert, and then Function. (However, *we strongly recommend that you always initiate a formula with the equal key* to keep you safely in the muscle-memory swing of things.) If you choose Insert Function, Excel inserts the mandatory = key for you. Now go to step 4.

3. Select Insert then choose Function, or press the Function Wizard button in the formula bar. See Figure 4.16.

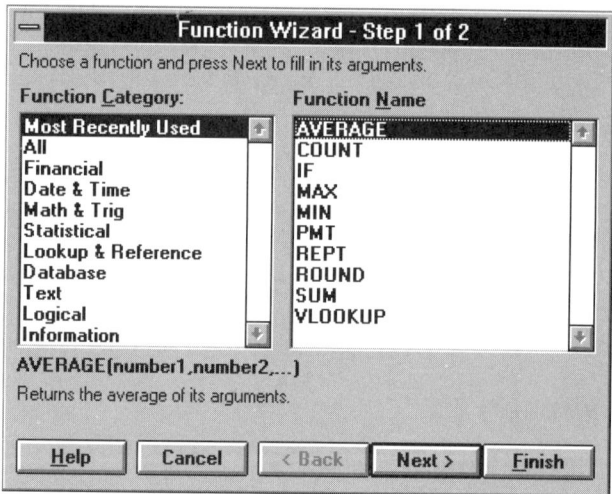

Figure 4.16 A Wizard, a True Star

4. From here on out, it can't get much easier. You can choose a Function Category and then select the desired function from the associated Function Name list. The ubiquitous Help button is there if you need it. If you can fast-forward a VCR, you can use Function Wizard!

5. To complete the example, select the Statistical category and then choose AVERAGE from the Function Name list. Notice that Function Wizard displays the current function's argument list below the Function Category list box. To get more detailed help, press the Help button.

6. Click Next.

7. Click on B2 and drag down to B6.

8. Click Finish.

Excellent, isn't it? Yeah, we think so, too. You can also use Function Wizard to inject a function into the middle of a formula. It's just a mouse-click away.

Function Mechanics

Now that you've seen Function Wizard wave its magic wand, shake that fairy dust-induced reverie off and let's open up the hood on functions!

In programming terms, a **function** is a series of instructions (a.k.a. commands or statements) that return a value. Returning a value is a function's raison d'être.* This book consistently uses the term "function" in this context, so here's your Underground function mantra, "A function returns a value, a function returns a value,…"

Function

In Chapter 10 we'll talk about the subtle, mind-bending differences between terms like macro, procedure, program, routine, subroutine, and function. It turns out that in VBA a function adheres to the "returns a value" definition. (Thank someone for small favors, eh?) We'll refer to this variety of function as a VBA function. Clever, huh?

VBA function

Another species of function is lurking about, as you might well have imagined given the fun we had on our recent Function Wizard joyride. This type of function exists within the confines of an Excel sheet, and we'll refer to it as a worksheet function, which is consistent with usage in Microsoft publications on the subject.

Worksheet function

A worksheet function has three parts, from left to right: =FunctionName(Arguments).

1. The equal sign—This is required, required, required.

2. The function's name—You don't have to type it in as capitals; Excel automatically converts it for you after you press ENTER. In fact, in Chapter 5 we suggest that you always type function and range names in lowercase. If Excel recognizes the name (that is, it has no typos), it automatically converts it to uppercase for functions and matches the case of your range names after you press ENTER. This alerts you to errors in your formula because *if a name doesn't change case, you know you typed it in wrong.* (But hey, why bother typing, use Function Wizard instead!)

3. The function's arguments, contained inside parentheses—Most functions have one or more arguments. Some functions have no arguments, for example,

---

*The term "function" can be used in a more general sense to refer to a subroutine. Confusing? You bet. Here's the *Microsoft Press Computer Dictionary* definition for function: "The purpose of or the action carried out by a program or routine; *a general term for a subroutine*; in some languages, a subroutine that returns a single value." (Emphasis ours.)

NOW(). Note that parentheses are still required even if the function has no arguments. Other functions have one argument, for example, SQRT(16). If a function supports more than one argument, the arguments are separated by commas. For example, the AVERAGE() function supports between 1 and 30 arguments, so something like AVERAGE(100,200,500) works quite nicely.*

Argument

Yes, it is...
No, it isn't...
Yes, it is...

An **argument** is a piece of information you give a function. In any conversation about functions, "argument" is a *good* word, not something to be avoided as in a relationship. You may occasionally (or even frequently, depending on how excited we get) hear propeller heads like us say "pass that function an argument." When translated into English that means "pass me some nails 'cuz I've got some serious home improvement to do." In this construction analogy, the result of construction (function) is a completed home to your specifications. The arguments might be— this is only a partial list, mind you—materials like concrete, lumber, dry wall, nails, plumbing, wire, and paint and parameters like floor plan dimensions, paint color, and light fixture choices. The house reflects the components put into it, as a function reflects (returns) a value depending on the arguments you supply to it.

Any of the following items can be arguments—a numeric value, an equation, a range reference (remember, a range reference can point to either a single cell or a group of cells), a chunk of text, logical values like TRUE or FALSE, logical comparisons, an error value like #N/A, *even other functions*. Arguments are instructions that enable a function to calculate a value and return a result for you. You can inspect any function's architecture and argument list either while in Function Wizard (press Help), by searching the help file for the phrase "alphabetic list of worksheet functions," or by looking it up in the *Microsoft Excel 5 Worksheet Function Reference*, which, by the way, does not come with Excel.

 Microsoft should unhesitatingly include the *Worksheet Function Reference* or at the very least the contents of this book as a help file that ships with every copy of the product. We're serious. This reference material is far superior to the bare-bones information provided on functions in the help file that does come with Excel. Everyone reading this, stop right now, walk over to your PC, fire up CompuServe, type GO MSEXCEL, and send a public message to All on this subject. Let's start a grassroots movement. *Power to the people, right on!* For a heavily quantitative product like Excel, the essence of which is its function set, this omission is inexcusable. Soapbox OFF.

---

*We use AVERAGE(100,200,500) here for simplicity and to emphasize the existence of multiple arguments for functions that many folks use for years with only one argument (a range reference containing the source values). For example, with the values 100, 200, and 500 in cells A1, A2, and A3 respectively, a typical use of AVERAGE() in this context would be AVERAGE(A1:A3). To carry this to its logical conclusion, an example of calculating the average of values stored in a group of discontiguous ranges would be AVERAGE(A1:A3,B4:B6,Z100:Z102).

As we said a few sentences back, it is possible to put a function *inside* another function. Enter the formula

```
=SUM(SQRT(16),AVERAGE(100,200,500))
```

in a cell and out comes `270.6667`. No problemo.

Using range references (either absolute, relative, or named) as function arguments is the real meat-and-potatoes of the function smorgasbord. This way you can build formulas that look to locations outside themselves for argument values, and thereby change whenever the underlying data changes. Remember the MENSA average IQ formula that Spreadsheet Sam built? It was `=AVERAGE(B2:B6)`. By storing the IQ data in cells B2 through B6, Sam didn't have to edit the formula to change any IQ data that was wrong because he needed to update some faulty scores or he had made a typo when entering the data into the worksheet.

Propagating Formulas with Ctrl + Enter

If you need to build and copy a formula to a range in one fell swoop, here's how (see Figure 4.17). Highlight the range that will house the cloned formulas. Then enter the formula as usual, but instead of pressing ENTER to complete the formula, press CTRL + ENTER. This works when you enter the formula manually or via Function Wizard.

	A	B	C	D	E	F	G
1		Sam	Mary	Fred	Earl	Shirley	
2	Year 1989	200	225	205	195	195	
3	Year 1990	165	225	210	165	205	
4	Year 1991	160	220	210	160	195	
5	Year 1992	120	230	205	115	205	
6	Year 1993	105	225	205	105	200	
7	Average						
8							

Figure 4.17 Propagating Formulas with CTRL + ENTER

AutoSum: A Very Popular Function

> I do benefits for all religions—I'd hate to blow the hereafter on a technicality.
>
> Bob Hope

Light a stick of incense for the ExcelGods; all praise to the AutoSum feature! Legend has it that the Microsoft usability lab rats proved beyond a shadow of a doubt that Excelites, day in and day out, add numbers in rows and columns by the

AutoSum button

zillions. Wow! (Ever wonder how much dinero they spend to find this stuff out?) Anyway, from this research the AutoSum button was born.

All kidding aside (a pretty good trick for us), the Excel Development Team did a major good thing with the AutoSum button (or ALT + =, if you are button challenged). It's fast, flexible, and effective. You enter some numbers, place the active cell below (for columns) or to the right (for rows) of those numbers and click the AutoSum button. Bam! An =SUM formula is magically inserted into the cell, and Excel guesses what cells to add and enters the range in the formula. In case it guessed wrong, Excel highlights those cells with the marching ant marquee. Hit ENTER or click a second time on the AutoSum button and Excel enters the formula. See Figure 4.18.

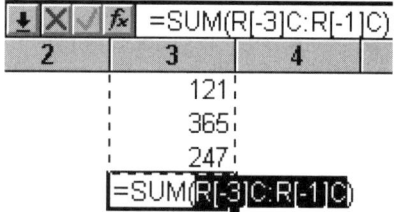

Figure 4.18 Automagic AutoSum!

You can change the active selection here in case you want a different range. Now, AutoSum sometimes guesses wrong. If you have an empty cell in the row or column to be added, AutoSum stops short of that cell. If a cell contains text, AutoSum stops short of that cell, unless you have a number formatted as text, in which case AutoSum includes it as though it were a value. (As we discussed earlier, the SUM function adds numbers that are formatted as text.)

The AutoSum function is quite flexible. Consider the table in Figure 4.19.

	7	8	9	10	11
10		Qtr 1	Qtr 2	Qtr 3	
11	Copra	90	37	155	
12	Gold bars	22	15	18	
13	Watches	375	299	100	
14					

Figure 4.19 AutoSum Down, Across, and Crossfoot

If you highlight the table of constants as shown in Figure 4.19, including the empty row (14) and the empty column (11), and click on AutoSum, you immediately get =SUM formulas that add each column down

```
=SUM(R[-3]C:R[-1]C)
```

and each row across

```
=SUM(RC[-3]:RC[-1])
```

including row 14, which totals all the column totals. No marquee, just instant formulas.

If you only select the constants (R11C8:R13C10) and click AutoSum, you only get formulas adding each column down. If you want to only sum the columns across, highlight R11C11:R13C11 and AutoSum produces formulas that add the rows across only. You can also make a noncontiguous selection of the appropriate cells to get formulas entered into only those cells. For example, highlight R11C11:R13C11 *and* the range R14C8:R14C10 to add the rows across and the columns down.

AutoSum in Excel 5 is one smart feature. In addition <*groan*> to sums, it can do grand totals by adding up the subtotals within a given range. Consider Figure 4.20.

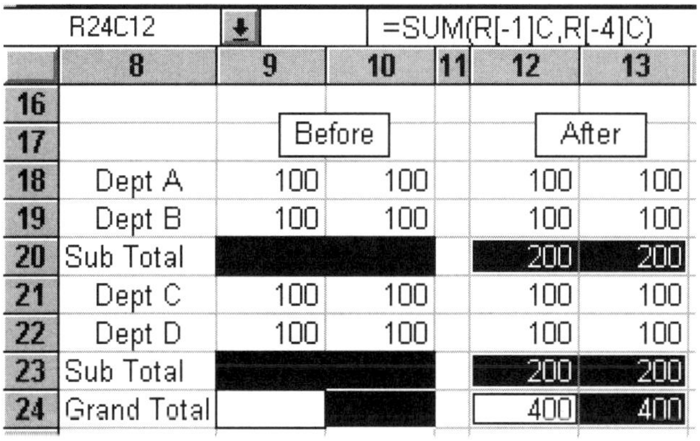

R24C12				=SUM(R[-1]C,R[-4]C)	
8	**9**	**10**	**11**	**12**	**13**
16					
17		Before		After	
18 Dept A	100	100		100	100
19 Dept B	100	100		100	100
20 Sub Total				200	200
21 Dept C	100	100		100	100
22 Dept D	100	100		100	100
23 Sub Total				200	200
24 Grand Total				400	400

Figure 4.20 AutoSum Does Subs and Grands, Grandly!

If you do a noncontiguous selection, highlighting the cells on rows 20 and 23 as well as the grand total on row 24 in columns 9 and 10, and then you click the AutoSum button, you get the results shown in columns 12 and 13. The subtotals and grand total formulas are automatically entered using the correct cell references.

Keen Formula and Function Stuff

> To have plenty is to be perplexed.
>
> Lao-tzu
> *The Way of Lao-tzu*

Now that we've covered function mechanics, let's delve into a potpourri of more advanced formula and function concepts.

A Whole Lotta Operators Goin' On

Arithmetic operators   Excel supports the standard arithmetic operators for addition, subtraction, negation, division, multiplication, percent, and exponentiation (see the *User's Guide*, page 127). Here they are in their symbolic form: + - / * % ^. The evaluation order of arithmetic operators in Excel is shown on page 128 of that guide. If you want to see the differences between evaluation order for Excel and Lotus, search for the help topic "operators, mathematical, Lotus 1-2-3." For whatever reason, this helpful information—at least to Lotus converts—is provided only in the help file, not in the *User's Guide*. Go figure.

Comparison operators   Excel supports standard comparison operators for comparing two values and producing TRUE or FALSE as a result (see the *User's Guide*, page 128). They are equal, greater than, less than, greater than or equal to, less than or equal to, and not equal to. Here they are in their symbolic form: =   > < >= <= <>.

Text operator   Excel uses an ampersand to represent the text operator (a.k.a. the concatenation—a \$64-word meaning "link some stuff together"—operator). The text operator joins two or more text strings together.

As we discussed earlier in this chapter, you can always use parentheses to override Excel's default operator evaluation rules.

Excel is, by design, very forgiving about mixed data types in formulas. You might think that a formula like

```
="MY SECRET PASSWORD IS "&9876
```

would give Excel fits. After all, the formula uses the text operator to join a text string and a number. For Excel, this is a mere walk in the park on a sunny day. It merrily allows the text operator to rule and converts the numeric value 9876 **to a text string. Free. Gratis. No charge. The formula results in the string** MY SECRET PASSWORD IS 9876**. There are limits, however. The formula**

```
="MY SECRET PASSWORD IS "/9876
```

yields #VALUE! **because this text string cannot be readily converted to a value.**

Excel supports reference operators for range (:), intersection ( ), and union (,). By now the range operator is part of your deep subconscious, like B2:B6 or R2C2:R6C2. The intersection reference operator is a space. We discuss range intersections in a later section in this chapter. An example of a union operation is a formula like

```
=SUM(B2:B6,D2:D6)
```

in which the SUM function operates on all cells in the union of the ranges B2:B6 and D2:D6. In other words, the values in all cells in those two ranges are added together.

Comparison Operators

Comparison operators deserve a touch of special attention, just so's the notion sinks in. Let's say Spreadsheet Sam wants to display whether or not his MENSA peers' IQs are higher than his. The easy way to do this is with a formula that compares his IQ with each peer's IQ and displays one of Excel's built-in logical values TRUE or FALSE, accordingly. He could enter the following formula below each average calculation cell:

```
=R[-1]C>R[-1]C2
```

This formula asks the question, "Is the value in the cell one row above me greater than the value in the cell one row above me way over in column 2 (my average IQ)?" See Figure 4.21.

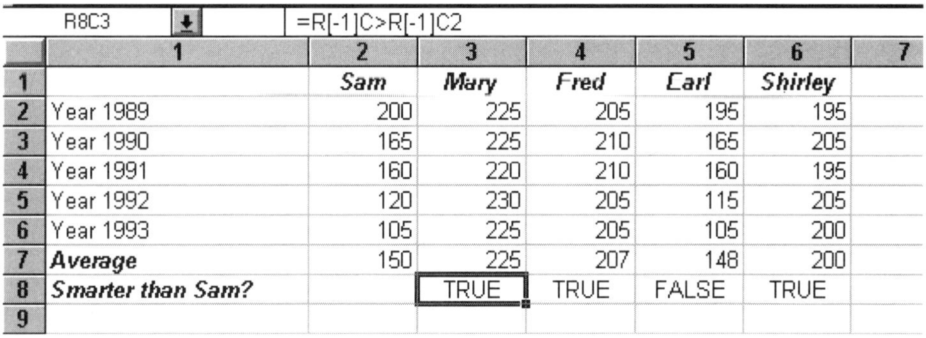

R8C3		=R[-1]C>R[-1]C2					
	1	2	3	4	5	6	7
1		Sam	Mary	Fred	Carl	Shirley	
2 Year 1989		200	225	205	195	195	
3 Year 1990		165	225	210	165	205	
4 Year 1991		160	220	210	160	195	
5 Year 1992		120	230	205	115	205	
6 Year 1993		105	225	205	105	200	
7 *Average*		150	225	207	148	200	
8 *Smarter than Sam?*			TRUE	TRUE	FALSE	TRUE	
9							

Figure 4.21 Truly Sam's a Genius (Not!)

Everybody Freeze: Converting Formulas to Values

If you want to *permanently* convert a cell's formula to the current value, take these steps:

1. Select the source cell or range. You don't have to explicitly recalculate with this method because, *unlike the Paste Special Values and* CTRL + *drag methods covered momentarily*, it forces a recalculation of the current range, even if you have Tools Options Calculation set to Manual.

2. Activate the formula bar (double-click the cell or click in the formula bar).

3. Press F9 to convert the formula to its resultant value. *This action doesn't quit Edit mode.*

4. Press ENTER to quit Edit mode and finalize the conversion or press ESC to abort the conversion.

The F9-to-recalc-and-paste-values technique does not prompt you before doing the replacement, it just does it. In Chapter 5, we explore this powerful F9 feature in greater detail. (Treat F9 as you would any power tool—always wear safety glasses, gloves, and other protective armor.) To undo the conversion after you press ENTER, assuming you've done nothing to clear or replace the undo buffer, select Edit Undo Entry (the keystroke equivalent is CTRL + Z).

There is another way to convert to values—Paste Special Values. It comes in two flavors depending on where the values are to be pasted.

To paste values to the current cell or range (in other words, if the source and destination ranges are the same), take these steps:

1. Recalculate the sheet, if appropriate.

2. Select the source range.

3. Copy the selection to the clipboard.

4. Select Edit Paste Special, select Values in the Paste frame, then click on OK. Now the Paste Special dialog box is gone. Values have been pasted into the destination range, but the source data is still on the clipboard.

5. Press ESC and you're done. Do not, we repeat, do not press ENTER. (Say what?) You heard us. Don't press ENTER, press ESC instead. The reason is fundamental to the way Excel pastes from the clipboard, as we'll explain shortly.

To paste values to another range (in other words, if the source and destination ranges are different), walk this way:

1. Recalculate the sheet, if appropriate.

2. Select the source range.

3. Copy the selection to the clipboard.

4. Select the destination range.

5. Select Edit Paste Special, select Values in the Paste frame, then click on OK. Now the Paste Special dialog box is gone. Values have been pasted into the destination range, but the source data is still on the clipboard.

6. If you want to continue pasting values elsewhere, repeat steps 4–5 until you get to the last destination range, in which case you'll press ESC instead of ENTER to complete the cycle.

Here's why you must press ESC and not ENTER. Excel is trying to be your **Press** ESC
friend. It really is. It leaves the copied range on the clipboard, including the formula, formatting, value, and so on for each cell in the range. Once the Paste Special dialog box is gone, if you press ENTER to terminate the Paste Special operation, *Excel assumes you want the entire source range to land in the destination range.* So it does exactly that. Plop. Formula and all. You sit stunned, slack-jawed, and completely disoriented that the cell (or cells) still contains the formula. Don't say we didn't warn ya! Seriously, there is an upside here. Remember, these are power tools. Once you know how they work, they're your best friend. But if you don't RTFM,* well, caveat emptor.

If you want to paste values to more than one location, then it's a real good thing that the entire range hangs out on the clipboard, allowing you to Paste Special Values, click on OK, select the next destination, Paste Special Values, click on OK, select the next destination, ad infinitum. (It's a good thing because you don't have to repeat the copy operation; the source data is already on the clipboard. Whenever you see the marquee surrounding a range after a copy operation, it means that the source data is still on the clipboard.)

A third option for converting to values is the CTRL + right-button drag technique. As dyed-in-the-wool mouse-o-philes, this method gets our vote. Here's the drill:

1. Recalculate the sheet, if appropriate.

2. Select the source range.

3. CTRL + right-button drag the range to its new destination (*which could even be back on top of itself*), choose Copy Values from the shortcut menu, and the clipboard is cleared, no fuss no muss. Try it, you'll like it!

Rated X: Explicit and Implicit Intersection

Returning to our exploration of the human condition, particularly as reflected by the MENSA members' meaningless IQ scores, let's say Spreadsheet Sam needs to

---

*RTFM—Read The <expletive deleted> Manual.

build a formula to show the amount and direction of any change in scores from the prior year. Basically, this would be 1992's score subtracted from 1993's score for each subject. See Figure 4.22. (We have named the relevent rows and columns using the row and column labels in this example.)

		1	2	3	4	5	6	7
R10C2			=Year_1993-Year_1992					
		1	**2**	**3**	**4**	**5**	**6**	**7**
1			*Sam*	*Mary*	*Fred*	*Earl*	*Shirley*	
2	Year 1989		200	225	205	195	195	
3	Year 1990		165	225	210	165	205	
4	Year 1991		160	220	210	160	195	
5	Year 1992		120	230	205	115	205	
6	Year 1993		105	225	205	105	200	
7	*Average*		150	225	207	148	200	
8	*Smarter than Sam?*			TRUE	TRUE	FALSE	TRUE	
9								
10	*Change from Prior Year*		-15	-5	0	-10	-5	
11								

Figure 4.22 Intersection, Implicitly Speaking

He might be tempted to put the formula

```
=(YEAR_1993 SAM) - (YEAR_1992 SAM)
```

into cell R10C2. Translated, that states "the intersection of the YEAR_1993 row and the SAM column, minus the intersection of the YEAR_1992 row and the SAM column." That's algebraically dandy for the SAM column (column 2).

Before we explore what happens if you copy the formula across in columns 3 through 6, let's drill a tad deeper into this formula. The (YEAR_1993 SAM) component is a classic example of explicit intersection referencing, where the intersecting row and column are explicitly named. We might have easily overlooked the lowly space—sittin' pretty between the two range names—which is really the super powerful *intersection operator*...give it a public phone booth and a red cape and it's able to intersect ranges with a single space.

Now let's see what happens if you copy the formula across in columns 3 through 6. At the outset of this chapter, we said Excel uses absolute references to define range names, and here's where that issue comes home to roost. The formula gets propagated into the neighboring cells as is and continues to refer to the absolute ranges referred to by the intersections YEAR_1993 SAM (cell R6C2) and YEAR_1992 SAM (cell R5C2). Implicit intersection to the rescue! (And you won't feel guilty after you've done it, either.)

The formula

```
=YEAR_1993-YEAR_1992
```

is the preferred formula and makes good use of implicit intersection. Excel tears into this formula and spits out the following calculation. Excel finds the cell in the current column (column 2) that intersects with the range YEAR_1993. The implied intersection is cell R6C2. Ditto for the subtrahend. Now you can copy the formula across and get the expected results.

Over in column 3 Excel plows through the same logic. In column 3 Excel's looking for the implied intersection between the current column and the range YEAR_1993. Ditto for the subtrahend. And so on. Excel knows the formula is referring to the current column by virtue of the absence of an explicit reference to the contrary; therefore, it's an *implied* reference, thus the term **implicit intersection**.

You should use explicit intersection when the formula containing the reference is outside the row and column housing the named ranges. For example, if you wander off into the Black Forest of Sheet1, say somewhere around R16360C250, and enter the formula

```
=YEAR_1993-YEAR_1992
```

Excel's gonna return zero. That's because Excel's still doing implied intersection, and the YEAR_1993 row intersecting with column 250 is an empty cell (returns the value zero), ditto for the YEAR_1992 row intersection column 250. Zero minus zero is, you guessed it, zero.

The correct approach here would be the longer, but very explicit <*groan*> formula

```
=(YEAR_1993 SAM) - (YEAR_1992 SAM)
```

which returns -15. In the discussion thus far, we assume YEAR_1993 refers to row 6 *in its entirety*. What if you limit YEAR_1993 to the current boundaries of the table, that is, YEAR_1993 is R6C2:R6C6?

In R16360C250, the formula

```
=YEAR_1993-YEAR_1992
```

returns the #VALUE! error instead of zero because the intersection of R6C2:R6C6 and column 250 (the current column) does not exist. Therefore the formula cannot return a meaningful value.

{Array Formulas}

Array formulas provide a way for you to perform arithmetic on arrays (ranges of data on a sheet) in Excel.

An array formula is easily identified by the curly braces { } that surround it. For example,

```
{=C2:C4/B2:B4}
```

is an array formula that puts the quotient of the two ranges into the array containing the array formula. But you don't enter the braces explicitly with the keyboard, instead you enter the formula as you ordinarily would, and then press CTRL + SHIFT + ENTER to finish it. Excel automatically detects that this is to be an array formula and inserts the braces for you.

You can edit an array formula as you would a nonarray formula, but watch out because, by design, *as soon as you initiate the edit, the curly braces go away.* Don't panic! When you finish the edit, to return the formula to an array formula, press CTRL + SHIFT + ENTER. (In ExcelSpeak, this is called **array-entering**.)

Our example of array formulas encompasses all of three data categories with three observations each, doing some straightforward division and summation. If you're interested in learning about more esoteric applications of arrays and array formulas, we refer you to the *Microsoft Excel 5 Worksheet Function Reference.* Check out its bibliography in the "For More Information" section, or research other standard reference texts on applied mathematics, business statistics, engineering statistics, and so on at your local library.

In our example, a hypothetical consulting company is interested in an executive summary, for each of its clients, that shows an effective hourly billing rate. The numerator is gross billings (including billable person-hours and any other out-of-pocket or miscellaneous line items in all invoices for a particular client). The denominator is the internal hours logged by all staff involved in all that client's projects. See Figure 4.23.

D2		{=C2:C4/B2:B4}		
	A	**B**	**C**	**D**	**E**
1	**Client**	**Internal Hours**	**Gross Billings**	**Effective $/Hour**	
2	3-squaredM	100	$15,000	$150.00	
3	Bank of Andromeda	200	$25,000	$125.00	
4	Specific Motors	50	$3,750	$75.00	
5					

Figure 4.23 Putting Array Formulas to Work

The steps to array-enter the formula are as follows.

1. Select the array D2:D4.
2. Activate the formula bar.
3. Press the = key.
4. Select the numerator range C2:C4 and enter a / (division operator).
5. Select the denominator range B2:B4.
6. Press CTRL + SHIFT + ENTER.

Excel displays the formula

{=C2:C4/B2:B4}

in all three cells in the array in the Effective $/Hour column. The formula moves through each row of the referenced ranges, divides the current row's Gross Billings value by its Internal Hours value, and places the quotient in current cell of the array. The primary benefit of using an array formula here is that you save memory. Even though the array formula appears in all three destination cells, *Excel stores it internally as a single formula.*

Now for the downside. You can't change an array in the way you've grown accustomed to working with regular cells and ranges. For example, if you select row 3 and attempt to insert a row, Excel produces the error shown in Figure 4.24.

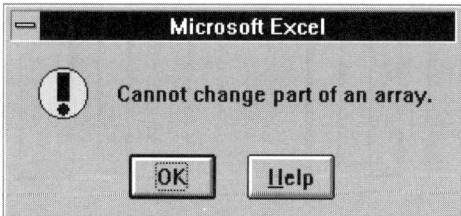

Figure 4.24 An Array is an Inviolable Unit

Inserting a row here would "break apart" the array. (To "see" the array on screen, select at least one cell in the array then press CTRL + / or Edit Go To Special Current Array.) Excel doesn't allow you to do anything that violates an array's integrity. So, to change array formulas, you have to select and modify the entire array. To reduce or enlarge the array's size, you have to eliminate the array (or temporarily convert it to values), insert/delete ranges on the sheet as needed, and array-enter the formula again.

One additional note on array formulas. Array formulas can also optimize your models by eliminating intermediate formulas. The *User's Guide* contains a good example of this in the "Working with Arrays" section.

How Calculation Works

> Rise like Lions after slumber
> In unvanquishable number—
> Shake your chains to earth like dew
> Which in sleep had fallen on you—
> Ye are many—they are few.
>
> Percy Bysshe Shelley
> *The Mask of Anarchy*, 1819

When Excel calculates a book, it works through a "calculation chain," examining each formula to determine if any of the formula's precedents (the values that feed into it) have changed. If at least one precedent of the current formula has changed, Excel recalculates the formula based on the new value; otherwise, Excel avoids the unnecessary calculation for this cell and moves on.

The pattern Excel uses to move through a book is this. Excel starts in the upper left corner of the top (uppermost) sheet and moves left to right and top to bottom until it reaches the lower right corner of the sheet. When it's done with the current sheet, it moves on to the next "lower" sheet in the sheet stack. Excel skips any empty, undefined cells. Figure 4.25 shows the Calculation filecard of the Tools Options dialog box.

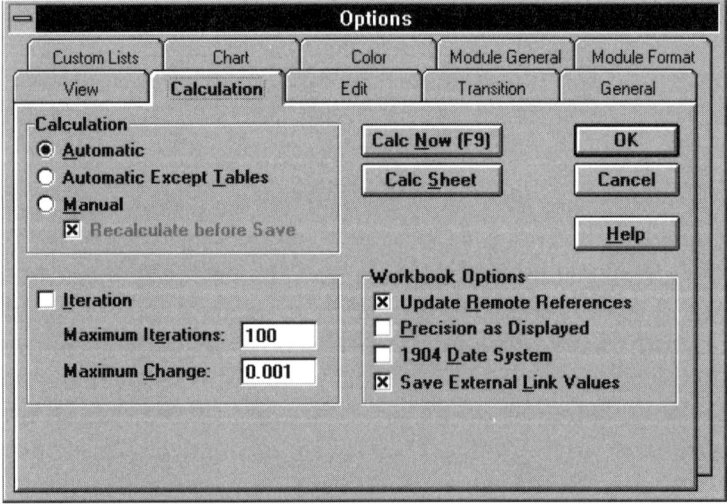

Figure 4.25 Calculation Options

If you have Tools Options Calculation set to Automatic (the default), Excel calculates all formulas in the current book whenever you edit an existing formula or enter a new one. This default setting is fine for many smaller models, but as your model grows in complexity, you may find it handy to set Calculation to Manual and get in the muscle-memory swing of pressing F9 whenever you want to explicitly recalculate the book, or SHIFT + F9 to explicitly recalculate only the current sheet.

Here's a list of the activities that trigger recalculation in Excel (deferred if Calculation is Manual; immediate if Calculation is Automatic).

- Press F9.
- Change (including deletion) any cell that is a precedent of any formula in the book.
- Change (including deletion) a range name that is explicitly used in any formula in the book.
- Insert, delete, copy, or move a cell, range, row, or column anywhere in the book.
- Select Tools Options Calculation Calc Now.
- Change Tools Options Calculation from Manual to either Automatic or Automatic Except Tables.
- Select Tools Options Calculation Calc Sheet.

Excel contains a special class of functions called volatile functions. They are AREAS(), CELL(), COLUMNS(), INDEX(), INDIRECT(), NOW(), OFFSET(), ROWS(), RAND(), and TODAY(). When you first open an Automatic calculation mode book containing one or more volatile functions, Excel automatically does a recalculation. Using NOW() as an example, the function itself acts as a data entry automaton. It is as though, upon opening the book, you were to run frantically around inside the book entering the current date/time serial number in every location containing the NOW() function. This volatility—an immediate change in value—triggers recalculation. The side effect is that any book containing a volatile function will, when you attempt to close it, think that it has been changed *even if you didn't manually make any changes*. Therefore, Excel will prompt you to save it.

If you're working with a very large model and want to save it without recalculating it, select Tools Options Calculation, clear the Recalculate before Save check box, and click on OK. This *deactivates* Excel's default safety net behavior of always recalculating before saving.

Calculation options are saved with each book, but this doesn't happen in a vacuum (unless you force it to be so, as we'll explain shortly). The calculation options of the first book opened in an Excel session *persist and overwhelm the calculation options of any other books you open throughout the current Excel session* (unless you manually override the session settings, at which point your new settings rule the roost). This means that if you open MANUCALC.XLS (a Manual mode book) first in a new Excel session, your session's calculation options are now set to Manual. So if you open AUTOCALC.XLS (originally an Automatic mode book) and then save and close AUTOCALC.XLS, the next time you open AUTOCALC.XLS in a vacuum (the only open book), you'll notice it's a Manual mode book.

To preserve a book's calculation options, make sure you open, manipulate, and save/close it in a vacuum, that is, with no other books open. Alternately, you could write a VBA auto macro for AUTOCALC.XLS to always force the desired settings, regardless of what settings the book "picked up" on its way out of a session.

For those of you in a hackin' kind of mood, here's the VBA code. You know the drill...open an existing (or insert a new) module, type in the following Auto_Open() procedure, close and save the book. When you next open the book, it'll be set to Automatic. QED.

```
Sub Auto_Open()
  If Application.Calculation <> xlAutomatic Then
    Application.Calculation = xlAutomatic
  End If
End Sub
```

It is possible (and sometimes useful) to have a formula refer back to itself. This is called a **circular reference**. A circular reference is usually constructed (as opposed to one that is the result of a mistake in a formula) to solve a simultaneous equation. Here's an old standard from Accounting 301. You decide to give a bonus of 5% to a manager based on the net income figure for that person's department, but the net income number has to reflect the bonus as a departmental expense. Algebraically that's stated as:

```
Net Income = Revenue - (Expenses + (Net Income * .05))
```

This is a simultaneous equation because the unknown, Net Income, is on both sides of the equal sign.

Under normal circumstances, Excel cannot resolve circular references. Consider the equation set up in a simple table in Figure 4.26.

Cell B23 is named "NetIncome" and the bonus calculation in B22, =NETINCOME*0.05, refers to this named cell. Net Income (B23) contains a formula

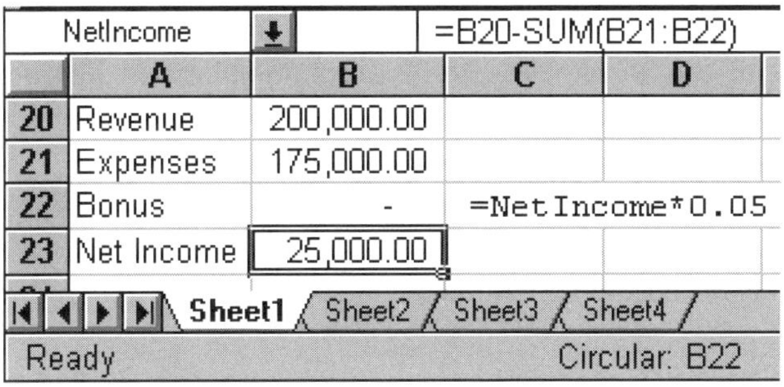

NetIncome	↓	=B20-SUM(B21:B22)		
	A	**B**	**C**	**D**
20	Revenue	200,000.00		
21	Expenses	175,000.00		
22	Bonus	-	=NetIncome*0.05	
23	Net Income	25,000.00		

Sheet1 / Sheet2 / Sheet3 / Sheet4 /

Ready Circular: B22

Figure 4.26 Circular Reference

that refers to B22 and hence a circular reference. When you enter the formula, Excel alerts you with a message box that it can't resolve the circular reference. Once you acknowledge the error message, the status bar reminds you of the circular reference condition and displays the exact cell reference, in this case B22.

It's interesting to note that the use of the range name causes the formula to display a single dash. The same formula constructed using cell references instead of range names returns zero.

Excel is, however, more than capable of dealing with this problem. All you have to do is turn on Iteration via Tools Options Calculation and check the appropriate check box. The defaults of 100 for Maximum Iterations and a Maximum Change of 0.001 are adequate. These settings tell Excel to stop after 100 iterations or when all values change by less than 0.001. You can adjust these settings, depending on the accuracy you need to resolve your calculation.

Once you turn on Iteration, Excel recalcs a number of times, each new calculation based on the results of the last, until the result no longer changes by the set threshold or the maximum number of iterations is reached. See Figure 4.27.

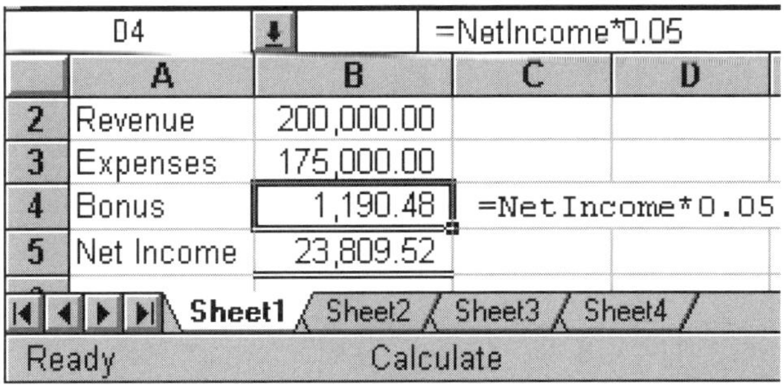

D4	↓	=NetIncome*0.05		
	A	**B**	**C**	**D**
2	Revenue	200,000.00		
3	Expenses	175,000.00		
4	Bonus	1,190.48	=NetIncome*0.05	
5	Net Income	23,809.52		

Sheet1 / Sheet2 / Sheet3 / Sheet4 /

Ready Calculate

Figure 4.27 Iteration Saves the Day!

You need to know what you are about when using Iteration to resolve formulas. You can wind up with faulty logic, divergent results (where each iteration resolves to a number *farther away* from the correct answer), and all sorts of issues. The order of calculation for Iteration is based on cell dependencies *not* on the usual row and column order, so you need to make sure that your formula does not depend on the order of calculation. Be careful with this puppy!

You can use VBA to define custom functions, also called user-defined functions. You can then use these custom functions as you would any of Excel's built-in functions. We cover custom functions in Chapter 10.

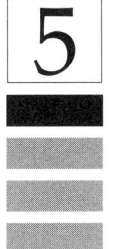 5 Auditing—It's a Good Thing

But I've bought a big bat. I'm all ready, you see.
Now my troubles are going to have troubles with me.

Dr. Seuss
I Had Trouble in Getting to Solla Sollew

We're talking bugs pilgrim. Not software bugs, not Microsoft's bugs. Your bugs. Little gremlins that creep into your model. The errant cell reference. The column of figures that doesn't foot. The formula that's one row short of a correct total. These little model anomalies will, well, *trouble* you. And that's what we're going to talk about now; how to ferret out these little troubles and squish them, but good.

One word of explanation about the examples in this section. Due to space limitations, we do not work with the more typical models that contain hundreds of rows and columns—the kind where little troubles creep in and are almost invisible. Our examples are brief, and often the errors may appear quite obvious. Just pretend you're working with huge models.

Chapter 4 stressed the many benefits of using range names instead of cell addresses for formula references. But to make it easier for you to track the conversation back to the figures *in this chapter only*, we use cell addresses where ordinarily range names would be more appropriate.

DEFCON1—THE BIG PICTURE

Oh, that's you all over.

Tin Man
The Wizard of Oz

You'd be surprised how a spreadsheet model takes on a life of its own. It's bad enough with models you build completely yourself, but on models you inherit it's unbelievable. Tables get added on over here; input areas wind up over there; stuff gets tacked on and strewn around all over the place.

After the model is built and all these pieces are sewn together, you had best check to see that the model is doing what it is designed to do. You had better *audit* it! And the first step is to make sure you understand what the model is supposed to do and how it's laid out.

A Trail of Bread Crumbs

Quod periit, periit.*

Plautus
Cistellaria, ca. 250 BC

When you first begin the construction of a model, you need to start laying the foundation for future maintenance. Since you're dealing with a programming environment (notice how we keep working this into the conversation?), you can use some of the conventions that programmers use when writing program code.

Document, Document, Document

Please document your models. If the model has already been written, you need to document it retroactively. But document it you must! Here is a list of the basic information you should track for every spreadsheet you build or inherit:

- *Author*—this is the original author of the model, the primary builder. If this person is building the model to meet someone else's needs, include a reference to the specification document that details the model's requirements.
- *Purpose*—twenty-five words or less on what the heck this spreadsheet is supposed to be used for and/or accomplish. We're talkin' big picture here.
- *Date of origin*—when construction began.
- *Date of last update*—the date of the last modification and the name of the person who modified it.
- *Description of last change*—what was changed last and why. If something starts causing trouble in a model that has been working fine, odds are that the last change is at fault.

How you track this information is, of course, up to you. We like to reserve the upper left corner of the primary worksheet for this kind of stuff. With the new multisheet capabilities of Excel 5, you could dedicate a sheet just for this type of information. Type it into cells or put it in text boxes. Or you can put this information in a cell note.

*What is lost is lost.

However you do it, *please* start documenting your spreadsheets. When you change something, note it. When you experience odd behavior in your model, note that, too. They have a saying in the astronomy field that is mentioned in the book *The Cuckoo's Egg*: "If you didn't write it down, it didn't happen." Write it down.

Jot Down a Quick Note

Next you can start using Excel's Note feature. This is not a new feature, rather it's another one of the little gems hidden away in Excel that doesn't get used nearly as much as it deserves.

All kinds of things lend themselves to "noting." If you write a complex formula, you should document the logic of the formula as a note attached to the cell that contains the formula (or the first cell containing a formula if that formula is used across a row or column). If you use a constant in a cell (or formula) and the source of the constant is, er, ambiguous, shall we say, you might want to note the name of the person who gave you the key figure, the date, the time, their Social Security number, home phone,…you get the idea?

Nota bene

How do you add a note? Easy. Select the cell to which you want to attach the note and hit `SHIFT + F2`. You could also click on Edit Note or use the note button on the Auditing toolbar. Any of these methods gets you to the Cell Note dialog box. See Figure 5.1.

Attach Note button

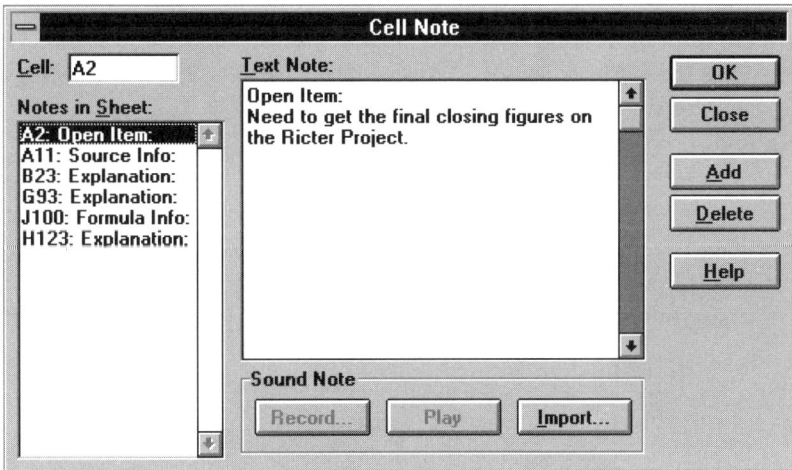

Figure 5.1 Cell Note Dialog Box

You don't have to first select the cell to which you want to attach the note, because you can pop up the Cell Note dialog box and enter the cell reference in the Cell edit box. But *we* always select the target cell first. This way you are less likely to attach a note to the wrong cell, and if you're detailing a formula's logic, it's helpful to have the formula visible in the formula bar.

Now, your first inclination is to start typing the note text over in the Text Note edit box. Resist this urge. The Notes in Sheet list box contains a list of every cell in the worksheet with a note attached to it. Each item consists of the cell reference *and all of the first line of the note that fits in the list box.* As the first line of any note you enter, type a description of the *type* of note you are entering.

Huh, what? That's right, it's a good idea to start each note with a short 12- to 15-character designation. If you start typing your note, you wind up with entries in the Notes in Sheet list that are truncated like this when displayed:

```
A2: Need to get the
A11: This was a re
B23: This should d
G93: The final clos
```

Not too clear, is it? With a mess like this, you have to read each note in the sheet in order to find, for example, all notes relating to open items.

Consistency is *not* the hobgoblin of little minds. If you want to stay sane, get in the habit of putting a short description on the first line of each note. You should also pick a few general classification names like the ones that were shown in Figure 5.1 and stick to them (no more than a dozen or so). If every time you want to describe information about a formula's construction you use a different description, you'll be right back where you started.

If you are part of a workgroup, buy a pizza and have a meeting. Get everyone to agree to use the same dozen or so descriptions for cell notes. You *will* thank us later. Hey, you're welcome, in advance.

And, *speaking* of notes... As a final note on notes, we should mention that, yes, you can now attach sound bites to cells. Oh, it's all very hip, fur sure. And *if* you have the necessary sound hardware, and *if* you have almost unlimited disk space (sound eats up disk space like Fido eats Gravy Train), and *if* you can think of something useful to say without 10 or 12 takes to get it right, go right ahead and indulge. Assuming, of course, that anyone you share this spreadsheet with (you aren't really going to record voice notes to yourself, are you?) has the necessary hardware to hear the notes, and *if* you don't think the note will be jotted down on paper anyway, and *if* you don't want a hard copy of the notes printed...you get the idea?

Three Miles High

> For I dipp'd into the future, far as human eye could see,
> Saw the Vision of the world, and all the wonder that would be...
>
> Alfred, Lord Tennyson
> "Locksley Hall," 1842

Back in Chapter 1 we discussed the mechanics of zooming the view of a spreadsheet. The ability to zoom out and get a general "lay of the land" is really handy. You can save a lot of time by zooming as opposed to scrolling around one screen at a time trying to figure out what is where.

To jump back and "see" the whole enchilada when you are documenting or auditing a worksheet, do this:

1. Click on the Full Screen button.

2. Do a CTRL + END to move the active cell to the last row and column of the worksheet containing data.

3. SHIFT + CTRL + HOME, which selects the sheet from the active cell back up to cell A1.

4. Pull down the View menu and click on Zoom.

5. In the Zoom dialog box, click on Fit Selection and hit OK.

Full Screen button

Excel sets the zoom percentage to display only the selected area on your screen, with the caveat that Zoom percentages are limited to between 10% and 400%. Consider Figure 5.2.

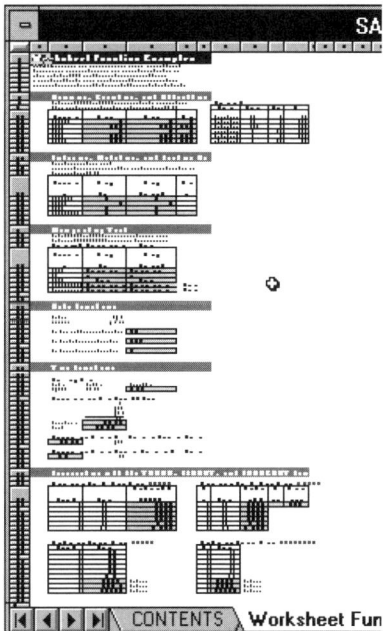

Figure 5.2 Zoom Out!

Okay, you can't actually read anything, but you can get a good idea of the sheet's layout. You can click on a cell and see the exact coordinate in the Name Box, so you can start mapping the sheet, noting the range coordinates of the different areas. Armed with this information, you can zoom in to review the details.

Trappin' Errors with Formulas and Formats

> We need education in the obvious more than investigation of the obscure.
>
> Oliver Wendell Holmes, Jr.
> New York City, February 15, 1913

Seldom is thought given to that which we feel is obvious—and that is one of the big problems with computer-generated spreadsheets. The output *looks* great. The rows of numbers all look so, well, official. And if it came off a computer, it can't be wrong. *Don't you believe it!*

Dahling, you *look* maaahvelous

If you are ever presented with some snazzy lookin' spreadsheet printouts that someone is using as Exhibit A to convince you to make some kind of financial decision, break out your old 10-key calculator and, as we say in the CPA trade, "run those numbers." You'll be amazed at how often they just don't add up. And we don't mean any fuzzy assumptions either. We're talking about 2 + 2 = 3 and other even more pedestrian errors.

We'll talk about finding errors in spreadsheets shortly, but for now let's concentrate on nipping in the bud those little troubles that creep in when you least expect it.

Trap Settin'

> Contrariwise, if it was so, it might be; and if it were so, it would be; but as it isn't, it ain't. That's logic.
>
> Tweedledee
> *Through the Looking Glass*

First, get in the habit of always testing for what may seem obvious. Take a simple example of a table of values that you've added down and across. See Figure 5.3.

This is pretty typical. You add the rows across and the columns down. Are your totals right? No errors in formula ranges? Is there any chance someone (even you) might have overwritten a formula with a constant? Let's check.

To test if the totals across equal the totals down, you can enter a crossfoot formula in cell G7, like this:

```
=IF(SUM(C7:F7)<>SUM(G4:G6),"Red Light","Green Light")
```

G6	↓		=SUM(C6:F6)			
A	**B**	**C**	**D**	**E**	**F**	**G**

		1st Qtr	2nd Qtr	3rd Qtr	4th Qtr	Totals
2	Northwest Divison					
4	Widgets	98	101	112	75	386
5	Doohickeys	110	92	98	75	375
6	Thingys	109	86	104	79	378
7	Total	335	279	314	229	

Figure 5.3 Foot and Crossfoot

Okay, so we're being a little facetious with the returned strings, but we want the formula to print all on one line. You should really use more descriptive strings. You can replace "Green Light" with "OK", and "Red Light" with "Error Northwest Division table. See cell G7".

This example makes good use of the conditional IF function and some of the logical operators, namely, "not equal to" <>. The IF function is a real workhorse of a function. If follows the basic "If...Then...Else" programming construct as in:

```
=IF(condition to be tested, do this if condition is true,
do this if condition is false)
```

IF statements can be nested up to seven levels deep to create small decision trees.

Error Tables

Now why would you want to put something like "See cell G7" in your error trap when the trap formula is in cell G7. Goooood question. Maybe you don't put the error-trapping formula in G7. After all, who knows where throughout a model you may need error-trapping formulas. What will you do to check them? Scroll the entire model looking for errors? We think not.

Consider a section of your worksheet, or a dedicated worksheet within a book, with all of your error-trapping formulas contained in a single table. Something like Figure 5.4.

You can use a simple conditional statement to trap simple errors. If a key figure should always fall within a given range, test for it. If, within a range of values, no figure should ever exceed some other value, test for it. If a value should never go below 0, or 3251, or whatever, *test for it!*

By the way, in this example (see Figure 5.3), the table does not crossfoot. The formula in cell C7 got overwritten with a constant and so does not add down correctly. But you probably noticed that, right? *Heh, heh, heh.*

	A	B	C	D	E	F
1	MULTIEXP.XLS Divisional Worksheets Error Traps					
2						
3	OK	OK	Error Northwest Division table. See cell G7			
4	OK	OK	Error Southeast Division table. See cell G7			
5	OK	OK	OK			
6	OK	OK	OK			
7	OK	OK	OK			
8	OK	OK	OK			
9	OK	OK	OK			
10						
11	Formula in C3:					
12	=IF(SUM(NWDivision!C7:F7)<>SUM(NWDivision!G4:G6),					
13	"Error Northwest Division table. See cell G7","OK")					

Figure 5.4 Error Trap Table

Custom Formats

Your custom formats can also do some limited error or logic testing. The *User's Guide* has this example of a custom format:

```
[Blue][>1000]#,##0;[Red][<-1000]#,##0;[Green]#,##0
```

This format displays values according to the definitions in Table 5.1.

Table 5.1 Conditional Custom Formats

Values In This Range	Display In
Greater than 1000	Blue
Less that −1000	Red
1000 to −1000	Green

The conditional is enclosed in square brackets like the color settings. You can also create a custom format like this:

```
#,##0;[Red]"Error"
```

which displays the text string "Error" in red if the cell returns a negative value.

Format conditionals have their place, but they are not as versatile as the IF function because you must look at the cell to discern an error. As you saw in the previous example, the IF function can be placed anywhere and be made to test conditions far removed from the location of the testing function.

DEFCON2—THE AUDITING TOOLBAR

> The nation which forgets its defenders will itself be forgotten.
>
> Calvin Coolidge
> July 27, 1920

It's time to take that big stick and go looking for troubles in your spreadsheet. Excel 5 has some really crackerjack tools built in to help you do just that. These tools can be readily accessed from the Auditing toolbar. See Figure 5.5. With these tools you can trace precedents, dependents, and errors; pop up the Cell Note dialog box; and access the info window for the active cell.

Figure 5.5 Auditing Toolbar—First Line of Defense

Engage Toolbar, Commander Riker

First, display the Auditing toolbar. You can manually display this toolbar by using either View Toolbars, check the Auditing check box, and hit OK, or Tools Auditing and click Show Auditing Toolbar on the flyout menu.

We think that the Auditing toolbar is such a massively useful thing that we strongly suggest you force this toolbar to display every time you fire up Excel. That way, if you turn the Auditing toolbar off during the course of an Excel session and forget to turn it on, it shows up the next time you start Excel.

For this you need a short VBA program, so unhide your PERSONAL.XLS book (Window Unhide). Activate Module1. Go to the end of the module (CTRL + END), and press ENTER to start a new line. Type in the following VBA code:

```
'
' Auto_Open Macro to display Auditing Toolbar
' Written xx/xx/xx by YourNameHere
'
'
Sub Auto_Open()
  If Not Toolbars("Auditing").Visible Then
    Toolbars("Auditing").Visible = True
```

```
    End If
End Sub
```

You'll notice that we started to document this little VBA program. From now on, pilgrim, you'll document *everything!* The apostrophes in the program indicate *remarks*, and any lines beginning with one are not executed. This gives you a way to comment your code. We also suggest you start indenting your code to make it more readable. The Tab key indents a line four spaces.

To Excel 5 the Auditing toolbar is toolbar number 10 (each toolbar is numbered according to its position in the Toolbars dialog box list) and can be referred to by number, as in "Toolbars(10)," or by name as shown in the example code. Setting the "Visible" *property* for the Auditing toolbar *object* to "True" causes it to be displayed.

Don't sweat the vocabulary right now. We'll talk more about all this in Chapter 10. Oh, don't forget to hide the PERSONAL.XLS book.

Mr. Custer, What Do All Them Arrows Mean?

The Auditing toolbar has buttons that allow you to trace cells flowing into and out of a given formula's result. Sounds confusing, but it is really simple in action. First, we need a spreadsheet to audit. How about the one in Figure 5.6?

	A	B	C	D	E	F	G
1							
2		Southeast Divison					
3			1st Qtr	2nd Qtr	3rd Qtr	4th Qtr	Totals
4		Widgets	99	121	112	116	448
5		Doohickeys	105	94	98	90	387
6		Thingys	109	80	109	100	398
7		Total	313	305	319	306	1233
8							
9		Quarterly Goals	300	300	300	300	
10		Variance to Goal	13	5	19	6	

Figure 5.6 Ready to Audit!

What Has Gone Before

Trace Precedents button

Now let's talk about precedents. **Precedents** are cells that affect the current cell. A constant does not have any precedent cells. Ah, but a formula typically does. Let's start with cell C10, which contains the formula =C7-C9. Select this cell and click on the Trace Precedents button (the first button) on the Auditing toolbar.

Some cool blue lines appear on your worksheet, *tracing* the cells whose contents affect the current cell. The first level displayed is called **direct precedents**. These lines are objects on the graphic layer of the worksheet and, as such, print with your sheet unless you remove them. Click the Trace Precedents button again and you get the next *level* of precedence cells, called **indirect precedents**. See Figure 5.7.

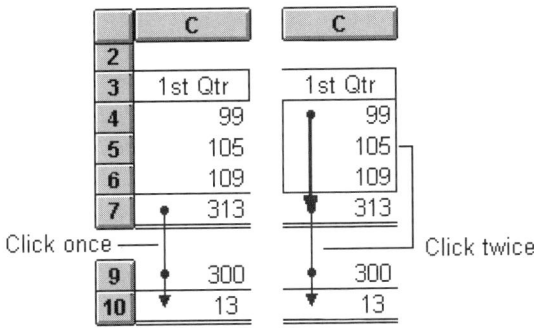

Figure 5.7 Multilevel (Indirect) Precedents

On the first click, you see that cells C7 (=SUM(C4:C6)) and C9 (constant 300) are both direct precedent cells to C10. The second click reveals that the range C4:C6 is indirectly precedent to C10 as that range affects the total in C7, which in turn affects C10. Once you have traced all the precedent levels, subsequent clicks on the button produce a beep. The lighter weight arrows show single-cell precedents, and the heavier weight arrow shows that the precedent is a range of cells.

Double-clicking on an arrow segment moves the active cell up and down the arrow's path from precedent cell to precedent cell and back.

You can remove the arrows by making the active cell a cell that contains an arrow head and clicking on the Remove Precedent Arrows button. (This button looks like the Trace Precedents button except for the little minus sign.) If the active cell is at the end of a multilevel set of precedent arrows, each click on the Remove Precedent Arrows button removes one level of precedent arrows.

Remove Precedent Arrows button

What Comes After

> There was only one catch and that was Catch-22, which specified that a
> concern for one's own safety in the face of dangers that were real and
> immediate was the process of a rational mind. Orr was crazy and could
> be grounded. All he had to do was ask; and as soon as he did, he would
> no longer be crazy and would have to fly more missions.
>
> Joseph Heller
> *Catch-22*, 1961

Trace dependent cells; remove dependent arrows The next two buttons on the Auditing toolbar trace dependent cells. The first button (with the plus sign) traces dependent cells, and the button to the right (with the minus sign) removes dependent arrows. See Figure 5.8.

Figure 5.8 Trace Dependents
and Remove Dependent Arrows

This is useful if you want to determine every cell that a given cell's result impacts. Say you want to trace all cells that are affected by a change in cell F5 (constant `90`). Select F5 and click the Trace Dependents button until it beeps to show all levels of dependent cells. See Figure 5.9.

	D	E	F	G
3	2nd Qtr	3rd Q	4th Qtr	Totals
4	121	112	116	448
5		98	90	387
6	80	109	100	398
7	305	319	306	1233
8				
9	300	300	300	
10	5	19	6	

Figure 5.9 Trace Dependents

Cell F5 flows into G5 (direct), which flows into G7 (indirect). F5 also flows into F7 (direct), which flows into F10 (indirect), and the shin bone's connected to the ankle bone,…you get the idea. A change in F5 impacts four cells on this worksheet (two directly and two indirectly). Since the arrows are of the lighter weight, you know that they indicate a single cell as the dependent (you saw the heavy arrow used to indicate a range of cells in the precedent example). Ah, but what's the story with the dashed black lines that point to the little sheet icons?

These arrows are indicating that a cell in another worksheet is dependent on this value. It may be a worksheet in the same book or another book entirely. (Off-sheet references are shown with the dashed line and the worksheet icon for both precedents as well as dependents.) Double-clicking on the dashed arrow pops up the Go To dialog box with only the off-sheet dependent-cell locations listed. The Go To dialog box, when called up this way, does not list range names but only the cells involved in the current trace. See Figure 5.10.

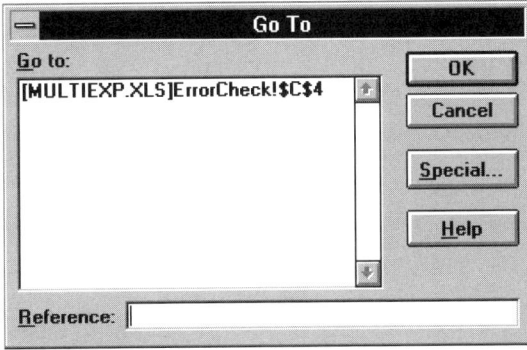

Figure 5.10 Special Trace Listing

You can remove the dependent arrows using the Remove Dependent Arrows button in the same manner described for the Remove Precedent Arrows button. If you want to immediately remove all arrows, both precedent and dependent, click on the Remove All Arrows button. Instantly, all the arrows are bye-bye.

Remove All Arrows button

Tracing Errors

Use the Trace Errors button when you have a formula that is returning an error, like #DIV/0, #VALUE, or #N/A, the source of which is caused by some other cell referred to in the formula. It doesn't work if the error is caused by that formula itself, like =100/0. Often an error in one cell may make the whole worksheet break out in error conditions as if it has chicken-pox. The Trace Errors button displays the entire upstream chain of precedents, following the errors and giving you a way to find the offending cell. Error precedents are shown using *red* arrows.

Trace Errors button

Now, if you select a cell that is displaying an error and hit the regular Trace Precedents button, it too uses red arrows. And you can keep clicking on the button to move back through indirect precedents, but it does not zero in on specific cells with the vengeance that the Trace Errors button does. Using Trace Precedents, you get entire ranges as precedents if the range is used in a formula along the chain.

With Trace Errors, only the cells with error values are traced, and the trace immediately goes back upstream as far as it can until it hits the source error cell, the precedent path branches to two or more errors, or a circular error is encountered. If you encounter a jump to another worksheet, go to that sheet via the special trace listing Go To dialog box discussed earlier (double-click on the dashed arrow) and immediately hit the Trace Errors button again when in the upstream worksheet.

Trace Errors also halts if it encounters existing trace arrows, so you might want to hit the Remove All Arrows button before you try to trace an error.

Notes and Info

The last two buttons on the Auditing toolbar are the Attach Note button (with the little thumbtack on it—get it...note, thumbtack...no? well, it'll grow on you) and the Show Info Window button. See Figure 5.11.

Figure 5.11 Attach Note and
Show Info Window Buttons

The note button is cool—it lets you do the cell notes we explained in an earlier section. Since you're going to leave the Auditing toolbar displayed at all times (you are, aren't you?), you can use this button to pop up the Cell Note dialog box instead of using the SHIFT + F2 method shown earlier. Far out.

The Show Info Window button pops up the good old Info window (figures, huh?). This is not new, it has been around forever. If you have never heard of it, don't feel bad. It's not considered a hot feature, and a lot of Excel users have never heard of it. You used to pop up the Info Window from the Window menu, but now you have to go to Tools Options View and check the Info Window check box in the Show group or use this button on the Auditing toolbar.

Before the Trace buttons became available in Excel 5, the Info window was the only way to get a list of precedent and dependent cells. You can display the information shown in Table 5.2 about the current cell in the Info Window.

Table 5.2 Info Window Settings

Default Items	Additional Items
Cell:	Value:
Formula:	Protect:
Note:	Names:
	Precedents:
	Dependents:

The cell, formula, and note contents are displayed in the Info window by default, and if you want to see any of the other items, you have to pull down the Info menu and turn each one on individually. They should all be on by default, but alas, the ExcelGods didn't ask us.

If you decide you want to see this type of information displayed as you move around a worksheet (*we* prefer the Trace buttons, but it's a free world), the best method is to resize the current book and the Info window so that they are both visible on screen.

DEFCON3—THE MANY FACES OF EXCEL

> Mother—what's the phrase?—isn't quite herself today.
>
> Norman Bates
> *Psycho*

Excel has many faces or layers. One face is reflected in a cell's content (constant, formula, text, and so on) as you see it in the formula bar. Another face is reflected in a cell's result, which can be formatted to appear much differently from its content, for example, a constant like 34547 formatted as Aug-94.

You can exploit these different layers to find all sorts of troubles that wind up wreaking havoc in a model.

Da Flipper—X-ray Vision

> They call him Flipper, Flipper, faster than lightning.
>
> *Flipper*
> 1960s TV Sitcom

You've seen this next trick in both Chapters 1 and 2 where you "flipped" the worksheet and made it display the formulas instead of their calculated result in the cells.

You can flip a sheet between formulas and results using the CTRL + ` (back apostrophe) key combination as you saw previously. But since we think it is such a useful tool, let's add it to the Auditing toolbar as a custom button.

Formula Flipper Button

You know the routine by now. Unhide the PERSONAL.XLS, go to Module1, CTRL + END to go to the end of the module, and hit ENTER to start a new line. Here's code that toggles between displaying formulas and their results:

```
'
' Formula_Flipper Macro to flip worksheet display
'    between formula and results
```

```
' Written xx/xx/xx by YourNameHere
'

'

Sub Formula_Flipper()
On Error GoTo EndMacro
  ActiveWindow.DisplayFormulas = Not ActiveWindow.DisplayFormulas
EndMacro:
End Sub
```

Now let's hook this code up to a custom button on the Auditing toolbar.

1. Pull down the View menu and choose Toolbars.

2. In the Toolbars dialog box, click on the Customize button.

3. Scroll down the Categories list and choose Custom.

4. Here you have a choice:

   a. If you like one of the custom buttons displayed here, by all means choose one.

   b. If you don't find any of the available buttons suitable, choose the blank button face (third row, second on the right).

5. Drag the button of your choice to the Auditing toolbar and drop it to the right of the Show Info Window button, leaving a skosh of space between the Show Info Window button and the new button you're adding.

6. Choose the Formula_Flipper macro in the Assign Macro dialog box when it pops up and click on OK.

7. Here's another choice:

   a. If you chose some button other than the blank one you're done and can click on OK. You could go back to Chapter 1 and review how to snatch a button from WinWord back when we customized the Standard toolbar if you think Word has a button face that you want.

   b. If you went with the blank button face and want to customize it yourself, right-click on the blank button you just dropped on the Auditing toolbar and choose the Edit Button Image option. While editing the image, you are on your own. Here's how we customized our Formula Flipper button. Take it or leave it, beauty is in the eye of the beholder, and all that stuff.

8. When you're done, OK out of the Customize dialog box and you're all set.

Our Formula Flipper button design

While you're at it, you had better deal with two rough corners that could stand some sanding.

First is the status bar text to be displayed when you click on the Formula Flipper button. Pull down the Tools menu and choose Macro. Select Formula_Flipper and click Options. Click on the Status Bar Text text box (third from the bottom) and type the text you want displayed, like `Toggle display between formulas and results`. Click on OK, then Close.

Next, pop over to Module2 where you left the macro you created to change the toolbar tip for the FileClose button back in Chapter 1. Make sure you count the correct button number for the Formula Flipper button. If you added it to the default Auditing toolbar and dropped it to the right of the Show Info Window button, it's number is 13. If you left a space between the Show Info button and the Formula Flipper, it's 14. Remember to *count spaces*!

Change this line of the NameSetter() macro from this:

```
Toolbars ("Standard"), ToolbarButtons(4).Name = "Close"
```

to this:

```
Toolbars ("Auditing"), ToolbarButtons(14).Name = "Formula
Flipper"
```

Remember to count buttons and spaces and make sure that you use the correct number. Run the NameSetter() macro and then place the mouse pointer on the new flipper button on the Auditing toolbar. You should see "Formula Flipper" as the ToolTip and "Toggle display between formulas and results" should appear in the status bar. Be sure to hide the `PERSONAL.XLS` book via Window Hide.

Flippin' da Worksheet

Now you have a flipper button. What's the big deal about flipping the sheet as regards auditing? It's a lifesaver. Remember the worksheet you started with? Let's look at that table of information after flipping the sheet. See Figure 5.12.

	B	C	D	E	F	G
1						
2	Southeast Divison					
3		1st Qtr	2nd Qtr	3rd Qtr	4th Qtr	Totals
4	Widgets	99	121	112	116	=SUM(C4:F4)
5	Doohickeys	105	94	98	90	=SUM(C5:F5)
6	Thingys	109	80	109	100	=SUM(C6:F6)
7	Total	=SUM(C4:C6)	305	=SUM(E4:E6)	=SUM(F4:F6)	=SUM(G4:G6)
8						
9	Quarterly Goals	300	300	300	300	
10	Variance to Goal	=C7-C9	=D7-D9	=E7-E9	=F7-F9	

Figure 5.12 Flipped to Reveal Formulas

When the sheet is flipped, the constants and formulas are clearly differentiated. You can scan a sheet and, uh oh, what's that there in D7? Hmmm, it should be a formula, but it appears that it has been overwritten with a constant. That could throw off the total for the second quarter and the variance for that quarter as well.

But the amount must be correct or else the error-checking crossfoot formula in G7 would have...Whoa! There is no error-checking crossfoot formula in G7, just a regular old =SUM function. That formula should be an =IF construct to check that the sum of G4:G6 is the same as the sum of C7:F7. Good thing you *audited* this, no?

Pretty clever them ExcelGods. On to the next section and we'll try to fix the errors you just uncovered.

Shields Up—R1C1

Cassis Tutissima Virtus*

d'Ablaing Family Motto, reg. 1814

Earlier we showed you how Excel deals with relative and absolute cell references, and how the A1 notation style differs from R1C1.

Well, good ol' R1C1 notation is a great tool in the spreadsheet auditor's kit. In fact, it is so useful that—you guessed it!—we're going to add another button to the Auditing toolbar to toggle worksheets between A1 and R1C1.

The R1C1 Button

Same drill. Unhide the PERSONAL.XLS, go to Module1, CTRL + END to go to the end of the module, and hit ENTER to start a new line. Here's the code you need to toggle the display between A1 and R1C1:

```
'
' Style_Flipper Macro
' Written xx/xx/xx by YourNameHere
'
'
Sub Style_Flipper()
  If Application.ReferenceStyle = xlA1 Then
    Application.ReferenceStyle = xlR1C1
  Else
    Application.ReferenceStyle = xlA1
  End If
End Sub
```

*A helmet is the best defense.

It's déjà vu all over again as you hook this code up to a custom button on the Auditing toolbar. If it seems as though you already did this, it's because you did. The steps to add this button are the same as those for adding the Formula Flipper button you added in the last section.

1. View Toolbars Customize.

2. Scroll down the Categories list and choose Custom.

3. Choose one of the custom buttons or choose the blank button face. Drag it to the Auditing toolbar and drop it to the right of the Formula Flipper button, leaving a skosh of space between the Formula Flipper button and the new button you're adding.

4. Choose the Style_Flipper macro in the Assign Macro dialog box when it pops up and click on OK.

5. If you want to customize the blank button face, right-click on it and choose the Edit Button Image option. Now you are on your own (again).

Here's how we customized our Style Flipper button. And save those cards and letters because we *already know* that we have no artistic ability.

Assign some appropriate text for the status bar; Tools Macro, select Style_Flipper and click Options. Click on the Status Bar Text text box (third from the bottom) and type the text you want displayed, like `Toggle display between A1 and R1C1`. Click on OK, then Close.

Our Style Flipper Button Design

If you want to add some ToolTip text, modify the NameSetter() macro in Module2. Be sure to count the buttons and spaces on the Auditing toolbar carefully or you'll wind up changing the wrong button. Don't forget to hide the `PERSONAL.XLS` book.

Using R1C1 to Audit

Let's see how R1C1 can help you when auditing a worksheet. In the last section, you saw how flipping the sheet to reveal formulas helped you spot two errors in the table of formulas and constants, one where a formula was overwritten by a constant and the other where a formula was constructed improperly. So far, so good.

Having the formulas in the right cells, or even having the right functions in the formulas, does not ensure that the formulas are correct. So, after you flip the sheet, you need to audit the formula contents to see if the formulas in the worksheet are correct. Consider the simple group of formulas in Figure 5.13.

Based on your review of this worksheet's layout, you know that row 77 is supposed to sum from rows 28 through 76 for each column in this table of data.

	B	C	D	E
76	2745	3796	2593	2991
77	=SUM(B28:B76)	=SUM(C28:C76)	=SUM(D28:D76)	=SUM(E28:E76)

Figure 5.13 Auditing Formulas—The Hard Way

To check that each formula is adding the correct range, you might zoom out and trace precedents to make sure that the arrows run through the proper cells. At some point, however, you're going to have to study the formulas themselves.

Using R1C1 can save you a lot of time staring at formulas and muttering things like, "Hmmm, column C, check, rows 28 to 76 check, ah, column D, check, rows 28 to 76...." You get the idea. Sure this is way oversimplified, but the basic technique applies to much more complex models. Honest.

Since you know that each of the =SUM formulas deals with the same range of rows and that the references in the formulas are relative, each formula is really the same identical formula. Eureka! Let's look at the same example only, in addition to having the sheet flipped to show formulas, we'll toggle on R1C1 notation. See Figure 5.14.

	2	3	4	5
76	2745	3796	2593	2991
77	=SUM(R[-49]C:R[-1]C)	=SUM(R[-49]C:R[-1]C)	=SUM(R[-49]C:R[-1]C)	=SUM(R[-49]C:R[-1]C)

Figure 5.14 Auditing Formulas—The Easy Way

There you have it, pilgrim. It's pretty easy now to determine if all the formulas are identical or not. Using this technique, you only have to check one formula for correct construction, logic, and result. All relative formulas based on the first must be identical, and in R1C1 style you can readily see if they are identical. If one of the formulas is out of whack, it'll stick out like a sore thumb.

Troubleshooting Formulas—Piecemeal

> Break it down for 'em Obie!
>
> Well wisher to Oblio
> Harry Nilsson, *The Point*

A single formula can be a simple thing, its purpose revealed by simple examination. Or it may be a convoluted creature whose unraveling requires pencil, paper, a calculator, the *Function Reference*, a comfortable chair, and a pot of coffee.

Here is a great trick that helps you with formulas that fall into the latter category. But, beware, it is a trick that is *fraught with peril*. It's like a power saw, great if used correctly, but get careless and people will start calling you Lefty. Get the picture?

Consider the following formula located in cell S345, which is not giving you the result you think it should:

```
=IF(AND(E346+F346=0,E345+F345>0),SUM($E$10:E345)-
SUM($F$10:F345),"")
```

If you want to know what is sitting in E346, you can start scrolling all over the sheet or you can edit the formula (hit F2, double-click on the cell, or click in the formula bar), select the E346 reference, and press F9—*but don't press any other key.* This causes only that portion of the formula to recalculate, and your formula then looks like this:

```
=IF(AND(8160+F346=0,E345+F345>0),SUM($E$10:E345)-
SUM($F$10:F345),"")
```

Here you see that E364 currently returns 8160 (bolded for dramatic effect). Now listen up:

YOU MUST HIT ESCAPE OR YOU WILL PERMANENTLY CHANGE THE REFERENCE IN YOUR FORMULA TO THE VALUE!

Sorry to shout like that, but it is important. If you hit ENTER, the cell reference in the formula is replaced by the value. In effect, you are executing a Paste Special Values. Hit the Escape key and you end the edit process and all is well with your formula.

If you highlight one of the large ranges like $E$10:E345 and hit F9, you will see each cell's return value displayed as an array,* like this:

```
=TF(AND(E346+F346=0,E345+F345>0,SUM({2650.65;11550;0;0;0;0;
0;0;0;0;0;0;0;0;0;0;0;0;0;0;0;0;0,14030.29;0;0;0;0;406.9;0;0;
0;0;0;0;0;0;0;0;0;0;0;0;0;12.12;0;3323.85;0;0;0;0;0;
1287.5;0;0;0;0;0;0;0;0;0;0;0;550;0;0;0;0;0;0;2350;0;0;0;0;0;
0;0;0;0;0;0;0;0;0;0;0;0;5322.33;0;0;0;0;0;0;0;0;"I'M_AN_
ERROR";0;0;0;0;2700;9543.55;0;0;0;0;0;0;0;0;0;0;0;0;0;0;2447
.66;0;0;0;0;0;0;0;0;0;0;0;0;0;0;0;0;0;0;0;0;0;0;2643.75;0;
0;0;0;0;0;0;0;0;0;0;0;0;0;0;1051.02;2687.5;0;0;0;0;0;5385;
0;0;0;0;0;0;0;0;0;0;0;0;0;0;0;0;0;15626.99;0;7725;0;0;0;
0;0;0;0;0;0;0;0;0;0;0;0;0;6251.4;0;0;0;0;0;0;0;0;0;0;0;0;0;
```

*If an array is too large for Excel to display in the formula bar, Excel displays the #NUM! error.

```
0;0;0;0;0;4830;0;0;0;0;9153.2;0;0;0;3018.88;0;0;0;0;0;0;0;0;0;
0;0;0;0;0;0;0;0;0;0;0;0;0;0;0;1899.54;0;0;0;0;0;0;0;0;0;0;0;0;0;
0;0;0;0;0;0;0;0;0;0;1000;0;0;0;3865.66;9660;0;0;0;0;0;0;0;0;0;
0;0;0;0;0;0;0;0;0;0;0;0;0;0;0;0;312.5;0;0;0;0;0;0;0;0;0;0;0;0;
0;0;0;0;0;6425;0})-SUM($F$10:F346),"")
```

Since this range should only contain values, a text string showing up might explain why the formula is not working properly.

You can highlight and calculate a cell reference like E346, a range like $E$10:E345, or a segment of the formula. If you highlight E345+F345 and hit F9, that part of the formula returns 6111.95. But, if you highlight E345+F345>0 and hit F9, it returns TRUE since the sum of the two cells is greater than zero.

By checking what each part of a formula is returning you can quickly discern where the problem is within your formula.

DEFCON4—EDIT GO TO SPECIAL

> If fight we must, let's go in there and shoot the works for victory with everything at our disposal.
>
> Mark Clark
> *Power and Diplomacy*, 1958

Last, but certainly not least, in our arsenal of trouble trappers are the features provided in the Edit Go To Special dialog box. This dialog box presents an impressive array of tools for finding problems in spreadsheet models.

Go To Special is a way to select a number of cells within a worksheet simultaneously, based on specific criteria. Set the criteria by selecting one of several radio buttons (sure, sure, "option" buttons if you prefer). After you have the cells selected, you can use the Tab key to jump from selected cell to selected cell through the worksheet.

A Tactical Weapons Display

> Praise the Lord and pass the ammunition.
>
> Attributed to Howell M. Forgy
> Pearl Harbor, 1941

To get to the Edit Go To Special dialog box is a little convoluted, but we'll fix that in a minute. You have to pull down the Edit menu, click Go To, and then, from the Go To dialog box, click the Special button. Whew, finally the Go To Special dialog box is displayed. See Figure 5.15.

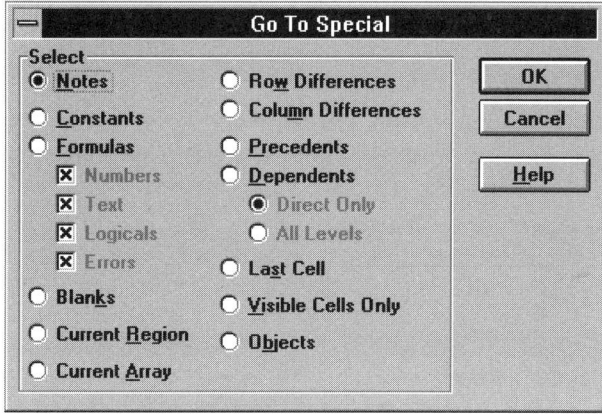

Figure 5.15 Go To Special

Here is your tactical weapons display for hunting down spreadsheet troubles. "Hey, kids!" they said, using their best Mickey Rooney impersonation (which is none too good), "Let's put on a show…er, let's add a toolbar button to bring up the Go To Special dialog box!" Great idea, Mickey, really.

By now you're a button-adding expert. Here's VBA code that pops up the Go To Special dialog box:

Button, button, add another button

```
'
' GotoSpecial Macro
' Written xx/xx/xx by YourNameHere
'
'
Sub EditGotoSpecial()
  If TypeName(ActiveSheet) = "Worksheet" Then
    On Error Coto EndMacro
    Application.Dialogs(xlDialogSelectSpecial).Show
  Else
    Beep
  End If
  Exit Sub
EndMacro:
  If Err = 1004 Then
    MsgBox "No cells (or objects) found.", vbExclamation
  End If
End Sub
```

The VBA "If...Then...Else" construct causes the program to beep if a Worksheet is not the ActiveSheet. The On Error statement lets the program exit gracefully if no cells match your criteria.

The steps for adding a button were detailed earlier in this chapter. Refer to those steps if you need to and hook this code up to a button on the Auditing toolbar.

Here is our Auditing toolbar as it is now. See Figure 5.16. For our Go To Special button face we snatched one of the button faces from WinWord 6.

Figure 5.16 Fully Loaded Auditing Toolbar!

Now that you can quickly gain access to the Go To Special dialog box, we'll discuss the different options or criteria you can set for selecting cells. Be aware that, if you start with only a single cell selected in your worksheet, when you run this dialog box, Excel searches the entire worksheet for cells that match your criteria. Although this is useful on occasion, more often you'll want to highlight a range within your worksheet and then run the Go To Special feature.

Notes, Last Cell, Objects, and Other Stuff

There are several options that you'll only use occasionally. Let's get them out of the way first.

Notes

If you want to highlight all the cells with attached notes in a sheet, you select a single cell in the sheet and pop Go To Special. The Notes button is selected by default so click on OK and every cell in the sheet with a note attached to it is highlighted. It's as though you went through the entire sheet making a number of noncontiguous cell selections.

The question is, why would anyone ever want to do this? You can get a list of cells containing notes by calling up the Cell Note dialog box. All cells with notes are listed in the Notes in Sheet list box. And it is not necessary to select a cell with a note in order to read the note.

If you want to delete all the notes in a sheet, select the entire sheet and do an Edit Clear Notes. Sorry, we can't come up with a good reason why you would use this option. Guess it's nice to know that it's there in case you ever come up with a reason to use it.

Last Cell

This does the same as the CTRL + END key combination you learned about earlier. Hmmm, CTRL + END seems easier.

Objects

This option lets you select all objects on the sheet's graphic layer. Unlike the other options, this one cannot be limited to a given area of the worksheet. Excel selects *all* graphic objects, text boxes, arrows, embedded charts, all of 'em.

This is really useful if you have lost track of, or don't want to go scrolling for, a graphic object some place way off in the distant reaches of the worksheet. Do a Go To Special Objects and the graphic objects are selected. Hit the Tab key and you can cycle through each object in turn.

If you have a bunch of objects on a sheet and want to move them all a little bit to the right, this option is the way to go. Sure, you can use the selection tool to group graphic objects together, but if they are widely dispersed around your sheet, the Go To method is faster.

And it's the fastest way to select all the graphic objects at once so you can delete them if you want.

Constants, Formulas, and Blanks

If you look closely at the Go To Special dialog box, you can see that an attempt was made to try to group the Constants, Formulas, and Blanks buttons together. Maybe it's just Constants and Formulas. Then again maybe we stared at it too long. Anyway, these options should be grouped together because they all deal with your basic cell contents.

Remember, the power of the Go To Special feature is that once you have all the cells selected, you can cruise through them with the Tab key. They may be scattered all over your worksheet but Go To Special makes them easy to find and review.

Constants

Want to see which cells contain constants? No problem, select your range and run this option. You can refine this criteria because as soon as you click on the Constant button (or Formulas, for that matter), the check boxes for Numbers, Text, Logicals, and Errors become available.

This is very useful if you want to see where the numbers are in a given range, for example. It works like the R1C1 and flipping techniques seen earlier, but it can more readily be applied on a larger basis.

Combine the weapons in your auditing arsenal! Zoom out on a large range, select the displayed area, and Go To Special on Constants. If a number is lurking where a formula should be, it'll stick out like a beacon.

Maybe you want to see where your text labels are. Uh oh! Text. If you have a number formatted as text, you have to deal with some inconsistency (so what else is new?) in how Go To Special works. The Constants option with the Text box checked deals with numbers formatted as text like this (see Table 5.3).

Table 5.3 Watch Text as Numbers!

Cell Contents	Constants / Text
100 (using Text format)	Not selected
'100	Selected
="100"	Not selected

Formatting the number as text does not enable Go To Special (with Constants Text) to find it. The ="100" is really a formula. Beware of how Excel deals with numbers formatted as text!

Formulas

These work like the Constants option except that you select only cells containing formulas. You can filter the formulas by what type of result they return, for example, Numbers, Text, Logicals, or Errors, or check them all.

Blanks (As in Shooting Same)

Blanks mean precisely that. Cells that do not have contents. Why should you concern yourself with blank cells when auditing a worksheet? Glad you asked.

Even though *you* know that the space is the intersection operator, and *we* know that the space is the intersection operator, a lot of ex-Lotus users still think that entering a space in a cell deletes a cell's contents. Hey, they can't help it, it's muscle memory. But, a space does not an empty cell make. So you can use the Blanks options to make sure cells that should be blank, really are.

Also, some cells may appear blank but not be (you know how appearances can be deceiving). For example, if a cell is formatted with the old standby custom format of ;;; to hide cell contents, it may well be nonblank (select the cell and look in the formula bar to be sure).

The Current Region

> ...the pellet with the poison's in the flagon with the dragon, the vessel
> with the pestle has the brew that is true.
>
> Mildred Natwick
> *The Court Jester*

This is as tricky to define as keeping track of that "chalice from the palace" (Jim's
a big Danny Kaye fan). Let's see what the *User's Guide* has to say about it. Hmmm,
nothing in the index on "current region." Nothing under "region" either. Let's try
the help file. Ah, ha!

Current Region

*Selects a rectangular range of cells around the active cell. The range selected is an area
bounded by any combination of blank rows and blank columns.*

So the current region depends on where the active cell is and how the sheet
thereabouts is laid out. A worksheet can therefore have a zillion "regions," and
the current one is dependent on where the active cell happens to be—and on
what's in the general vicinity, of course.

If a cell is surrounded by empty cells, that one cell is the "current region" all
by itself. If you are in a cell that is adjacent to cells with contents, Excel applies its
definition to come up with the current region. You'll have to experiment with this
one until you get the hang of it.

Once you have the current region selected, you can then search it using any of
Go To Special's other options.

The Current Array

This one is a slam dunk. If you put the active cell on a formula that is an array-
entered formula entered into a number of cells, this option highlights the entire
range of cells containing the array formula.

What's Wrong with This Picture?—Row and Column Differences

> It were not best that we should all think alike; it is difference of opinion
> that makes horseraces.
>
> Mark Twain
> *Pudd'nhead Wilson*, 1894

The differences options are another handy-dandy addition to your bag of tricks.
Select a segment of a row or column. Then run one of these options depending on
whether you are dealing with a row or a column.

The active cell in the selection is used as the comparison cell, and all other cells in the range are compared one by one to this cell. Any cells whose contents differ from the comparison cell are selected. This is great for checking formulas that use those pesky relative cell references. You know, where each formula looks different, but they are really identical.

Earlier we showed you how to flip the sheet and change the notation style to R1C1 to find formula errors. Those techniques are fine for small ranges, but these Go To Special options are killers for large ranges. You can tab directly to the offending cells.

Precedents and Dependents

These options act pretty much like the Trace Precedents and Dependents buttons on the auditing toolbar—only not as well, in our opinion. You click on a cell with a formula and run the option and the precedent cells (or dependent, if you ran that option) are highlighted.

We just feel that the arrows that the Trace buttons draw on the sheet are much more elegant and deal with branching in a clearer fashion. And the Trace buttons display graphically where trails lead off the sheet. The Go To Special precedent and dependent options do not deal with off-sheet trails at all.

Visible Cells Only

This is a cool option. Say you have some hidden rows and columns in a worksheet and you want to copy *only* what is visible on the sheet. If you highlight the range that contains the hidden rows and/or columns, copy it, and paste that selection somewhere else, the hidden stuff is copied with it. But, if you highlight the range and then run the Go To Special Visible Cells option, the selection does not appear to change *but the hidden rows and columns are not selected and the range can then be copied without them.* Way cool.

And there you have it. You're armed to the teeth, pilgrim. Lock and load. Over the top, and don't shoot till you see the whites of their eyes. Grab that big stick and dive in. Start giving your spreadsheet troubles some trouble of their own.

6 The Output—Formatting, Charting, and Printing

There is nothing worse than a brilliant image of a fuzzy concept.

Ansel Adams
Recalled on his death, April 22, 1984

What do formatting, charting, and printing have in common, you say? Well, they all directly affect how the output looks—how the results of the numbers appear, rather than the production of those numbers. All this takes place after the fact (or should anyway) of building the model. You've crunched the numbers, audited the results, calculated the calcs, formulated the formulas, you get the idea. Now to make it look good.

FORMATS—PUT ON A HAPPY FACE

Don't get us wrong. We are *violently* of the opinion that it is far more important that your numbers balance and have a high degree of relevance, accuracy, truth, justice, and the American Way than for them to look pretty. Substance over form and all that is the credo we try to live by. But, that said, it certainly doesn't hurt if your reports look nice, persuasive even. *Heh, heh, heh.* Providing, of course, that you don't spend two minutes on the numbers and two hours on the formatting.

Substance over form—but looking good helps.

Formatting the Hard Way

Excel makes formatting cells and groups of cells a snap. Select the cells and apply the formatting. Ah, but therein lies the rub.

A Plethora of Choices

Having a healthy selection of choices is good as long as you do not experience sensory overload. Let's take a look at Excel's formatting options in the Format Cells dialog box:

1. Pull down the Format menu.

2. Select Cells.

Here's where you access all the attributes that can be added to a cell. See Figure 6.1.

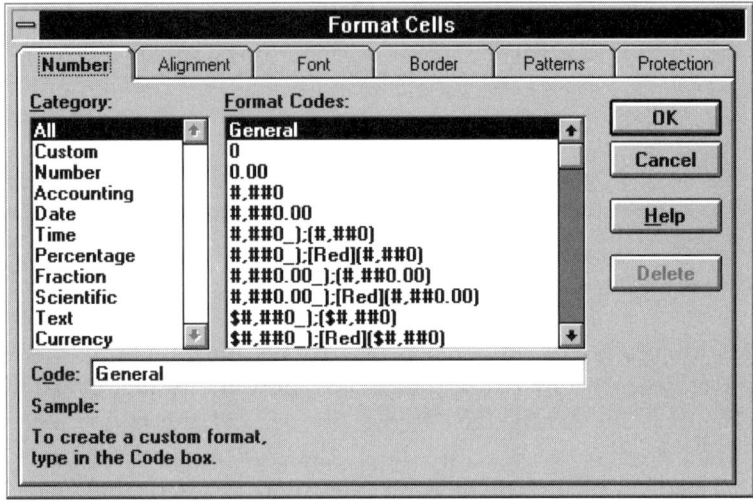

Figure 6.1 Format Cells Dialog Box

The Long Way Around the Barn

Now you start to see the dilemma. You can start off by slogging through over 36 choices for your basic format codes—not counting, of course, any custom format codes that you may have created along the way. Then you can choose from 16 or so alignment options, set a font and maybe some font effects, or borders, colors, patterns...well, you get the idea. Too many choices.

Start applying all this drek cell by cell (or even range by range), attribute by attribute, and you will soon be old and gray.

AutoFormat or AutoConformance?

> ...conformity is the jailer of freedom and the enemy of growth.
>
> John F. Kennedy

One click formatting The Redmond Rangers have gone a long way to make formatting on a large scale easier. To this end they came up with AutoFormat. Select a range of cells and run AutoFormat. AutoFormat lets you choose from a list of preset formatting options, which apply themselves to your selected range.

1. Select at least two cells in a worksheet.

2. Pull down the Format menu.

3. Select AutoFormat.

The AutoFormat dialog box is displayed. See Figure 6.2.

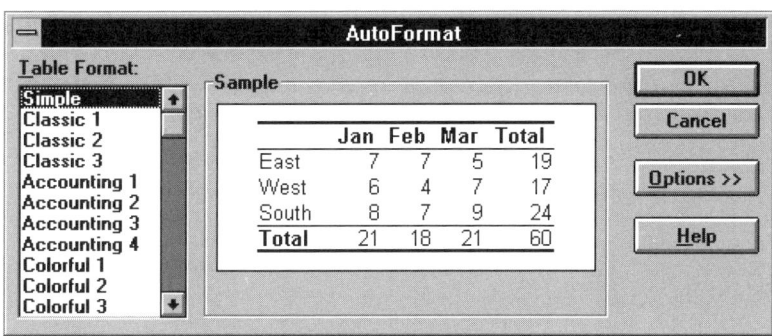

Figure 6.2 AutoFormat Dialog Box

If you choose the Simple Table Format, your selection gets formatted in the manner of the table shown in the Sample display. Column headings become bold and centered with a semi-heavy border on top and a standard border below. The data area is formatted with the 0 number format. The total line is formatted with bold text in the first column, and general formatting for the column total cells. The borders are as shown.

Trapped!

So what's the problem with this method? The problem is that you have to use a formatting scheme that someone else dreamed up. It is impossible to add your own Table Formats nor can you modify the ones provided. And, quite frankly, some of the built-in Table Formats are *stinkeroo!* You can forget about half of them if you plan to print on anything other than a color laser printer, and you have a couple of those floating around, right?

What you can do is eliminate different categories of formatting provided in the Table Format of your choice. For example, you can turn off the border attributes for the Simple Table Format and you still get all the other attributes. Then you can apply the borders you prefer. To switch off some of the attributes for a built-in format, click on the Options button and clear the appropriate check box.

Close, But No Cigar!

This is where the gears of the AutoFormat machine really fail to mesh. If you have to apply manual formatting to get it like you want it, you are back to doing it the hard way.

If begging disgusts you, skip down to the next paragraph. *Ahem, oh Microsoft, yoo hoo, please, pretty please, let us define custom AutoFormats, please, with sugar on top? Be your best friend!* And if you could let us define AutoFormats using style names well, golly, we'd think we'd died and gone to heaven, that's what.

When Microsoft lets us modify or create our own Table Formats within AutoFormat, we will embrace it and sing the praises of AutoFormat from the highest mountain (like the Matterhorn at Disneyland *<grin>*) because you can't beat formatting everything with a single click. Until then, you'll have to do it with style(s).

Do It With Style

> Mrs. Robinson, you're trying to seduce me, aren't you?
>
> Benjamin
> *The Graduate*

We made a lot of noise in Chapter 1 to entice you to think about styles because we feel strongly about them. In our experience, styles are among the most underutilized features in Excel. And what a great feature it is, too.

All standard formatting for each class of entry you make—labels, numbers, currency, totals, column headings, and so on—can and should be formatted by applying the appropriate style.

The virtues of styles
Now you old-hand word processor types know all about the virtues of styles—ease of use, standardization…all the usual reasons. But if you are not accustomed to the wonderfulness of styles or do not do much in the way of formatting in your worksheets, we had better discuss these massively useful critters.

Think of a style name as a bucket. Into the bucket you put formatting attributes like bold, center, borders, shading, and so on. When you apply a style to a range of cells, you "dump" the bucket and the range takes on all the attributes of that style. Simple, no?

The Lazy Man's Way to Custom Formatting

We just have one word for you: *styles*. You'll love 'em. Sure they're more work than AutoFormat, but you get something that is customized exactly the way you want to format your spreadsheet. Consider Figure 6.3.

	A	B	C	D	E
1	**Budget Report**	**1st Qtr**	**2nd Qtr**	**3rd Qtr**	**4th Qtr**
2	Revenue				
3	Fees	$100	$100	$100	$100
4	Services	10	10	10	10
5	Total Revenues	$110	$110	$110	$110
6	Expenses				
7	G & A	$30	$30	$30	$30
8	Travel	10	10	10	10
9	Outside	55	55	55	55
10	Total Expenses	$95	$95	$95	$95
11	**Total**	**$15**	**$15**	**$15**	**$15**

Figure 6.3 A Sample Table

This table was easy to create because we didn't bother to format anything while we built it. When you build your models, your attention should be focused on making your numbers and calculations accurate and meaningful.

Once we entered the data, we applied the styles listed in Table 6.1.

Table 6.1 Breakdown Formats per Style

Figure 6.3 Range	Selected Formats	Style Name
A1:E1	bold; horizontal centered; left, right, top, bottom borders; shaded	RptColHead
A2:E2, A6:E6	Shaded	RptHead
A3:A4, A7:A9	;;;____@; right borders	RptLines
A5, A10	right, top, bottom borders	RptSub
A11	bold; horizontal centered; right, top, bottom borders; shaded	RptTotal
B3:E3, B7:E7	$#,##0	Num1stLine
B4:E4, B8:E9	#,##0	NumLine
B5:E5, B10:E10	$#,##0, top, bottom borders	NumSubLine
B11:E11	$#,##0, top, bottom borders; bold	NumTotLine

So how did we get these styles? We developed them over time to fit the way we like to present spreadsheet tables. One of us being of the CPA persuasion likes to have the first number of a column formatted for currency with a dollar sign, so we have a style for that (Num1stLine) chosen right from the provided currency formats.

Set a Good Example

Styles are most easily created "by example." Format a cell or range manually, get it exactly the way you like it, click in the Style drop-down list box you added to the formatting bar back in Chapter 1, type in the name of the style you want to create, and hit ENTER. That's all there is to it. Now you have a style that contains all the formatting attributes of the selected range.

Style names   When you name a style, we suggest you keep it short and simple. Do describe what the style should be used for (for example, RptTotal). *Do not* describe the format attributes (BoldItalic$) because the style name remains but the attributes may get redefined over time.

Spaces can be used in the style name for clarity, but we prefer the capitalization convention as shown in Table 6.1. Use a naming convention that lets you know which styles are used for numbers ("Num" prefix in our examples) and which are for labels ("Rpt" prefix in our examples).

To use styles, once created, you

1. Select the cell or range you want to format.

2. Pull down the style list on the formatting bar.

3. Click on the style name.

Styles can be modified via Format Styles.

A style can be set to only apply selected cell attributes. There are six basic attribute categories as shown in the Style Includes group box (see Figure 6.4). A style can include all, some, or one of the attribute types. This lets you have a style that applies some formatting but that does not disturb other format attribute types that have been manually applied.

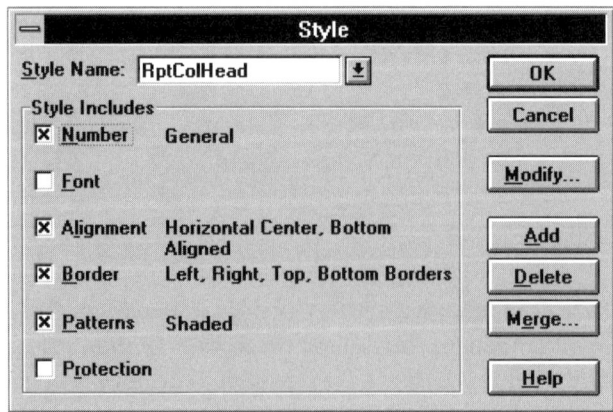

Figure 6.4 Control Style Attributes

We talk about managing your styles across books in Chapter 8 when we discuss templates.

Some Custom Formats

Line items we like to indent four spaces (for example, RptLines). This requires the creation of a custom format. Creating custom number formats is not a big deal:

1. Format Cells Number.

2. Select the Category you want to have your custom format listed under.

3. Type in the format you want in the Code text box.

If you aren't sure how to create the format you want, fire up help and search on "number formats, codes for" (bet that wouldn't have been your first guess).

Custom Indents

For example, in the RptLines style we used the text placeholder, the @ symbol, along with the underscore character to create a custom format that indents text entries like so:

Four underscores followed by the @ sign (each underscore tells Excel to indent by the width of a single space character). Anything typed into a cell so formatted is indented four spaces.

Custom Rounding

In Excel 5 you can use a custom number format to round by thousands. Place a comma at the end of a number format to round the value as in:

#,##0,

Some Stuff We Couldn't Figure Where Else to Put

A final note on formatting (and we use the term here loosely). Excel 5 provides several buttons that present pull-down palettes of tools for things like bordering and drawing, which can be considered formatting of a sort. You'll also see this palette concept for chart types on the chart toolbar.

We talked briefly about the drawing and bordering buttons back in Chapter 1 and strongly suggested that you add them to your formatting toolbar. What we didn't mention is that the palettes that these buttons display can be dragged onto the sheet thereby creating mini-toolbars.

Floating palettes

In Figure 6.5 you see that after clicking on the Borders button, which displays the border palette, you can tear-off the tool palette by clicking and dragging the displayed tool palette onto the sheet. These mini-toolbars do not appear in the Toolbars list (View Toolbars). To remove a tear-off palette, click once on the control icon on the palette's title bar (upper left corner).

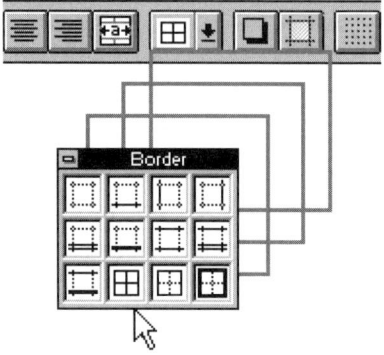

Figure 6.5 Tear-off Tool Palette

AS YOU CAN SEE BY THIS CHART

Get it right or let it alone. The conclusion you jump to may be your own.

James Thurber
Further Fables for Our Time (New York, 1956)

We thought of starting this section off with the old saw about "one picture is worth a thousand words," but that observation oversimplifies this topic.

It's easy to be bad.   Displaying numbers as pictures dates way back and is one of the sharpest double-edged gizmos we have *ever* come a'cropper with. The creation of a chart is not hard at all, especially given some of the nifty features in Excel, but creating a *good* chart is a science and discipline in and of itself. It's easy to create bad charts—"bad" meaning that the chart fails to convey the message or worse, conveys a misleading message.

We are not going to try to do a "10 Easy Steps to Creating Excel Charts." The *User's Guide* does a very good job of this already. We do touch on the basics, but our intent is to stay focused on some of the more…well…underground aspects of charting.

There really is a lot to this topic. We could do an entire *Underground Guide* on charting alone. Honest. If you want to get into this subject big time, we refer you to the landmark work *The Visual Display of Quantitative Information* by Edward

Tufte (Graphics Press). Tufte makes big bucks designing and analyzing charts and dealing with "data-ink ratios" and the "non-redundant display of data-information." Despite the weird terms, it is one nifty book.

Where the Left and Right Brains Meet

> We will control the vertical. We will control the horizontal. We can change the picture to a soft blur or sharpen it to crystal clarity.
>
> The Control Voice
> *The Outer Limits*

The trick to charts is to take numeric data and present it using a creative symbology to show some relationship. The chart needs to make the relationship clear and should do so without requiring the observer to analyze the underlying quantitative data. It must have "clarity, precision, and efficiency" according to Tufte. When you pull it off, it's great; when you don't, *oh, brother*.

Charts in Excel are either in a separate chart sheet linked to numeric data in a worksheet or embedded in a worksheet's graphic layer. Usually you embed a chart in a worksheet when you want to show the chart and the supporting data on the same page or screen.

Excel has some great tools for creating charts quickly and easily (some are new in Excel 5, some have been around for a while).

The Chart Wizard

The Chart Wizard is great. Select the cells that contain the numeric data you want to chart, and then fire up Excel's chart wizard to do all the work.

If you want to embed the chart on the worksheet, you can engage the wizard by clicking on the ChartWizard button. If you want to create the chart in a separate sheet, you insert a Chart sheet and the wizard starts up automatically.

ChartWizard button

If you go the embed route, you click the ChartWizard button and the mouse pointer changes to an icon very much like the Fill Handle Grabber™, kind of a drawing cross-hairs with a chart thingy attached. Drag this across your worksheet to draw the chart on the sheet.

The Chart Wizard itself pops up and guides you through the five basic steps to create a chart:

1. Pick the range of cells containing the data to be charted.

2. Choose a chart type (from a smorgasbord of 15 basic chart types).

3. Select a format for the chart type you picked (for example, do you want your donut chart completely or partially exploded?).

4. Adjust data series, x-axis labels, and legends.

5. Add a legend, chart title, and axis titles.

The choices do not really end here. You can go on to tweak the chart to your heart's content with too many options to try to discuss without doubling the size of this book. But never forget this: step 1 is where you make or break it. The numbers you select to chart either make sense or they don't. Once you go on to step 2, everything is formatting, which makes it look good or bad, depending. In step 1 you either pick the numbers that make your point or you don't.

The New Chart Sheet Display

New and improved
Excel 5 displays charts somewhat differently than Excel 4 when the chart is in its own sheet. Excel 4 resizes the chart to match the size of the sheet window in which it's being displayed. This can cause the chart to appear distorted, depending on the size of the sheet. In Excel 5 the chart appears in a view much like Print Preview. The chart size remains constant, and you deal with the chart by zooming in and out to size it within its window.

If this bugs you, you can switch to the Excel 4 display method by activating the chart sheet, Tools Options, click the Chart filecard, and check the Chart Sizes with Window Frame check box. We think the new display is a big improvement, but to each his own.

In-Sheet Editing

When you have a chart sheet and you activate it, some of the Excel 5 menus change. This is consistent with the way charts worked in Excel 4, except that the menus do not change as radically. The Data menu disappears entirely, but all the other menus remain and some suddenly contain commands specific to working with charts. The Chart toolbar also appears automatically.

In Excel 4, if you had a chart embedded on a worksheet and you double-clicked on it, a chart window opened, displaying the chart. The chart menus appeared, and you could then edit the chart. However, in Excel 5, you double-click on an embedded chart and, unless you watch closely, nothing appears to happen. Bang! Then it hits you—the Data menu has disappeared. A Chart toolbar has appeared. Hmmm, but where is the chart window that used to pop up? There ain't one, pilgrim.

Embedded charts
Welcome to the world of in-place editing. The embedded chart on the worksheet is fully editable *right where it is!* No more popping up a chart window. To get out of the chart editing mode, click anywhere on your worksheet outside the embedded chart. Done deal.

This is not without a downside though. If you have a *small* embedded chart and you liked the old chart window because you could maximize that window and see the chart better for editing, you might feel cramped. You can work around this inconvenience. One technique to is resize the chart graphic (a messy solution we think) or zoom in on the worksheet (only a little better).

Ah, but there is another way to get an embedded chart in a resizable window. Restore the book so that it is not maximized and the worksheet containing the embedded chart graphic is visible. Next resize the book smaller than the displayed chart graphic. See Figure 6.6.

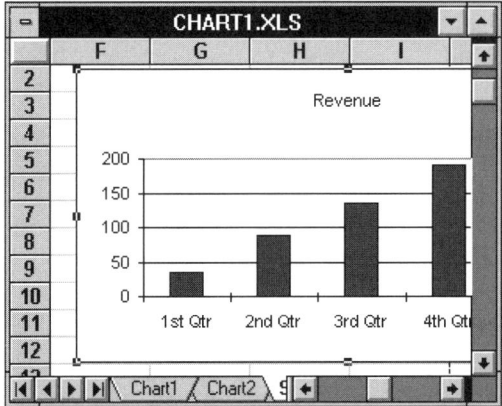

Figure 6.6 Embedded Chart in Resized Book

Now double-click on the embedded chart. Shazam! Holy moley, Captain Marvel, a chart window! See Figure 6.7.

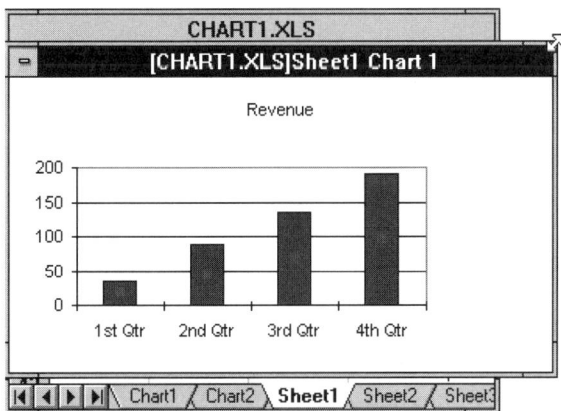

Figure 6.7 Double-Click on Embedded Chart

Hmmm, this chart window is missing one very useful thing. *A Maximize button!* Oh well, it *is* an imperfect world after all. You'll have to manually resize this chart window to make it larger. Works great though. The chart menus are displayed, and you can edit whatever you want. When you're done, close the window from its control menu (double-click on the hyphen control thingy, natch). The embedded chart is updated, and all is right in the world.

Adding Data to Charts—A New Trick

Drag-and-plot   Excel 5 offers a new method for adding a data series to an embedded chart (or new data to an existing data series). Highlight the new data and then click on any edge of the selected cells and *drag* these cells to the embedded chart and release the mouse. This is called the **drag-and-plot** method. See Figure 6.8.

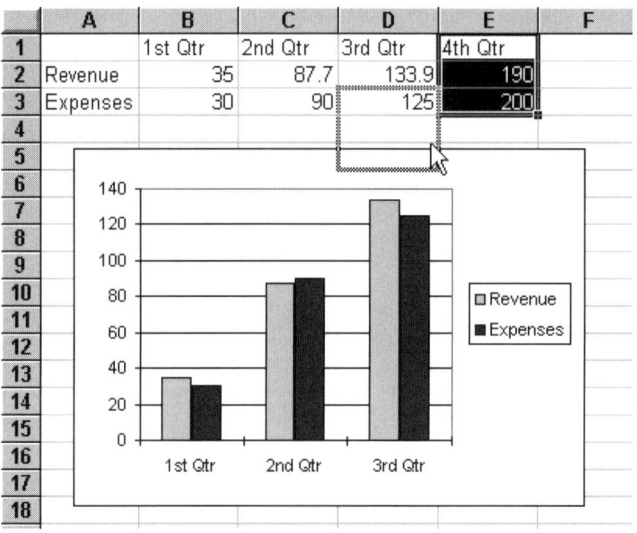

Figure 6.8 Drag-and-Plot on Embedded Chart

It's middlin' cool and saves you from having to edit series formulas, which are odd cryptic things that look something like this:

```
=SERIES(SHEET2!$A$2,SHEET2!$B$1:$D$1,SHEET2!$B$2:$D$2,1)
```

This technique works best when you can drop contiguous ranges of data on the chart in a single operation. If the data ranges are noncontiguous, it's best to re-drag-and-plot the old and new data in one fell swoop. If you want to do this little trick with a chart in a separate sheet, you copy the data, switch to the chart sheet, and paste the data.

Dynamic Charts—An Old Trick

The following dynamic charting method was used before the drag-and-plot trick (discussed in the previous section) made its debut in Excel 5.

Let's set up a plausible scenario. Say you have a chart showing sales versus sale inquires by month. Each month you have to update the chart to include the previous month's data. We'll embed this chart only in the interest of saving space, that is, we can show you the chart and the data in one figure. See Figure 6.9.

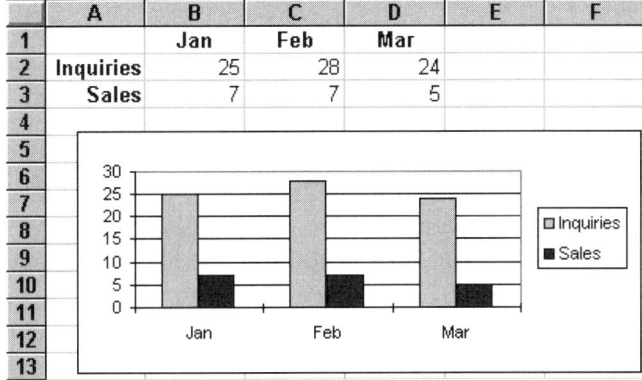

Figure 6.9 A Dynamic Chart Setup

Looks pretty ordinary, no? All the tricksy stuff is out of sight, but what it does is pretty neat. When you enter the data for April in cells E1:E3, this chart automatically includes the data. No kidding, one second it's just Jan through Mar, and the next it's Jan through Apr. Here's how it works (most of the time, *heh, heh, heh*).

The first step is to create some named formulas in the sheet (`SalesInfo`), one for the x-axis data and one for each data series you want charted. See Table 6.2.

You remember named formulas, don't you? Select any cell in `SalesInfo`, select Insert Name Define, enter `XAxis` in the Names in Workbook text box, enter the formula shown in Table 6.2 in the Refers to text box, click Add, and continue until the remaining named formulas are defined.

Table 6.2 Dynamic Named Formulas

Range Name	Named Formula
XAxis	=OFFSET(SalesInfo!$A$1,0,1,1,COUNTA(SalesInfo!$B$1:$M$1))
YInquiries	=OFFSET(SalesInfo!$A$1,1,1,1,COUNT(SalesInfo!$B$2:$M$2))
YSales	=OFFSET(SalesInfo!$A$1,2,1,1,COUNT(SalesInfo!$B$3:$M$3))

The OFFSET() function is very useful in that it lets you designate a range of cells that starts some number of rows and columns from a starting point. In this case, you use "SalesInfo!$A$1" as the starting point. The next argument tells OFFSET() how many rows down (if positive) or up (if negative). Then comes the number of columns down or up. The next two arguments define the size of the range you want: the height and the width.

Take the XAxis named formula as an example. It says start at A1, go zero rows down (no change), go one column right, the defined range is 1 row high, and the width is determined by the COUNTA() function. COUNTA() returns the value of the number of nonblank cells in the range "SalesInfo!$B$1:$M$1" which covers the 12 months that'll ultimately be charted.

This use of COUNTA() for nonblank cells, and COUNT() for nonzero cells is the trick that makes this technique work. As you add data to the chart each month, x-axis data on row 1, and y-axis data on rows 2 and 3, the range of cells to chart is not fixed but *dynamic*. It changes each month. The OFFSET() formulas automatically determine the cells that contain data and provide a handy reference to that range.

This takes care of the data in the worksheet, but how do you use the named formulas in the chart? And why do you have to do a named formula at all? Well, meanwhile back in the chart...

The easiest way to create the chart for this example is by using the existing data in the SalesInfo sheet. Create the chart and then edit the =SERIES() formulas for each data point in the chart itself. See Table 6.3.

Table 6.3 A Dynamic Duo of Series Formulas

Data Point	Named Formula
1	=SERIES(SalesInfo!$A$2,DEMO1.XLS!XAxis,DEMO1.XLS!YInquiries,1)
2	=SERIES(SalesInfo!$A$3,DEMO1.XLS!XAxis,DEMO1.XLS!YSales,2)

The syntax of the =SERIES() formula is

series_name, x-axis, y-axis, order number

For the x-axis and y-axis you substitute the appropriate defined formula names. This smoke-and-mirrors approach is required because Excel doesn't let you use other functions within the SERIES() function.

 This technique does work, honest. However, you might go crazy *trying* to make it work. This is due to Excel's, uhm, *unique* way of updating the named formulas and the series formulas, which are treated by Excel as pseudo-external references. If you look at the =SERIES() formula, you see that it

refers to a book (`DEMO1.XLS`) and then to a range within that book. Yep, that's an external reference all righty. You could call it a link, but Excel does not recognize it as a link. Pull down the Edit menu and the Link command is grayed out (assuming that you don't have any other links set up in the sheet). This is so weird that we keep expecting Rod Serling to be standing behind us saying "...next stop, the Excel zone."

There's no consistent method to get the link, er, nonlink to update in, well, a *consistent* manner. Rather than try to document all the possible permutations for updating problems, just remember this: If you wind up with a chart that doesn't update properly, close it and then reopen it.

As long as we're on the subject of the strange and unusual, you can forget trying to use the Paste Names button or the F3 shortcut key when editing the =SERIES() formula. They just don't work. So type carefully.

That's all there is to it (*heh, heh, heh*). Add data to the worksheet and the chart uses it—although you may have to close and reopen it to make it update correctly. *But other than that, how did you like the play, Mrs. Lincoln?*

In Picture Viewing

We hesitate to talk about this next trick as it can easily contribute to chartjunk (which we talk more about shortly). But what the heck, when used judiciously, it can be very effective.

In Excel 5 it is possible to embed a chart on a chart sheet. First, create the chart in the chart sheet. Then you create a chart embedded in a worksheet. Select the embedded chart and copy it. Switch to the chart window and paste. Simple as that. See Figure 6.10.

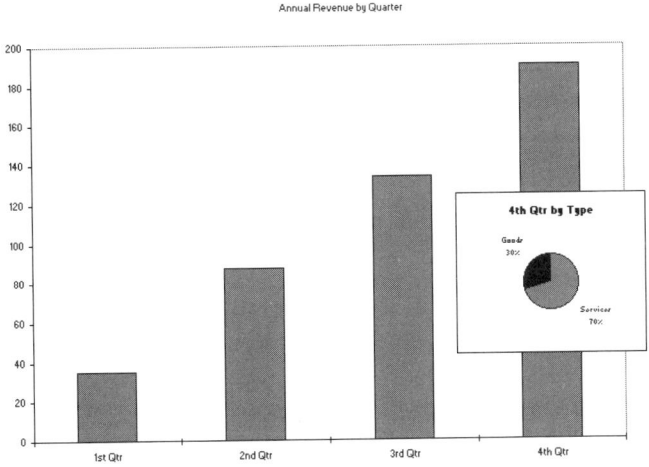

Figure 6.10 Embedded Chart on a Chart Sheet

You might want to show a series of data and then break down one of the data points using a different chart type. In Figure 6.10 a pie chart breaks down one of the columns into component parts.

Charting Dangerous Waters

Problems can arise from the way you construct your charts as well as from the computer environment (i.e., bugs). Here are a couple of gotchas to watch out for when creating visual representations of your numeric data.

Keep Your Thumb Off the Scale

> —where due to a terrible miscalculation of scale the entire battle fleet was accidentally swallowed by a small dog.
>
> Douglas Adams
> *The Hitchhiker's Guide to the Galaxy*

Here's one of the most basic things to watch for when charting. The scale. This is typically the y-axis and shows the underlying series values. Consider the chart in Figure 6.11.

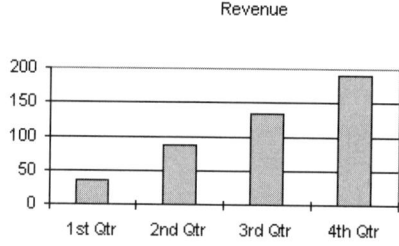

Figure 6.11 A Strong Showing

Looks good, a nice steady and substantial rise in revenues. Now contrast this chart with Figure 6.12.

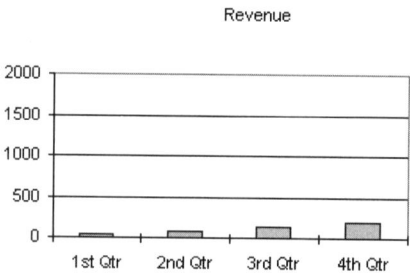

Figure 6.12 Not So Impressive

The revenues don't appear nearly as impressive. Barely any growth at all. *But both charts are based on the same data!* The trick here is one of scale. Double-click on the y-axis and you can tweak the scale to suit your purpose. You can adjust the scale to make a trend more pronounced or less apparent. Watch out that someone doesn't sucker *you* in with this trick.

The Amazing See-Through Chart

Here's a bug dealing with Hewlett-Packard laser printers using the PCL printer language that can make you crazy when printing charts embedded on worksheets.

If you wind up placing the chart object over some cells that have contents, those cells are covered by the chart and are not visible. So far so good. Hmmm, would you ever want to hide something with a chart object? Probably not, but it's conceivable to have a situation where a chart might wind up covering some stuff on a worksheet.

Whether you do this cover-up job by design or by accident, the important thing is that everything is hunky dory until you print the worksheet, at which time all the underlying cell contents get printed *on top of your chart!* Bummer. Print Preview looks OK, but the printed output is fouled up.

Mangled printing— beware!

According to Microsoft, this is a problem whenever PCL is used to print, but they do offer some workarounds. Redmond suggests you use ATM or Bitstream fonts (versions 1.1 and 1.2, respectively) if you have such animals on your system. Or use the native fonts Modern, Roman, or the ever popular Script *<oh, sure>*. Finally, they suggest setting TrueType as Graphics (File Page Setup Options Options and check the Print TrueType as Graphic check box).

This problem does not occur when you embed a chart object in a chart sheet.

Chart Junk

> Everyone spoke of an information overload, but what there was in fact was a non-information overload.
>
> Richard Saul Wurman
> *What-If, Could-Be* (Philadelphia, 1976)

People get carried away with charts, it's a fact. The trick is not to get carried too far. It's easy to add circles, and arrows, and color, and cross-hatching, and horizontal gridlines, and vertical gridlines, and text boxes, and pictures, and on and on. Use restraint.

Just like in word processing where you don't want your letter to look like a ransom note, you don't want to create a chart that takes longer to figure out than analyzing the underlying data would take. We think the "keep it simple" rule should be applied often and liberally.

An old architectural maxim says "use decoration in your construction, but do not construct decoration." Keep in mind that a chart is a visual display of numeric data. Its purpose is to make clear some relationship within the data. Its job *is not* to impress your audience with how many pieces of clip art you can work into a single screen. Or win an award for the busiest graphic ever designed.

Take Gridlines, Please!

Avoid non–data-ink   Consider something simple like gridlines. The more gridlines, the better right? Major and minor gridlines on the x-axis, major and minor on the y-axis, great right? No, although you'd be surprised how many chart makers seem to think so. Stick to major gridlines only and do not use both x- and y-axis gridlines on the same chart unless you have a very compelling reason. Gridlines fall into the category of non–data-ink and as such should be used sparingly.

Hey, better yet, how about no gridlines at all or only a single gridline at the breakeven point (or whatever threshold needs to be emphasized)? How do you get a single gridline? Easy, turn off Gridlines and draw an arrow on your chart. Make it perfectly horizontal (or vertical, depending on your needs), and lose the arrowhead (select the arrow, Format Object and under Arrowhead Style choose the option that has no arrowhead). This trick lets you use only the gridline(s) that you need to get your chart's point across.

Clip Art Columns

Bleccch!   The use of cute pictures in place of the bars or columns usually seen in a chart is generally something to avoid. Consider the chart in Figure 6.13.

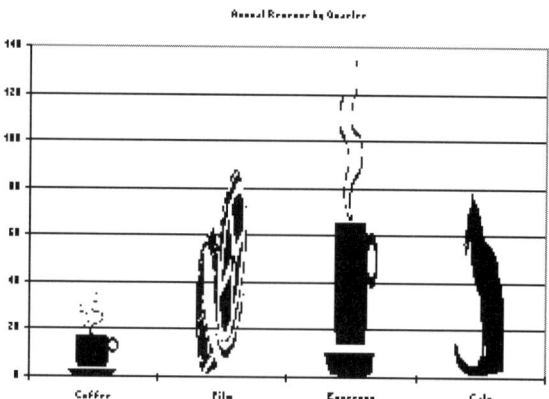

Figure 6.13 Typical Coffee, Film Violence, Espresso, Cats Chart

This is a nonsensical chart that uses clip art in place of the usual dull bars. Now, there may be a time when this is actually an effective presentation method. We can't think of such a situation, mind you, but we concede that it is within the realm of theoretical possibility.

How do you do it? Copy a graphic to the clipboard, switch to Excel, click on the data point to change, and Paste. Please, don't make us regret having told you how to do this.

Cross-hatching

> ...are so amazingly primitive that they still think digital watches are a pretty neat idea.
>
> Foreword
> Douglas Adams, *The Hitchhiker's Guide to the Galaxy*

Back in the olden days of PC-generated charts when we all thought dot matrix printers were a pretty neat idea, you used cross-hatching on the columns to differentiate them. If you still like to use a jillion different cross-hatchings on your charts, try to cut back. It can get real ugly. Don't let Figure 6.14 happen to you.

Real charts don't wear plaid.

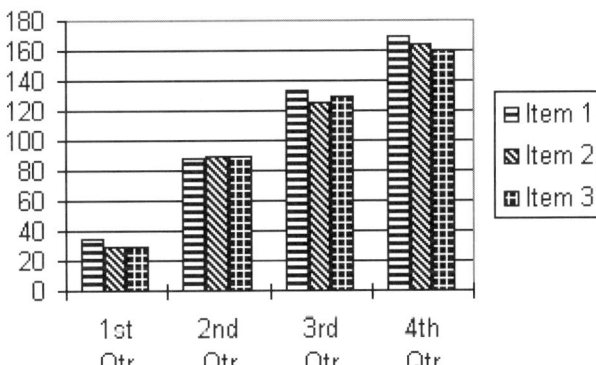

Figure 6.14 Cross-hatching at Cross Purposes

When you are showing your charts on the screen, color is where it's at for differentiating columns or bars. But when you print in black and white, the colors get translated into shades of gray. And this is as it should be.

A 3-D, Radar, Donut-Like, Area Chart

Excel has bunches of chart types. Donut charts (for pie charting multiple data points), radar charts, and area charts just to name a few of the more exotic. And like that cinematic masterpiece, "Jaws III," you can do them in 3-D!

Fly low and avoid the radar.   Now don't get us wrong. If you ever need to display a continuous variance in volume where you have several data series, an area chart can't be beat. But it's the pits if you're trying to show a breakeven analysis. And there must be, oh, at least 20 people in the world who can figure out a radar chart. The point is, don't think that because Excel has a lot of different chart types you must embark on a crusade to use each and every one of them in every presentation you do.

Think of the chart types as different tools. When you need a hammer, use a hammer. Using a screwdriver may be inventive, but it doesn't get the job done. If you have to explain what your chart shows, maybe it still needs some work.

Each Data Series in a Chart Can Be a Chart

Strong drink and large automobiles don't mix. Some discretion should also be exercised when mixing different chart types together. No, we don't mean a nice straightforward overlay chart where you want to show one data series as a line chart type over another displayed as a column chart. This is very useful, especially when you want to show a second y-axis. You see this type of chart when showing how a given business's performance stacks up against the overall industry figures.

But Excel 5 lets you use a different chart type for each data series in the chart. In a fit of *chartis junkis*, you may think that combining a bar chart with a radar chart is peachy, but trust us, you'll hate yourself in the morning.

PRINTING—THE FINAL FRONTIER

> Cut! Print it!
>
> Movie director's call

The printed page. The final output. The end of the journey. The report at the end of the tunnel. (Substitute the cliché of your choice here.)

At some point you'll want to go with a printed or "hard" copy of your model, and this section discusses the hows and whys of generating that copy.

Print Basics 101

The first task is seeing that Excel prints the area of the sheet that you want printed. There are several methods for doing this and we shall explore each in turn.

Remember, you are dealing with over 3000 square feet of worksheet. It wouldn't do to print every cell now would it? Unless, of course, you had some wallpapering to do.

Default Printing

The easiest, slam-dunk, nothing-but-net way to print an Excel sheet is to make that sheet active and click on the Print button on the standard toolbar. Excel then metaphorically engages autopilot, overrides all manual control, communes with your printer, and as if by magic your printer starts spitting out pages.

Print button

What the Print button does is start the print process using the default settings in the Print dialog box. You get one copy of the selected sheet(s). If you make Sheet1 active and click the Print button, you get one copy of Sheet1. Make several sheets active and you get one copy of the several sheets—assuming, of course, that there is something on the sheet(s) to print. Try to print an empty sheet and Excel complains with a "There is nothing to print in the specified pages" message box. Fair enough.

So what does Excel print if the sheet is not empty? Well, if the sheet is a chart or module, you get the chart or the code printed, natch. But, if the sheet is a worksheet, Excel prints the area of the sheet defined by cell A1 and the end cell (the intersection of the last row with contents and the last column with contents). Contents in this regard also includes graphic objects floating over the sheet cells.

The alternative to the Print button is to whistle up the Print dialog box (File Print) and take manual control, as it were. See Figure 6.15.

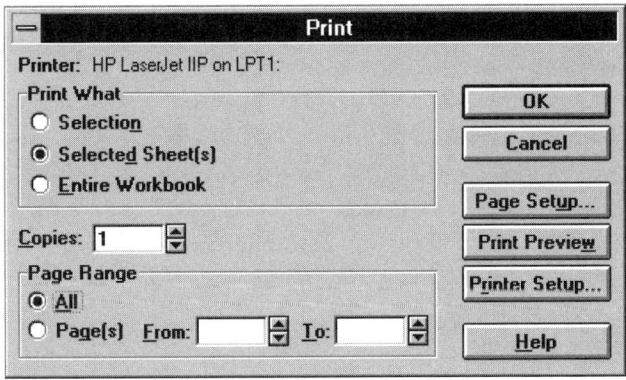

Figure 6.15 Excel's Print Dialog Box

Using this dialog box you can tell Excel what you want—how many copies you want, whether to print everything or only a specified range of pages. We hope that one day Microsoft will standardize the print dialog boxes between its applications. As it is now, WinWord, Excel, and Access each have just enough differences to be really annoying. Gives us all something to look forward to, eh?

Print What—Selections Galore

In the Print What group box you can specify that Excel print just the Selection; Selected Sheet(s), which is the default setting; or the Entire Workbook (every sheet in the book).

Bypassing Print_Area

The "Selection" means the active cell or range of cells in each selected sheet. If you choose the Selection option button, it overrides the Print_Area range should the sheet being printed have one.

Note that, under any of the three settings, if you have set print titles (discussed shortly), they are printed as well.

But the preferred way to define what should be printed is to use the Print_Area range name.

Set Print_Area

In the golden days of Excel, you learned to highlight a range of cells, pull down the Options menu, and click on Set Print Area. Back in Chapter 1, we broke the bad news that Set Print Area disappeared along with the Options menu in Excel 5.

Set Print Area button

Fortunately the Redmond Rangers provided a button to set the print area. Practical jokers that they are, they left it off the standard toolbar. This we fixed in Chapter 1 by adding said button to the toolbar. So you can readily define a range name called Print_Area by highlighting the cells to be printed and clicking on the Set Print Area button. Print_Area is always a sheet-level name, so you can have one on each sheet.

The Print_Area name is one of Excel's "built-in" range names (discussed in Chapter 4), so don't use it for anything you don't want *printed!*

Say you have named the different areas of a single worksheet. You can easily make Print_Area refer to several other range names. Create a range name called Print_Area (Insert Name Define) and in the Refers to edit box, type in the references to the range names like this:

```
=Sheet2!Lobster,Sheet2!MainReport,Sheet2!Snout
```

Each range prints on a separate page. (Thanks Don!)

Save a Tree—Print Preview

Print Preview is a big time saver! It lets you check out how your sheet will lay out without having to actually print the physical pages. Print Preview saves you from having to scroll around your worksheet looking for the dotted page delineation lines to see where the page breaks are.

You can get to Print Preview from either the Print dialog box command button labeled (what else?) Print Preview, or you can click on the Print Preview button on the standard toolbar.

Print Preview button

In the Print Preview screen, you can click on the Margins command button and see the physical margins *and* the column width markers for the sheet displayed. If you are so inclined, you can resize column widths (but not row heights) right here by dragging the column width markers. The width value is displayed on the status bar as you drag, but it can take a loooooong time to repaint the screen, depending on the complexity of your model.

If you call up the Page Setup box via the Setup command button from within Print Preview, you cannot see nor set the Print_Area or Print_Titles ranges in the Sheet filecard.

Page Setup

> ...it's a setup, boys!
>
> Jack Napier
> *Batman*

You can get to the Page Setup dialog box from the File menu, the Print dialog box, or the Print Preview screen. This is where you set up the format you want for your printed output.

This dialog box has four filecards for controlling settings: Page, Margins, Header/Footer, and Sheet. Most of the stuff is pretty routine. Options like orientation, paper size, margins, and so on, are straightforward so we won't rehash them. But there are some topics of real interest that we should mention about Page Setup. *Oh, yeah!*

Print_Area Defined!

On the Sheet filecard you can set the attributes for the sheet you're printing. The print section lets you print gridlines (if you want) or the sheet notes (if there are any). Pretty standard fare.

Ah, but how Excel now deals with the print range is different. If you have created a range name called Print_Area, either manually or via the Set Print Area button discussed earlier, the absolute range coordinates appear in the Print Area text box. This is new in Excel 5.

If you have not defined the Print_Area range name in your sheet, you are supposed to enter the range to print in this text box. You can type in the coordinates manually, specifying multiple ranges by separating them with a comma, or (get this) you can highlight the range with the mouse. That's right, when the cursor is in the Print Area text box, you can select cells in your sheet. As you drag your mouse across the sheet, the range coordinates appear in the text box.

Ahem. We have a problem with this. Two problems, actually. First, it's deucedly difficult to select ranges with the Page Setup dialog box obscuring 45% of your screen. Second, it seems to us that it contradicts the Windows "select then do" paradigm. There is no way to highlight the range prior to calling up the Page Setup dialog box. It feels *wrong, wrong, wrong!*

We've started having this recurring nightmare lately. In it the Microsoft lab rats decide that they like the old Lotus verb/noun paradigm better than the Windows noun/verb method. (That's where you click on a command like Copy and then select your range instead of the other way around.) Do us a favor and write your congressperson and tell them if Microsoft decides to declare this old method as a new standard, it will cost corporate America billions in lost productivity and retraining.

Paste Names button

As an alternative you could type a range name into the Print Area text box. Or, you can use the Paste Names button to select *any* existing range name as long as the cursor is in the Print Area text box. If you use any range name other than Print_Area, remember that Page Setup converts the range name to its absolute cell coordinates when you click on the OK button and it no longer tracks these coordinates back to the range name that you started with. The setting is no longer dynamic, and changes to the range name will not update to the Print Area setting.

Print_Titles

Set Print Titles is another casualty of the demise of the Options menu in Excel 5. This menu command has been replaced with the Print Titles section of the Sheet filecard in the Page Setup dialog box.

In this filecard you have two text boxes, one for Rows to Repeat at the Top and another for Columns to Repeat at the Left. The idea here is the same as the Print Area text box we just discussed. Click on the Rows to Repeat at the Top text box, for example, and then you click and drag across the rows you want in your Print_Titles. The row numbers appear in the text box. The same technique applies to the Columns to Repeat at the Left text box.

Once you have made a selection for one or the other or both and click on OK in the Page Setup dialog box, Excel takes the row and column coordinates and creates a range name of Print_Titles (ah, just like the old days!)

You could create this range name yourself if you wanted to bypass the Page Setup dialog box altogether. Select the rows and columns you want and create a range name called Print_Titles. No problem.

From Head to Footer

The Header/Footer filecard provides access to the custom header and/or footer dialog boxes, which remain largely unchanged from Excel 4 and are very intuitive and easy to use.

The prebuilt headers and footers that are provided with Excel 5 are truly new and cool. There is a drop-down list box for each. See Figure 6.16.

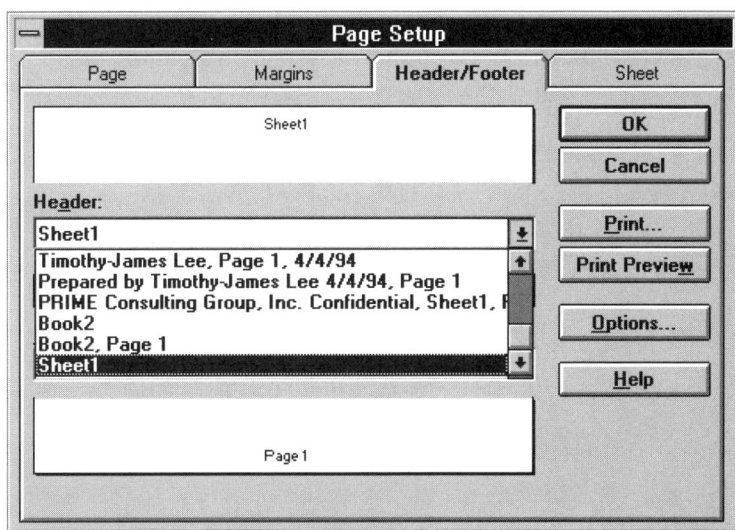

Figure 6.16 Prebuilt Headers List

You can choose from 17 prebuilts (you get the same list of choices for footers as you do for headers). This can *really* save you some time if you can conform your wants to one of the prebuilts provided. (In Chapter 8 we discuss templates and how to have new sheets get the header and footer you want by default.)

Marginal Utility

The Margins filecard lets you set and change just that: margins. A little Preview graphic in the middle of the filecard is supposed to show you how the margin settings affect the page layout, but it does not always perform as expected. Sometimes the graphic responds to changes in the settings and sometimes it doesn't.

If you want to tinker with the margins visually, pop into Print Preview; click on the Margins command button, which displays the margins on screen; and drag the margin marker handles to change them.

Page Control

Finally, on the Page filecard, we've saved the best for last. Here you can adjust the Scaling. What does this do for you? It lets you escape this type of vicious circle.

You have a spreadsheet and you need to print it out. Now. You print it and the last two columns print on the page 3 of the printout by themselves. You don't want these two columns to print on page 3; you want the whole spreadsheet to print on two pages. So you fiddle with some of the column widths. You check it out in Print Preview, and now you only have one orphan column on page 3. You tweak some more columns and finally you get it down to two pages. You print it out. Arrrrgh! Now some of the columns are too narrow, and a bunch of numbers are displayed as a series of repeating pound signs (###).

Using the Scaling option, you can set a percentage to scale the printout (increase it 20%, decrease it 10%, whatever) or you can force the printout to a certain number of pages. To avoid the agonies of the previous example, you click on the Fit to option button and set the number of pages you want the printout to fit on. The Scaling option has been around since Excel 4 and is one nifty feature.

Scenic Views Ahead

> Memory, Officer Starling, is what I have instead of a view.
>
> Hannibal Lector
> *Silence of the Lambs*

The View Manager is another one of those underutilized gems that lurk within Excel. Not only is it used to control screen layouts, but it can also store multiple print settings for a single sheet.

View Manager is an add-in and as such takes a few seconds to come up the first time you run it. This is called "on-demand" loading. The Add-in is not loaded until you access it. Add-ins also impact system resources. On our test machine (486DX2/66 with 16 megs RAM), the View Manager (VIEWS.XLA) consumed 1% of available resources.

Before you create a View, you need to set up your sheet layout and print options. Just as you create styles "by example," you set all the display and print attributes for a sheet and then save all those attributes as a "View."

Display Attributes

Display attributes include all the options found on the Tools Options View filecard. See Figure 6.17.

Store freeze pane settings.   In addition to the Window Options attributes, the View Manager can store split screen and freeze pane settings. This is very handy for creating views for

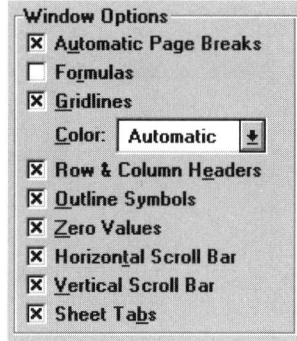

Figure 6.17 Window Options in the View Filecard

input, where you have rows and columns frozen on screen. By switching views, you can instantly go from a sheet view with frozen (or split) panes to one where you can scroll freely through the entire sheet.

Finally, the view stores the window size of the book, its position, the current zoom percentage, and last, but not least, the active range selection. Whew! Is this a cool feature or what?

Print Attributes

Print attributes are covered by anything you can set in the Page Setup filecards (Page, Margins, Header/Footer, Sheet). If you have several different sections of a single sheet that require changing between portrait and landscape, margin changes, gridlines, whatever, View Manager is the way to control switching between settings.

View Manager Add-In

Okay, you've set up your display, you've set all the print attributes you want. Now what? Ah, simplicity itself.

1. Pull down the View menu.

2. Click on the View Manager option.

If View Manager does not appear on your View menu, you'll have to install the View Manager add-in. Pull down the Tools menu, click Add-Ins, check the View Manager check box, and click on OK.

Install View Manager add-in.

As we've said, since this is an add-in, it may take a few seconds to load initially. But patience is a virtue, and soon you are rewarded with the View Manager dialog box. See Figure 6.18.

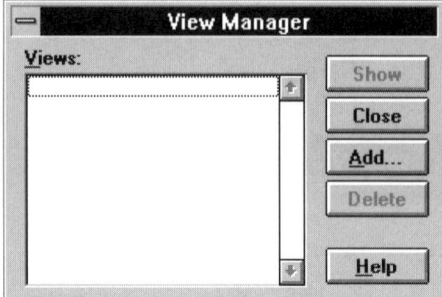

Figure 6.18 View Manager

 Now the Excel Help file tells you that the View Manager lists all the views defined in the active *workbook*. Wrong! It lists all the views in the active *worksheet*. It could be that the original spec for Excel 5 called for this "views in the active workbook" feature since there is even a tip in the help file saying that you should include the sheet name in the view name so you can tell which view goes with which sheet. But either this is a bug or the feature didn't make the cut.

In any event, views are local to each sheet and the View Manager dialog box *lists the views for the active sheet only.*

To create a new view, click on Add. You get the Add View dialog box <what else?>. See Figure 6.19.

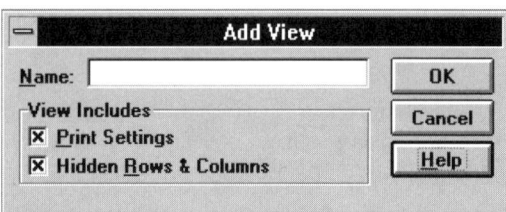

Figure 6.19 Name That View!

Including the current print attributes in your view is optional (check or uncheck the box, as appropriate). If you have hidden any rows or columns in the sheet, you can either include the hidden aspect of these rows and columns or not.

The Hidden Rows & Columns option is whiz-bang if you do any financial reporting. It used to be that you'd spend hours writing macros to hide and unhide columns when you have a 12-month financial report with columns for Budget, Actual, and Variance. Views to the rescue!

Here's the only downside to View Manager that we've come across. A view comprises a complete set of parameters. Change to another View and you get all of the settings stored in that View. At some point, you'll want to update a View so that it has different settings. To update an existing View, you must perform the following unintuitive steps. We assume that you are currently in the View to be updated and that you have changed the settings you want modified.

Select View View Manager, select the View to be updated—*even though it's the last view activated, and even though it's not necessarily at the top of the Views list box list* (another peeve of ours; this list should preselect the current View, dammit)—then click Add, type in the name of the current view in the Name text box (we're not kidding), make sure the appropriate check boxes are checked, click on OK, and if you're *really lucky* you get the message box "Overwrite existing view '[view name]'" and you can click on OK.

Updating a view

The View Manager is awesome, but its user interface could stand some work.

Report It!

> Genghis always wanted one damn report after another.
>
> Amok Shing, Mongol
> *My Years in the Horde* (from the modern translation by K. Tibet, 1972)

Hand in hand with the View Manager, the Print Manager feature makes managing complex printouts involving several sheets within a workbook a piece of cake.

Here's what you do:

1. Pull down the File menu.

2. Click on the Print Report option (if there is no Print Report option, nip on over to Tools Add-ins and check the Report Manager box).

Here is the Print Report dialog box in all its glory (see Figure 6.20).

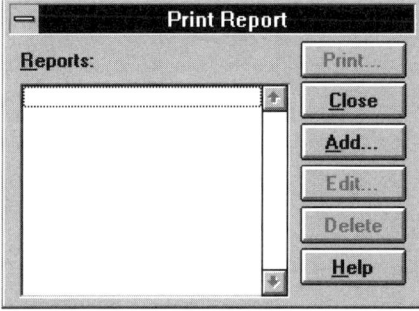

Figure 6.20 Report Manager, er, Print Report

If you think it odd that you have to load an add-in called Report Manager to get a menu option called Print Report, *we're with you!* We suspect that this is one of those Microsoft lab rat mysteries that will never be explained satisfactorily by human science. Anyway, the Print Report dialog box is your gateway to the Print Manager. Select the report you want to print and click the print button. The rest is, as they say, history.

Ah, but if you have not created any Print Reports, you should click on Add and the dialog box shown in Figure 6.21 appears. Give your report a name (up to 100 characters, but limit yourself to 20–25 so you can actually *see* your report name in the Print Report dialog box), and then add sections to it. Since Report Manager is another "on-demand" add-in, you can expect another 1–2 % resource hit when you initially invoke it.

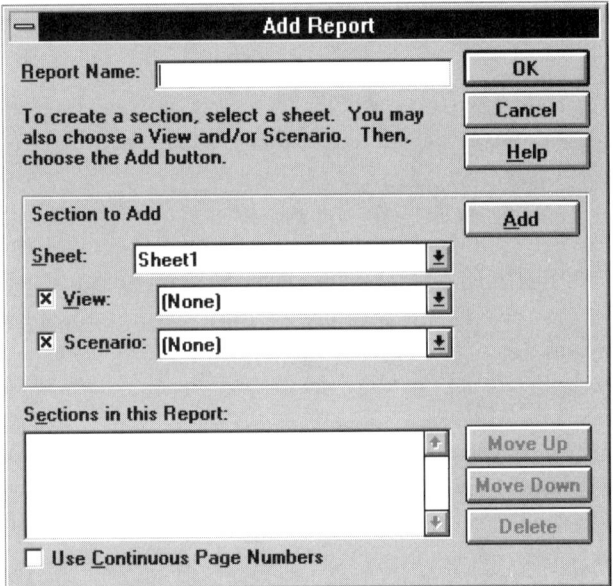

Figure 6.21 Report Management Made Easy

Section to Add

Each section is made up of three parts:

- Sheet
- View
- Scenario

The Sheet drop-down list shows you all the sheet names for the active book. A valid sheet name is the minimum requirement needed for creating a report. If you do not specify a View or Scenario, the specified sheet is printed using the default print settings for that sheet.

The View drop-down list shows you the names of all the Views (if any) for the selected Sheet.

The Scenario drop-down list shows the various Scenarios (if any) for the selected sheet.

After you pick a Sheet, you can optionally select a View and/or a Scenario. Then you click the Add button to add this section to the report. Each report can have multiple sections. Each section can be a different Sheet or a different View/Scenario of the same Sheet.

We have never banged into the upper limit for sections, not having ever gone beyond 100 sections in a single report. One of Redmond's finest speculated that you are only limited by available memory. Hmmm. The help file says, "Maximum number of views...Limited only by available memory, although the View Manager dialog box lists the first 256 views only." Then later on it says that the maximum number of *named* views, reports, and scenarios is "limited only by available memory." Draw your own conclusions, pilgrim.

Section limitations

Editing Reports

It's possible to edit existing Reports...sorta. Choose a Report in the Print Report dialog box and click Edit. Looks good so far, no? Although you can add, delete, and change the section order (via the Add, Delete, Move Up, and Move Down command buttons), you *cannot edit an existing section in the Sections in this Report list box!* This is not a real heartbreaker, but it is not so cool either. You have to delete the old, add the new, and reshuffle the list.

Page Numbers

When checked, the Use Continuous Page Numbers check box is supposed to force each page in each report section to be consecutively numbered. When doing a complex report spanning several sheets, it would be very nice indeed to let Excel worry about the page numbering. Unfortunately there is a bug in this feature.

Continuous page numbering doesn't work unless you force the First Page Number setting on the Page filecard in Page Setup to "1" instead of the default "Auto" in the *first view used in the first section of the report.* Whew, what a pain. Let's hope Microsoft fixes this one soon. Because what if the first section has no view? It looks like there is simply no way to have continuous page numbering unless you create a view at least for the first section (sheet)! Ridiculous, no?

7 Data Analysis—the Quest for Fire

I am…a liberal, a conservative, a Texan, a taxpayer, a rancher, a business-man, a consumer, a parent, a voter, and not as young as I used to be—and I am all these things in no fixed order.

Lyndon Baines Johnson

Extend the life span of the known universe! With keen-edged tooth and unrelenting claw, join us in the eternal fight against entropy! As the motion of air stirred by the gentle beating of a butterfly's wing on Earth affects the orbits of distant stars, so can your list and data organization efforts ripple throughout the cosmos. (Or at least across the vast plane of your hard disk platter.)

MANAGING LISTS OF STUFF

We're drowning in information and starving for knowledge.

Rutherford D. Rogers
New York Times, February 25, 1985

Stuff *n.*   1. the material or substance out of which anything is or can be made; raw material   2. constituent elements or basic nature; essence; character (*Webster's New World Dictionary*, Third College Edition)

Stuff. We've all got it to some degree, in quantities small and large. It's sitting in our Excel workbooks begging to be sorted, collated, sliced, diced, squeezed, transmogrified, and charted for all the world to see. Uhm, or maybe you just need to get the damn report to your boss by noon, eh? Let's inspect a new weapon in your burgeoning arsenal—*the list.*

The list as a tactical weapon

List: A Database by Any Other Name

> No knowledge is so easily found as when it is needed.
>
> Robert Henri
> *The Art Spirit*, 1923

In Excel 5, a **list** is a database. The End. If you know what a database is, you know what an Excel 5 list is and can skip ahead to the section on data forms; otherwise, let's punch it up to Warp 9 for a run through the Database Quadrant.

A List is a Flat File is a Database is a List is a ...

> "The rule is, jam tomorrow, and jam yesterday—but never jam today."
> "It must come sometimes to 'jam today,'" Alice objected.
> "No, it can't," said the Queen. "It's jam every other day: today isn't any other day, you know."
>
> Lewis Carroll
> *Alice's Adventures in Wonderland*, 1865

Database defined

Database—"Loosely, any aggregation of data; a file consisting of a number of records (or tables), each of which is constructed of fields (columns) of a particular type, together with a collection of operations that facilitate searching, sorting, recombination, and similar activities."(*Microsoft Press Computer Dictionary*, 2nd ed.)

"Loosely" eh? The only way to go. *Heh, heh, heh.*

Ah, but there's more. Much more. Database books by the jumpin' jillions! Let's cut to the chase, Executive Summary style. A record is a row in a database. A field is a column in a database. Each record (row) contains information about one specific entity and no other. Each field (column) represents data of a particular type. For example, in a hypothetical address book database, the fields might be First Name, Last Name, Company Name, Detailed Description of Most Embarrassing Moment Ever, Phone Number...you know, mundane stuff like that.

Flat file database defined

Databases come in two flavors—flat file and relational. (We've heard tales of database engineers falling off the edge of a flat file, but that couldn't be true, could it?) In a **flat file database**, there's no relationship between individual records, not even a torrid one. In your address book database of the flat file variety, let's say that record 17 contains your mother's address data and record 987 contains Zaphod Beeblebrox's address data. Record 17 doesn't know squat about the data in record 987. As for **relational databases**, we turn again to the dog-eared *Microsoft Press Computer Dictionary*:

"A type of database…that stores information in tables—rows and columns of data—and *conducts searches by using data in specified columns of one table to find additional data in another table*" (emphasis ours). See Microsoft Access.

Relational database defined

An Excel 5 list is a flat file database. Amen.

Translated into ExcelSpeak, this means you've got a sheet with rows organized as records and columns organized as fields. But, you might be wondering, what *exactly* do I have to do to tell Excel that this-here stuff is a list? Glad you asked!

List defined

Creating a List

The answer to the question you just asked is: *Excel already knows it's a list!* Any contiguous range of rows and columns is a list. To expedite the Excel feature set that deals with lists, there is some homework you can do first.

Here are our two key rules governing the creation of a list in Excel:

- Rule 1—The first row should contain your list's column labels (a.k.a. field names, for example, "Company Name" or "Street Address"). Excel looks at the first physical row in a list and, using built-in heuristics, figures out if that first row contains column labels or raw data and it reacts accordingly, thereby saving you time. (Later in this chapter ,we explain the heuristics Excel uses.) If Excel thinks the first row is data not labels, it proposes boilerplate column labels like "Column A." Fair enough. (Note that the terms "column labels" and "header row" are synonymous.)

Our rules for clean list living

- Rule 2—A list can't contain blank rows or columns.

That's it! There are additional precepts you can follow to make managing your lists easier (discussed shortly), but the two preceding rules are all you need for a jump start.

Excel's list management feature set is extensive, and we cover 'em all. Here's a teaser list to wet your whistle:

List management features

1. Sort data in a list (although it is true that you can sort without using AutoFilter).

2. Filter a list to display only rows that match your search criteria.

3. Calculate and display automatic subtotals and grand totals.

4. Create cross-tabulation pivot tables.

5. Add, change, and delete records in a list using an automated creature called a data form.

In addition to our hallowed Rules 1 and 2, here are a few noncritical but beneficial precepts to enhance your list management chores.

List Extremities

The smallest possible list is a single cell. This is merely a bit of Excel trivia, of course, since such a list has no practical value, but Excel can deal with it. The largest possible list is an entire sheet—16,384 records and 256 fields. (You'd better have 128 MB of RAM on hand for that one because, as was discussed in Chapter 1, it's almost impossible to utilize an entire Excel worksheet.)

One Sheet, One List

It is possible to have more than one list on a sheet, but AutoFilter can only be active for one list at a time. The optimal strategy is to have one sheet for each list in a particular workbook.

However, if you need multiple lists on a single sheet, *separate each list from its siblings with at least one blank column and row and use the diagonal offset technique described in Chapter 2.* This avoids any confusion about where each list begins or ends, and also prevents any filtering activity on one list from affecting lists (or data of any kind) to the left or right of the current list.

Field Content, Rooting and Grubbing

> Discovery consists of seeing what everybody has seen and thinking what nobody has thought.
>
> Albert Szent-Györgyi von Nagyrapolt
> *The Scientist Speculates*, I. J. Good (ed.), 1962

The content of fields in your list can affect sorting and searching. There are three issues here: capitalization, formulas, and leading spaces. Capitalization only affects sorting if you explicitly select the Sort Options dialog's Case Sensitive check box. Formulas in a list are sorted based on their return values. Leading spaces at the beginning of text in a cell are legitimate characters and definitely affect sorting. Excel's default ascending sort order puts spaces smack in between the characters "9" and "!" so you should only prefix with spaces if you've got a damn good reason.

Target Lock on Column Labels

Column labels benefit you when sorting, filtering, and creating pivot tables, features that are discussed later in this chapter. Without column labels, data in a list is a mass of undifferentiated stuff, like a basketball game scoreboard with no "Home" and "Away" labels above the two team scores. How are you gonna know who's winning? Similarly, in an Excel list, how are you gonna know what the data below represents unless there's a column label above?

- Sorting—Column labels allow the Sort dialog to automatically stuff your list's labels into its Sort By controls, thereby saving you time. See Figure 7.3 later in this chapter.

- Filtering—If your first row is *not* a header row, AutoFilter blithely treats your first data row as a set of labels, thereby omitting those values from the automatic filtration process. Hey, you gave it no other choice! (See Figure 7.12 later in this chapter.)

- Creating pivot tables—The PivotTable Wizard's layout panel field buttons are based on data values instead of field names. Unreadable. Unusable. Fubar.

A common format for column labels is a quick click on the Bold or Italic buttons. You can apply any Alignment, Font, Border, or Pattern attributes that distinguish the labels from the rest of the list. Amazingly clever, those Redmond Rangers, 'cuz even a change in case provides Sort with a target lock.

Common format for column labels

Format your column label cells differently from the rest of your list. Excel can use this distinction to "see" that the first row is a header row.

Applying a style called MyHeader or something similar also does the trick, *just make sure that the MyHeader style is indeed different in at least one respect from the rest of the list.* (If you were wondering, yes, we do lose lots of sleep testing this stuff in the lab. One of us actually performed the following little experiment. Create a style called MyHeader with no attributes different from the rest of the list cells, just a different style name. Does Sort automatically recognize the first row as a header row? No. Proof that a different style name is not *by itself* a sufficient distinction.)

Of all the cell formatting attributes you can change that in turn trigger Sort's recognition of a header row (Alignment, various Font attributes, Border, Patterns, and a differentiated style), only Alignment doesn't give Sort a case of amnesia when changing the attributes back to what they were originally. In other words, change Alignment and Sort recognizes the header row, then change it back and Sort still recognizes the header row. Not so for the other aforementioned cell formatting attributes. Weird.

Our general guidelines for naming column labels are mostly common sense. Use normal capitalization, for example, "Ship Region" instead of "ship region." Don't worry about avoiding spaces because Excel doesn't object to them at all, for example, "Ship Region" is vastly more readable than "ShipRegion" and, after all, humans build computers not vice versa. Keep a name's total character count at or under 30 characters for readability in the list itself, data forms, and the PivotTable layout panel.

Name That List

Naming a list is a good idea, and naming it Database is optimal. First, there's the standard perquisite that a named range is easy to refer to. Second, as we mentioned in the preceding paragraph, if your list's column labels are not formatted differently from the rest of your list, Sort assumes the current range has no column labels, *even if the current range is a list with AutoFilter activated.* Naming the list Database guarantees that Sort sees the first row as a header row every time, whether it's formatted differently from the rest of the list or not.

Now before we explore the innumerable, intricate wonders of AutoFilter, we must first cut our teeth on data modification and sorting. Then we can tackle filtering head-on and no holds barred. What better place to begin than with the utilitarian data form.

The Data Form: Presto Chango

> Nous avons changé tout cela. (We have changed all that.)
>
> Molière
> *Le Médecin Malgré Lui,* 1666

A data form is an instant dialog box produced by Excel to contain your list's column labels, a text box for each one, and a complete set of button controls for viewing, adding, changing, deleting, and searching records in your list. It's better than a Chia Pet 'cuz you don't even have to add water! See Figure 7.1.

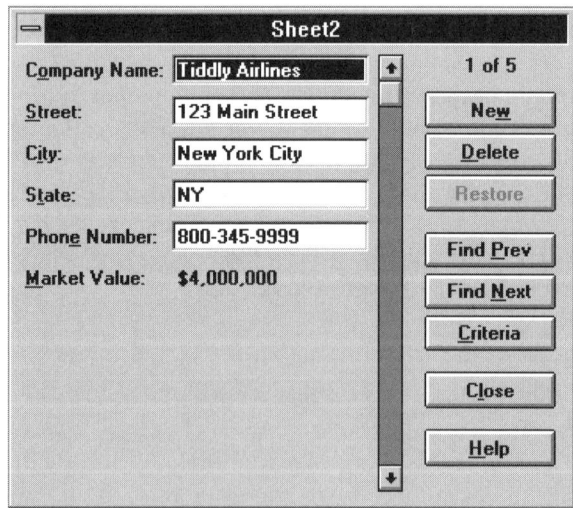

Figure 7.1 Flying the Friendly Data Form

A data form can display a maximum of 32 fields. If you have more than 32 fields in your list, you'll have to either reduce the field count (not always a viable option, we grant you) or hide one or more columns until the total displayed field count is no more than 32. This latter workaround doesn't do you much good if you need to view and/or modify more than 32 fields simultaneously, in which case, you're a good candidate for an industrial-strength relational database management system like Microsoft Access.

Data form can show 32 fields maximum.

The contents of editable fields appear in text boxes. Calculated values and protected fields are displayed on the data form, but you can't edit them. (In Figure 7.1, Market Value is a calculated field.)

To view records, click the View Next or View Previous button or move along the scroll bar. To add a record, click New or drag the scroll box to the bottom of the scroll bar (all fields are cleared and the record counter in the upper right corner reads "New Record"). To delete a record, click Delete.

When you're browsing with a data form, have a liter-size jug of bug repellent handy (preferably the custom juice that John Goodman used to good effect in "Arachniphobia"). Set up a simple five-item list and select Data Form. The displayed list starts on the first record (Record Number Indicator reads "1 of 5") and the scroll box is at the top of the scroll bar. So far so good. Click Find Next once and notice that the scroll box doesn't move down. Continue clicking Find Next and the scroll box sticks to the top of the scroll bar. Click Find Next all the way to the last record in the list and the tab's still stuck.

You can click on the scroll bar's up and down arrows to move one record at a time, which brings up the next record as appropriate, updates the Record Number Indicator, and moves the scroll bar tab. It sure looks to us as though the scroll bar and the Find buttons march to the beat of two entirely different drummers. It gets worse. With the last record displayed, click once on the scroll box. The Record Number Indicator now shows "1 of 5" while the record displayed is the last record (5 of 5)—that's right, the displayed record doesn't change! "Red Leader, we've got bandits at five o'clock high!"

To search for records that match search criteria (one or more chunks of information that you're looking for inside a list):

1. Click Criteria.

2. Enter the desired search criteria (as explained in the next paragraph).

3. Press Find Next or Find Prev to locate the next record that matches the criteria (but the scroll box still stays riveted at the top of the scroll bar).

To clear all criteria and return to the first record in the list:

1. Click Criteria.
2. Click Clear.
3. Click Form.

On to criteria searching, bug jug in hand. Using the procedure just described, say the first record's Company Name field contains "Charlie Airlines" and you enter a criterion of "charlie"—without the quotes—then press Find Next. (Assume that there is only one record that matches to this criterion.) The form displays the correct record, but it beeps. Why? We understand why it beeps when you click Find Next a *second* time (because there's only one matching record so there's no next record to be found), but beeping on the very first hit is incomprehensible. Go figure.

Perform one criteria-based search that returns at least one record. Now specify an entirely new set of criteria that are guaranteed to return no records and click Find Next. The data form beeps and displays the very last record you looked at in your previous criteria-based search, implying that this record matches your current criteria, *which it decidedly does not*. Go figure, again *<sigh>*. At the very least there should be a message box indicating that no matching records could be found.

Fair warning about changing records with a data form—changes are permanently, irrevocably saved when you take any of these actions: press Enter, click the New button, click the Close button, or move to another record via the scroll box. If, before you take any of these actions, you want to restore the record to the way it was originally, click Restore.

Oddly, if you make a change and then press Find Next or Find Prev, Excel actually throws away your changes *without asking you*, as though there's an automatic background Restore being done for you every time you press Find Next or Find Prev. Thanks, but no thanks.

Since column labels can be as long as the maximum length of text in a cell (255 characters), you might be tempted to use some ridiculously long field names (we were, *heh, heh, heh*). The resulting data form doesn't object to the label's length, but it sure does look funny when the form is twice as wide as the video display and the text boxes and command buttons are stacked up like cordwood in a Montana winter (see Figure 7.2).

In Excel 5 you can build your own data form as an Excel 5 dialog hooked up to VBA macros. If you have a data form that's a vestige from Excel 4, rest assured that you can retrieve and convert that form into an Excel 5 dialog. This conversion process is well documented in the *User's Guide* and the help file.

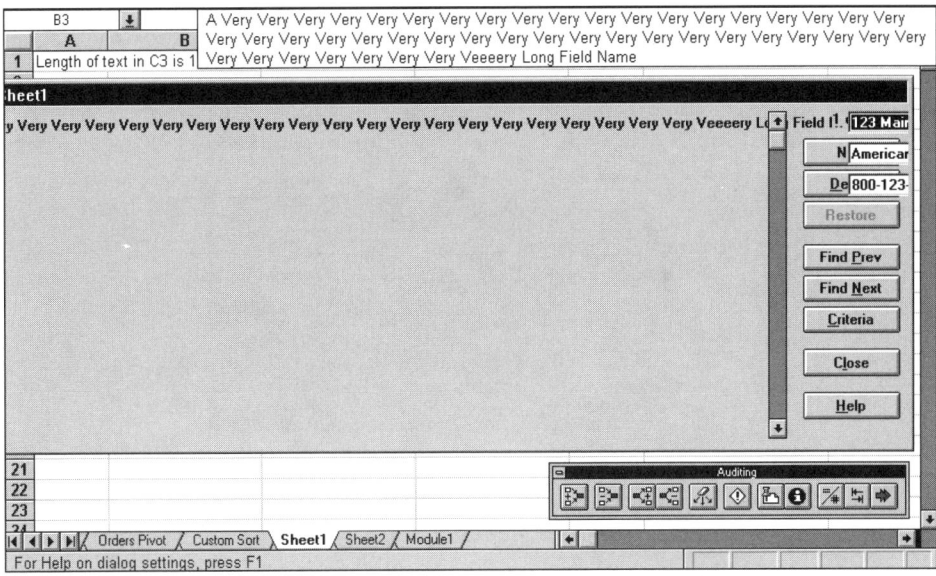

Figure 7.2 Data Form Goes Cubist

Sorting a List

> Order and simplification are the first steps toward the mastery of a
> subject—the actual enemy is the unknown.
>
> Thomas Mann
> *The Magic Mountain*, 1924

Filtering a list and sorting a list are two entirely different processes. When you
filter a list, you may end up with no rows, a few rows, all the rows in the list, or
somewhere in between. It all depends on what you ask Excel to search for. When
you sort a list, you always end up with the same number of rows as when you
started, only they're in a different order. This explanation may seem as plain as the
inevitability of Microsoft's being the first software company to achieve a nuclear
strike capability, but it's an important distinction to bear in mind because—
filtering a list does *not* automatically sort that list.

Filtering changes the display of the list so that it reveals only the records that
match your search criteria *but the resulting records are left in their original order*. In
order (pun intended), let's explore sorting and then filtering.

**Filtering leaves
records in their
original order.**

Do This First or Else!

You can sort a list whether it's AutoFilter-enabled or not. Select any cell inside the
list, select Data, and choose Sort. Excel's Sort dialog pops up (see Figure 7.3). If

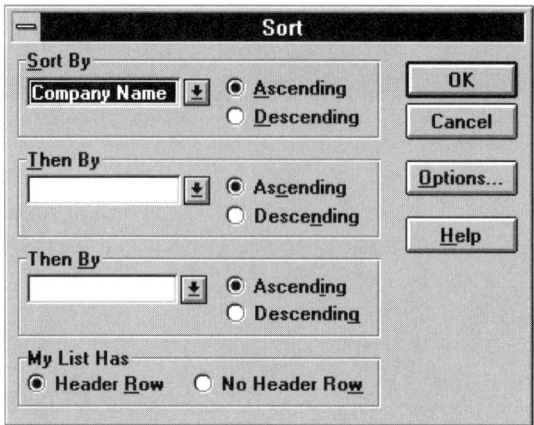

Figure 7.3 The Sanguine Sort Dialog Box

you accidentally select more than one cell in the list, Excel detects the adjacent data and asks you if you want to expand the selection or continue with the current selection. Typically you want to expand the selection. See Figure 7.4.

	A	B	C
1	*Company Name*	*Street*	*City*
2	Tiddly Airlines	123 Main Street	New York City
3	delta Lower Case Airlines	234 Secondary Street	San Clemente
4	Delta River Airlines	3456 Tertiary Street	Los Angeles
5	Bavarian Airlines	989 Polygon Place	Jacksonville
6	Leading Space Airlines	899 Hexagon Circle	Atlanta
7			
8	**Sort Warning**		
9	Microsoft Excel found data next to your	**Sort...**	
10	selection. Since you have not selected		
11	this data, it will not be sorted.	**Cancel**	
12	What do you want to do?		
13	● Expand the selection	**Help**	
14	○ Continue with the current selection		
15			

Figure 7.4 Sort Warning When You Select More Than One
Cell But Less Than the Entire List

If there is the slightest possibility that you'll someday need to return your list to its original order, insert a new column somewhere in the list that contains unique record numbers for each row. The fastest way to do this is...you guessed it...*AutoFill!* Then hide this column until the dark and stormy night when you'd pawn the family jewels for it.

Default Sort Order Rules

> Had I been present at the creation, I would have given some useful hints for the better ordering of the universe.
>
> Attributed to Alfonso X

A set of default sort order rules govern sorting. Excel sorts data first by type and then within type by the additional rules discussed here. For an ascending sort (one that moves up the series, for example, the alphabet in ascending order is A..Z but in descending order is Z..A), Excel arranges data as follows:

1. Numbers—from the smallest negative to the largest positive, treating dates and times as values, for example, a cell containing `NOW()` is sorted as a number based on its value of `34431.7439047454`, not on its formatted appearance as `4/7/1994 5:51:13 PM`.

2. Text—character sort order is number characters, followed by various punctuation marks, and then the letters of the alphabetic (see the *User's Guide* for the precise sequences and how to change character sort order by nationality). Remember that the space character comes in between the "9" character and the standard punctuation characters but before the alphabet characters, like this

    0 1 2 3 4 5 6 7 8 9 (space) ! " # $ % & ' ( ) * + , - . / : ; < = > ? @ [\ ] ^ _ ` { | } ~ A B C D E F G H I J K L M N O P Q R S T U V W X Y Z

   > **The space comes after "9" and before "1!"**

3. Booleans (logicals)—FALSE then TRUE.

4. Errors—appear together in their original order, that is, are all weighted equally.

5. Blanks—always last, *whether the sort is ascending or descending*.

   > **Blank records are always last.**

See Figure 7.5 for a sample ascending sort that includes all the data types. Be aware that this figure is for demonstration purposes only. It's very unusual to mix data types like this in a database column. Strictly speaking, it's verboten.

A descending sort of the list based on the Field of Dreams column would reverse the order of rows 7 through 18, with two notable exceptions:

- Rows 19 and 20 would remain the lowly Blank This Company and Blank This Too Company, respectively, because blanks always, always, always get trail sweep duty.

- Erroneous Co. would still appear before Another Erroneous Co. because error values have the same sort ranking among themselves, regardless of direction.

	6	7	8
6	**Company Name**	**Field of Dreams**	**Original**
7	Minus One, Inc.	-1	7
8	Plus Two, Ltd.	2	8
9	Time Warner, Inc.	4/7/94 17:51	11
10	Leading Space, Inc.	800RealBigGorillas	13
11	Bavarian Airlines	800-234-5678	1
12	Charlie Airlines	800-345-9999	2
13	Big Gorilla, P.A.	800BigGorillas	12
14	Normal Everyday Text Co.	Hello world	14
15	Falsely Logical Company	FALSE	6
16	Truly Logical Company	TRUE	5
17	Erroneous Co.	#DIV/0!	9
18	Another Erroneous Co.	#VALUE!	10
19	Blank This Company		3
20	Blank This Too Company		4
21			

Figure 7.5 Up Up and Away! (Ascending Sort Based on "Field of Dreams" Column)

Sure-fire Cure for Xenophobic Data

The *User's Guide* suggests that if a column contains mixed numeric and text data, and you want the contents to be sorted as if all the data is text, you should insert an apostrophe prefix into each numeric cell. This works, but can take a long time to do manually. Yes, you could write a macro to do this for you, but we're opposed to this idea on general principle because it alters the original data.

Don't touch that data! Instead, insert a column to the right of the source data, copy the formula

```
=TEXT(RC[-1],0)
```

into each cell, and then use this new column for the sort. You can hide or delete it after the sort, as appropriate. You may have to use a format text parameter other than 0 in the TEXT() function, depending on your specific needs. Keep in mind that a sort based on the result of this TEXT() formula is really a pure text sort.

For example, in an ascending sort, if your source values are 100.13 and 100.12 (in their original order) and your adjacent sort formula is =TEXT(RC[-1],"0.#"), don't be surprised when a sort does *not* put the row containing 100.12 ahead of 100.13! Wuzzat? These two different numeric values are both being sorted as the identical text strings "100.1" based on the function's parameter "0.#". However, change the format text parameter to "0.##" and the sort behaves as you desire. Moral of the story: Watch your significant digits when converting numbers to text, friend.

Here are a few miscellaneous sorting morsels for you to masticate:

- The positions of hidden rows in a list don't change during a sort unless they're part of an outline. (Note: In Excel 4, the opposite is true—hidden rows do get sorted whether in outline mode or not—so be careful if you're accustomed to the old Excel 4 behavior.)

- Sort options are sticky from one sort action to another (on the current list) until you explicitly change an option. And the stickiness persists across Excel sessions.

- The Sort dialog supports a maximum of three separate fields. Therefore, for deeper sorts, sort the three least important fields first and then proceed with the remaining fields as appropriate.

Tailor-made Sort Orders

> Surfer No. 1: Man, that was an epic session.
> Surfer No. 2: Yeah, but you shoulda been here *yesterday*.
>
> Ubiquitous surfer dialog

Excel provides a way for you to roll your own sort order. Here's an example using Lee's surfing diary. Note the use of a four-item custom list to describe, in SurfSpeak (*hey bro', killer barrel*), the overall quality of a particular surf session. From worst to best, the list is: "Sleep in," "Why not?," "I'm out there," and "Epic."

By keying one of the four possible rankings into a column in the list, you can sort the list in the custom sort order—*this is not a traditional alphabetic sort*. In fact, that's the whole point of a custom sort order. In an ascending sort that uses this custom sort order, "Sleep in" comes before "Epic" even though alphabetically "E" precedes "S." Righteous, dude!

Here's the drill. Create the custom list via Tools Options Custom Lists. Select Data Sort, select Rank in the Sort By drop-down and Ascending. Click the Options button, select the "Sleep in,..." list from the First Key Sort Order drop-down (see Figure 7.6).

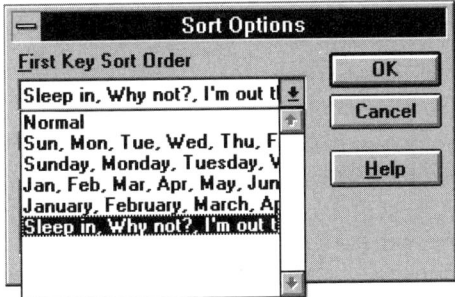

Figure 7.6 Applying a Custom Sort Order

Click OK to close the Sort Options dialog and click OK again to close the Sort dialog and engage the sort.

The resulting list, custom sorted in order from worst to best, looks like Figure 7.7.

	A	B	C	D	E	F	G	H	I	J
					Avg Swell	Swell	Swell			Tide
1	Date	Rank	Location	Time	Height	Origin	Interval	Wind	Tide	Direction
2	11/4/93	Sleep in	1st Street	8:00 AM	2.0	290	12	Onshore	4.0	Incoming
3	11/7/93	Sleep in	1st Street	8:00 AM	0.5	275	6	Onshore	1.0	Outgoing
4	11/10/93	Why not?	1st Street	7:00 AM	2.5	275	8	Calm	2.0	Outgoing
5	11/11/93	Why not?	1st Street	7:30 AM	2.5	275	8	Calm	1.5	Outgoing
6	11/1/93	I'm out there	The C-Spot	7:00 AM	4.0	290	14	Offshore	3.5	Incoming
7	11/3/93	I'm out there	The C-Spot	9:00 AM	3.0	290	14	Calm	4.5	High
8	11/17/93	I'm out there	The Park	7:00 AM	5.0	275	10	Offshore	3.0	Incoming
9	11/18/93	I'm out there	The Park	7:30 AM	4.0	275	10	Calm	4.5	High
10	11/19/93	I'm out there	The C-Spot	8:00 AM	3.5	275	10	Calm	4.0	Outgoing
11	11/27/93	I'm out there	The C-Spot	7:30 AM	5.5	295	14	Calm	3.0	Incoming
12	11/26/93	Epic	The C-Spot	7:00 AM	6.0	295	14	Calm	1.5	Incoming

Figure 7.7 Gnarly Custom Sort, Dude

Microsoft Query and ODBC

> Life is a foreign language; all men mispronounce it.
>
> Christopher Morley
> *Thunder on the Left*, 1925

Friends, pilgrims, fellow Excel worshippers, gather round the camp fire. We've got an announcement. Some of you have expressed curiosity about Microsoft Query and ODBC. Fair enough. Here's the tale.

The keys to Get External Data

These two creatures, when melded with Excel, provide access to data that resides somewhere in the ether outside Excel (a.k.a. "foreign database"). Maybe an Access, FoxPro, dBASE, or Paradox database; or even a SQL database living a happy, charmed life on a host mainframe. You will undoubtedly be treating this data as a list inside Excel, so that's why we're mentioning Query and ODBC at this juncture.

Query is a data-access application that can either stand on its own two feet or join forces with Excel via the Query Add-in. The Add-in allows either you or Excel's macro languages (XLM and VBA) to interact with Query and, ultimately, the foreign database. Alternately, you can use the ODBC Function Add-in to interact with foreign databases *without using Query*.

You access Query from *inside* Excel via the Data menu, like this. Select Data then choose Get External Data to start Query. Now you can "go up against" external data (as the database gurus say). If Get External Data isn't on your Data menu, pop over to Tools Add-Ins and check the MS Query Add-In check box. If MS Query Add-In isn't there, check the *Excel User's Guide* or the *Query User's Guide* for specific installation instructions.

ODBC is an acronym—*who the hell makes these up without asking us common folk!*—for open database connectivity, and it represents a set of specifications used to provide access to various data sources. ODBC exists as a set of drivers implemented as DLLs (dynamic link libraries), a driver manager, and an administrative Windows Control Panel utility. Each data source has its own DLL driver. This hoopla all ships with Excel. If you can't find a specific component on your system, check the *Excel User's Guide* or the *Query User's Guide* for specific installation instructions. With that tale woven, in the very next section on AutoFilter, we provide detailed steps for going up against an Access database.

Acronym soup

AutoFilter: More of That Microsoft Magic

"I weep for you," the Walrus said:
"I deeply sympathize."
With sobs and tears he sorted out
Those of the largest size,
Holding his pocket-handkerchief
Before his streaming eyes.

Lewis Carroll
The Walrus and the Carpenter

Throughout this section we deal with a list that contains individual in-process orders to a variety of customers, each order identified by a unique value in the Order ID field. Here are the steps for getting this data using Excel's Get External Data feature:

1. Create a new workbook and select cell A1 in Sheet1.

Steps for grabbing external data

2. Select Tools Add-Ins. If MS Query Add-In is listed and checked in the Add-Ins Available list box, proceed to step 3. Otherwise, refer to the *User's Guide* for installation instructions.

3. Select Data Get External Data. This starts Microsoft Query and the Select Data Source dialog box appears. If you did a typical Excel installation, you'll see NWind in the Available Data Sources list box. This represents the Northwind sample database that ships with Excel 5. *But don't select NWind.* Why not? Because this particular database is in dBASE format and has only 39 records in the Orders table, which is not a rich enough data source for our purposes. This chapter's examples work with the industrial-strength version of the Northwind sample database that ships with Microsoft Access. The Access version contains 1078 records in the ORDERS table. So, to follow along with our examples, you need the Access version of the Northwind database.

4. Press the Other button.

5. Select MS Access Databases in the list in the ODBC Data Sources dialog then click on OK.

6. Scroll to locate the NWIND.MDB database file and once this file is selected, click on OK.

7. MS Query returns to the Select Data Source dialog with MS Access Databases already selected in the Available Data Sources list box. Click the Use button.

8. From the Add Tables dialog, select the ORDERS table, press Add, and then press Close.

9. Double-click the asterisk at the top of the ORDERS table frame (immediately above the Customer ID field name). This selects all fields and all records, and places them in the data pane. See Figure 7.8.

10. Select File Return Data to Microsoft Excel. Query automatically returns focus to Excel, where you see the Get External Data dialog. Accept the default selections—Keep Query Definition check box selected, Include Field Definitions check box selected, Include Row Numbers cleared, and a Destination of

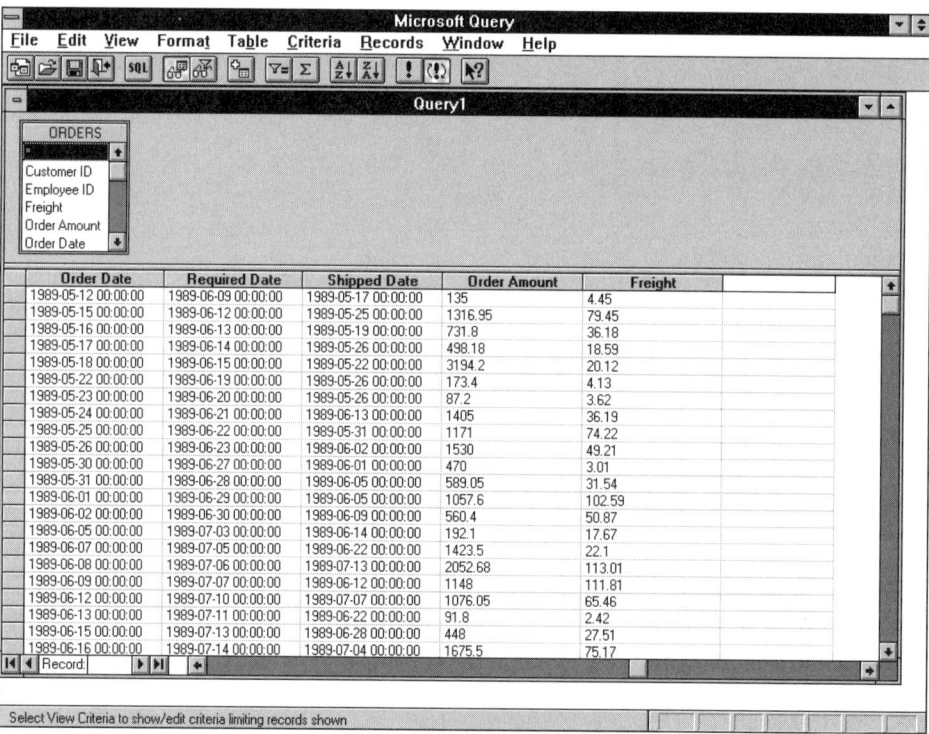

Figure 7.8 MS Query at Work on the NWind Orders Table

Sheet1!$A$1. (BTW, if you select the Help button here, Excel's title bar starts flashing annoyingly. *Don't panic!* It means Excel wants the focus back. Ignore it, read the help text as needed, and then simply `Alt + Tab` to return to Excel as usual. The title bar will stop convulsing.)

11. Click OK and stand back for the fireworks. For about 5–10 seconds, your screen dances about, the status bar reading "Getting data..." When the dust settles—look for "Ready" on the status bar—you've got yourself an external database sitting pretty in Sheet1.

To activate AutoFilter, select any single cell inside the list, select Data Filter, and choose AutoFilter on the flyout menu. *Remember that, even before you activate AutoFilter, your sheet contains a valid list.* But it's not until you activate AutoFilter that you can put AutoFilter's first class feature set to good use. See Figure 7.9.

	A	B	C	D	E	F
1	Order ↓	Customer ID ↓	Employee ID ↓	Ship Name ↓	Ship Address ↓	Ship City ↓
2	10000	FRUGF	6	Frugal Feast Comestibles	Evans Plaza☐ 531 - 2nd Ave.	Eugene
3	10001	MERRG	8	Merry Grape Wine Merchants	304 King Edward Pl.	East Vancouver
4	10002	FOODI	3	Foodmongers, Inc.	418 - 6th Ave.	Walla Walla
5	10003	SILVS	8	Silver Screen Food Gems	12 Meikeljohn Ln.	Helena
6	10004	VALUF	3	ValuMax Food Stores	986 Chandler Dr.	Austin
7	10005	WALNG	5	Walnut Grove Grocery	33 Upper Arctic Dr.	Buffalo
8	10006	FREDE	8	Fred's Edibles, Etc.	1522 College Blvd.	Bellingham
9	10007	MORNS	4	Morning Star Health Foods	45 N. Terminal Way	Helena
10	10008	FUJIA	3	Fujiwara Asian Specialties	72 Dowlin Pkwy.	Phoenix
11	10009	SEVES	8	Seven Seas Imports	90 Wadhurst Rd.	London
12	10010	SILVS	8	Silver Screen Food Gems	12 Meikeljohn Ln.	Helena
13	10011	WELLT	6	Wellington Trading	16 Newcomen Rd.	Sevenoaks
14	10012	LIVEO	6	Live Oak Hotel Gift Shop	7384 Washington Ave.	Portland
15	10013	RITEB	3	Rite-Buy Supermarket	2226 Shattuck Ave.	Berkeley

Figure 7.9 AutoFilter Activated

The drop-down arrows that Excel adds to the column label cells are your visual clue that the list is now in AutoFilter mode. To turn AutoFilter off, select Data Filter and again choose AutoFilter on the flyout menu. (When turning AutoFilter off, it doesn't matter if the active cell is inside the list or not.) If you ever select more than a single cell but less than your entire list before AutoFiltering, Excel interprets this range as a list within a list.

Drop-down arrows appear in the column label cells.

Now that AutoFilter is active, let's ask the list some questions. To find out how many orders are destined for Kirkland, click on the Ship City down-arrow (see Figure 7.10). You can filter to include all records, perform a Custom filter, select from an alphabetized list of field contents to filter by, and filter all blanks or all nonblanks.

	E	F	G
	Ship Address	*Ship City*	*Ship Regio*
	2817 Milton Dr.	[All]	NM
	2817 Milton Dr.	(Custom...)	NM
	2817 Milton Dr.	Albuquerque	NM
	2817 Milton Dr.	Aloha	NM
	2817 Milton Dr.	Anacortes	NM
	2817 Milton Dr.	Anchorage	NM
	2817 Milton Dr.	Auburn	NM
	2817 Milton Dr.	Austin	NM
	2817 Milton Dr.	Albuquerque	NM
	2817 Milton Dr.	Albuquerque	NM

Figure 7.10 AutoFilter's Drop-down Arrow Control

Scroll down and select Kirkland (or press the K key), press Enter or double-click, and the list is distilled to the three records that match Kirkland. (See Figure 7.11.) Yo! This is righteous! To return the list to its full display (no filtering), select Data Filter and choose Show All on the flyout. (There's no Edit Undo for AutoFilter.)

	A	B	C	D	E	F	G
1	Order ID	Customer ID	Employee ID	Ship Name	Ship Address	Ship City	Ship Regio
428	10574	TRAIH	4	Trail's Head Gourmet Provision	722 Dynamite Blvd.	Kirkland	WA
429	10577	TRAIH	9	Trail's Head Gourmet Provision	722 Dynamite Blvd.	Kirkland	WA
430	10822	TRAIH	6	Trail's Head Gourmet Provision	722 Dynamite Blvd.	Kirkland	WA
1080							

Figure 7.11 Filterin' It on Down

The visual clues AutoFilter provides are awesomely keen, eh? Marvel at the *electric blue* coloring of the Ship City's drop-down arrow control and the *electric blue* row headers for the matching rows. The status bar message "3 of 1078 records found" is a nice touch, too.

What's AutoFilter doing in the background? It asks the list to return only those records that match your search criterion. In the Kirkland search, the English version of the query goes like this, "Yo, List, if it's not too much trouble, please show me the rows that contain exactly the string 'Kirkland' in the Ship City field. Thank you kindly." Logically translated as, "Show Rows Where Ship City = Kirkland." AutoFilter supports all of Excel's standard comparison operators.

Figure 7.12 shows you the penalty for not having a header row; namely, cells in the first row get substituted as column headings and these values are therefore eliminated from the set of available filtration values...sorta. In this case, "New York City" is not in the drop-down's list of filtration values. You can still use Custom AutoFilter and manually type in "New York City," but this starts to get very confusing, not to mention self-defeating. The way to avoid the confusion is to...guess what...*use an explicit header row in a list!*

	A	B	C	D	E	F
1	Tiddly Airlines	123 Main Street	New York C	NY	800-345-9999	$4,000,00
2	Delta River Airlines	3456 Tertiary Street	(All)	CA	800-987-6543	$2,500,000
3	delta Lower Case Airlines	234 Secondary Stree	(Custom...) Atlanta	CA	800-987-6543	$3,000,000
4	Bavarian Airlines	989 Polygon Place	Jacksonville	FL	800-234-5678	$1,000,000
5	Leading Space Airlines	899 Hexagon Circle	Los Angeles San Clemente	GA	800-222-3334	$250,000
6			(Blanks)			
7			(NonBlanks)			
8						

Figure 7.12 No Header Row Omits a Filtration Value

Custom AutoFilter

To build your own custom search, including wildcard characters and a logical AND or a logical OR (say that five times real fast) of values *in the same field*, you need Custom AutoFilter. Say you want to see all foreign orders. It's as easy as rolling downhill.

1. Click on Ship Country's down-arrow.
2. Choose (Custom...). Excel displays the Custom AutoFilter dialog box (see Figure 7.13).
3. Choose <> from the comparison operator drop-down.
4. Choose USA from the field drop-down.
5. Click on OK.

374 records lickety-split.

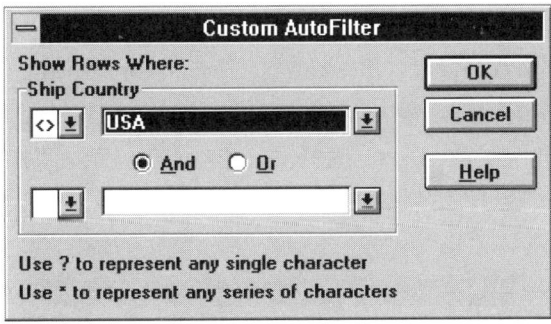

Figure 7.13 Making It Easier with Custom AutoFilter

The only weird thing about Custom AutoFilter is the null item at the top of the comparison operator drop-down list. Click it and then click on OK. Excel prompts you: "Error in parse line." Yeah, like, right. The associated help topic text is gonzo cryptic (clearly meaningful to those brave souls who relish building their own SQL queries, square brackets, and all). Chalk it up as a "Previously Unreported Requirement" (the latest MicroSpeak euphemism for "bug.") *Heh, heh, heh.*

Advanced Filter

> The folly of mistaking a paradox for a discovery, a metaphor for a proof, a torrent of verbiage for a spring of capital truths, and oneself for an oracle is inborn in us.
>
> Paul Valéry
> Introduction to the *Method of Leonardo da Vinci*, 1895

Advanced Filter comes into play when your search criteria cover more than one field or involve a comparison that's too complex for the basic AutoFilter. For example, if you want to see all foreign orders with a value in excess of $2000, the logical expression is

Show Rows Where (Ship Country <> USA) AND (Order Amount >= 2000)

Instead of using AutoFilter's drop-down controls, you need to set up a **criteria range**, ExcelSpeak for a range on the sheet that's separate from the list and containing both the names of the fields to be searched and the search criteria for each field like this:

"How many foreign orders in excess of $2000?" Here's how...

1. Insert three rows above your list's header row. This is where the criteria range will live.

2. Copy the column label Ship Country to A1.

3. Copy the column label Order Amount to B1.

4. Type <>USA into A2. This is the search criterion for the Ship Country field.

5. Type >=2000 into B2. This is the search criterion for the Order Amount field.

6. Select Data Filter and choose Advanced Filter on the flyout menu. Excel displays the Advanced Filter dialog box (see Figure 7.14).

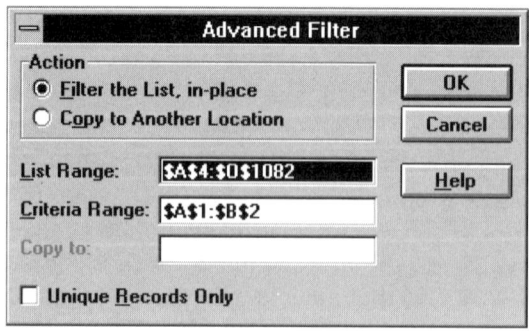

Figure 7.14 The Advanced Filter Dialog Box

7. Click in the Criteria Range text box, highlight A1:B2 on the sheet, and click OK. Excel reveals the 83 records with off-shore orders valued at $2000 or more. If you do an Edit Go To now or walk the Name Box list you'll see the built-in name Criteria defined as $A$1:$B$1. Excel creates it for you automatically whenever you perform an Advanced Filter. If you already have a range named Criteria in the sheet, that range's coordinates appear in the Criteria Range text box. Also, when Advanced Filter creates the range name Criteria, it creates it as a sheet-level name *not* as a book-level name.

The built-in range name Criteria

Complex search criteria can get, well, complex. Twist your brain into a swollen pretzel real quick, yes indeedy. This powerful but complex feature can be extraordinarily useful in certain circumstances, so check out the *User's Guide* for examples. Here are the high points:

- Criteria on the same row are evaluated with a logical AND.

- Criteria on different rows are evaluated with a logical OR, that is, same-row criteria get evaluated first, then offset row criteria are OR'd to each other.

- Criteria can include wildcard characters. A tilde "~" prefix treats a wildcard as a normal character.

- Absolute and relative range references (named or unnamed) are valid within criteria expressions.

- Formulas are valid criteria; in ExcelSpeak these are **computed criteria**.

Now that you've got some answers, where do you put them? In-place filtration is the default, but by selecting the Copy to Another Location radio button in the Advanced Filter dialog, Excel allows you to specify where on the sheet to place the filtered records. If your list contains duplicate records, you can exclude all but the first of any set of duplicate records by selecting the Unique Records Only check box in the Advanced Filter dialog.

Where to put your answers?

Here's how to quickly find out if in fact any duplicates are lurking about in your list. Start with an unfiltered list, select Data Filter Advanced Filter, clear the Criteria Range text box, make sure the Unique Records Only check box is cleared, and click on OK. Note the number of filtered records (x). Now select Data Filter Advanced Filter, clear the Criteria Range text box, check the Unique Records Only, and click on OK. (Fair warning—this can take several seconds; for example, on a 486 DX2/66 with 16 MB of RAM, excluding duplicates in a 1080-row list took 18 seconds.) Note the number of filtered records (y). If the number of records match, there are no duplicates. Otherwise, the list contains $x - y$ duplicate records.

Counting duplicate records

List Subtotals

> Bring us together again.
>
> Richard Milhous Nixon
> Speech in New York City, October 31, 1968

Excel's automatic subtotal feature provides a variety of functions you can automatically (no surprise!) apply to a list. Far more than a one-dimensional summation across the entire list, subtotaling includes some superlative group breakdown capabilities.

Automatic Subtotals

If it's possible to outshine the AutoSum feature, automatic subtotals does so with candlepower to spare. (Don't ask us why the ExcelGods didn't name this feature something like AutoSubtotal, 'cuz Security kept throwin' us out of the marketing meetings!)

Let's go back to our in-process orders list. Say we're curious about order amount subtotals by destination country. Like your first dance lesson at an Arthur Murray studio, it's one two three kick turn...

1. Sort your orders by Ship Country. You must always do an initial sort on the primary column of interest. The documentation calls this "grouping" the list.
2. Select Data Subtotal. Excel displays the Subtotals dialog box (see Figure 7.15).

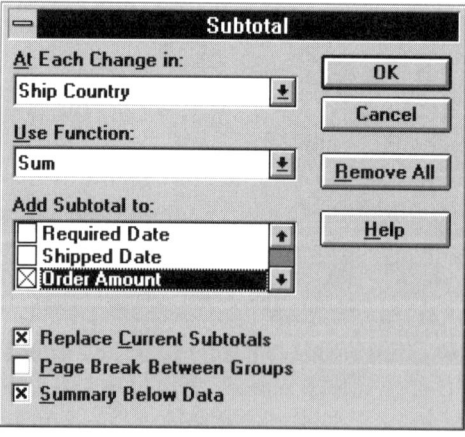

Figure 7.15 The Sublime Subtotal Dialog Box

3. Select Ship Country in the At Each Change in drop-down.

4. Accept the default Sum function. (The dialog discerningly defaults to Sum for a column of numbers and Count for text.)

5. Select Order Amount and select Freight in the Add Subtotal to list box, if it isn't already selected.

6. Select or clear any of the three check boxes that govern formatting, depending on your taste.

7. Click on OK.

Excel automatically outlines the list, leaving it fully expanded. To collapse it one level, press the row level 2 outlining symbol (see Figure 7.16, which shows the outlining symbols, the subtotals by country, and the grand total).

Automatic subtotals use Outlining (automatically, natch).

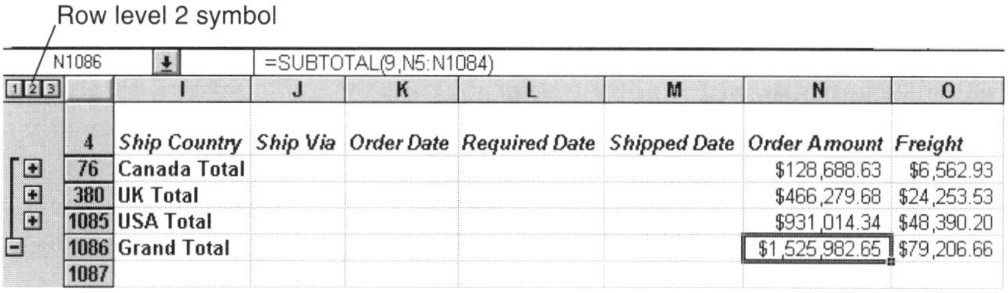

Row level 2 symbol

		I	J	K	L	M	N	O
		Ship Country	Ship Via	Order Date	Required Date	Shipped Date	Order Amount	Freight
	4							
⊞	76	Canada Total					$128,688.63	$6,562.93
⊞	380	UK Total					$466,279.68	$24,253.53
⊞	1085	USA Total					$931,014.34	$48,390.20
⊟	1086	Grand Total					$1,525,982.65	$79,206.66
	1087							

N1086 · =SUBTOTAL(9,N5:N1084)

Figure 7.16 Order Amount and Freight Subtotaled by Country

Note that Excel inserts the appropriate subtotal formula for you. If you browse the list in its fully expanded state (click the row level 3 symbol), you'll see that Excel also automatically inserts subtotal rows between the breaks between each country (group). Nifty. The other summary functions provided are Average, Max, Min, Product, Count Nums, StdDev, StdDevp, Var, and Varp.

Complex Subtotals

There are scads of subtotal permutations awaiting you deep in the heart of your list. You can subtotal a filtered list so that only the resulting (unhidden) records are subtotaled. You can sort a subtotaled list. You can subtotal across more than one group at a time, for example, Order Amount subtotaled by Ship Region within each Ship Country (see Figure 7.17). Multiple functions for groups, you wonder? Sure! Not to mention the use of `COUNTIF()`, `SUMIF()`, and other database functions to report statistics about records in a list that match complex criteria. And so on.

We discovered two nested subtotaling bugs. First, if there are blank cells in a subtotal column (in this list's case, there are 244 UK orders with a blank Ship Region), those blank cell rows get incorrectly included in the subtotal of the last nonblank group for that column (remember, blanks always appear at the bottom of the sort regardless of the sort's order—ascending or descending). In this list's case, the UK's 244 blank Ship Region orders are melded with the Suffolk orders. The overall UK subtotal is correct, but the breakdown of that subtotal is misleading. It certainly would be a surprise to the sales manager responsible for Suffolk orders!

Second, Excel incorrectly displays the subtotal of the last group of the second level in a nested subtotal *below* (instead of above) the subtotal for the first level. Or maybe the first-level subtotal is hiked up one row too far. By either description, something's rotten in the UK. (See Figure 7.17.) For example, Excel displays Essex, Kent, Lancashire, and N. Yorkshire above the UK subtotal, but it displays the Suffolk subtotal *after* the UK subtotal. The group 1 subtotal values are correct except for Suffolk, as we pointed out earlier.

Judging by the arrangement of the outline detail symbols, this appears to us to be an outlining bug, not a subtotaling bug. Bug or no, the key to a nested subtotal is to sort first (by Ship Country by Ship Region), subtotal normally on the first group (Ship Country), and then subtotal on the second group (Ship Region), *clearing the Replace Current Subtotals check box*. (Note: For visual clarity, we moved the Ship Region column to the right of Ship Country. This is no way affects the bug's behavior.)

1 2 3 4		H	I	J	K	L	M	N	O
	4	Ship Country	Ship Region	Ship Via	Order Date	Required Date	Shipped Date	Order Amount	Freight
⊞	76	Canada Total						$128,688.63	$6,562.93
·	77		BC Total					$128,688.63	$6,562.93
⊞	92		Essex Total					$14,602.15	$503.32
⊞	103		Kent Total					$6,657.25	$226.25
⊞	116		Lancashire Total					$7,202.80	$426.75
⊞	127		N. Yorkshire Total					$10,654.81	$405.91
⊞	385	UK Total						$466,279.68	$24,253.53
⊟	386		Suffolk Total					$427,162.67	$22,691.30
⊞	399		AK Total					$17,466.43	$1,084.53
⊞	418		AZ Total					$15,047.23	$818.86

Figure 7.17 A Nested Subtotal Bug

There are two workarounds to this nested subtotal bug. One, use PivotTable (discussed later in this chapter). Two, do all subtotaling backwards, relative to the initial grouping of the sort. It's counterintuitive and clumsy, but it works.

DATA ANALYSIS

> Given for one instant an intelligence which could comprehend all the
> forces by which nature is animated and the respective positions of the
> beings which compose it, if moreover this intelligence were vast enough
> to submit these data to analysis, it would embrace in the same formula
> both the movements of the largest bodies in the universe and those of the
> lightest atom; to it nothing would be uncertain, and the future as the past
> would be present to its eyes.
>
> Pierre Simon de Laplace
> *Oeuvres, vol. VII, Théorie Analytique des Probabilitiés*, 1812–1820

Excel's analytical capabilities are legion. Stellar. Superlative. Rife with possibility.
The mind boggles and sputters when confronted with this vast permutational
plane. But that's what data analysis is all about, eh? Twisting and turning your
data. Tweaking it. Calibrating it. Analyzing it to the left; analyzing it to the right;
analyzing it until it cries out *"Uncle!"* Sifting grains of sand for the mother lode—
causality, correlation, statistical significance. Praise be to the scientific model. So
let's get crackin'.

TextWizard

**Sometimes it's the simple things that bring the greatest joy. Perhaps because
it's so easy to appreciate them? Well, enough philosophizing. What we're
talkin' about here is TextWizard. No middleware protocol-conversion layer on
steroids. No, sir. TextWizard is clean, simple, elegant, and *effective as hell*. If
you've ever gyrated and danced and pleaded and cajoled and cursed while
trying to import some textual data into an Excel sheet, curse no more.**

The mighty TextWizard starts automatically when you open a text file. You
have to be a little careful regarding what Excel recognizes as a text file. An ASCII
file with a .TXT extension is a safe bet. A file with .CSV as an extension is treated
as a comma-separated value file whether it is one or not. Anyway, open a text file
and instead of standing there helplessly like Billy Batson, you're suddenly Captain Marvel with incredible power at your disposal.

If you already have a mass of unparsed text in your sheet, select the text, pull
down the Data menu, and click Text to Columns to invoke the TextWizard.

TextWizard starts off by analyzing the incoming data or text file very
intelligently—offering you choices between delimited and fixed width file types,
starting import row, and file origin. But it usually has already made these choices
correctly. Our favorite of its three dialogs is Step 2 where you choose between
delimiters and text qualifiers, *and get to preview the incoming file in columns inside
the dialog* (see Figure 7.18). Shazam, fer sure.

**Intelligent text/
data file
parsing and
previewing**

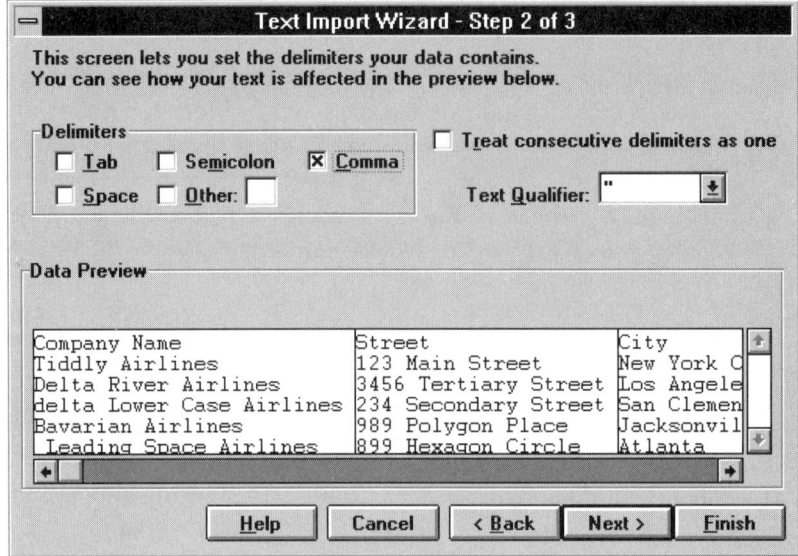

Figure 7.18 TextWizard, the Delta Force of Text Importation

With TextWizard you can parse text data any way you like. Soon you'll have every datum in its proper field (column). Excel has really come a long way in this regard. Kudos, Microsoft.

Pivot Tables

> I am the very model of a modern Major-General.
> I've information vegetable, animal, and mineral,
> I know the Kings of England, and I quote the fights historical,
> From Marathon to Waterloo, in order categorical.
>
> Sir William Schwenck Gilbert
> *H. M. S. Pinafore*, 1878

We're definitely going long on Microsoft stock. *Spend a couple of minutes with pivot tables and you will, too.* **Hell, you'll hock the ranch, your retirement plan, and your kids' college fund, and bet it all on MSFT.**

Slicing and Dicing That Data

Pivot tables are the sharpest way to cut up that data for easy analysis. You won't believe your eyes. How much would you pay for this tool that no kitchen, er, database should be without?

There's no better way to learn about pivot tables than to plunge in head first. Throughout this section we're working with the familiar orders list. We'll put on our financial analyst hat, roll up our shirtsleeves, and get some instant answers to some complex questions. This is gonna be fun!

1. Select Data PivotTable in the book containing the orders list and click on Next.

2. Point to the range containing the source data. (We use the range name Database throughout this example.) Click on Next.

3. Drag the Ship Country field button and drop it in the Row area. Notice the smooth, sleek, voluptuously rounded corners—all the fields appear as buttons stacked neatly in their source list's column order.

4. Drag the Ship Region field button and drop it in the Column area.

5. Drag the Order Amount field button and drop it in the Data area. Excel defaults to a Sum function. (*If you don't have goose bumps by now, you're probably dead!*) See Figure 7.19 for the final layout. (In a moment, we show you how to change the summary function that PivotTable applies to the data.)

Surely this is magic!

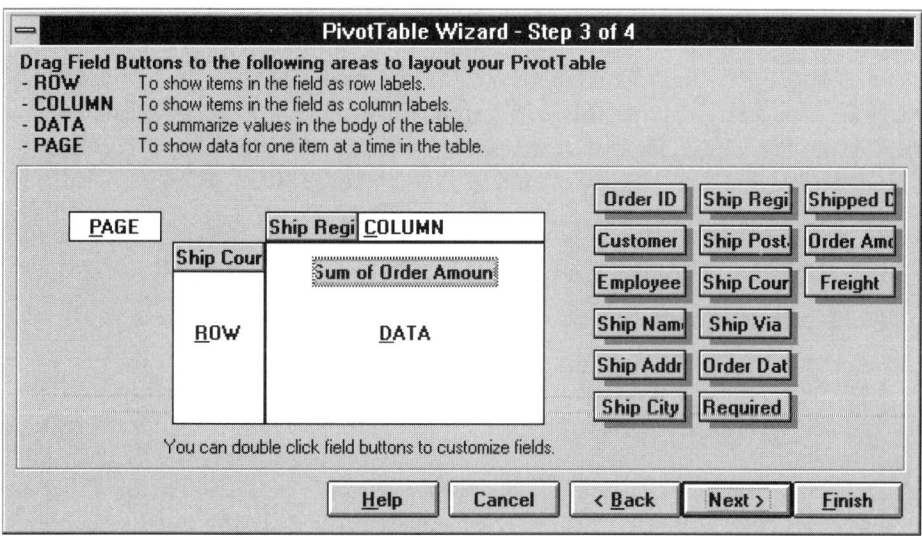

Figure 7.19 A Pivot Table Is Conceived

6. Click the Next button and then click Finish to accept all of step 4 of 4's defaults. Excel inserts a new sheet with the pivot table on it. It's your first pivot table, and it's a masterpiece (see Figure 7.20).

	A	B	C	T	U	V
1	Sum of Order Amount	Ship Region				
2	Ship Country	AK	AZ	WY	(blank)	Grand Total
3	Canada	0	0	0	0	128688.63
4	UK	0	0	0	405252.79	466279.68
5	USA	17466.43	15047.23	11441.63	0	931014.34
6	Grand Total	17466.43	15047.23	11441.63	405252.79	1525982.65
7						
8				Query and Pivot		
9						
10						

Figure 7.20 PivotTable, a Thing of Quintessential Beauty

Note that we hid columns D through S for clarity although you do not need to do so. (Note on the note: You can either hide columns or use PivotTable's PivotTable Field feature to selectively hide items; it's six of one and a half dozen of the other).

There you have it! It's amazing, it's unbelievable. But wait, there's more!

Once the pivot table exists, you can manipulate it with the Query and Pivot toolbar. (In case you're following along, to keep you in step with the precise appearance of our subsequent figures, you need to apply a Currency style to the Sum of Order Amount—click the PivotTable Field button, click the Number button, choose the third Currency format code from the top, and click on OK twice. Or you can perform this formatting once the pivot table is finished by clicking the PivotTable Field button and proceeding from there. Your choice.)

For our next miracle, let's see what the average order value is by Ship Country and by Ship Region. Watch this, folks, only five deft mouse strokes to analytical bliss:

PivotTable Wizard button

1. Click the PivotTable Wizard button.

2. Double-click Sum of Order Amount in the Data area.

3. Select Average in the Summarize by list box.

4. Click OK.

5. Click Finish.

If you get any #DIV/0 error values, they simply indicate that a particular item's denominator is zero, that is, no orders for that region.

Pivot tables are, quite simply, the cat's pajamas. (Okay, okay, so our age is showing, they're *burly!*) But there's still more. Exciting, huh!?

Viewing data in chunks as easily as turning pages in a book

If you want to page through a particular group one at a time, say, examine each individual employee's orders by Ship Country and by Ship Region, that's easy.

1. Click on the PivotTable Wizard button.

2. In the layout panel (Step 3 of 4), drag-and-drop Employee to the Page area.

3. Double-click on Sum of Order Amount and change the summary function to Sum.

4. Click on OK, and then click Finish.

5. In the resulting pivot table, click on the Employee ID's drop-down arrow to spin through the Employee ID values from (All) to 9, and choose 1. (Each employee in the orders list is represented by an identification number from 1 through 9.) See Figure 7.21.

	A	B	C	R	S	T	
1	Employee ID	1					
2							
3	Sum of Order Amount	Ship Region					
4	Ship Country	AK	AZ	WY	(blank)	Grand Total	
5	Canada	$0.00	$0.00	$0.00	$0.00	$13,660.05	
6	UK	$0.00	$0.00	$0.00	$53,959.00	$66,751.63	
7	USA	$3,550.84	$2,715.24	$1,369.20	$0.00	$128,315.22	
8	Grand Total	$3,550.84	$2,715.24	$1,369.20	$53,959.00	$208,726.90	
9							

Figure 7.21 Flip Through Group Values Like Pages in a Book (Here by Employee ID)

But you say you still haven't had enough? You say you want us to do the *impossible*? Well, how about seeing the smallest, largest, and average order values in a table individually by country as well as world-wide? Would you buy one then? Well, step right up, pilgrim, step right up.

Multiple summary functions like that (snap your fingers).

1. Click the PivotTable Wizard button.

2. Drag Employee off the Page area, drag Ship Region off the Column area, drag Ship Country to the Column area, drag the Order Amount button (from the button stack, not from the Data area), and drop it below the existing Sum of Order Amount in the Data area.

3. Repeat this action.

4. Double-click on the first Sum of Order Amount, click on Min in the Summarize by list box, and click on OK.

5. Ditto for the second Sum of Order Amount, only this time select Max.

6. Ditto for the third Sum of Order Amount, and this time select Average.

7. Click OK and then click Finish. See Figure 7.22. (Note that there are no hidden columns in this figure.)

There you have it! We bet you're reachin' for your wallet right now and screaming "*Are those operators standing by to take my order?*" But wait, you can't buy

	A	B	C	D	E
1		Ship Country			
2	Data	Canada	UK	USA	Grand Total
3	Min of Order Amount	$57.50	$28.00	$12.50	$12.50
4	Max of Order Amount	$10,835.24	$13,333.22	$16,387.50	$16,387.50
5	Average of Order Amount	$1,812.52	$1,538.88	$1,322.46	$1,415.57
6					

Figure 7.22 Do This in a Flat Second!

this amazing product because it is absolutely 100% free! That's right, it's included free in every box of Microsoft Excel. It won't rust, won't tarnish, and is the slickest thing to hit data analysis since the scientific method.

Remember the nested subtotal bug back in Figure 7.17? Well, here's additional proof of its insectoid nature, since the pivot table properly differentiates between the UK's blank and nonblank regions (see Figure 7.23). Small comfort to the Suffolk regional manager who just lost $405K by the click of a mouse, eh? *Heh, heh, heh.*

	A	B
1	Ship Country	UK ↓
2		
3	Sum of Order Amount	
4	Ship Region	Total
5	Essex	$14,602.15
6	Kent	$6,657.25
7	Lancashire	$7,202.80
8	N. Yorkshire	$10,654.81
9	Suffolk	$21,909.88
10	(blank)	$405,252.79
11	Grand Total	$466,279.68
12		

Figure 7.23 PivotTable Corrects Nested Subtotal's $405K Bug

PivotTable vs. AutoFilter

Aside from PivotTable's overcoming the nested subtotal bug, let's review the key differences between AutoFilter and PivotTable.

- AutoFilter processes a list in place (although you can opt to copy to another location by using Advanced Filter), whereas a pivot table always appears in a different location from the source data. (Technically, you can drop a pivot table right on top of its source data, but that is such an unusual—let's be honest, inconceivably weird—act that we deem it moot.)

- AutoFilter's not designed to rearrange a list or the resulting summary function values dynamically; PivotTable is.

- AutoFilter does not provide any predefined custom calculations (although you can create them yourself with formulas); PivotTable does.

- AutoFilter is not designed to individually group or ungroup aggregations of data, or to hide/reveal item detail in a breakdown format; PivotTable is.

- AutoFilter is priceless for doing complex searches, so in this arena AutoFilter and PivotTable can work hand in hand. To analyze a particular subset of records, grab 'em with AutoFilter, copy the filtered subset to another location, and then PivotTable the resulting extract. Feature synergy! *We love this product!*

A PivotTable Treasure-trove of Teasers

PivotTable, like the horizon, is a feature that teases you eternally, always offering more wonderment and adventure around the next bend. We could write an entire book on the subject. So where does that leave you? We hope you're duly impressed (how about sockless and slack-jawed?) with the feature's fundamentals and as curious as a nine-lived cat to dig into the rich infrastructure of this marvelous analytical tool.

To entice you to continue, here's a smattering of the amazing things you can accomplish as a PivotTable disciple. It's all right there at the tips of your digital extremities.

- Data Sources
  - Use a traditional Excel list.
  - Use external data (you'll need to hook up MS Query and ODBC).
  - Use multiple consolidation ranges.
  - Use another pivot table.
  - Convert from an Excel 4 crosstab table.
- Layout
  - Use drag-and-drop in the pivot table itself to delete fields.
  - Drag-and-drop pivot table fields from column to row to page status.
  - Use the layout panel to add fields.
  - Introduce new summary calculations.
- Formatting—a veritable plethora of options…
  - Use the familiar AutoFormat.
  - Use the PivotTable Field dialog to change field formatting.
  - Automatically generate a new sheet to house each PivotTable page.
  - Create linked charts that update for each flipped page.

Other powerful PivotTable features aplenty

- Analysis—ad infinitum

  - Toggle subtotal and grand total displays.

  - Sort by field labels or actual data values.

  - Double-click an item to drill up or down on its associated details.

  - Double-click a data area cell to create a new sheet containing only the associated records that comprise the cell's value.

  - Rearrange fields with drag-and-drop right on the pivot table (you don't have to go back to the layout panel).

  - Perform custom calculations (choose from eight pre-defined types ranging from "Difference From" to "Index").

  - Create groups on the fly based on numeric, date, and time value ranges.

If you've enjoyed learning about AutoFilter and PivotTable in this chapter, and if you've got an iota of strength left from all that provocative rooting and grubbing, additional rewards await you. We encourage you to explore on your own Excel's what-if, goal-seeking, scenario management, consolidation, engineering function, and statistical function tools.

8 Supercharging Excel

A, B, C, D, E, …Your public library has arranged these in ways that make you cry, giggle, laugh, love, hate, wonder, ponder, and understand.

American Library Association
Advertising slogan, 1961

In this chapter we look at some of Excel's infrastructure and how to deal with security issues when working in a group. How to control what happens when Excel starts, how Excel maintains certain settings…things like that. This type of stuff often is overlooked when you first start out learning Excel, and it has been our experience that a lot of users never get around to going back and picking it up. Granted, you may not use startup switches or INI settings every day, but when you need them, they can really save your bacon. You may create, edit, review, and use your own models without another user ever seeing them, but you can still use some of the annotation techniques discussed in this chapter.

Infrastructure stuff

Templates, though, *are* something that you should be using daily. WinWord 6 power users have come to appreciate the power and flexibility that templates provide for word processing, but not too many spreadsheet users are aware that Excel is also template based.

Whenever a new book or sheet is created, it is based on a template. Phooey you say? If Excel has templates where are they? And just what is a *template* anyway? Glad you asked, pilgrim.

TEMPLATES

You are the bows from which your children are as living arrows sent forth.

Kahlil Gibran
The Prophet, 1923

Templates in Excel often extract from us somewhat mixed emotions. Sometimes we love them. Sometimes they make us want to reprogram good ol' Excel with an

Hand me the ax…

ax. We'll present the facts (as we see 'em, *heh, heh, heh*), and let you draw your own conclusions.

You've used templates lots of times. Sure you have. A cookie cutter is a template. So is a sheet of paper from a yellow pad (the lines are already on the page; you don't have to draw them).

Okay, okay, a formal definition: a **template** is a master file that contains all the static information needed to create a new file in the mold of its master. Forge ahead and with some examples you'll be able to master <*groan*> the concept.

Cookie Cutter Deluxe

> Temples fall, statues decay, mausoleums perish, eloquent phrases declaimed are forgotten, but good books are immortal.
>
> William Vernon
> Sermon, Western University, Kansas, 1900

Oatmeal-raisin templates Let's hypothesize that you have read this book and decide you want some information recorded on Sheet1 of every book that gets created based on some of the tips you found in Chapter 5. Hey, stop laughing, it could happen. To further complicate things, pretend you want each book created to have four sheets, and these sheets should be named General, Input, Calcs, and Reports. See Figure 8.1.

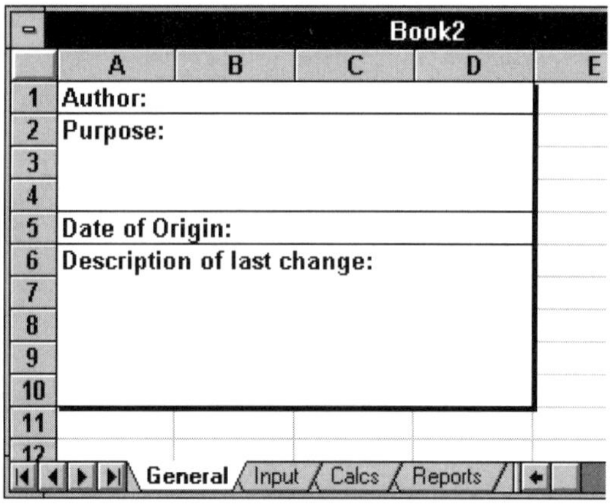

Figure 8.1 A Customized Book Template

A Template Recipe

To make like magic and have each book you create pop up looking like this , take the following steps:

1. Create a new book. Adjust the number of worksheets in the book to four, and rename the Tabs as shown in Figure 8.1.

2. Enter the boilerplate information. This could be text, numbers, graphics, styles, formatting, skeletal model components like row and column labels, formulas, whatever.

3. Pull down the File menu and click on Save As.

4. In the Save As dialog box, pull down the Save File as Type list box and choose Template. This automatically gives the file name an extension of XLT.

5. Change to the XLSTART directory. It's found beneath the Excel program directory.

6. Name the file BOOK.XLT and click on OK.

7. Close the BOOK.XLT file.

Now create a new book and be prepared to be suitably impressed.

You can have prebuilt sheets of any flavor (worksheet, chart, and so on) in the BOOK.XLT template, and each time you create a new book you get sheets that "contain all the static information." There you have it. That's what an Excel template is all about.

Where the Wild Templates Are

> And when he came to the place where the wild things are they roared their terrible roars and gnashed their terrible teeth...
>
> Maurice Sendak
> *Where The Wild Things Are*

The only tricky part of creating a template is making sure you save it to the XLSTART directory. WinWord is much more friendly in this regard. When you tell WinWord to save a file as a template type, it seeks out the appropriate directory on its own. Excel puts the burden for this on you. Actually you can save it to the XLSTART directory or the Alternate Startup File Location (AS) directory if you have defined one.

The AS directory was discussed back in Chapter 1. Its raison d'être is to allow the storing of templates (and files to be loaded automatically, like PERSONAL.XLS) in more than one place. This is most often used in network situations in which some templates are available to a group of users on a shared drive, and others are stored on a local drive to be used only by the person at that station. Go Tools Options General for access to the AS directory setting.

There's a context element to the XLSTART and AS directories. If you have a BOOK.XLT file in both locations, *the one in the AS directory wins*. AS wins whenever there is a duplication of file names in both startup directories, no matter what the type of XLT.

Template precedence

As far as other files go, any file in either the XLSTART or the AS directory is automatically opened when Excel is loaded. This is why your PERSONAL.XLS file is always handy when you need to write a VBA program. Any Excel book you want to have opened every time you start Excel should be in either the XLSTART or the AS directory.

MTP—Multiple Template Personalities

> I've wrestled with reality for 35 years, and I'm happy, Doctor, I finally won out over it.
>
> Elwood P. Dowd
> *Harvey*, 1950

You say you like the concept but not the implementation? You say ya want to be able to choose from several different book templates, not just one all-powerful one? Is that what's bothering you, bunky?

Well, never fear. You want multiple templates, you get multiple templates. Let's modify the one you just created under the assumption that you suddenly realized that this template is only going to be used when building models for a specific project and not *all* books should start off life like this one.

Über Book

> Betcha' can't open it.
>
> Pandora's sister

First, you have to open the BOOK.XLT template. That sounds easy enough doesn't it? *Heh, heh, heh.* Try it. When you do a standard File Open on BOOK.XLT, you get not the template, but *a new book based on the template!* This is not a bug, but rather it's "by design." The Redmond Rangers have made it difficult to open a template to prevent accidental modifications.

Hold down the Shift key. The trick is to open the template *while holding down the Shift key*. No kidding, try it. Right before you click on OK in the File Open dialog box hold down the Shift key. See. Cool, huh? To use Excel's most recently used (MRU) file list—File1, File2, File3,.or File4—to open a template, you've got to hold down the Shift key as you click on the template name.

Now that you have BOOK.XLT open, save it under the name LOBSTER.XLT (why Lobster? uhm, why not?) and close it. Using whatever method you favor, delete BOOK.XLT from the XLSTART directory.

Next, create a new book by clicking on the File New icon on the Standard toolbar. Interesting, yes? See Figure 8.2.

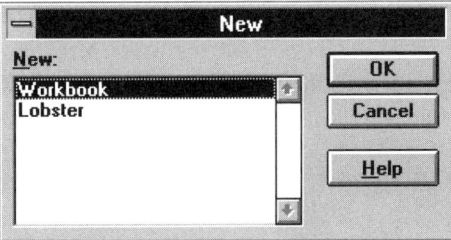

Figure 8.2 Viva la Choice!

The default "Workbook" now gives you precisely that—a default book created by Excel itself. "Lobster" however, is another matter. A new book based on Lobster gives you a book like the one in Figure 8.1. And its default name is "Lobster1." Cool? Man this is subzero! Unfortunately there will be a thaw very shortly.

You can create a book template for each type of model that you regularly build. Each template should contain whatever is needed to build a model of that type, like styles, custom formats, whatever.

All this is not without a confusing aspect (do you feel it getting warmer all of a sudden?). When you create some custom book templates, those template names appear in the File New dialog box (as shown in Figure 8.2). But if you are in an existing book and you want to insert a new worksheet in that book, things start getting weird. If you right-click on the sheet tab and choose Insert, you get the dialog box shown in Figure 8.3.

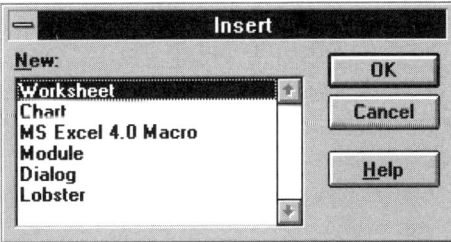

Figure 8.3 Something New Has Been Added

Look there at the bottom of the list. Lobster! Yep. If you create a template named BOOK.XLT to modify the default book, you've got no worries, mate. But if you create some additional book templates, they also show up in the Insert dialog box. Futhermore, if you choose Lobster in this example, you get the four worksheets in Figure 8.1 *added to the current book*.

More than you bargained for

Now that we're completely enslaved by our master templates *<groan>*, let's polish up our lamps and make some wishes—more information about styles with templates, sheet templates, dialog templates, macro templates, and a table of *Underground Guide*lines with a cherry on top. Read on, pilgrim.

Managing Styles in Templates

We promised that we'd expound on how to move styles between books, and, more importantly, between templates. This is something you need to know because, if you're starting to see the light as far as using templates, most of your styles exist only in books that you have already created.

To move a style between books or templates, the source and destination files must be open. Make the destination file active, pull down the Format menu, and click on Style. From the Style dialog box, click on the Merge command button. You get the Merge Styles dialog box (see Figure 8.4).

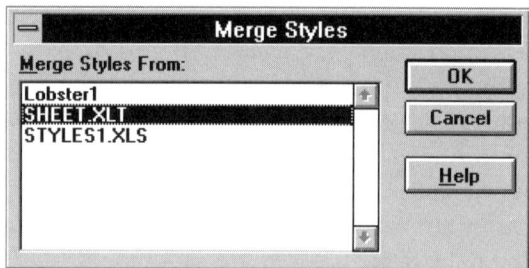

Figure 8.4 Move Styles Here, There, Everywhere...

Choose the source file and click on OK here and on OK or Close in the Styles dialog box. Bang! The styles from the source are in the destination quick as a wink.

Other XLTs

> Round up the usual suspects.
>
> Inspector Renault
> *Casablanca*, 1942

We have pierced the mysterious veil surrounding book templates, but what about when you insert a lowly sheet into an existing workbook? Can you create a template for that as well? You bet!

Individual sheets   Excel supports a `SHEET.XLT`, a `DIALOG.XLT`, as well as a `MACRO.XLT` template. Here's the scoop. To make a template as a model for inserted worksheets, you create a new book. Eliminate all the sheets in this book except those you want to pop up when you insert a worksheet. Huh, what?

That's right. When you insert a worksheet into an open book, and you have created a custom SHEET.XLT, *and* that XLT has, oh, say, two worksheets and dialog sheet, that's what you get inserting into the book…two worksheets and a dialog sheet. Weird, huh?

If all you want is a single worksheet when you perform an Insert Worksheet (not an unreasonable want, in our opinion) you must eliminate all but *a single worksheet* from the SHEET.XLT.

It all boils down to a lot of smoke and mirrors. There is nothing magical about the SHEET.XLT, DIALOG.XLT, **and** MACRO.XLT **file names. If you do not create these files, Excel knows exactly what type of sheet to insert when asked. But, when you create any of the** SHEET.XLT, DIALOG.XLT, **and** MACRO.XLT **templates, all bets are off. Excel inserts everything (sheetwise) it finds when you do an insert, based on what it finds in the template file.**

If you create a MACRO.XLT template and put a dozen dialog sheets in it, that's what Excel inserts into your book when you insert a macro sheet. Ditto for SHEET.XLT and DIALOG.XLT. Confusing? You bet. Maybe this will help. See Table 8.1.

Table 8.1 Guidelines for Working with Custom XLTs

If you want to do this…	Create this…
Modify Excel default book.	BOOK.XLT, containing all sheets, styles, boilerplate, etc., that you want in each new book created.
Modify Excel's default worksheet.	SHEET.XLT, which should contain only one sheet (a worksheet).
Modify Excel's default dialog sheet.	DIALOG.XLT, which should contain only one sheet (a dialog sheet).
Modify Excel's default Excel 4 macro sheet.	MACRO.XLT, which should contain only one sheet (an Excel 4 macro sheet).
Create a custom book template.	filename.XLT, containing all sheets, styles, boilerplate, etc., that you want in each new book created.*
Create a custom single sheet.	filename.XLT, containing one modified sheet of the type of sheet you want to insert.*
Create a custom module template.	Sorry, no can do (see next section).
Create a custom chart template.	Sorry, no can do (see next section).

*This file name appears in the Insert dialog box and when selected the sheet from this file is inserted into the current book.

The Ignoble MODULE.XLT and CHART.XLT Templates

How do you modify Excel's default module and chart sheets? You don't! Despite what you read in the *User's Guide*, you can't modify the Excel defaults for these type of sheets.

If you go to the trouble to create a MODULE.XLT, Excel ignores it. If you whip up a CHART.XLT, Excel ignores it, too. Then the next time you start Excel, it complains with an error message telling you to use the Chart AutoFormat feature.

WHAT HAPPENS WHEN YOU START EXCEL

> Captain, the Romulans are powering up their forward disrupter array.
>
> Lieutenant Commander Worf
> *Star Trek: The Next Generation*

Jumping through hoops When you first power up Excel, you can make it jump through some hoops by specifying any of several command line switches. A command line switch in Excel is a backslash followed by a single alpha character. You use the command line switch when Excel is first started. This is most often done from the Program Manager.

Excel's Startup Command Line Switches

The command line switches can be entered in the ProgMan Item Properties dialog box, which starts Excel from the icon in Program Manager. You can also type in the switches if you start Excel from the Run dialog box. Excel 5 supports the three switches listed in Table 8.2.

Table 8.2 Excel's Startup Switches

Switch	Function
/r or /R *c:\path\filename.ext*	This switch is used in conjunction with a path and file name that specifies a file that you want Excel to open upon loading. The switch causes the file to be opened as *read-only*.
/p or /P *c:\path*	This switch is used in conjunction with a path to specify a directory to be used as the default directory for that session of Excel.
/e or /E	This switch is used to prevent Excel from opening the default BOOK1 book (Excel starts *empty*).

You can combine these switches. For example, to start Excel from an icon in Program Manager, without a default book, and specifying a default directory, the ProgMan Item Properties dialog box might look like Figure 8.5.   **Switches in combination**

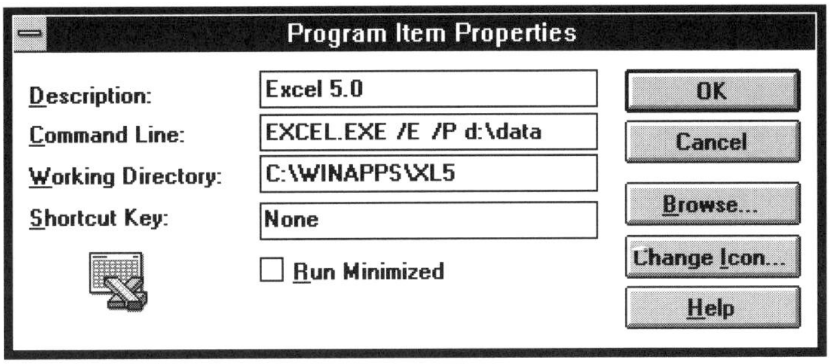

Figure 8.5 Switches In Action!

The odd thing about Excel's startup switches is that you *cannot* use them on the LOAD= or RUN= lines of the WIN.INI file! Why? Dunno, just can't.

The Magical Mystical EXCEL5.INI File

> Among scientists are collectors, classifers, and compulsive tidiers-up; many are detectives by temperment and many are explorers; some are artists and others artisans. There are poet-scientists and philosopher-scientists and even a few mystics.
>
> Sir Peter Brian Medawar
> *The Art of the Soluble,* 1967

When Excel needs to write a note to itself, it does so in a file called EXCEL5.INI. This file is located in your Windows program directory. It's a little ASCII text file, and you can display it in Windows by opening it up in Notepad. Here is the EXCEL5.INI file from one of our testing computers. Indented lines belong to the line above them and are indented due to space constraints because INI files do not support a line continuation character.

```
[Microsoft Excel]
Options5=3735
Comment=The open=/f lines load custom functions into the
   Paste Function list.
Options3=0
User=Timothy-James Lee
Font=Arial,10
```

```
AltStartup=c:\altxl
Maximized=2
StickyPtX=400
StickyPtY=238
MRUFuncs=5,4,1,0,102,27,7,6,59,345
DefaultPath=D:\DATA
DefSheets=1
Pos=4,2,795,594
Default Chart=
Basics=1
CBTLOCATION=C:\WINAPPS\XL5\EXCELCBT
AutoFormat=8
AutoFormat Options=63
Options=23

[Init Commands]
reports=10, File, Print
    R&eport...,'C:\WINAPPS\XL5\library\REPORTS.XLA'!mcp01.
    PrintReport.,----,,Print or define document reports,
    MAINXL.HLP!1731
views=10, View, &View
    Manager...,'C:\WINAPPS\XL5\library\VIEWS.XLA'!STUB,,,
    Show or define a named view,MAINXL.HLP!1730
XLQUERY=10,Data,&Refresh Data,'C:\WINAPPS\XL5\library\
    msquery\XLQUERY.XLA'!doRefresh,,,Refreshes the data
    range,MAINXL.HLP!1841
XLQUERY1=10,Data,Get E&xternal Data...,'C:\WINAPPS\XL5\
    library\msquery\XLQUERY.XLA'!doGetData,,,Inserts data
    from an external query,MAINXL.HLP!1840
solver=10, Tools, Sol&ver...,'C:\WINAPPS\XL5\library\
    solver\SOLVER.XLA'!STUB,--,,Find solution to worksheet
    model,MAINXL.HLP!1830

[WK? Settings]
Comment=This section controls Lotus file open and save
    settings.
Load_Chart_Wnd=1
AFE=2
Monospace=1
Gridlines=0
```

```
[Line Print]
Comment=This section controls Lotus macro line printing
   settings.
Options=2
LeftMarg=4
RightMarg=76
TopMarg=2
BotMarg=2
PgLen=66
Setup=

[Spell Checker]
Speller=Spelling 1033,0
Custom Dict 1=C:\WINDOWS\MSAPPS\PROOF\CUSTOM.DIC
Ignore Caps=0
Suggest Always=1

[Recent File List]
File1=C:\WINAPPS\XL5\XLSTART\XL5GALRY.XLS
File2=D:\DATA\PCG\ACCTING\NEWCHECK.XLS
File3=D:\DATA\PCG\ACCTING\PCG_CKBK.XLW
File4=C:\WINAPPS\XL5\XLSTART\DOG1.XLS

[Converters]
conv1=Microsoft Multiplan (*.*) ,C:\WINAPPS\XL5\
   xlconvmp.dll,*.*

[Help]
XLREADME.HLP=C:\WINAPPS\XL5\XLREADME.HLP
```

Whoa! That's a bunch of stuff Excel is keeping track of.

If you really want to get into some of the more esoteric settings, we refer you to the *Excel Developer's Kit* (EDK). Sure, you can find some of this information in Excel's help file, but the EDK goes into more detail. Not complete detail, of course, Microsoft likes to keep some secrets, but with the EDK and a little experience you should be able to grok a lot of what isn't spelled out.

Excel controls most of the key word settings and updates them when you change something so it can keep track of your change for the next time you start Excel. It is generally better to let Excel control these key word settings and to not go mucking about in this file, but there are some settings that you can change or set yourself with relative safety.

The [Microsoft Excel] Section

In the Micorsoft Excel section you find most of the stuff that is of general interest.

Options5= (and its sibling key words, like Options= and Options3=) control the various settings you make via Tools Options. Don't mess with 'em. Make changes in Excel and let Excel update these guys.

A lot of the settings in this section are pretty intuitive. User= and AltStartup= specify your author name and the Alternative Startup File Location, respectively. DefSheets= is the number of default worksheets per book setting. Some key word settings, however, are pretty cryptic, and it's always a good idea to leave alone what you're not sure of.

One key word discussed in the EDK that you should know about is Open=. This keyword can be used to make Excel open a specific file, or several files if you like. You would do it like this:

```
Open=c:\winapps\xl5\library\reports.xla
Open1=d:\data\pcg\general.xls
```

You can keep incrementing the setting, that is, Open2, Open3, and so on, to open additional files. This is yet another way to get files opened when Excel starts up. The more common way is to copy the files to open to the XLSTART or the AS directory. This INI setting method is of use to Excel developers who want to control what files get opened under different circumstances without moving them from directory to directory.

Control add-in loading.   Excel uses these Open= to load Add-ins that you specify via Tools, Add-ins.

If you do ever make any manual changes to the EXCEL5.INI file, Excel must be closed and reopened before those settings take effect.

Do You Know Where Your Files Are?

What happens if the EXCEL5.INI file gets deleted? Probably not much. You lose all the custom settings that Excel tracks in that file. It might be a pain, but it is not the end of the world.

What about the EXCEL5.XLB file? Hmmm, that's a scary thought. You'd lose your custom lists, all your custom buttons. Not so good. You might want to give some special thought to these "setting" files when next you consider file security and data backup.

WORKING WITH OTHERS

People don't work the way they used to.

Arthur Burns

If you develop spreadsheet models solely for your own use, you need only protect your work from yourself. But, if you're like most of us, you are part of a user community and must consider how your model will be used and possibly abused by others.

This brings us to the subject of passing spreadsheets around. Someone (or perhaps some group) develops a model, someone else may review and make changes, and still another may actually enter data and generate reports. Looks like we need to face facts and talk about safe spreadsheeting.

No spreadsheet is an island.

Security is the way to prevent bad things from happening to your otherwise defenseless spreadsheet. It is reasonably effective and can be implemented in such a way as to still allow someone to annotate the model.

Controlling Access to Files

Once the toothpaste is out of the tube, it's hard to get it back in.

H. R. Haldeman
American Chronicle, 1987

If you build a model and employ good development practices like those discussed in this book, you stand a reasonable chance of being able to work productively on the model long after the initial construction is done. This could involve troubleshooting a newly discovered problem or maybe adding some new functionality to the model.

But, what if you open the spreadsheet in question, this very child of your creative and technical abilities, who you sent out into the cold hard world, and discover that someone has made undocumented changes to it? Formulas changed, new tables added, things moved around, sheets renamed. *Thieves, pillagers, assassins, VANDALS!*

Fear, fire, foes!

It can really get you down. So let's give your spreadsheets a little armor before they are sent out to do battle. Before we can go any further, we had best define terms and talk about what passwords do and don't do in Excel 5.

First, there is what Microsoft calls the **Protection Password**. This password locks the file. Excel won't load the file if you don't have this password. Finí. End of story. Period.

Next is the **Write Reservation Password**. This one is confusing until you get used to it (so what's new?). If you don't know the Write Reservation Password, you *can only open the file as read-only.* Okay, so what's the story with this **read-only**? When you open a file as read-only, you can muck about with it until the cows come home (subject to some other constraints we cover shortly), but you cannot, no how, no way, save the file using its original file name. You *must* rename the book, thereby preserving the original unsullied and unchanged.

But, if you *do* know the Write Reservation Password, you can open the file *either* read-only (purely voluntarily on your part) or you can open the file with what Microsoft calls **write-access.** All write-access means is that you *can* save the file under its original file name.

Setting a Password

To set a password on the file, do a File Save As and click on the Options button. See Figure 8.6.

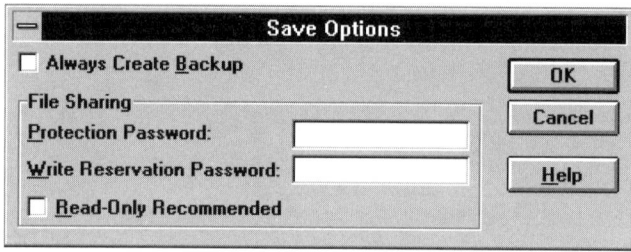

Figure 8.6 What's the Secret Word?

Passwords can be up to 15 characters and can include spaces, symbols, and numbers, according to the help file, or "any combination of letters, numbers, and symbols" according to the *User's Guide.* That pretty much covers it.

Keep it simple and watch the case. Here's our take on passwords. Keep it simple, but not too simple. Forget about using your name, your dog's name, the middle names of your kids. And for Pete's and everybody else's sake don't use "password" as a password. (Hey, we've been out in the trenches on point, *and it happens.*) We recommend using the technique made famous on the CompuServe Information Service (CIS): Pick two words that don't normally go together and separate them with a symbol.

Oh, and etch this into your neural synapses:

Passwords are case sensitive!

That means DOG does not equal DOg. Unless you have a really good memory, maybe you should get in the habit of using either all lowercase or all uppercase letters when doing passwords.

Meanwhile, back at the dialog box, you enter a Protection Password, a Write Reservation Password, or both, and click on OK. Next, Excel asks you to reenter the password(s) you just entered to make sure there were no typos. This is needed because, as you type in the password, the text box only displays asterisks. This keeps someone from reading your password over your shoulder, don't you know. After that, you can proceed to save the file.

Habits of the Protect Document Password

Boris darling, when Moose puts cake in oven...KABOOM!

Natasha Fatale
The Adventures of Rocky and Bullwinkle

If you have a file with a Protection Password and you open it, Excel prompts for the password. See Figure 8.7.

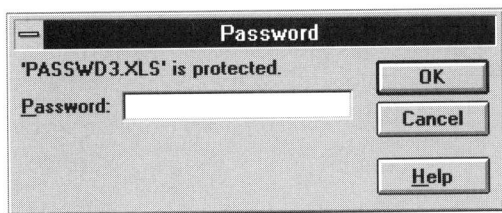

Figure 8.7 Say the Secret Word and Win a Prize

Type the correct password in, click on OK. Boom! The file is loaded into Excel, assuming there is not a Write Reservation Password. If there is a Write Reservation Password, well, you still have some decisions to make.

Hey, if this is a password-protected *template* that you're trying to open, remember to hold down the Shift key while clicking on OK.

The Confusing Write Reservation Password

Roskolnikov Natasha! Fearless Leader now say *don't* kill Moose and Squirrel!

Boris Badinoff
The Adventures of Rocky and Bullwinkle

If there is a Write Reservation Password on the file, you get the modified Password dialog box shown in Figure 8.8.

Now, maybe you have the Write Reservation Password or maybe you don't. At this point in the File Open process, you can click on the Read Only command button and the file is loaded as read-only. No password is needed to do this, but even if you type in the password, the Read Only button opens the file as read-only. Ipso facto.

No password needed to open read-only.

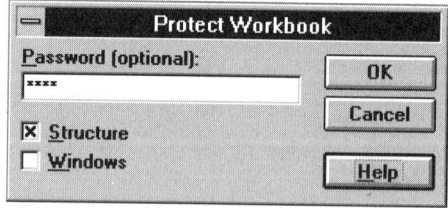

Figure 8.8 Say the Secret Word or Read-Only!

If you *have* the Write Reservation Password, you can type it in. Once you type in a password, the OK button becomes available and if you click on it (and, of course, you typed in the correct password) you get *full write-access to the file!* In other words, the Write Reservation Password can unlock the read-only aspect of the file.

Once the File Is Opened

> Catch-22 says they have a right to do anything we can't stop them from doing.
>
> Joseph Heller
> *Catch-22, 1955*

The file is finally open. Ah, but that is only the first line of defense. Additional layers of protection, again in the form of passwords, can be applied to books and even to individual sheets.

Book-Level Protection

Protection can be applied to the workbook itself via Tools Protection Protect Workbook. See Figure 8.9.

Figure 8.9 Protection at the Book Level

The password itself is optional when protecting. *Remember that an actual password is optional here.* You can use either book- or sheet-level protection without actually entering passwords to prevent careless mistakes.

If you do not use a password, the protection can be easily removed via Tools Protection Unprotect Workbook, but you must take a conscious action to do so, which *should* make you more careful in making changes.

In this dialog box, you have two options—Structure and Windows—which determine the type of protection to enable. You *must* pick one, the other, or both. The Structure option prevents adding, deleting, moving, hiding, unhiding, and renaming sheets within the book. The Windows option prevents resizing the book, splitting the view of a sheet, maximizing and minimizing, moving windows, and eliminates the child window control box (the hyphen thingy).

Sheet-Level Protection

Regardless of whether or not the book is protected, each individual sheet can be protected. Protection is enabled and disabled in the same manner as the book protection discussed earlier via Tools Protection Protect Sheet. See Figure 8.10.

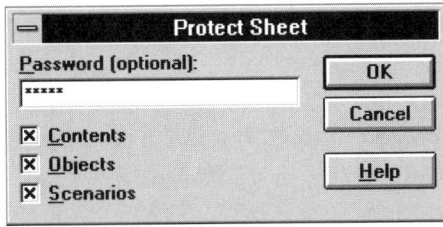

Figure 8.10 Protection Sheet by Sheet

Each worksheet within the book can be protected for Contents, Objects, and Scenarios. Module and dialog sheets can only be protected from editing, so no check boxes appear when you go to protect them. Chart and macro sheets support both contents and objects, so both of those check boxes appear when protecting those types of sheets.

The most common type of protection extended to worksheets is for cell contents. We generally leave the Objects check box unchecked for reasons discussed shortly.

Cell-Level Protection

You got the file open. The book and the sheet are protected. Now, does this mean you cannot enter or edit the contents of cells? Maybe yes and, then again, maybe no. It all depends on a cell formatting attribute that we have not talked about yet—the Protection attribute, which you set from the Format Cells dialog box. See Figure 8.11.

Protection as a cell attribute

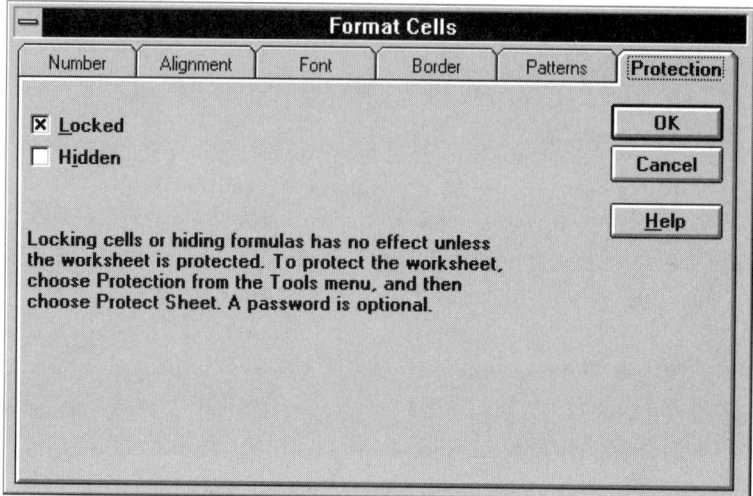

Figure 8.11 Default Cell Level Protection Attributes

A cell can be Locked, Hidden, neither, or both. The Locked attribute prevents a cell from being entered into or edited. A Hidden attribute prevents a cell's contents from being displayed in the formula bar. Use this to keep all those top secret formulas hidden from spying eyes.

Neither of these settings has any effect until the sheet is protected via Tools Protection Protect Sheet! Zip, nada, no impact, doesn't do a blessed thing. Once you protect the sheet, these attributes become *live.* If a cell is unlocked, it can be entered into and edited even though the worksheet is protected.

You control the cell-level locked attribute in order to create a worksheet where a user can input only into selected cells. All cells are locked and not hidden by default. Table 8.3 shows how cell protection affects the worksheet.

Table 8.3 Worksheet Protection vs. Cell Locked Attribute

Worksheet is:	Cell Attribute is:	You can:
Not Protected	Locked	Enter and edit
Not Protected	Unlocked	Enter and edit
Protected	Unlocked	Enter and edit
Protected	Locked	No changes allowed!

If you have a protected sheet and some of the cells are not locked to allow entry, the Tab key moves the active cell from unlocked cell to unlocked cell (left to right, top to bottom) through the worksheet.

Bypassing Password Protection

> Q: What keeps people honest?
> A: Witnesses.
>
> Anonymous

At this point we have some good news and some bad news. The good news is that now you know all about passwords. The bad news is that for a couple of hundred bucks anyone can buy a password recovery utility that breaks every level of password security in Excel. Well, maybe it's not so bad. You be the judge. Hey, people break into banks, so do you really think you can keep out someone really determined to get in?

Is anything really secure?

Keep in mind that Microsoft tells you up front that if you forget your password, you're out of luck. So if you have a lapse of mental acumen, are you to toss out all your password-protected files and books? If a trusted employee joins the Foreign Legion or turns out to be not so trustworthy after all, do you abandon all your files? No. If that were the case, no one would ever use passwords. But what do you do?

You call up the nice folks at AccessData 800-658-5199 (801-224-6970 outside the United States), and they'll sell you an amazing program for breaking Excel 5 passwords. They've got utilities to crack all the major programs, including WordPerfect, Novell, and WinWord. *And they're all perfectly legal.*

The ability to break a password should give you the confidence to use them! If knowing that AccessData sells these utilities gives you nightmares, relax. They are responsible folks and if you need a little extra security, you can call them and they'll tell you about a "security character" that you can use in your passwords. When their product finds a password that includes this character, it refers you to AccessData who, after verifying you actually own the file in question, will open it for you at no extra cost.

Only a fool uses a lock with no key.

Don't despair if you are a developer of add-on utilities for the Excel after-market either. You can get, free of charge, a registered password from AccessData to use in your add-on that the AccessData utilities will refuse to break.

Comments and Annotations

> Meet is it changes should control
> Our being, lest we rest in ease.
>
> Alfred, Lord Tennyson
> *Love Thou Thy Land*, 1842

If you're working on a fair-sized spreadsheet project, there are generally several review cycles where someone looks at your model from a construction standpoint; perhaps someone else reviews it from a user interface point of view; changes are recommended, implemented, and tested; and the next cycle begins. In a perfect world, only a limited number of team members are allowed to actually make changes to the model. So how do you gather feedback from everyone else on the project?

Let me draw you a picture.   Here's a method that works for us. We generally lock the sheets but leave the Objects check box unchecked. Then everyone with a comment can annotate the sheets right there on the sheet in question, using several of the graphic objects that Excel provides.

Now, although there are bunches of graphic gizmos in Excel, we have found that three provide all the annotation capabilities we need: text boxes, circles, and arrows.

Text on the Sheet

Text boxes are spiffy for jotting down some text and displaying it right on the sheet. Wait a minute, can't you do that in cells, you ask? Yes, but it's a real pain to type in a paragraph of text and get it to display correctly. And you have to deal with the 255-character limitation. Text boxes are much, much better (with 10,240 characters maximum to boot). Besides, the sheet is locked, so no one can change anything in the cells anyway.

Text Box button

Creating a text box is quick and easy. Click on the Text Box button and drag the graphic cross-hairs across the sheet where you want the text box to appear. You can type in the text box, and your text wraps automatically within the box. You can format the text much like you can in a word processor. Click outside the text box and see your handiwork. See Figure 8.12.

	A	B
1		
2	A cool text box	
3	floating above	
4	the worksheet	
5	on the graphic	
6	layer.	
7		

Figure 8.12 A Sample Text Box

CTRL, ALT, and SHIFT when dragging graphics   If you type more text than the text box can display, no problem. Enlarge the text box: click on the box to select it, and drag one of its handles. Move the box by dragging one of its borders.

You can copy graphic objects by dragging while holding down the Control key. Hold down the Alt key while dragging a graphic object and the object snaps to the sheet's gridlines.

Last but not least, hold down the Shift key and you can only drag the graphic in line horizontally or vertically to its previous position. To put the cursor in the text box so you can edit the text, click on it twice.

The graphic object (a fancy way to say text box) can be formatted from the Format menu or from the right-click-on-the-text-box shortcut menu.

To give your text boxes some substance, select the box and click once on the Drop Shadow button and once on the Light Shading button (see Figure 8.13). It looks good on screen and prints out nicely, too.

When making a comment or an annotation, a text box is perfect.

Figure 8.13 Drop Shadow and Light Shading Buttons

Circles and Arrows

The other two graphic gizomos that are needed when marking up a spreadsheet are circles and arrows. Both can be easily drawn on the sheet's graphic layer in much the same way as the text box.

Both of these drawing tools are found on the Shape palette. As discussed in Chapter 6, these palettes can be drug off their buttons and become mini-toolbars. This is a very cool technique because it provides all the drawing tools you need for annotating in one handy place (including the text box tool) and stays visible while you review the book.

Click on the Shape button and drag the palette off the formatting toolbar and onto the sheet. See Figure 8.14.

Shape button

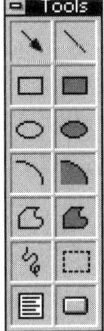

Figure 8.14 Shape Tools Palette

The arrow tool is the first tool in the first column. You draw the arrow from the starting point to the point where you want the arrowhead to appear. The circle tool is the ellipse in the third row, first column. You can make a perfect circle by holding down the Shift key while dragging the drawing tool cross-hairs across the sheet, but we find the elliptical shape of more use in circling cells, which are rectangular in shape to begin with.

To format the graphic objects, you select them and access Format Object (either menu bar or shortcut menu). You can move objects by selecting them and then dragging them with the mouse.

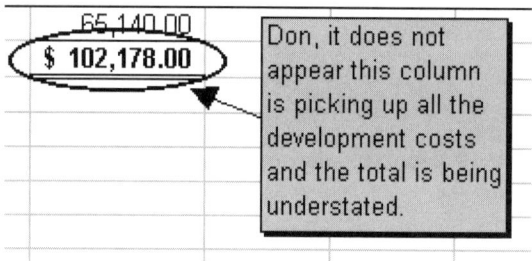

Figure 8.15 An Annotated Sheet

Be aware that these graphic objects are no different than the embedded charts discussed earlier in that they are subject to the PCL printer bug (see Chapter 6, The Amazing See-Through Chart). If you place the text box, for example, over cells with contents, those cells print *on top of* the graphic.

9 OLE 2.0 Where Marketing Meets Technology

> All visible objects, man, are but as pasteboard masks...strike, strike through the mask!
>
> Captain Ahab
> Herman Melville, *Moby Dick*, 1851

This is it, pilgrim. The crowd falls silent, Bill Gates take his place in front of his programming orchestra. He taps his baton on the podium and prepares to conduct the dawn of a new age.

Information shared, data embedded, compound documents, messaging, common languages *<camera pulls back as lightning flashes across the sky>*, the earth shakes, *<music swells>*, the tower of Babel falls! *<fade to black>*.

Right. Well, so much for the future. What you actually have of this vision today is OLE 2.0. That's short for Object Linking and Embedding (we've always thought it should be Linking or Embedding, but as we have lamented, Microsoft doesn't ask us). It's not bad, but don't believe everything you read in the papers.

Keep in mind that we like and endorse this technology, honest. One of our most popular courses is our "Putting OLE & DDE to Work" (now for OLE 2.0, VBA, & DDE) training seminar. Hundreds of developers, support personnel, and end users have attended this class and the reviews have been phenomenal. OLE either has, or will, change the way you use a personal computer.

Putting technology to work

INFORMATION AT YOUR DIGITAL EXTREMITIES™

> And now for something completely different.
>
> *Monty Python's Flying Circus*

The compound document is the first step on the path leading to the document centric computing paradigm. Wazzat? Glad you asked—otherwise, this would be a very short chapter.

Today's computing model is **application centric**. You have an *Excel* file, your colleague has a *PowerPoint* file. Each application saves its data files in a proprietary binary file format. One application may be able to translate to and/or from another application, but the files are fundamentally the product of the application that created them.

Where the computing model is headed is called **document centric**. In the future you'll use your computer to create documents, but those documents won't be the product of a given application. They will most likely be the product of the operating system (*ka-ching!* Somewhere up north we hear a cash register ringing, don't you?). The operating system will contain a number of toolsets that will be used to construct the document.

Good-bye operating system; hello operating toolset. You'll have a spreadsheet toolset, a word processor toolset, a charting toolset, and so on. Different companies will sell toolsets that plug into the operating system, but it's quite likely that the operating system will come with a pretty complete set to start with. *Ka-ching!*

As we said, the first step toward this brave new world is the **compound document**. Compound documents are created using OLE 2.0. They are documents that, although they still belong to some application, contain embedded or linked data that was created and formatted in other, different applications.

Compounding Those Documents

No, 'tis not so deep as a well, nor so wide as a church-door; but 'tis enough, 'twill serve...

Mercutio
William Shakespeare, *Romeo & Juliet*

A WinWord 6 document can contain an Excel chart. The chart is said to be **embedded** in the WinWord 6 document. What gets embedded is the entire book that originally contained the chart. OLE makes it possible for another application to display data that is native to Excel, which is really pretty amazing.

When it comes to editing the Excel data, however, WinWord is helpless. It does not have the tools to deal with Excel data. To edit the data, you need Excel.

A compound Excel document (book) might contain data embedded from other applications like WinWord and/or PowerPoint. This foreign data is displayed as though it belongs to Excel, but without the **source applications** that created that data, it cannot be edited.

Fields, Functions, and Other Hooks That Go Bump in the Ether

> Make things as simple as possible, but no simpler.
>
> Albert Einstein

Data (and you had best get in the habit of calling this an object or a data object) can be **linked** to a compound document as opposed to embedded within it. A discussion of embedding is coming up shortly. This difference between object linking and object embedding confuses a lot of users new to OLE. It all boils down to where the actual data resides. If you embed data from another application in an Excel sheet, *all* of the data is stuffed into the Excel binary file that makes up that workbook.

If, on the other hand, data in another application is linked to an Excel 5 sheet, the data remains external to Excel. A representation, or perhaps more accurately, an echo of the data is displayed in the Excel sheet. If the linked data in the external application is modified, the data in the Excel sheet is updated to reflect those changes.

When where is who, what, and why

The thing to remember when dealing with links is that the data isn't really in Excel at all, only its reflection is.

Simple Cell Links

> Unfortunately, in these times the simple man or the simple answer is not enough.
>
> Edmund G. Brown
> *Reagan: The Political Chameleon*, 1976

Let's look at a simple example. In Figure 9.1 you see a single paragraph linked from a WinWord 6 document to an Excel 5 worksheet.

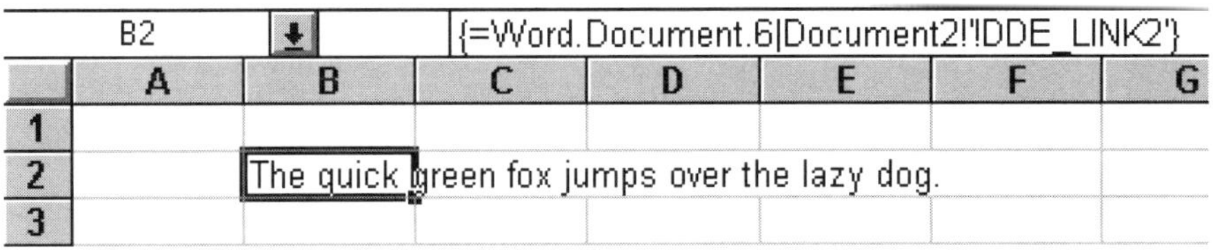

Figure 9.1 Simple Link to WinWord 6

Note the strange looking stuff in the formula bar. This array-entered formula was created following these steps:

1. Select and copy the paragraph in WinWord 6.

2. Switch to Excel 5.

3. Select the destination cell.

4. Pull down the Edit menu and click Paste Special.

5. In the Paste Special dialog box, select Text in the As list box, click the Paste Link radio button, and then click on OK. See Figure 9.2.

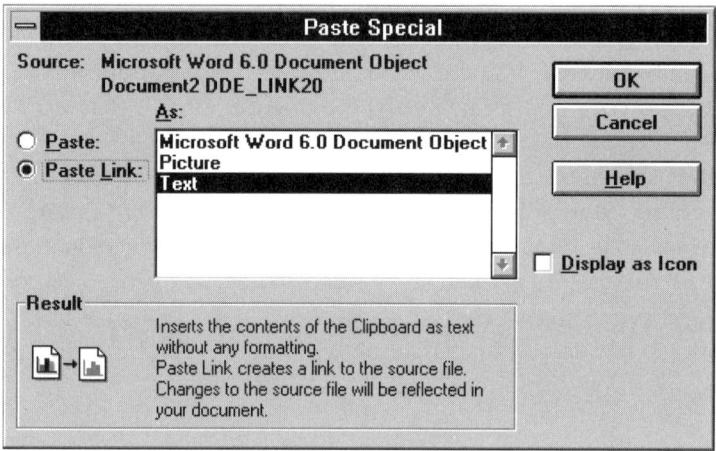

Figure 9.2 Paste Special Settings for Linked Text

Excel automatically enters this link as an array formula although in this simple example, an array entry is not required. In fact, you could type the following formula directly into a cell:

```
=Word.Document.6|'D:\DATA\TUGEXCEL\LINKTXT2.DOC'!Lobster
```

Assuming that the path was to a valid WinWord 6 file *and* that file has a bookmark called "Lobster," any text contained within the bookmark would be displayed in the cell. The text is subject to the 255-cell character limitation, of course. An invalid file name wins you a #REF error in the cell. Remember that a bookmark in WinWord is analogous to a range name in Excel.

Hidden windows   Even if WinWord were not running, it would still be possible to update the link. Naw, it's not magic (we wish it were). It's smoke and mirrors, well, actually it's smoke and *hidden windows*. That's as in "I know that application is running somewhere on this PC *but I can't find it!*" More on that cryptic remark shortly.

Double-click on the cell with the formula and the source application is loaded with the specified data file. If the source application or the data file is not available, you get this error message. See Figure 9.3.

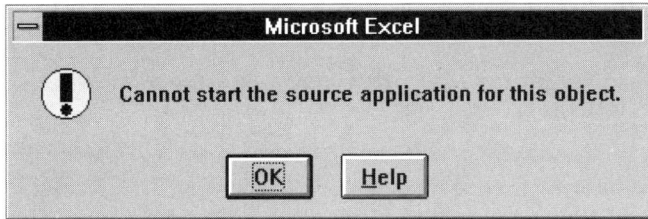

Figure 9.3 No One at Home

Your Honor, I Object!

You can beat the cell character limitation by linking the data as an object (see the first selection in the As list box in Figure 9.2). This way you get the linked data reflected as an object. See Figure 9.4. In Figure 9.4 the object is selected to show you its formula, which is visible in the formula bar.

Picture 1		=Word.Document.6|'D:\DATA\WINWORD\DOCS\DELETE1.DOC'!'DDE_LINK12'							
A	**B**	**C**	**D**	**E**	**F**	**G**	**H**	**I**	**J**

1 If on the other hand data in another application is linked to an Excel 5 sheet the data remains external to
2 Excel. A representation, or perhaps more accurately, an echo of the data is displayed in the Excel sheet. If
3 the linked data in the external application is modified the data in the Excel sheet is updated to reflect
4 those changes.
5
6
7

Figure 9.4 Paste Special as Linked Object

Double-clicking on the linked object has the same effect as that described in the last section, namely, the source application loads (if not already running) and opens the data file (if not already open) and the linked data is selected. You can also achieve the same result by selecting the object and then clicking on the Object option on the Edit menu or from the Edit Object option on the object's shortcut menu. We talk more about objects later.

Managing Links—Good News, Strange News

The good news is that links can be managed from the Links dialog box. See Figure 9.5. The strange news is how these links behave. You would think that an Automatic link would, well, update automatically right? Links are finicky creatures, but if you know their habits, you should be fine. But don't *ever* feed one after midnight.

Select Links from the Edit menu and you see the screen in Figure 9.5.

You select the links you want to work with (click, SHIFT + click, and CTRL + click all work as you would expect in the Source File list box). You can force the links to update, you can open the source application (or switch to it if it is already

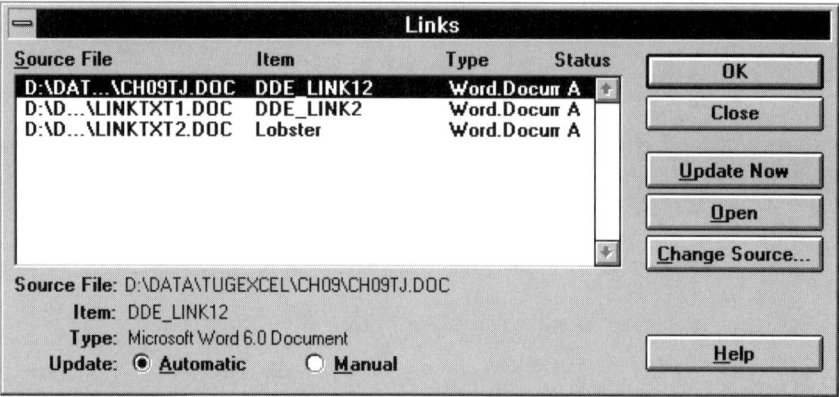

Figure 9.5 Edit Link Central

open), or you can modify the source by making the link point to a different file or application altogether.

 You should be able to lock a link, but you can't. Keep it from updating until you decide to unlock it. There is no provision to break a link either. That's where you might be linked to all sorts of data in other applications that's subject to change. When the data is all finalized, you want to break all the links so the data in Excel becomes static. Ah, well. Of course, WinWord 6 has locking and a break link command in its Links dialog box. Don't the WinWord mavens at Microsoft *ever talk to the Excel gurus!* Come on, at least slip the occasional note under the door.

Finally, you can change a link from Automatic to Manual and vice versa.

Romulan Warbirds Decloaking off Starboard!

> When a thing is funny, search it for a hidden truth.
>
> George Bernard Shaw

There is indeed something funny going on. We don't mean funny "ha ha"; we mean funny "sheesh."

When you fire up an Excel 5 book that contains a link (or several for that matter), a lot depends on whether the source application is running or not. By default Excel informs you that links exist. See Figure 9.6. In the Tools Options Edit filecard there is a check box called "Ask to Update Automatic Links," which, if cleared, causes Excel *not* to ask about updating links but rather to force updates automatically.

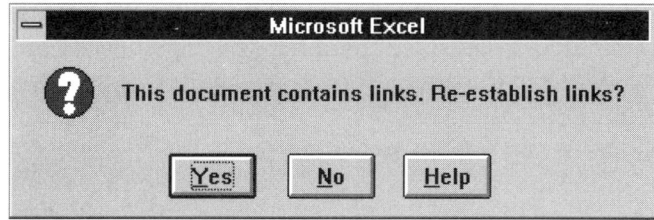

Figure 9.6 Update Them Link Critters, Pardner?

If you click Yes (or you have configured Excel to force updates automatically) and the source application is running, then no worries, mate. Excel chats with the source application and cajoles it into peeking at the file (at the other end of the link) and updating the data to the latest and greatest.

If you click Yes and the source application isn't running, here's what happens. Let's use WinWord 6 as the example. WinWord 6 is launched and it loads the specific data file that contains the linked data. Let's see, have we left anything out…oh, all this launching and loading happens in a *hidden* window. It's invisible and, to you the user, inaccessible. Yeah, Microsoft has perfected a cloaking device and uses it to hide entire applications running on your computer from you.

Check out Task List. There's no clue that another application was just launched. Your only hint is the amount of time it takes to do the update. Same delay as when you start WinWord from Program Manager. Hmmm, resources take a hit commensurate with starting WinWord. Now try starting WinWord and loading the source document. You get a message like the one in Figure 9.7.

Links, it's all timing.

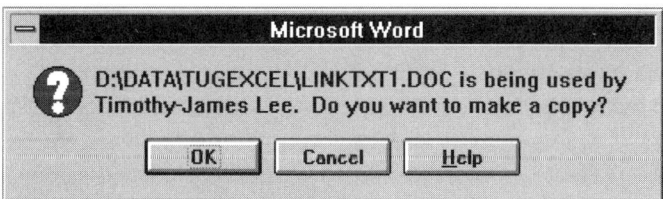

Figure 9.7 Must Be My Evil Twin

Now you might think, If that's me, who am I? But thinking like that can make your head explode. It's the hidden version of WinWord that has opened the data file.

Close the Excel linked file and the source file (or files) in the hidden WinWord window close(s). But not WinWord itself. Huh, what? That's right, pilgrim, WinWord stays running in its cloaked condition. Close Excel altogether. You guessed it. *WinWord stays running!* How do you get this hidden instance of WinWord to close? Easy, close Windows. *Ouch!*

We'd prefer that OLE 2.0 exhibit more robust clean-up procedures. Ah, well, at least updating links upon subsequent file openings doesn't launch multiple instances of WinWord.

When Automatic Isn't—Or Just Say No...

When you open an Excel 5 file with links you get the "Re-establish links?" message (see Figure 9.6). If you click No, the links do not update, but this has significant consequences.

The links are now manual. If you pop open the Links dialog box, the Automatic radio button is still lit, but changes in the source application are not updated. The links can only be updated via the Update Now button (see Figure 9.5). There's no way to reestablish the links as automatic short of closing the file and reopening it and responding by clicking on the Yes button to the "Re-establish links?" message.

The bottom line is that you have to be really careful with links.

REACH OUT AND TOUCH SOME OBJECTS

> ...communication is one of the persistent dreams of the inhabitants of the oblate spheroid on which we move, breathe, and suffer for lack of beer.
>
> Don Marquis
> "The Almost Perfect State," *The Best of Don Marquis*, 1927

Communication is what OLE is all about. Application A chatting away with application B. Ah, can't you hear that digital highway hum? But what are your applications talking about? Most likely they're going on about objects. So, like, what's an object?

No problem, fire up good ol' Excel's help engine and, hmmm, lot's of stuff on "object," but there's no friendly little green dashed underlined definition for the term. We looked at lots of help screens and never saw object defined. Okay, we'll look in the *User's Guide*. Here it is, from page 704, "you can include information, or *objects*, created in other applications." Uh, yah. Guess that an object must have something to do with information then (we're getting warm, pilgrim, *heh, heh, heh*). Let's see what Help in WinWord 6 has to say about what an **object** is.

Object defined   A table, chart, graphic, equation, or other form of information you create and edit, often with an application other than Word and then insert and store in a Word document.

By George! We think that's got it! Replace "Word" with "Excel" and you have a definition that will see us through this section. Whew! With that in mind, here we go on a whirlwind tour of dealing with objects.

In-place Activation

> If you have form'd a circle to go into,
> Go into it yourself and see how you would do.
>
> William Blake
> *To God*

Excel 5 has the new and improved OLE 2.0! It may not be faster than a speeding bullet, but it *can* leap tall applications in a single bound. The way cool whiz-bang feature in OLE 2.0 is in-place activation (a.k.a. in-place editing). Huh? Despair not, pilgrim, read on!

What Has Gone Before...

To appreciate in-place activation you have to understand how OLE 1.0 worked. Prior to OLE 2.0, when you wanted to activate an embedded object...no, wait, come back! Terms like "embedded object" are only scary because they're new. Remember that an "object" is only some information, probably created with an application other than Excel, and when you insert that information into Excel, it is said to be "embedded." Like most things in life, it's easy once you get the terminology sorted out.

To continue, prior to OLE 2.0, when you wanted to activate an embedded object in your Excel 4 spreadsheet, you double-clicked on it and the conversation went like this:

Excel 4:	Hmmm, now what's this stuff that the user double-clicked on? Yuck, it's not mine, that's for sure. Jeez, look at that stuff, oh, sez here "Property of: Word for Windows." Guess it must be word processing stuff. Yoo-hoo, WinWord. Wakie wakie, up and at 'em.
WinWord 2:	WHAT!
Excel 4:	Somebody wants to edit some stuff in my spreadsheet and it's your stuff so I'm sending it to you. Just dump it in a document thingy or do whatever it is you word processors do and when you're done send it back.
WinWord 2:	Okie dokie.

WinWord 2 would pop up and you'd be presented with a pseudo-document in WinWord with a title like "Object in Sheet1." You could work on it in WinWord 2 and, when done, you'd notice that the Save command on the File menu changed to Update. Update or close the document and the data is pumped via the OLE communications channel back to Excel.

What did this WinWord 2 data look like in Excel you ask? *Heh, heh, heh*. It looked like a WinWord icon. The first time we saw it, one of us called a friend at Microsoft. The official response was "it's by design," which is a euphemism for "it's not a bug, it's a feature." When we asked how they envisioned users implementing it, they said they'd look into it. They never got back to us on that one. True story.

How it is Now

First, you can forget about the stupid embedded icon stuff (although it is an option if you want it). You can now embed WinWord 6 text in an Excel 5 spreadsheet in a text frame (which looks like the text box graphic object you created in Chapter 5). See Figure 9.8.

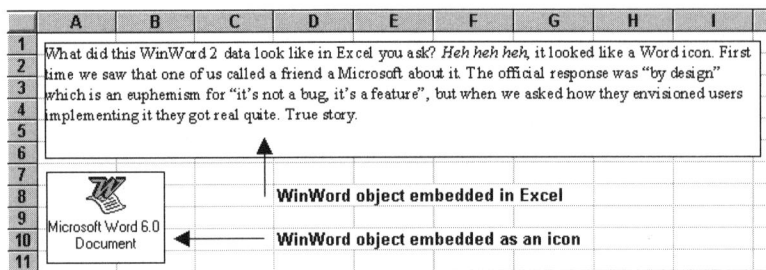

Figure 9.8 WinWord 6 Objects Embedded in Excel 5

With OLE 2.0, your embedded data doesn't have to go the source or host application, unless you have it embedded as an icon (see Figure 9.8). Instead, the host application comes to your data. 'Tis true, by golly. When you double-click on the WinWord 6 object in Excel 5 to activate it, through the miracle of modern programming, the conversation now goes something like this:

Excel 5:   WinWord data initiated. WinWord activate and standby for menu and toolbar lock.

WinWord 6:   Commands mapped and synchronized, Excel. I relieve you, sir!

Biff, boom, bang, Excel's toolbars are swapped out for WinWord's. Excel's menus combine with WinWord's. *WinWord's native command set is active and can be used to edit the embedded object right there in the spreadsheet*. It stays this way until you click back in the sheet (outside of the embedded object). This is also known as **in-place activation**, or **in-place editing**.

Can you see that wonderful document-centric world off in the distance? Somewhere on the road to Cairo. Coming someday to a computer near you. Meanwhile...consider Figure 9.9 where a WordArt object embedded in Excel has been double-clicked on for activation.

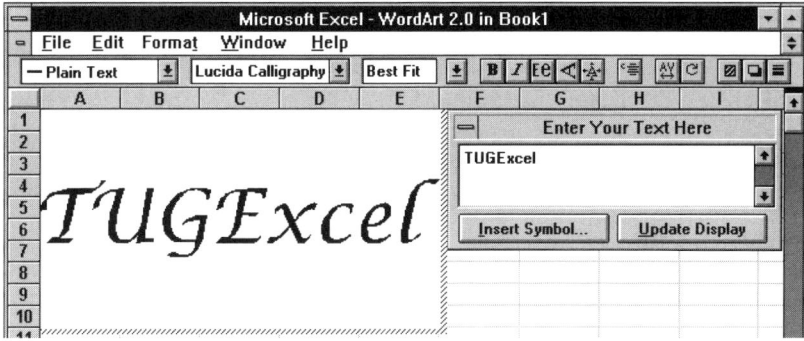

Figure 9.9 This is Excel???

Excel has never looked like this! The menu bar is WordArt's, not Excel's. Ditto for the toolbar. Faster than a palace coup, WordArt takes control.

All is not sweetness and light, of course. Take a WinWord 6 object being edited in-place in Excel 5. Sure, any standard toolbars displayed in WinWord appear in the Excel window. But we mean the standard toolbars. If you have a custom toolbar, it goes missing. Ditto for any customizations you may have made to any of the standard toolbars.

Table 9.1 lists some of the Microsoft Office/Windows applications and show which support in-place editing.

Table 9.1 Office 4.0 Object Classes That Support In-place Editing

Object Class Name	Supports In-place Editing?
Drawing	No
Equation 2.0	Yes
Excel 5.0 Chart	Yes
Excel 5.0 Worksheet	Yes
Graph	No
Paintbrush Picture	No
PowerPoint Presentation	No
PowerPoint Slide	No
Sound	No
Word 6.0 Document	Yes
Word 6.0 Picture	Yes
WordArt 2.0	Yes

State of the Object: Edit, Open, Play, and Convert

Embedded OLE objects look and behave much like the graphic objects that were discussed in Chapter 8 until activated. You select an OLE object by clicking once on it. The expected sizing handles appear. Notice in the formula bar, however, that the object is represented by an embed function:

```
=EMBED("MSWordArt.2","")
```

That's a pretty good clue when you are not sure if a graphic object on a sheet is a plain old Excel graphic or an embedded OLE object.

As seen, you can double click on an object to activate it. This lets you edit the data contained in the object using the source application's command set, and other options are available.

Object, I command thee!   If you select the OLE object and pull down the Edit menu, the Object option is no longer grayed out. Select it and several commands appear on the fly-out menu. The available commands are determined by the type of object selected and can include:

- Edit—has the same effect as double-clicking on the object.

- Open—bypasses the in-place editing, opens the source application, and loads the object data (like the old OLE 1.0 method).

- Play—runs the object data, for example, an embedded .WAV file that when played is run using the sound recorder (SOUNDREC.EXE).

- Convert—presents you with a list of formats that the data can be converted into. See Figure 9.10

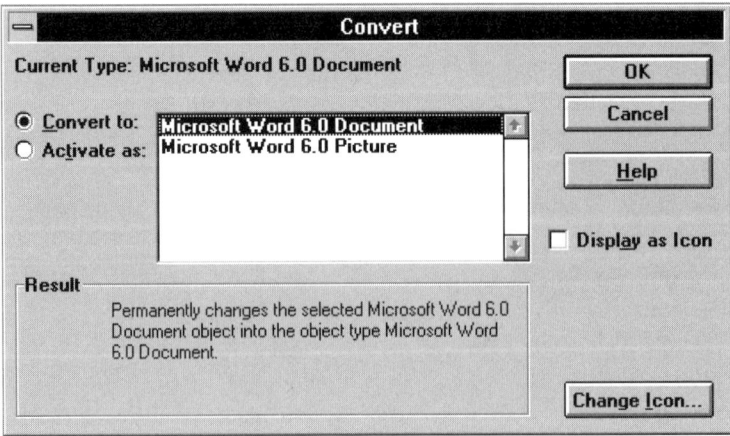

Figure 9.10 Embedded Data Can Be Converted

Sizing, Scaling, and Formatting

Once you have your object embedded in the container document, getting it to look the way you want it can be a challenge. Not all objects scale in the same manner. (If you drag on the sizing handles to scale the object, does that make it a dragon scale operation? *<groan—sorry, couldn't resist>*) WordArt objects, for example, scale nicely, so making the displayed object larger or smaller does not present much of a problem. WinWord 6 objects are another story.

Consider Figure 9.11, which shows several WinWord 6 objects embedded in an Excel 5 worksheet. The top object in the figure appears as first embedded (100% × 100%).

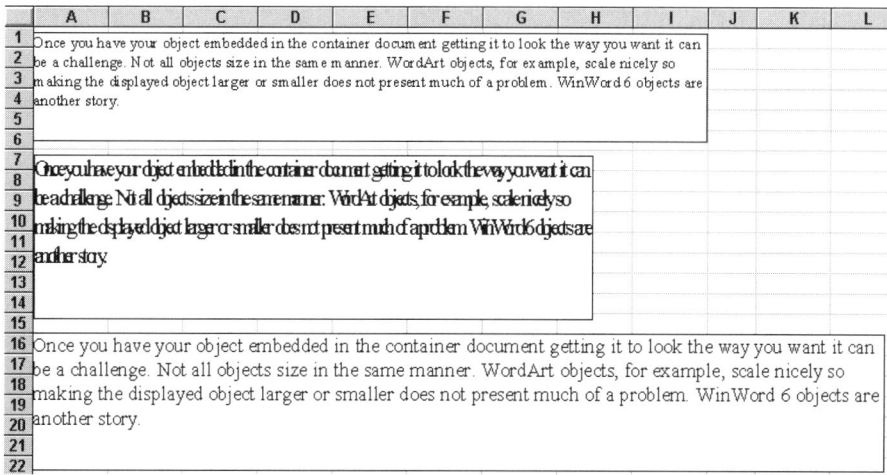

Figure 19.11 Scaling Can Be a Trick

The middle object was scaled by dragging the fill handles to 83% × 150% (watch the status bar while dragging the handle to see the scaling percentages). Not so good, is it? The object does not behave like a text box. The data does not wrap, so no matter what the size of the object, you get the same number of lines. The result is that the displayed text gets squished.

Sizing can be taxing.

The bottom object was scaled while holding down the Shift key (which maintained the proportions) and is displayed at 124% × 124%.

To resize the object and change the wrapping or point size of the text, you have to edit the object. This is most easily accomplished via the double-clicking technique. See Figure 9.12.

By dragging the object's sizing handles when it is activated, you can change the way the displayed text wraps. Notice the odd border surrounding the activated embedded WinWord object. That's called a **hatched border** and is a visual clue that the object is being edited in place.

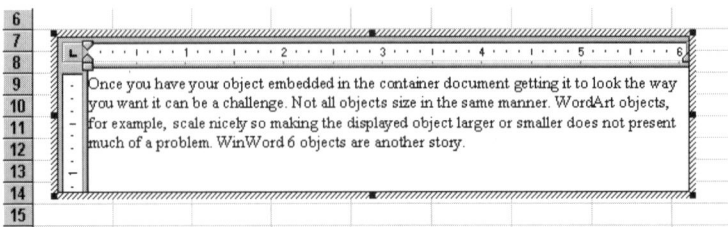

Figure 9.12 In-place Editing for Resizing

The embedded OLE objects can be formatted in the same manner as Excel's graphic objects (text boxes, arrows, circles, and stuff like that). You select the object and choose Object from the Format menu or Format Object from the shortcut menu.

Be the First on Your Block to Drag-and-Drop

Americans have been conditioned to respect newness, whatever it costs them.

John Updike
A Month of Sundays, 1975

This is the hot feature of OLE 2.0 that Microsoft is spotlighting big time in its advertisements for Office. You've seen them—"cross-application drag-and-drop makes it easy to share data between applications." Yum! Real wowie-pow-zowie stuff for sure. But is it practical? Will it play in Peoria?

Intraapplication Issues

We can sum up the issues involved with dragging objects from sheet to sheet and from book to book quite simply. There aren't any. That's for the simple reason that you can't drag anything from one book to another. Since you can't display two sheets at the same time without putting them in separate book windows, that lets out dragging from sheet to sheet as well.

OLE 2.0 primal scream therapy

The surprising, distressing, insane, unusual, (please supply the adjective of your own mood and mind-set) thing is that you *can* do this in WinWord 6. Tile two documents and you can drag objects from one to the other all you like. You might consider a primal scream every once in a while when things like this have you blathering incoherently. Works for us.

Interapplication Issues

This is what the hoopla is all about. Instead of clicking on a chart in Excel 5, copying it, switching to WinWord 6, positioning the cursor where you want the chart, and pasting it—that's uhm, about seven mouse clicks—you can drag-and-drop directly from Excel 5 to WinWord 6.

1. Minimize all open applications except Excel and WinWord.

2. Take one of these steps:

   a. Pop up the Task List and click on Tile.

   b. Manually resize each window so that both applications are visible.

3. Scroll WinWord so that the destination spot for the chart is visible.

4. Scroll Excel so that the chart is visible.

5. Click-and-drag the chart in the Excel window over to the WinWord window and drop it.

Ta da.

Doesn't seem all that quicker or easier to us, but that's admittedly a subjective opinion. It makes for a good demonstration though. Real sizzle. Oh, it only works on charts embedded in a worksheet. You can't drag-and-drop charts from chart sheets; you have to use the more pedestrian copy and Paste Special method.

The "between applications" drag-and-drop technique does the equivalent of a cut and paste in that the object is deleted from the source application. Holding down the Control key while doing the drag copies the object (hey, that's a consistent implementation of the Control key, right on!)

Knockin' down the Berlin Wall twixt apps

Once you've got the Excel object in another application, like WinWord 6, here are some things to watch out for. If the Excel object is a chart that you embedded via drag-and-drop, you *may* experience some, er, difficulties scaling or resizing it. We say "may" because we could not replicate the behavior on all of our machines. But it's mentioned in the Microsoft Knowledge Base, so beware. What happens is you go to resize or scale the embedded object and suddenly the graphic shows some other part of the original Excel sheet. Very bizarre. The recommended MS workaround is to *not use drag-and-drop!* They recommend copying the chart from an Excel chart sheet and doing a Paste Special in the container application.

Even with this chart workaround, the secret to resizing Excel charts embedded in other applications is to do an in-place activation and resize the resulting window. The good news is that we had no problems with any other Excel-embedded objects like sections of worksheets.

Resource Requirements

> Finally, it is ominously evident that these resources are in the course of rapid exhaustion.
>
> Theodore Roosevelt

OLE is really cool despite some of the problems we have found with it. And it's a harbinger of better things to come. But, boy oh boy, it takes some beaucoup computer resources to do this stuff—disk, processor, memory, and so on. Chances are that whatever you have is not enough.

You embed that cool little chart from Excel 5 in a WinWord 6 document. Hey, it's a small chart so what impact could that have on the WinWord file? Well, what about the four worksheets, three other chart sheets, two module sheets, and the odd dialog sheet that are also in the book along with the little tiny, teensy-weensy chart that you drugged over to WinWord and dropped on the poor unsuspecting document?

Better double-click on that embedded object, pilgrim. Whoa, Nelly! That's right, everything comes along for the ride. Embedding causes a file's size to swell so fast that you'll think it has a case of the mumps.

Open a few linked documents and two or three cloaked applications may be launched on your PC. Ross was wrong. That giant sucking sound is OLE slurping up your system resources.

How Do You Spell RAM? DASD? CPU?—M-O-N-E-Y

> Requires 640K.
>
> Ancient historical writing
> circa 1980

Ah, the good old days—when a standard PC came with a ridiculously small amount of RAM and a laughably tiny hard disk. Those were the days. And we're not talking about the old AT classic. We're waxing nostalgic about our last 386/33 with 8 megs RAM.

Listen up! Sixteen megabytes nowadays is *entry level. ENTRY LEVEL!!!* (To get the flavor of that statement, please imagine the late Sam Kinison screaming that at you. Thanks.)

A baseline OLE 2.0 PC configuration   And what about DASD (pronounced dass-dy, it's an old IBM term for storage systems)? You may think that the 130-megabyte hard disk that came with your computer is big, but it is a sad fact that there is no respect for the disk anymore. None. Applications think nothing about consuming 30 to 35 megabytes of disk. Operating Systems can eat 100 megs, no problem. Temp files, DLL's, DocFiles… you may not realize it but you're running out of space.

Better plan on half a gigabyte. Yeah, that's 500 megs. We'd yell it at you, but it is all so depressing. But that's the way it is. Wrap all this stuff up in a 486DX2 running at 66 megahertz.

Oh, and don't get too carried away with yourself once you have this setup (or if you already have it). It's entry level for fooling around with OLE, DDE, or simply cutting and pasting between two major applications. Don't believe us? Try installing Microsoft Office (Professional Version). Now, try loading *all* the applications that comprise Office. What a world.

Don't Forget Video Bottlenecks

> Video meliora, proboque, deteriora.*
>
> Petrarch
> *Sonnet 225, Canzone 21, To Laura in Life,* ca. 1327

Video? VIDEO? Arrrgghhhhhh! If you set yourself up a help desk or computer consultancy and simply answered every problem brought to you with this "The problem is your video drivers," you would be right *better than 50% of the time!* Eeeeeeeeek.

That's without worrying about OLE. Remember that with embedded and linked stuff, the container application (that's the application that has the compound document) has to be able to display the data from the source application. Drop an embedded Excel chart on another application and scale it. Chances are better than even money that the display goes gonzo and shows you some part of the underlying sheet at some huge size. Er, the problem seems to be your video drivers.

For video problems we don't have much better advice than take two aspirin and call the doctor in the morning. Best you can do is try to stay current with the latest drivers available for your video board.

I got those "Latest video driver version 2.358" blues.

A disconcerting note is that the cheaper SVGA boards seem to be much more well behaved than the super high-powered snakelike or fighter plane–like cards. Just a pattern we've noticed. Take it with a grain of salt.

OBJECTS.ENVELOPE.STRETCH WORKIT:=TRUE

> They were upon their great theme. "When I get to be a man!" Being human, though boys, they considered their present estate too common-place to be dwelt upon. So, when the old men gather, they say: "When I was a boy!" It really is the land of nowadays that we never discover.
>
> Booth Tarkington
> *Penrod,* 1914

*"I know and love the good, yet, ah! the worst pursue."

Attempting to take an operating system, an application, or a concept as far as it can go, and then beyond, is a fascinating process. It's guaranteed that you'll learn things along the way about the object of interest and about yourself. What the tacticians call a win-win situation. Right on.

New and improved user interface

In the following sections we poke and prod at the soft, fleshy parts of OLE 2.0 and provide you with some precepts to assist you in putting this amazing, magical, but still delicate technology to work for you in your day-to-day computing. Enjoy.

Objecti Incognito (Not Anymore)

> We must all hang together, or assuredly we shall all hang separately.
>
> Benjamin Franklin
> At the signing of the Declaration of Independence, July 4, 1776

An OLE 1.0–enabled application, like Excel 4 or WinWord 2, did not possess the user interface (UI) hooks to allow you to save an embedded object outside the bounds of the compound document. For example, if WinWord 2's COMPOUND.DOC contains an embedded Excel 4 worksheet and you edit that worksheet (it has a name like "Worksheet in COMPOUND.DOC"), there is absolutely no way you can take that one specific object and save it to disk as a separate, standalone file. No way, no ma'am, no sir, no how. Sure, you can copy it to the clipboard and paste it into a 100% true-blue Excel worksheet and save that worksheet to disk, but that's not the same as a direct, immediate, take-this-object-and-shove-er-save-it-to-disk-now option, is it? No. As they say in the consulting trade, that's TMT (too much trouble).

So, in grand style, OLE 2.0 provides both a programmatic specification and a UI specification for allowing us, the humble users (bothersome creatures, aren't they?) to save the object to a file. No clipboard juggling required.

The steps to save an OLE 2.0 embedded object, in its current state, out to a run-of-the-mill 8.3 DOS file name on your hard disk is as follows. (Not all OLE 2.0-compliant applications support this feature, for example, Equation Editor does not support saving its objects to files.)

Assuming you've got a WinWord document embedded in an Excel container worksheet, Open the WinWord document object, that is, do not in-place Edit it, rather, Open it. (Why is this? Because when the server's and container's menus are aggregated during in-place editing, the File menu system always remains exclusively that of the container. You have to Open the object—now its owner application completely takes over the application display space—in order for the server's File menu system to become available. Feeling vertiginous yet?)

Select File from the primary menu bar, choose Save Copy As, and then enter a legitimate file name as appropriate (see Figure 9.13). This saves the embedded object, *in its current state*, to a free-standing file. Of course, from this point forward

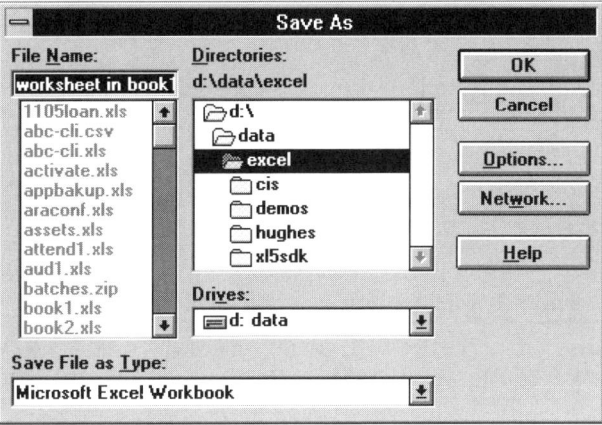

Figure 9.13 File Save Copy As Dialog for an Excel OLE 2.0 Object

there's absolutely no relationship between the new file and the embedded object. They are forever two separate, distinct entities spawned from the moment in time when you clicked on OK in the Save As dialog box. This is as it should be 'cuz this is an embedded object, not a linked object.

Conversely, when you use Insert Object to embed an OLE 2.0 object in the container document, note that the Object dialog has two filecards—Create New and Create from File (see Figure 9.14). OLE 2.0 allows you to spawn an embedded

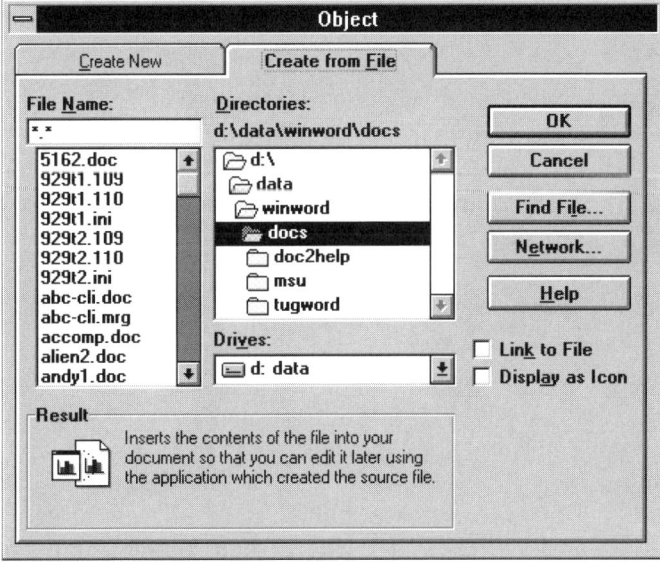

Figure 9.14 Insert Object Dialog's Create from File Options

object based on the data in a free-standing file (again, not all OLE 2.0-compliant applications support this feature).

For those of you interested in some of the technical arcana of OLE 2.0, dig this. The syntax for object class names has changed a bit from the OLE 1.0 days. Table 9.2 shows some application and OLE object class name changes from version 1.0 to 2.0. Note the use of the period (dot) separator. In Chapter 10, you'll see a lot of this "object.object.property" syntax.

Table 9.2 Object Class Names in OLE 1.0 versus 2.0

"Human" Form	OLE 1.0 Object Class Name	OLE 2.0 Object Class Name
Microsoft Excel Worksheet	ExcelWorksheet	Excel.Sheet.5
Microsoft Excel Chart	ExcelChart	Excel.Chart.5
Microsoft Word Document	WordDocument	Word.Document.6

Post-mortem on Roving Links

> What though the mast be now blown overboard,
> The cable broke, the holding anchor lost,
> And half our sailors swallow'd in the flood?
> Yet lives our pilot still.
>
> William Shakespeare
> *King Henry the Sixth*

Sadly, OLE 2.0 as implemented in Microsoft's current Office 4.0 suite of applications does not provide a mechanism for automatically tracking a source file's movements. For example, assume that the Excel compound document `CONTAINR.XLS` contains a link to some source data in the WinWord 6 document `SOURCE.DOC`. If you close `CONTAINR.XLS`, move `SOURCE.DOC` to a different subdirectory or volume, and reopen `CONTAINR.XLS`, you'll be stuck looking at a #REF error in Excel (as we explained earlier, it can't resolve the invalid path name or file name reference). But if you reverse this scenario, WinWord 6 handles this broken link situation far more gracefully—the container displays not an error, but instead the very last value of the linked source data. However, in WinWord 6 as with Excel, updating the link at this point is impossible.

The way it might have been... Furthermore, the object itself provides no visual clue that the link is "broken" or "out-of-date," a feature that was hinted at in Microsoft's *OLE 2.0 Design Specification* document. The document sketched one possible implementation—a linked object's border (a one-pixel wide *dotted* border to distinguish from an embedded object's *solid* border) would be presented in the Windows "disabled text" color if either the link was automatic and the update had failed or the link was manual. In our opinion, they're all good ideas that should have, but didn't, make the cut.

Back to link management. Both OLE 1.0 and 2.0 lack a dynamic link management feature. Strictly speaking, this is true from a native *user interface* point of view, but not from a programmatic point of view. We've been preaching in our seminars since 1991 that you can write DDE macros to overcome many of these OLE user interface limitations. (Here "user interface" refers primarily to Edit Paste Link.) This is because your macro manages the dependent-source (a.k.a. client-server) data relationship. A macro can be far more robust and situation specific than OLE's broad-band user interface feature set. But we digress.

...and the way it is

In Excel, when you edit a broken OLE 2.0 link, there's still no functionality for representing the state of the link. First, the Links dialog incorrectly reports the broken link's status as "A" (Automatic). Second, the Change Source button invokes a minimalist dialog box that's missing several controls (the help topic for Change Links describes controls that *simply aren't there*). See Figure 9.15.

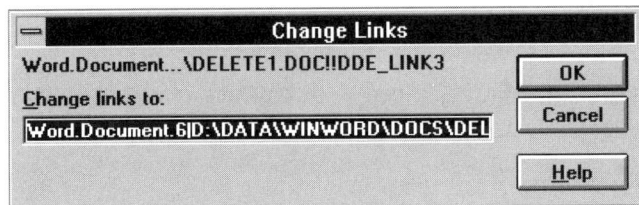

Figure 9.15 Excel's Minimalist Change Links Dialog (Compare to Figure 9.16)

Hey, wait a minute! Didn't we just say OLE 2.0 was new and improved? True, the specifications are new and improved, but guess what? The human beings who programmed Excel and WinWord are, well, different human beings. This isn't a judgmental stance we're taking, mind you, we're simply pointing out that they're not the same people. The Excel development team programmed the treatment of broken links differently from the WinWord development team. In this particular case, WinWord wins hands down.

In WinWord, when you edit a broken OLE 2.0 link, the Links dialog's Update column reads "N/A" (not available). Remember, this is more than OLE 1.0 did. (Which, BTW, was nothing. *Once an OLE 1.0 link was broken, you got no notification or indication anywhere. Nada, amigo.* Uh, except if you're Excel 5, and there's still nada.)

WinWord handles broken links better.

Another OLE 2.0 pleasantry threaded into WinWord is the button labeled Change Source. It fires up a dialog that looks much like the common File Open, with the notable addition of an Item text box containing the item description, so you can at least try to find the wayward source file (see Figure 9.16). It kindly points to the source file's last known directory and file name. Slick. There was no such feature under OLE 1.0. Still, it's a bummer that you have to *manually* (ugh) invoke this OLE 2.0 feature.

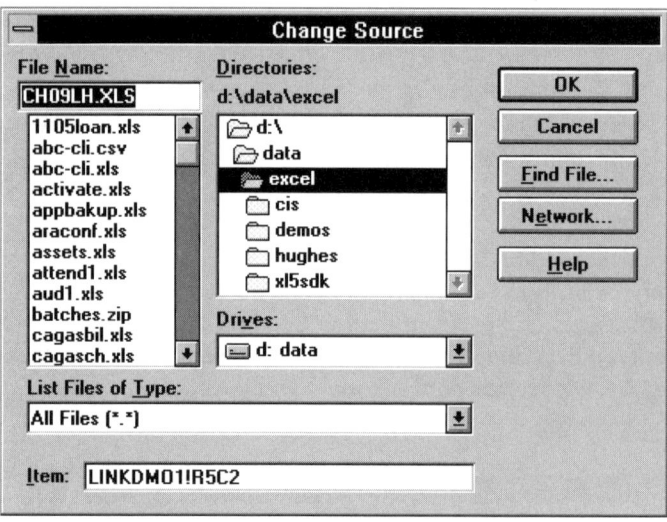

Figure 9.16 Word's Change Sources Dialog for Broken (Out-of-date) Links (This Is WinWord 6, Not Excel 5!)

Burrowing Objects and Links

> Behold! human beings living in an underground den...Like ourselves... they see only their own shadows, or the shadows of one another, which the fire throws on the opposite wall of the cave.
>
> Plato
> *The Republic*

OLE 2.0 supports nested embedded objects and embedded links. Sure, you're thinking. More vocabulary terms. Well, you're right! A **nested embedded object** is an object inside an object, which is in turn inside the outermost container or compound document. A **nested linked object** is a link to an object that's inside the container instead of outside of it (therefore, the link points to an object with no file name). Reads a bit stiff, eh? Well, the verbiage required to describe these cool features does get a bit convoluted, but the features are worth their weight in gold, so hang tough, pilgrim.

Nested Embeds

...plans within plans...

Frank Herbert
Dune

Imagine a scenario where an Excel worksheet serves as the compound document. Inside the sheet is an embedded WinWord document object. Inside the WinWord document object is an embedded WordArt object. See Figure 9.17. To set up this scenario, follow these steps:

1. Maximize Excel.

2. Open a new Excel 5 workbook and save it as `OLE2EM1.XLS`.

3. Select Insert Object, activate the Create New filecard, then choose Microsoft Word 6.0 Document and click on OK. The WinWord object is now embedded *and being edited in-place*.

4. Type in "Hello world." and press `ENTER`.

5. Select Insert Object (remember, you're working with Word's menu system aggregated with Excel's), activate the Create New filecard, select Insert Object, then choose Microsoft WordArt 2.0 and click on OK.

6. WordArt opens with its default text "Your Text Here," which will do for this little experiment, only let's make it blue for sport. Click on OK. At this point *if* you only see the WordArt object's border but not its true contents that's because you have Picture Placeholders turned on in WinWord—*and there's nothing you can do about it right now!* Lord knows, we tried. Pulled every rabbit out of every hat in our corporate HQ. The rule is: If the last time Windows "saw" WinWord and Word's Tools Options View Picture Placeholders check box was selected, meaning "show picture object borders but not the pictures themselves," you're not gonna see the WordArt object now. *And you can't access Word's Tools Options menu when it's aggregated.* Catch-22.

   A nested embed

7. The WordArt object is now embedded in another embedded object. This is called a nested embed. (BTW, if you're feeling dizzy and want to pinch yourself to prove that you're looking at a WinWord-aggregated-with-Excel menu system, select Help and notice that the About drop-down command reads "About Microsoft Word..." *Heh, heh, heh.*)

8. Click anywhere outside the WinWord object and you're back into the standard Excel display space. *Thank goodness.*

9. Save `OLE2EM1.XLS` (or discard it, at your discretion).

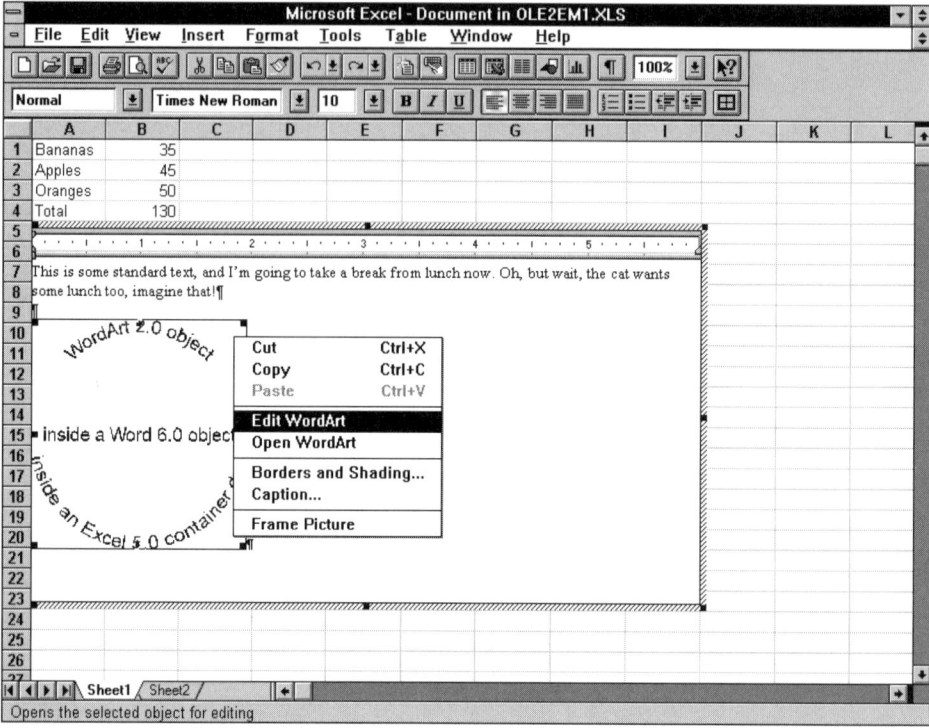

Figure 9.17 A Nested Embed

OLE 1.0 had no equivalent of in-place editing. Under OLE 1.0 you could access the WordArt object once you had opened the WinWord server application, *but WinWord then took the screen over from Excel*. At that point you could open the WordArt server application and it would "float" above the WinWord screen. *You could no longer "see" the true container application (Excel)*. OLE 2.0 to the rescue.

OLE 2.0 has in-place editing and it's a very, very, extraordinarily good thing. So you can now access the WordArt object *while the container application's screen persists*. Try this.

Keep your helmet lamp handy.

Assuming you're exactly where we left you in the last bulleted step,

1. Right-click inside the WinWord object, select Document Object, and then choose Edit. You're back into in-place edit mode.

2. Right-click inside the WordArt object and choose Edit WordArt.

With your very own eyes you can see that the server application (WordArt) is running inside the first embedded object's server's menu system (that's WinWord). Now pay attention, pilgrim, 'cuz this is a bit labyrinthine. Notice that the WordArt server is not full-screen, rather it's floating in what WindowsSpeak calls "windowed" or "restored" mode. *Hey, wait a minute!* Edit is supposed to aggregate the server's menus into the container's menus, right? So why is WordArt running windowed? Presumably because aggregation ends after the first embed, that is, for any nested embeds (no matter how deep into the dark cave you go spelunking—more on this later), you don't get the benefits of aggregated menus when you select in-place editing. Click Cancel to dismiss WordArt.

If you're keeping up with our steps on your PC, the WinWord object is still being edited in-place. Therefore, to return to Excel's standard display space, click anywhere outside the WinWord object. Now let's see what happens when you Open the WinWord object and then fiddle with the nested embedded WordArt object.

Take these steps:

1. Right-click on the WinWord object, select Document Object, and choose Open. Be sure that Tools Options View's filecard check box called Picture Placeholders is *cleared*.

2. Right-click on the WordArt object and choose Edit WordArt. Take note, pilgrim— *WordArt's menus aggregate with Word's menus.*

3. Select File from the primary menu bar, and then choose Close and Return to OLE2EM1.XLS (now there's a pull-down item we betcha haven't seen before) to dismiss WordArt and WinWord.

4. Right-click on the WinWord object, select Document Object and choose Open.

5. Right-click on the WordArt object and this time choose Open WordArt. WordArt appears windowed, as you'd expect.

6. Click Cancel to dismiss WordArt.

7. From within WinWord, select File Close and Return to OLE2EM1.XLS.

The moral of the story is…well, the story's not over. We want to take you on a journey deep into the caverns of OLE 2.0 nested embedding. (After all, this is the *Underground Guide*, eh?) When we emerge back at the cavern entrance, all smiling triumphantly, we'll divulge the moral.

How Deeply Can Objects Be Embedded?

> A man of genius makes no mistakes. His errors are volitional and are the portals of discovery.
>
> James Joyce
> *Ulysses*, 1922

We're really not crazy. Really. We're just very curious and very exacting. So, before you delve into this section, scratching your head mightily as to why we might even conceive of such an experiment, we'll tell you!

Didja ever inadvertently fire up multiple copies of a Windows app? Well, whether you personally have or haven't, *it happens all the time out there in the trenches.* When it happens, the user gets a nice, clean-cut, wholesome message box entitled "Application Execution Error" that states, "Insufficient memory to run this application. Quit one or more Windows applications and then try again." accompanied by a cheerful OK button. When the user clicks on OK, *Windows is still running and stable.* No GPFs. No system lockups. No (shudder) warm or cold boots. Does this same grace under fire permeate the world of OLE 2.0? A world where server applications can start up like wildfire, depending on the complexity of any given compound document? A world of DLLs on top of Windows on top of MS-DOS? Say one of your co-workers e-mails you a multiple-object compound document. Before you know it, as you navigate through it, you may find yourself in a nested embed situation or a nested link situation. It could happen. *Easily.* The question is, when you overload OLE 2.0, is Windows still running and stable? We're here to tell ya. Read on, pilgrim.

We performed an experiment to see how deeply OLE 2.0 objects can be embedded. To streamline things, we'll refer to the objects occasionally by their letter designation (A, B,...G)—see following list. Note that in conducting this experiment, we used in-place editing (Edit as opposed to Open) wherever the user interface allowed.

A word about our test machines. We ran this next experiment on computers set up to meet the recommended minimum PC configuration we described earlier, namely, 486DX2/66, 16 MB RAM, and 400–500 MB hard disk capacity, running the latest versions of Excel and WinWord.

- A—Excel worksheet—the top-level container (compound document) a.k.a. "The Big Kahuna"

- B—WinWord document embedded in A

- C—Excel worksheet embedded in B

- D—WinWord document embedded in C

- E—Excel worksheet embedded in D

- F—WinWord document embedded in E

- G—Excel worksheet embedded in F

Stretching the envelope

Pilgrim, don't try this at home unless someone is paying you or you're as crazy as we are. Question—do you think it's gonna work? Answer—yes, it works. With some caveats. *Heh, heh, heh.* (Uhm, if you decide to replicate this experiment, don't forget to do a full verified backup first. Maybe two. Seriously.)

The point of the experiment lies in the discovery of how OLE 2.0 responds to stressful situations. Does it behave gracefully? Or leave your PC locked up in some brake-squealing, stomach-churning, torso-wrenching fishtail like a souped-up Chevy playin' chicken with a timber-loaded 18-wheeler on some rain-slicked back-country road with no hospital within several hundred miles of your present location? Yeah, that's a feeling you'd better learn to live with if you decide to step so much as one angstrom beyond the boundary of what Microsoft considers "typical business application usage." Now about those usability lab rats and their due diligence…Oh, to hell with them, gird thy loins once again, pilgrim. Remember, they may be calling it "OLE 2.0" (emphasis on the "2.0" part), but in-place editing and everything that goes with it is really a first-time-out-the-door feature. A commendable feature, yes indeedy. But we don't subscribe to the "three is six" school of thought, so how 'bout "OLE 2.0 InPlace 1.0?" Read on.

It is not all that unreasonable to ask to exit an application, is it? *Well, in the course of testing this phenomenon, we saw Windows do stuff we had never ever seen before*. And we live for these kind of out-of-bounds conditions.

First, we start a completely new session of Windows to guarantee a clean environment. Then we embed objects (using Insert Object) one after the other until we're down at object G.

At this point we notice that everything works fine *as long as we back out in the proper innermost-to-outermost object order*. If, however, we are down inside object G, toggle over to the child window containing object A, and close A (accidentally or masochistically), *oh, brother*. In several of our tests, after about 30 seconds of hard disk activity, EXCEL.EXE GPFs (General Protection Fault). Once we dismiss that uplifting message box, WINWORD.EXE GPFs. Gaak. *Two GPFs for the price of one!* Not really that funny, is it? One test PC produces GPFs 100% of the time during this experiment, the other less than 25% of the time. Go figure. *But when we update and close each object in the proper innermost-to-outermost order, we never experience any problems!*

Always exit innie to outie.

We figure it's a timing problem in the shut-down and clean-up routines buried deep in an OLE 2.0 DLL. Regardless, watch for it. *The moral of the story is…*

- Never quit an application that's behaving as an active server until all nested embeds have been individually updated.

- Always perform these updates in the proper order, that is, update from the innermost object back out to the outermost container.

Pilgrim, this is important, so we'll repeat it. *Always update embedded objects from the innermost object back out to the outermost container*. To do otherwise is to tempt system suicide.

Nested Links

> Eas'd the putting off
> These troublesome disguises which we wear.
>
> John Milton
> *Paradise Lost*

Question—can you nest links? Answer—yes, but you'd best be prepared to treat them all as manual links 'cuz even if they're Automatic, they ain't. Sorry 'bout that pilgrim, but it's the unadulterated truth.

We conducted a simple experiment. We started with a traditional Excel container worksheet. We embedded a Word 6.0 Document object. In this document we entered a lead-in paragraph, created a small table of sales data, and then in the WinWord object we embedded an Excel 5.0 Chart object, selected the Chart object's Sheet1, and replaced the default data with data as paste linked text. Next we closed the Chart object, closed the WinWord object, and stood back to admire our work (see Figure 9.18). At this point we had an Excel container with an embedded WinWord document that in turn had embedded in it an Excel chart linked to the text in the WinWord document. Whew, this is a lot like trying to discuss time travel, isn't it?

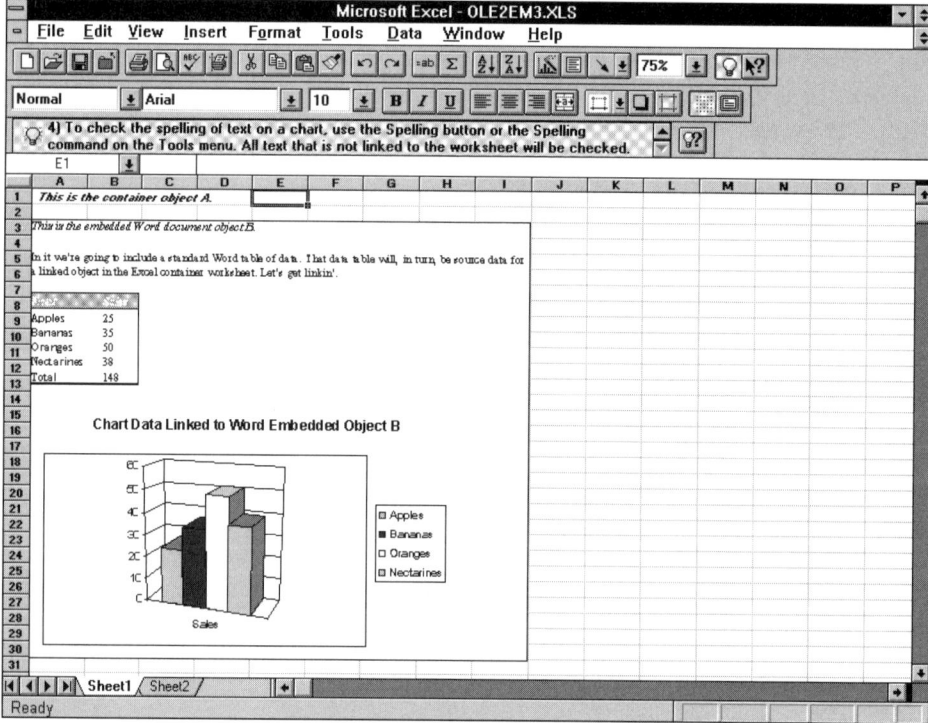

Figure 9.18 A Nested Link Scenario

We tightened up our hiking boots, climbed back down into the cavern, and discovered that when we changed the data in the WinWord object's table, *the Chart object did not update*. (Remember, *this is an automatic link*.) We had to physically open the Chart object, select the sheet containing the link, run the Links dialog, and press the Update Now button. Then the chart changed to reflect the new data. Sheesh. This is "making it easier"? *Oh, brother.* Remember, pilgrim, if the link that points to WinWord is inside a traditional Excel worksheet with no embedding (a straight link), changes in Word's source data immediately cause the Excel-dependent chart to change. So we know the linking technology works in that respect. Introduce just one level of nesting, and you have to grab the link by the throat and throttle it to get it to respond. Go figure.

Nested links aren't automatic.

A CAVEAT CORNUCOPIA

> But answer came there none—
> And this was scarcely odd, because
> They'd eaten every one.
>
> Lewis Carroll
> *Alice's Adventures in Wonderland*, 1865

To wrap things up, how 'bout a few OLE 2.0 tips and tricks we collected along the way.

The only non-mouse way we discovered to get out of an in-place edit is the Escape key. However, this does not discard any changes you've made during the in-place edit.

This means there's no way to roll back the results of the last edit performed on an embedded object unless you save the container document before you make every edit. Then when you find you're dissatisfied with the now-closed embedded object's changed appearance, you can close without saving the container document thereby manually rolling back. Hey, as we've said many times before, when the going gets weird, the weird turn pro (thanks, Hunter).

This is the scariest thing we encountered. While conducting tests with multiple nested embedded objects, Excel (the container application) GPFed. No problem, we thought (no more than usual anyway), but when we tried to exit Windows, we were informed via a system-level error message that we had to first save changes and exit WinWord before we would be allowed to leave Windows. Meaning, the server (WinWord) was still running in a cloaked (hidden) window. Meaning *we couldn't exit Windows without application-rebooting*.

When this happens to you, *don't panic*. At the very least, meticulously close all running applications except Program Manager to minimize any damage that may occur when you Vulcan-salute your PC.

10 VBA, the Programmatic Side of the Coin

A sufficiently advanced technology is indistinguishable from magic.

Arthur C. Clarke

How to spell global macro language— V-B-A

Until Excel 5 and Visual Basic for Applications came along, every Windows application was effectively an island unto itself. We, the innocent, industrious, happy inhabitants of these various islands, managed to communicate with each other by sending hapless messengers out in a fleet of rickety canoes—*HMS Dynamic Data Exchange*—across the deep dark waters of the Windows messaging ether. Very deep. Very dark. Occasionally a courier sent out on an inter-island mission never returned. Bon voyage and R.I.P.

Pre-Excel 5, we used Dynamic Data Exchange (DDE)—an inter-application communications protocol—to connect WinWord to Excel, Visual Basic to WinWord, Excel to PowerBuilder, and so on ad infinitum. DDE was a relatively effective solution, but not always. Messages did get lost, or were plain ignored, in cases where the recipient didn't recognize the nature of the incoming message or was too damn busy to reply in a timely manner. (Every millisecond, hell, every nanosecond, counts when you're a CPU in a non-preemptive multitasking environment, don't ya know).

Using a handful of DDE commands, software vendors and developers (ourselves included, if we do say so ourselves) managed to create some amazing hyper-applications. All technicalities aside, DDE was (and still is) cool for one very important reason—*Microsoft is not the only player supporting it*. That's right, you could then and still can today use DDE to communicate with non-Microsoft products ranging from Lotus Ami Pro to Intuit Quicken. DDE is not "proprietary."

Then along comes the dynamic (no pun intended) duo—OLE 2.0's Visual Basic for Applications (VBA, for short) and OLE Automation (OLEAuto). Pilgrim, it's a whole new ball game.

In one sentence, **OLEAuto** is a set of self-aware blueprints for an application, and **VBA** is the toolkit that we (the customers) use to enter, poke around in, and even modify that application and its components. When a Windows application is OLEAuto compliant, it can reveal secrets about itself and its components to knowledgeable folk; all you need to know are the right questions to ask. Then, if you're feeling declarative, you can command that application to sit up and bark at the moon if you want to. All you need to know are the right commands to issue. You can even, to a degree, get the application to tell you what commands it's prepared to deal with. The trick is, *you must utter the questions and the commands in some dialect of VBA*. Hello VBA, good-bye DDE. Sort of.

At the time of this writing, the on-the-shelf-so-you-can-buy-'em-right-now applications containing a dialect of VBA are Microsoft Excel 5 and Microsoft Visual Basic 3.0. The trade journals herald the delivery Real Soon Now of Microsoft Access 2.0 and Microsoft Project 4.0, both of which speak VBA. Interestingly, and sadly, Microsoft WinWord 6 is a half-breed in this regard—it can answer your VBA queries and respond to your VBA commands, *but it does not itself speak VBA*. Translation: WinWord 6 is OLEAuto compliant, but WordBasic is not a VBA language. (Yet. Perhaps by the time WinWord 7 rolls around it will be, but that's a story for the likes of John LeCarré to tell.) Instead, WinWord 6 relies on DDE to communicate with external applications.

OLEAuto is a Microsoft kind of thing—for now...   Notice how often "Microsoft" appears in the last paragraph? As in, before each and every application name? *This is important.* Until other big guns like Borland, IBM, Lotus, Novell/WordPerfect, and so on spawn OLEAuto-compliant applications, code that you write in VBA using OLEAuto conventions can only interact with Microsoft's family of OLEAuto-compliant applications.

Wait! Don't panic! VBA languages support all the necessary DDE commands to do inter-application communication the old-fashioned way. But if you're thinking VBA and OLEAuto are a panacea for multivendor interapplication communication, sorry. Sure, this is the direction in which Microsoft is heading. World dominion, oh, uhm, let's scale our crystal ball back a few years, yeah, what we mean is, Microsoft seeks to provide a truly common, operating-environment–wide, global macro programming language. Whether other vendors comply or not, well...MAPI, anyone? It remains to be seen if these "other vendors" will do it the Microsoft way, their own way, or deliver us more rattletrap canoes with which to chart the deep dark waters of interapplication communication. (Welcome to the world of delayed gratification. Déjà vu, eh?) Lotus is already touting LotusScript, its own proprietary equivalent of Microsoft's VBA. So let the games begin. *Caveat emptor.*

XLM VETERANS TAKE HEED

And slowly answer'd Arthur from the barge:
The old order changeth, yielding place to new;
And God fulfills himself in many ways,
Lest one good custom should corrupt the world.

Alfred, Lord Tennyson
Idylls of the King, 1859–1885

If you never used Excel's XLM macro programming language, skip this section. If you're of the XLM persuasion, onward into the breach…

Fair question: Is coding in VBA going to be different from coding in XLM? Honest answer: Yes, pleasantly different. Everything you learned while writing XLM code, particularly about the innards of Excel, is going to continue to be as invaluable as ever. It's easy in much the same way that riding a bicycle is easy… it's easy once you know how. VBA is considerably easier to write and read than XLM. Making the transition is a win-win situation. The one cautionary note we'd sound is this—as with *any* new language (computer or human), be prepared to immerse yourself in it until you reach that "hey, I'm dreaming in VBA" crossover point. Enjoy the journey. We did.

> **VBA is easy—once you know how.**

To ease the transition from XLM to VBA, here's a handful of tips:

- Bone up on the *Excel Visual Basic User's Guide*, Appendix B, "Switching from the Microsoft Excel 4.0 Macro Language."

- Study the `SAMPLES.XLS` workbook in the `\EXCEL\EXAMPLES` subdirectory created when you installed Excel. It contains samples of equivalent XLM and VBA code.

- Breathe, eat, and sleep the "Visual Basic Equivalents for Macro Functions and Commands" A..Z help topics. Here's the quickest way to navigate there. Select Help Contents, select the "Reference Information" jump topic, select the "Microsoft Excel Macro Functions Contents" jump topic, select the "Visual Basic Equivalents for Macro Functions and Commands" jump topic. Alternately, with WinHelp running, File Open `MACROFUN.HLP` and select the "Visual Basic Equivalents for Macro Functions and Commands" jump topic. (Note: By default, Excel's help files are stored in the `\EXCEL` directory.)

REQUIRED READING FOR EVERYONE

> I have tried to remove weight, sometimes from people, sometimes from heavenly bodies, sometimes from cities; above all I have tried to remove weight from the structure of stories and from language.
>
> Italo Calvino
> *Six Memos for the Next Millennium*, 1988

Your VBA toolkit   XLM veterans and Excel VBA newcomers alike, listen up. Here are several tools you absolutely must have velcroed to your body as you ramp up with VBA:

- Devour the *Excel Visual Basic User's Guide*. Yum.

- Review the `MAINXL.HLP` help file's relevant Examples and Demos lessons. (Select Help, Examples and Demos and then choose "Using Visual Basic.")

- Study the VBA_XL.HLP help file's numerous Reference Example code snippets.

- Buy a copy of the *Microsoft Excel 5 Visual Basic for Applications Reference*. Grab your Gold-plated Platinum card, pick up the phone, and dial 800-677-7377. *Do it now.*

- Hang out in the cyberspace of CompuServe's MSEXCEL forum Section 4 "VBA for Excel."

- While you're up on MSEXCEL, don't miss `XL5TOP.EXE`, described in the library summary as "The latest and greatest information on Excel 5.0 for Windows...This file is the newest information on Excel 5.0, info on macros, Visual Basic for Applications, and much more. The file uses full-text search so you can query on any word and the search engine will present a Topics Found dialog with titles of all articles with the specified word in them."

- Ditto for `XLOBJ.DOC`, described in the library summary as "XLObj.Doc provides a detailed overview of using Microsoft Excel 5.0 as a development platform. The document covers the creation of custom applications using Microsoft Excel's 128 programmable objects. Also included is an introduction to programming using Visual Basic for Applications as well as a discussion of Excel's support for OLE 2.0, ODBC, MAPI, and TAPI. The document also contains a chart depicting the Excel Object Model. The document was authored by Eric Wells, Product Manager for Excel." (Kudos to Eric Wells for an exemplary document.) There's plenty of other public-domain stuff that awaits you there in the hallowed MSEXCEL cyberspace stacks.

KICK-OFF: TOOLS OPTIONS MODULE SETTINGS

> Every vital development in language is a development of feeling as well.
>
> Thomas Stearns Eliot
> *Philip Massinger*, 1920

Before you write a single line of VBA code, tweak your Module Settings as follows:

Check Module Settings

1. Select Tools Options.

2. Click the Module General filecard. Four check boxes are displayed therein.

3. Check Auto Indent, check Display Syntax Errors, clear Break on All Errors, and check Require Variable Declaration (details in the paragraphs following this list).

4. Click the Module Format filecard.

5. Module Format parameters control cosmetics only, so these are completely up to you. Probably easy enough to stick with the defaults (since that's the way code appears in SAMPLES.XLS) for now and customize it downstream. Click on OK.

When Auto Indent is active, the VBA module watches your keystrokes and does a fairly good job of indenting your code when appropriate.

When Display Syntax Errors is active, the VBA module monitors each statement. When you press ENTER VBA reports any syntax errors it sees. For VBA neophytes, this is a good thing. As you become more experienced, you may opt to clear this setting because as you cut-copy-and-paste code snippets around, the module monitor nags you relentlessly. No problem. Clear the check box.

When Break on All Errors is cleared, standard On Error trapping statements in your code work normally. When this setting is checked, VBA ignores your On Error statements and breaks on any error. This can be handy for gnarly debugging sessions, but typically this setting is cleared (off).

We saved the best, and most important setting, for last. Require Variable Declaration should be on, on, on. Without stepping up on Ye Olde Soapbox and lecturing evangelically about the virtues of strong data typing like a bunch of feral Computer Science 301 professors, let's just say that we encourage you to explicitly declare variables. *Pretty please*. The benefits are as follows.

- Anyone who comes along later to maintain your code will kiss your feet for adhering to the convention of strong data typing. (Hell, come back to your own code after a one-week hiatus and if everything's neatly declared *you'll kiss your own feet*! Hmmm, on second thought maybe you should just treat yourself to a movie.)

- Your code will be more compact and efficient since without explicit declaration, Excel has no choice but to allocate excess memory to many variables that could be stored more compactly. (Without explicit declaration, everything is a Variant data type by default. Bleccch.)

OLEAUTO AND THE HEART OF GOLD

> Beneath it lay uncovered a huge starship, 150 meters long, shaped like a sleek running shoe, perfectly white and mind-bogglingly beautiful. At the heart of it, unseen, lay a small gold box which carried within it the most brain-wrenching device ever conceived, a device that made this starship unique in the history of the galaxy, a device after which the ship had been named—the *Heart of Gold*.
>
> Douglas Adams
> *Hitchhiker's Guide to the Galaxy*

When first we groked the essence and potentiality of OLE Automation, we thought instantly and metaphorically of the *Heart of Gold*. To share our vision of OLEAuto with you, we're going to extend and embellish the *Heart of Gold* metaphor a bit. (Hey, it's called "poetic license.")

Excel 5 is like the *Heart of Gold*. You can either pilot it internally (mouse and keyboard) or remotely (VBA and OLEAuto). All of the *Heart of Gold*'s capabilities are available in either piloting mode. The Excel 5 programmable object called Application is, effectively, Excel itself. **Application** is to Excel 5 as "the *Heart of Gold*'s potential behaviors" is to the *Heart of Gold* itself.

"Application" is an object.

Excel possesses 128 programmable objects, one of which is, you guessed it, Application. (An OLE Automation **object** is a programmable entity that you can access by name.) They are arranged in a logical hierarchy, as the *Heart of Gold* is assembled in a logical order. Other frequently used programmable objects are Workbook, Worksheet, Module, DialogSheet, and Chart, with objects deeper down in the object hierarchy like Border or Toolbar. Similar objects in the *Heart of Gold* might be called Cockpit, CargoBay, FuelTanks, Engines, ControlPanel, and so on.

Object.Method

As the remote pilot of the *Heart of Gold*, you can act upon it and with it. Ditto for Excel and OLEAuto. Let's call these actions or commands **methods**. You can fly the *Heart of Gold* with the Fly method, shut it down with the Quit method, or fill its tanks with the Fill method. Getting into the VBA syntactical swing of things, these commands might be in the form

```
Object.Method
```

where the period serves as a separator. For example,

```
HeartofGold.Fly
HeartofGold.Quit
HeartofGold.FuelTanks.Fill
```

Excel equivalent methods would look something like this:

```
Application.Calculate
Application.Quit
Application.ActiveWorkbook.Sheets.Add
```

Objects have **properties**, and here the term means what it sounds like it should mean in plain English. Where the *Heart of Gold* might have properties like Height, Mass, SurfaceArea, Temperature, and Velocity. Excel objects have properties like Caption(a property for the Application and many other objects) or Pushed (a property for the ToolbarButton object). You can get your hands on the contents of Excel's title bar by referring to Application.Caption.

Now, you (or we) may think that ActiveCell sounds more like an object than a property, but we're not espousing object-oriented programming theory here. The important thing to grasp is where and how these objects, properties, and methods relate to each other within Excel's "object model." Remember, too, that today Visual Basic 3.0 can remotely pilot Excel and its programmable objects, and by the time this tome hits the shelves, Access 2.0 and Project 4.0 will be able to pilot Excel, too. Powerful stuff. *Mind-bogglingly powerful.*

WELCOME TO YOUR NEW HOME, THE VISUAL BASIC MODULE

Slang—Language that takes off its coat, spits on its hands, and goes to work.

Carl Sandburg

Hello, we're the Neighborhood Module Welcoming Committee. Care for some cookies and milk? Seriously, you'll be rackin' up some hours here so take time to poke around. See Figure 10.1.

Welcome Wagon!

The Visual Basic toolbar and the module sheet's transmogrified menu pull-downs give you access to the components and features you need to get the job done. Keep in mind that you develop your custom dialog boxes in a completely different sheet type—a dialog sheet (more on this later).

Recording a Macro

Recording a macro is as easy as falling off a log. In the first example you build (coming up shortly), we walk you through the steps. The best feature of the VBA

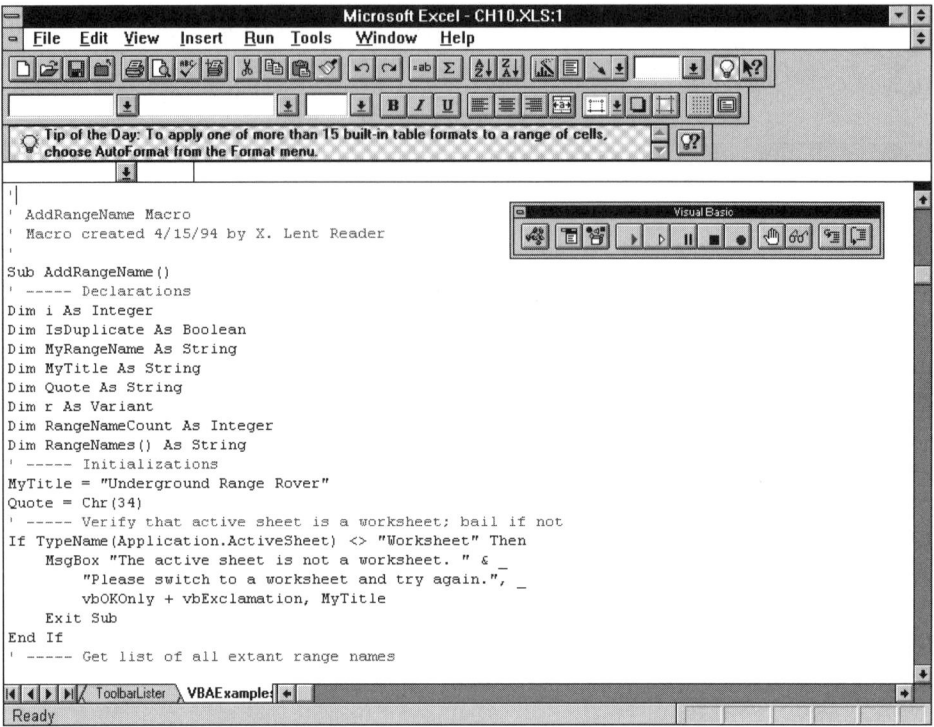

Figure 10.1 The VBA Module in All Its Glory

recorder is that you can tell the recorder, *before you turn it on*, exactly where you want the recorder to dump the recorded actions.

Editing a Macro

Whether you recorded a macro or typed it in by hand, editing a macro is straight-forward. Dig the color-coding scheme. Balk at the lack of drag-and-drop within a module. That's right, you gotta use old-fashioned cut-copy-and-paste techniques to copy or move statements around.

Need help with a particular object, method, or function in your source code? Place the insertion point next to (or anywhere inside) the object, method, or function name and press F1. In the ClearNavigationKeys example later in this chapter, should you want help on the TransitionNavigKeys property, you'd simply click in that statement and press F1. See Figure 10.2 for the resulting help topic.

Display module and worksheet   Splitting panes so you can see your VBA code and a target worksheet is probably the most painful *<groan>* aspect of the module's design. Here's the trick.

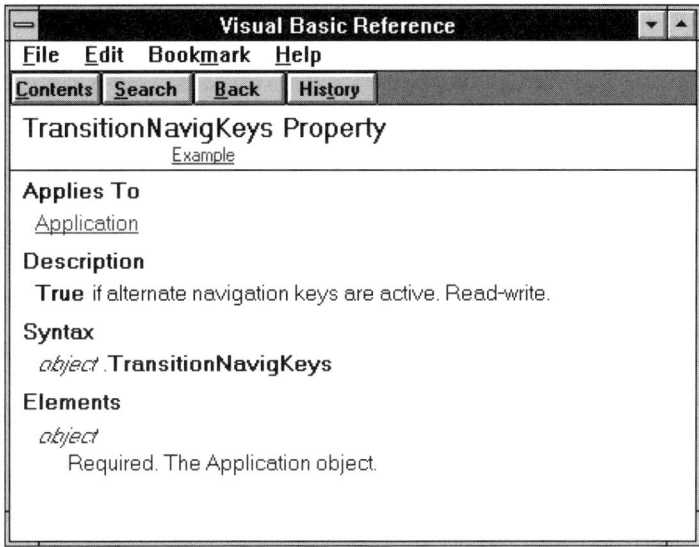

Figure 10.2 Help Is Always Just a Keystroke (F1) Away

Let's start by assuming you've got one worksheet named Sheet1 and one module named Module1.

1. Select Module1.

2. Select Window and choose New Window.

3. Select Window, select Arrange, select Horizontal, select the Windows of Active Workbook check box, and click on OK. Uh huh, that's right, your screen ain't quite there yet. One more step.

4. If you want your module on the top bunk and the sheet on the bottom bunk, activate the bottom window and click the Sheet1 tab. To flip things around, activate the appropriate window and then click the desired tab. Lock 'n load, soldier, you're ready for some big bear now.

Back to the issue of editing. If the macro of interest is right in front of you on screen, make your changes QED. However, you may find that in a large module, or a workbook with several modules, you desperately need a road map. Object Browser to the rescue!

Bobbing for Objects and Anything Else You Can Sink Your Teeth Into

> There was a child went forth every day,
> And the first object he look'd upon, that object he became.

> Walt Whitman
> *There Was a Child Went Forth*

There are two ways to navigate through the multilayered, object-oriented infrastructure of Excel objects while inside a VBA module:

1. Use the F1 key help method with the cursor on an object, function, or method name, and examine the associated help jump topics for the entity of interest.

2. Use Object Browser to get help on the entity and, where appropriate, look at it. And in some cases, insert VBA code based on the selected entity.

Object Browser button

Object Browser gives you quick access to all procedures in all loaded workbooks (including the typically hidden PERSONAL.XLS), and to all objects and modules in both Excel and VBA (see Figures 10.3 and 10.4). Simply click on the Libraries/ Workbooks drop-down to see the list of available entities. The dialog's two list boxes provide drill-down style access to deeper and deeper layers of the OLE Automation object model lurking within Excel 5. Object Browser is only available within a VBA module. If the entity is a procedure, you can edit it by clicking Show, and change its settings by clicking Options. If the entity is anything other than a procedure,

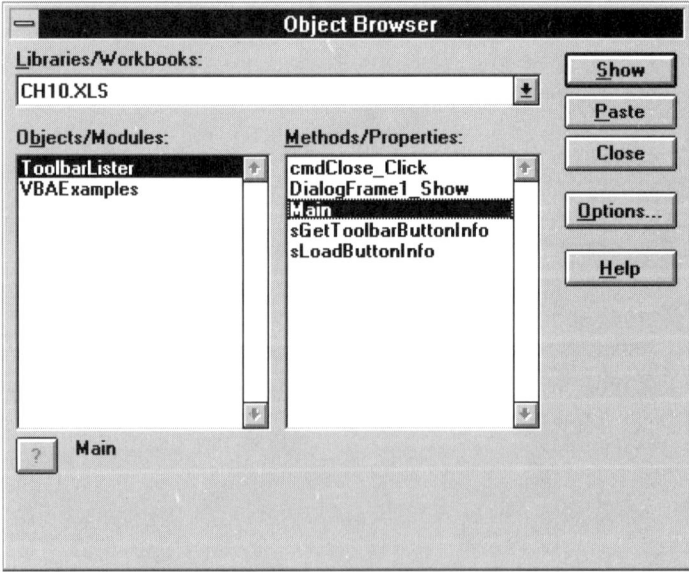

Figure 10.3 Object Browser Sniffs a Workbook

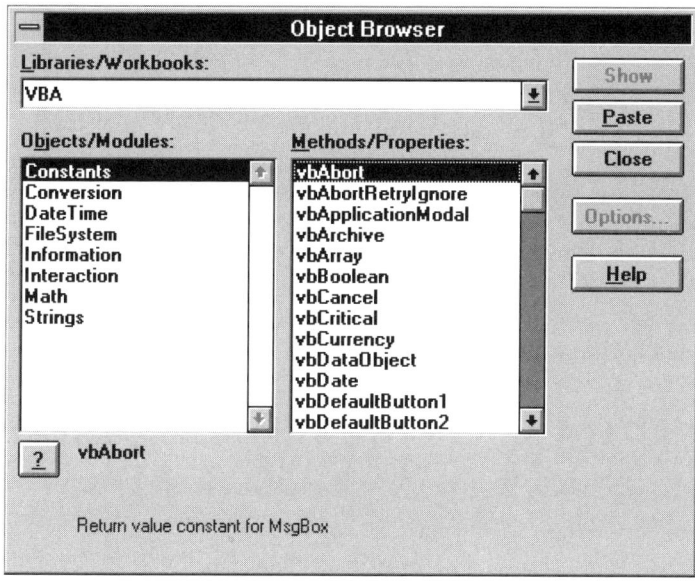

Figure 10.4 Object Browser Sniffs VBA

the Help button (below the Objects/Modules list box) is enabled. Click it to see the associated help. If the entity is a method or property, you can insert partial statement code into the module—wherever the cursor is—by clicking Paste.

For example, if you want to jump to the Main procedure in the ToolbarLister module stored in CH10.XLS,

1. Select CH10.XLS in the Libraries/Workbooks drop-down.
2. Select ToolbarLister in the Objects/Modules list box.
3. Select Main in the Methods/Properties list box.
4. Click Show (see Figure 10.3).

Then, to see a list of all the VBA built-in constants,

1. Select VBA in the Libraries/Workbooks drop-down.
2. Select Constants in the Objects/Modules list box.
3. Select whatever constant in the Methods/Properties list box interests you (see Figure 10.4).

Hey, Man, Where's the Start Button on This Thing?

There are many ways to run a macro. If you're in a module, you can select Run Start (or press F5), select Tools Macro Run, or press the Run Macro button on the

Multiple ways to start

toolbar. If you're outside a module, you can select Tools Macro and Run the macro of your choice. You can assign macros to objects like toolbar buttons and graphic objects in sheets, and, as you'll see in the Underground Toolbar Lister example, assign macros to controls in custom dialog boxes.

What About Debugging?

Yes, pilgrim, VBA has an extensive set of debugging tools. You can step through code line by line. You can also set breakpoints and watch expressions. VBA has an interactive debug pane with watch and immediate modes, along with a full set of error checking commands and functions.

DOING WITH A MACRO WHAT YOU'VE ALREADY DONE MANUALLY, ONLY FASTER

> In creating, the only hard thing's to begin;
> A grass-blade's no easier to make than an oak.
>
> James Russell Lowell
> *A Fable for Critics*, 1848

Put on your water wings. This section is not intended as an introduction to Visual Basic. The richness of the language and Excel's object model can't be done justice in these few pages. So we've opted for a jump-in-and-get-wet approach. To help you along, we provide some sample code you can key in and dissect. We're not going to wax philosophical about looping constructs, data typing, scoping, and so on, but that doesn't mean you can't start using these aspects of VBA by example.

Example 1: Force the Tools Options Transition Navigation Keys Option Off

> When you're lying awake with a dismal headache,
>   and repose is taboo'd by anxiety,
> I conceive you may use any language you choose to indulge in,
>   without impropriety.
>
> Sir William Schwenck Gilbert
> *Iolanthe*, 1882

Automate a manual process. In writing this VBA procedure, your mission (should you decide to accept it!) is a two-parter. First, examine the current setting of the Tools Options Transition filecard's check box called Transition Navigation Keys. Second, if it's cleared, do nothing (no need to change the setting because it's already set the way you want it—off); otherwise, clear it. You can do this as a human being with the mouse and keyboard. In fact, *you already did it!* That's right, waaaaaay back in Chapter 1. Since this is familiar ground to you as an operator, seems like a good place to start. When you're done writing this procedure, you'll have seen how VBA can accomplish the same actions a human operator can, but VBA does it transparently and much much faster. ("Electrons, full speed ahead." "Aye, aye, Cap'n.") Hands-free operation, it slices, it dices, er, sorry, we got carried away (and besides, we already did that bit). Let's get hackin'.

1. Create a new workbook.

2. Insert a module sheet and rename it VBAExample1.

3. Let's synchronize our watches. Let's all make sure that the Tools Options Transition filecard's Transition Navigation Keys check box is *checked*. (We're checking it so we can record the act of clearing it.) And make sure that the Microsoft Excel Menu or Help Key character is / (the forward slash character is the default).

4. Select Tools Record Macro Record New Macro.

5. Enter a macro name of ClearNavigationKeys and click on OK.

6. Select Tools Options Transition, clear the Transition Navigation Keys check box, and then click on OK.

7. Select Tools Record Macro Stop Recording.

8. You should see the following code in your module:

```
'
' ClearNavigationKeys Macro
' Macro recorded mm/dd/yy by X. Lent Reader
'
'
Sub ClearNavigationKeys()
With Application
   .TransitionMenuKey = "/"
   .TransitionNavigKeys = False
End With
End Sub
```

In a nutshell, this recorded macro uses the With...End With construct to loop through and set two properties of the Application object, TransitionMenuKey and TransitionNavigKeys. The former is set to the string "/" and the latter to the logical value False (read: *turn the damned thing off*).

Remember, as in our *Heart of Gold* example, an object is...well, *it all depends on context*. As we said earlier in this chapter, an OLE Automation object is a programmable entity that you can access by name. You can act on an OLEAuto object using the methods it supports. A method either causes an object to do something or changes one of the object's properties. A method is a command or action. A property, well, thank God, a property is a property.

Object.Method
and
Object.Property

We know that Application is an Excel OLEAuto object, TransitionMenuKey is a property of the Application object, and one possible setting of this particular property is the / character. Although the preceding code doesn't contain a method statement, if we add the line `Application.Quit`, then we'd be using the Quit method on the Application object to quit Excel.

The recorder magnanimously gave us the syntax and vocabulary for one property we don't care about—TransitionMenuKey. All we want to know is the correct name of the TransitionNavigKeys property and to confirm that it's Boolean (True or False). So let's toss out the baby with the bath water, uhm, we mean the TransitionMenuKey statement, throw in an If...Then...End If construct to toggle, and this sucker's a done deal.

1. Delete the following statement.

   ```
   .TransitionMenuKey = "/"
   ```

2. Surround the With...End With construct with an If construct that does what the original assignment stipulated, "...if [the Transition Navigation Keys check box is] cleared, do nothing (no need to change the setting because it's already set the way you want it—off); otherwise, clear it." Like so. (New statements are shown here in bold.)

   ```
   Sub ClearNavigationKeys()
   If Application.TransitionNavigKeys Then
     With Application
       .TransitionNavigKeys = False
     End With
   End If
   End Sub
   ```

3. File Save your book as VBATUGXL.XLS.

If the TransitionNavigKeys property is True, your macro turns it off; otherwise, your macro does nothing to the setting and ends. To test it, manually check the Transition Navigation Keys check box, run the macro, and then examine the Tools Options Transition setting. By golly, the check box is cleared. You're jammin' now, pilgrim!

Example 2: Underground Range Rover—Bomb-proof Add a Range Name to the Current Sheet

In writing this VBA procedure, your mission has three parts, a veritable VBA hat trick! First, ask the user for a range name to be added to the current sheet. Second, check this name against all existing names on this sheet to see if it's a duplicate (or null, or an invalid name). Third, add the name if it's kosher; otherwise, inform the user of the problem and ask the user to try again.

Query the user with VBA.

As with our first example, you can do all this with the mouse and keyboard. However, VBA can surround the process of entering a unique range name for the current selection with some input and error-checking not available with Excel's native Insert Name feature. This protects the user from a faux pas, for example, inadvertently defining the current selection with a range name that already exists in the workbook. This example is for you to read, study, and code in on your own if you're so inclined.

```
'
' AddRangeName Macro
' Macro created 4/15/94 by X. Lent Reader
'
Sub AddRangeName()
  ' ----- Declarations
  Dim i As Integer
  Dim IsDuplicate As Boolean
  Dim MyRangeName As String
  Dim MyTitle As String
  Dim Prompt As String
  Dim Quote As String
  Dim r As Object
  Dim RangeNameCount As Integer
  Dim RangeNames() As String
  ' ----- Initializations
  MyTitle = "Underground Range Rover"
  Quote = Chr(34)
  ' ----- Verify that active sheet is a worksheet; bail if not
  If TypeName(Application.ActiveSheet) <> "Worksheet" Then
    MsgBox "The active sheet is not a worksheet. " & _
      "Please switch to a worksheet and try again.", _
      vbOKOnly + vbExclamation, MyTitle
    Exit Sub
  End If
```

```
' ----- Get list of all extant range names
RangeNameCount = ActiveWorkbook.Names.Count
ReDim RangeNames(RangeNameCount)
i = 0
For Each r In ActiveWorkbook.Names
  ' Don't have to worry about index of -1
  '    because the For Each never executes if count is 0
  RangeNames(i) = r.Name
  i = i + 1
Next r
' ----- Input loop
On Error Resume Next
Do While True
  ' Initializations
  IsDuplicate = False
  ' Get the user's range name
  Prompt = "Please enter a range name " & _
    "for the current selection:"
  MyRangeName = InputBox(Prompt, MyTitle)
  If MyRangeName = "" Then
    ' Exit if user clicked OK (func returns empty string)
    Exit Sub
  End If
  If RangeNameCount <> 0 Then
    ' This is not the 1st range name so have to compare
    '    against all extant names until there's a match
    '    or at end of list
    For i = 0 To RangeNameCount - 1
      If UCase$(MyRangeName) = UCase$(RangeNames(i)) Then
        Prompt = "The range name " & Quote & _
          MyRangeName & Quote & _
          " already exists. " & _
          "Please enter a different name."
        MsgBox Prompt, _
          vbOKOnly + vbExclamation, MyTitle
        IsDuplicate = True
        Exit For
      End If
    Next i
  End If
  If Not IsDuplicate Then
```

```
      ActiveWorkbook.Names.Add Name:=MyRangeName, _
        RefersToR1C1:="=" & ActiveSheet.Name & "!" & _
          Selection.Address(ReferenceStyle:=xlR1C1)
      If Err = 0 Then
        Prompt = "The range name " & Quote & _
          MyRangeName & Quote & _
          " was added successfully."
        MsgBox Prompt, _
          vbOKOnly + vbInformation, MyTitle
        Exit Do
      ElseIf Err = 1004 Then
        ' 1004 is run-time error for an invalid range name
        Prompt = "The range name " & Quote & _
          MyRangeName & Quote & _
          " is not valid. Please enter a different name."
        MsgBox Prompt, _
          vbOKOnly + vbExclamation, MyTitle
        ' set Err to 0 so it doesn't remember prior error
        Err = 0
      Else
        ' Graceful exit trap for any other error
        MsgBox "Error " & Err & " occurred. " & _
          "Please contact your system administrator.", _
          vbOKOnly + vbExclamation, MyTitle
        Exit Sub
      End If
    End If
  Loop
End Sub
```

Example 3: User-defined Function fIsValidToolbarName()

Build your own functions.

In writing this VBA function procedure, your objective is to receive a string and check to see if this string matches the name of any existing toolbar. If it matches, return the Boolean True; otherwise, return False. This general-purpose function is handy if you ever need to create a toolbar on the fly. Pass `fIsValidToolbarName()`, the suggested new toolbar's name, and in a single call get back True or False so you know how to proceed.

You can add a VBA function procedure to Excel's list of available functions. VBA code you write can call it, or you can use it in a formula in a worksheet. *Dual personality functions, don't ya know!* Wondering about the function's semi-weird name? Once upon a time…Okay, seriously. Everybody and his brother has a set of variable and procedure naming conventions. Somewhere way back when (further back than we care to remember), we selected the convention of a lowercase "s" to prefix custom subroutines and a lowercase "f" to prefix custom functions; thereby setting these procedure names off from the application's own, built-in, "native" commands or functions. That tale told, let's pound out some code.

```
'
' fIsValidToolbarName custom function
' Ported from PRIME 6.0's WordBasic global procedure library
' (c) 1993-94 PRIME Consulting Group, Inc. All rights reserved.
'
Function fIsValidToolbarName(ByVal ToolbarName As String)
As Boolean
  ' Note use of ByVal to protect ToolbarName since we UCase() it
  ' ----- Declarations
  Dim t As Object
  ' ----- Initializations
  ToolbarName = UCase(ToolbarName)
  fIsValidToolbarName = False
  ' ----- Main body
  ' A toolbars collection is so small that it's not worth
  '   optimizing the list evaluation to quit once a match is
  '   found; besides, you'd have to poke each t.Name into an
  '   array, then loop *again*
  For Each t In Toolbars
    If ToolbarName = UCase(t.Name) Then
      fIsValidToolbarName = True
    End If
  Next t
End Function
```

Figure 10.5 shows how this user-defined function operates in a worksheet.

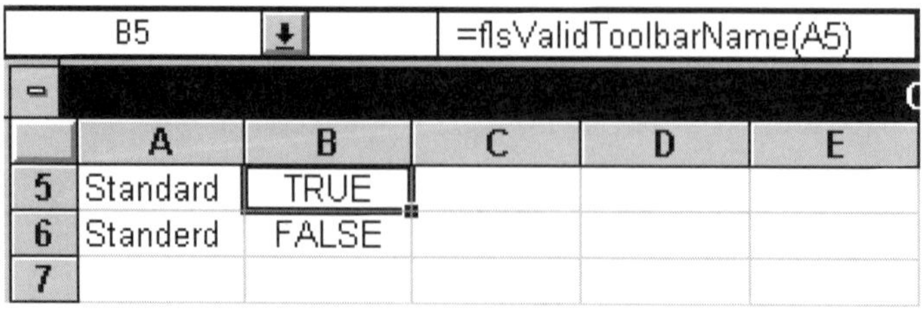

B5	⬇		=fIsValidToolbarName(A5)

	A	B	C	D	E
5	Standard	TRUE			
6	Standerd	FALSE			
7					

Figure 10.5 A User-defined Function at Work in the Trenches

For an example of a procedure calling `fIsValidToolbarName()`, see the subroutine `sGetToolbarButtonInfo()` listing in the next section.

Hooking macros to dialog box controls

Example 4: Underground Toolbar Lister

The Underground Toolbar Lister provides an example of how you can hook macros up to dialog box controls. To design the dialog box, we created a dialog sheet and added controls using the Forms toolbar features. In Figure 10.6 you see the finished dialog box. The figure also shows the screen display when you are changing control properties. The steps are: right-click a control (in Figure 10.6 we're working on the list box named "List Box 1") and then change properties as needed in the Format Object dialog.

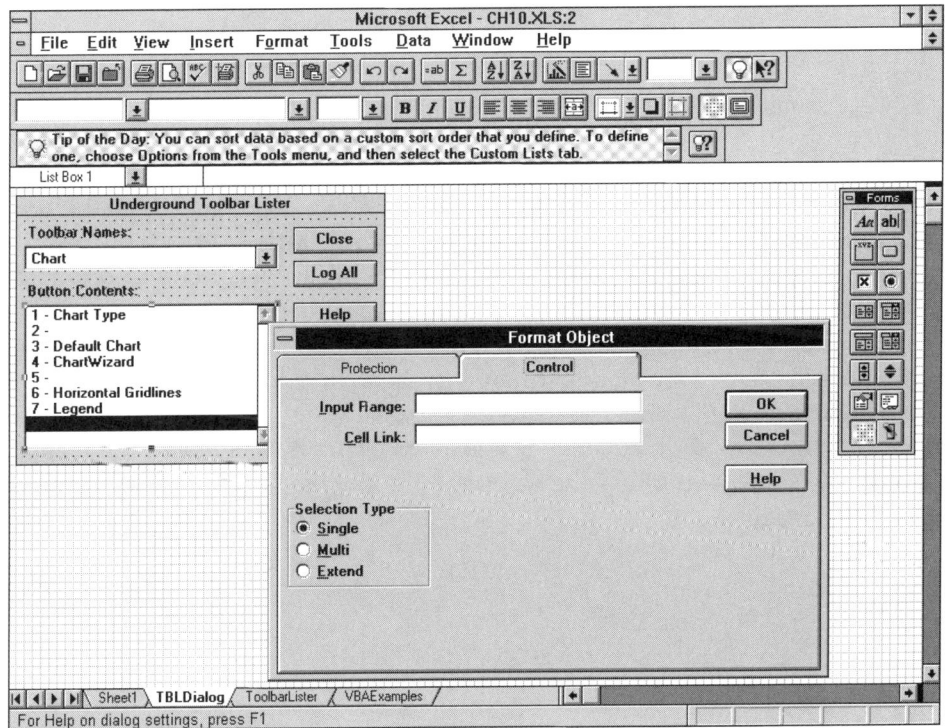

Figure 10.6 Underground Toolbar Lister's Dialog

To hook a control up to a macro, select the control, select Tools Assign Macro, select the desired macro and click on OK. In Toolbar Lister, we assigned DropDown1_Click to the drop-down control called "Drop Down 1" (see Figure 10.7).

Here's an interesting side note. We ASCII-ported this PRIME 6.0 application—our WinWord 6 add-on shareware package comprised of utilities like Toolbar Lister and a dozen others equally indispensable, if we do say so ourselves (call

WordBasic portability to VBA

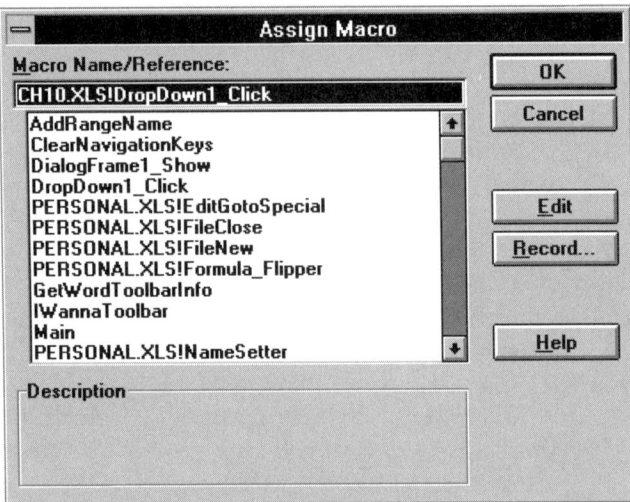

Figure 10.7 Assigning a Custom Dialog Control to a Macro

800-659-4696 to order)—from WordBasic to VBA in about four hours. QED. Admittedly we left out some of the PRIME 6.0 features (like logging all toolbar button assignments to a log file, and context-sensitive help), but it's very encouraging to see the easy portability of "basic" code not only from Visual Basic 3.0 to Excel VBA, but from WordBasic as well.

Sure, we hit some aggravating potholes. The two languages handle arrays within dialog list controls quite differently, the dialog editors produce different default names for controls, you have to explicitly assign VBA procedures to controls, and so on. But, all in all, it was a less back-breaking migration than we would have imagined, and some empirical proof of the beginnings of a common macro language.

```
'
' ToolbarLister utility
' Ported in part from PRIME 6.0's ToolbarLister utility
' (c) 1993-94 PRIME Consulting Group, Inc. All rights reserved.
' Wherever appropriate, the original WordBasic vbl names are
'    shown as remarks to facilitate version control.
'

Option Explicit

' ----- Declarations
Dim ButtonInfo() As String
Dim CountToolbars As Integer
Dim d As Object
```

```
Dim i As Integer
Dim Prompt As String
Dim Quote As String        ' Q$ in PRIME 6.0 version
Dim TabChar As String      ' Tab$ in PRIME 6.0 version
Dim TBIndex As Integer     ' Index in PRIME 6.0 version
Dim TheToolbarName As String
Dim TheToolbarNames() As String
Const DialogName = "TBLDialog"
Const MacroTitle = "Underground Toolbar Lister"


Sub ToolbarLister()
  ' ----- Declarations
  Dim t As Object
  ' ----- Initializations
  Quote = Chr(34)
  TabChar = Chr(9)
  Set d = DialogSheets(DialogName).DropDowns("Drop Down 1")
  ' ----- Main body
  Application.StatusBar = _
    "Gathering information about the available toolbars. " & _
      "Please wait ..."
  CountToolbars = Application.Toolbars.Count
  Application.StatusBar = ""
  ' To keep TUGExcel example simple, ignore case of 0 toolbars!
  ReDim TheToolbarNames(CountToolbars - 1)
  i _ 0
  For Each t In Toolbars
    TheToolbarNames(i) = t.Name
    i = i + 1
  Next t
  ' Note: The array gets built in the order of appearance in
  '    View Toolbars (which is *not* alphabetical; so for now
  '    we'll leave it in that same order and *not* sort
  DialogSheets(DialogName).Show
End Sub


Sub sLoadButtonInfo(ByVal TheToolbarName As String)
  Dim l As Object
  ' load up ButtonInfo() array used by the List Box 1 control
  Prompt = "Gathering button information about the " & _
    TheToolbarName & " toolbar. Please wait ..."
```

```
      Application.StatusBar = Prompt
      sGetToolbarButtonInfo TheToolbarName, ButtonInfo()
      Set l = DialogSheets(DialogName).ListBoxes("List Box 1")
      l.List = ButtonInfo()
      l.ListIndex = 1
      Application.StatusBar = ""
End Sub


Sub sGetToolbarButtonInfo(ByVal TheToolbarName As String,
ButtonInfo() As String)
' returns an array in redim'ed ButtonInfo(); each item is
' comprised of TheToolbarName's button info as 3 concatenated
' items: (1) button number (1-based), (2) " - ", and (3)
category
' item name; validates TheToolbarName and redims ButtonInfo()
' to 0 if bogus TheToolbarName
      ' ----- Declarations
      Dim CountToolbarButtons As Integer
      Dim t As Object
      ' ----- Main body
      If fIsValidToolbarName(TheToolbarName) Then
        Set t = Toolbars(TheToolbarName)
        CountToolbarButtons = t.ToolbarButtons.Count
        If CountToolbarButtons = 0 Then
          ReDim ButtonInfo(0)  ' don't allow redim to -1
          ' unusual case where toolbar exists but is buttonless
          ButtonInfo(0) = "The " & _
            TheToolbarName & " toolbar has no buttons!"
        Else
          ReDim ButtonInfo(CountToolbarButtons - 1)
          For i = 1 To CountToolbarButtons
            ButtonInfo(i - 1) = LTrim(Str(i)) & " - " & _
              t.ToolbarButtons(i).Name
          Next i
        End If
      Else
        ReDim ButtonInfo(0)
      End If
End Sub
```

```
Sub DialogFrame1_Show()
  ' Initialization (dbox)
  Application.StatusBar = ""
  d.List = TheToolbarNames()
  d.ListIndex = 1
  ' load up ButtonInfo() with the details from toolbar #1
  '    (0th in the array list)
  TBIndex = 0
  TheToolbarName = TheToolbarNames(TBIndex)
  sLoadButtonInfo TheToolbarName
End Sub

Sub DropDown1_Click()
  i = d.ListIndex
  TheToolbarName = TheToolbarNames(i - 1)
  sLoadButtonInfo TheToolbarName
End Sub
```

Example 5: WinWord Toolbar Sniffer

Here's an example of how Excel pilots the only OLEAuto-programmable object supported by WinWord 6—the object called "Word.Basic." For this distilled example to work, make sure WinWord 6 is already running.

Controlling WinWord 6 with OLEAuto

```
'
' GetWordToolbarInfo Macro
' Macro created 4/18/94 by X. Lent Reader
'
Sub GetWordToolbarInfo()
  ' ----- Declarations
  Dim CountToolbars As Integer
  Dim i As Integer
  Dim Quote As String
  Dim TheToolbarName As String
  Dim wb As Object
  ' ----- Initializations
  Set wb = CreateObject("Word.Basic")
  Quote = Chr(34)
  ' ----- Main body
  CountToolbars = wb.CountToolbars()
  For i = 1 To CountToolbars
```

```
      TheToolbarName = wb.[ToolbarName$](i)
      MsgBox "Word's toolbar #" & i & " of " & CountToolbars & _
          " is called " & Quote & TheToolbarName & Quote
   Next i
   Set wb = Nothing
End Sub
```

Assistance and Augmentation

There's no need to fear. Underdog is here!

Underdog
The Underdog Hour

Face it, we all need some help at one time or another. Here we show you where to turn when things get really bleak. Consultants, books, utilities, on-line services, you name it.

WHERE TO GET PROFESSIONAL HELP (YOUR SHRINK NOTWITHSTANDING)

Vell, Zaphod's just zis guy, you know?

Gag Halfrunt, brain care specialist
Douglas Adams, *Hitchhiker's Guide to the Galaxy*

The deadline is ticking. You're sure that Excel can be made to jump through the right hoop and solve your problem. But all it does is snarl and snap at you. Time to call for help, but as the age old question asks, "Who you gonna call?"

Real-Time Help from a Living Human Being

...able to leap tall buildings at a single bound!...It's a bird! It's a plane! It's Superman!

Announcer
Superman, 1940

Here's how to get a real live person on the line when you have a serious Excel problem. But remember, like we used to say to our parents when we were in college, "Send money." If you're looking for someone to chat with for free, well, we have some suggestions coming up later on for that (maybe not "free," but how about for connect costs?).

PRIME Consulting Group, Inc.

310-318-5212

Hey, it's us! Sure we do Excel consulting. As long as we're doing a shameless plug, let us say we do WordBasic and Visual Basic development and training as well. We also do a lot of what we call "utilization consulting." That's where we tell you that getting utility out of your software and systems is more important than dropping a computer on everyone's desk and giving them all a day's general training on a program's feature set. Then we tell you how you can up the utilization within your company. As Yoda would say, "Oh yes, young Jedi, add much to bottom line that will. Happy employees make."

Don't forget the "send money" part. *Heh, heh, heh.*

Donald A. Buchanan

818-843-7873

Don, among other things, is the Technical Editor on this here book. All complaints should therefore...no, really, Don is an amazing Excel developer we have been lucky to do business with over the years. He plays guitar and has been oft referred to as "the emir of comedy" due to his, uhm, unique sense of humor. Tell him we sent ya.

Directory of Microsoft Solution Providers

800-227-4679

This service is provided by Microsoft Corporation. It provides referrals to Microsoft Solution Providers around the world. You tell 'em what you want and where you are and they type in your zip code or some such geographical datum and out pops the lucky winner (or winners, depending on the density of consultants in your neighborhood).

Be prepared for what may well be the world's longest phone-voice menuing system announcement message. Have a cup of coffee on hand.

CompuServe Information Service

> To a considerable degree science consists in originating the maximum amount of information with the minimum expenditure of energy.
>
> Edward O. Wilson
> *Biophilla*, 1984

If you don't want to pop for a hired gun to help you deal with Excel in real time, you can go the cyberspace route on the CompuServe Information Service (CIS).

CIS is a great way to get answers to specific questions or to find out the latest news on bugs and workarounds. You can post a question and any of the best and brightest who hang out there may answer your question for free. Several Redmond Rangers monitor the forums discussed in this section, and they work hard at never letting a question go unanswered or a problem unresolved. You may have to wait a day or so, but you sure can't beat the price.

To sign up for a CIS membership, call 800-848-8990.

GO MSEXCEL

This is where to go on CIS for Excel advice. Section 4 for VBA stuff and section 6 for general Excel traffic. Library 3 is chock full of VBA and XLM sample code and applications. Note that the section numbers and titles change occasionally, so use your CIS shell program to browse and/or join them in real time, based on your personal interests.

Eric Wells (one of Microsoft's finest) is known to frequent the MSEXCEL forum and dispense Excel wisdom to all comers. If you exchange electrons with him, tell him we said "Hi."

GO PROGMSA

This is the Programming Microsoft Applications forum. Section 5 deals with Excel SDK issues (to order the *Software Development Kit*, call Microsoft Developer Services at 800-759-5474). You can get information on creating add-ins, XLLs, and complicated developer stuff like that there.

Your Local Bookstore

> A good heavy book holds you down. It's an anchor that keeps you from getting up and having another gin and tonic.
>
> Roy Blount, Jr.
> *New York Times*, June 2, 1985

Okay, you have the *Underground Guide to Excel*, but as hard as it may be to believe, your Excel library may not be complete. Sure, other books may not make as nice a gift as the *Underground Guide*, hint, hint, but consider the following tomes, available in a bookstore near you.

The Underground Guide to Word for Windows, Woody Leonhard (Addison-Wesley)

This book has nothing to do with Excel whatsoever! But, if you use Excel, you probably use WinWord as well, and if you don't, for cryin' out loud *why don't you?* If you have a copy of WinWord, you *need* this book. 'Nuff said.

Using Excel Version 5 for Windows, Ron Person (Que)

This is the book you need to supplement, well, *replace* really, the *User's Guide* that comes with Excel 5. It contains over 1200 pages of material covering Excel's feature set from A to Z. When you need a real reference book for Excel, this book is the hot tip.

Ron has written a number of books on various software products. His company does training in Excel and VBA for developers and developer wannabes. He cooks, is soft-spoken, married well, and is just one hell of a nice guy.

Microsoft Excel Visual Basic for Applications Step by Step, Reed Jacobson (Microsoft Press)

This tongue-twister of a title is a nifty introduction to the mysteries of VBA. It's done in a self-paced, do-it-yourself style and comes with a disk of practice files. Reed has done a really nice job on this topic.

Microsoft Excel 5 Visual Basic for Applications Reference (Microsoft Press)

This is the A-to-Z reference book for VBA and is the printed equivalent of the VBA information available in Excel's on-line help. Keep in mind that this is the same information that you already have in the help files. We mention it because some people like to look things up in books.

Microsoft Excel 5 Worksheet Function Reference (Microsoft Press)

This is the A-to-Z reference book for Excel's functions and is the printed equivalent of the worksheet function information available in Excel's on-line help, plus the underlying mathematical formulae.

OTHER NIFTY STUFF

Speaking of training courses (we were speaking about training courses weren't we?)…

Application Development Using Microsoft Excel 5.0 and Visual Basic, Applications Edition

(Microsoft Education Services Course Number 349)

Call 1-800-426-9400 for referrals to Microsoft Solution Authorized Training Centers in your area that are certified to teach this course.

Putting OLE 2.0, VBA, and DDE to Work: Integrating Windows Applications

This two-day, hands-on class explains the workings of both OLE and DDE protocols, with many live examples from several popular Windows applications, including Excel, Visual Basic, and WinWord. Attention is given to OLEAuto and DDE programming techniques using application programming languages.

Call 310-318-5212 for registration information. Does that number look familiar? It's us again. Oh, and if you're interested in WordBasic, we co-authored the Microsoft Education Services course *Application Development Using Microsoft Word 6.0* and were the first authorized training center to teach this course.

Microsoft Excel Software Developer's Kit

This is the official documentation for Excel 5's API and includes sample C source code. If you plan on building an Excel add-in you'll need this one.

CompuServe (Again)

If you're in the market for third-party utilities, either shareware or commercialware, haunt the cyberspace stacks up in MSEXCEL. Savvy developers hang their hats there, often with demo versions of their wares in the public-access libraries.

And here's one last shameless plug for PRIME Consulting Group. If you're in the market for an Excel 5 add-on, like what you've read here, and are groovin' on our dedication to perfection at any cost, have we got a product for you.

Index

& (ampersand), 61–62
' (apostrophe), 6, 120, 214
* (asterisk), 6, 66, 130, 249
@ (at symbol), 177
\ (backslash), 6, 94, 96
^ (caret), 130
, (comma), 131
{} (curly braces), 136–38
$ (dollar sign), 113, 114, 130, 175, 176
= (equal sign), 66, 125, 130
! (exclamation point), 99
() (parentheses), 116–18, 123, 125–26, 130, 131
. (period), 94, 96, 99
+ (plus sign), 66, 130
# (pound sign), 196
? (question mark), 6, 94, 96
: (semicolon), 6, 131
_ (underscore character), 94, 95, 98, 177

A1 notation style, 93, 111, 112, 113, 160–62
Abbott, Bud, 93
Access, 191, 217, 218
AccessData, 253
Adams, Ansel, 171
Adams, Douglas, 55, 186, 292, 311
Add button, 201
Advanced Filter table, 107
Advanced Search command button, 40
alignment settings, 61, 69, 70, 75, 207
ALT+ENTER, 64
ALT+PAGE DOWN, 9
ALT+PAGE UP, 9
ALT+R, 114
ALT+TAB, 121
AltStartup= setting, 246
American Library Association, 235
Amok Shing, 42, 51, 81, 198
ampersand, 61–62
annotations, 253–54
Antonius, Marcus Aurelius, 1
apostrophe, 6, 120, 214
Apply Names dialog box, 105
AREAS(), 139
arguments, definition of, 4, 126
Aristophanes, 53
arithmetic operators, 130
array(s)
   current, 169
   -entering, 136–37
   formulas, 136–38
arrow tool, 255–56
ASCII files, 305
   EXCEL5.INI, 243–46
   TextWizard and, 227

asterisk, 6, 66, 130, 249
at symbol, 177
Attach Note button, 145, 156–57
auditing, 143–70
   the Attach Note button and, 156–57
   documenting models and, 144–45
   Edit Go To Special and, 164–70
   error trapping and, 148–51
   flipping worksheets and, 157–59, 161, 167
   Info Window settings and, 156–57
   the Note feature and, 145–46
   the Show Info Window button and, 156–57
   toolbar, 47–50, 151–57, 166
   tracing dependent cells and, 154–55
   troubleshooting formulas and, 162–64
   using R1C1 notation and, 160–62
   the "vanishing formula" syndrome and, 49–50
   zooming and, 147–48
AUTOCALC.XLS, 140
AutoEntry™, 78, 79, 88
AutoFill, 80, 82–84, 212
AutoFilter, 206–8, 211, 217–26, 234
   activating, 219
   column labels and, 207
   naming lists and, 208
   PivotTable vs., 232–33
   turning off, 219
AutoFit, 74, 75
AutoFormat, 172–74
Auto Indent, 291
Automatic calculation mode, 139
Automatic Page Breaks check box, 38
Automatic radio button, 264
Auto_Open(), 140
Auto_ range names, 108–9
Auto Select, 9
AutoSum, 30, 127–29, 224
AutoSum button, 30, 127–29
AVERAGE(), 126
AVG, 124

Backslash character, 6, 94, 96
Bacon, Francis, 66
Bates, Norman, 157
binary files, 258, 259
Blake, William, 265
blank(s)
   auditing and, 167, 168
   cell content type, 61, 76
   cells, definition of, 76
   default sort order rules for, 213
Blount, Roy, Jr., 313
Bogus Color button, 35–36
Bold button, 34

BOOK.XLT, 238, 239
bookmarks, 12, 93
Boolean(s)
 cell content type, 61, 76
 default sort order rules for, 213
border(s), 69, 71, 207
 button, 35–36, 178
 hatched, 269
Break on All Errors, 291
Brown, Edmund G., 259
Buchanan, Donald A., 312
bugs. See auditing; error(s); error messages
Bullein, William, 97
Burns, Arthur, 247
buttons, customizing, 22–26

Calculate Now button, 4
Calculation filecard, 138–39
Calvino, Italo, 290
capitalization
 conventions, 176
 sorting and, 206, 207
Carroll, Lewis, 121, 204, 217, 286
cell(s). *See also* blank(s)
 active, definition of, 7
 converting the contents of, to
results, 67
 deleting vs. clearing, 86–87
 destination, 71, 74
 editing nonblank, 88
 hidden, 252
 -level manual formatting, 69–70
 -level protection attributes, 251–52
 naming, 12
 number of characters in, limitations on, 61
 references, relative and absolute, 97, 102, 110–15
 references, substituting range names for, 104–5
 selecting groups of, 10–11, 87
 selecting ranges of, 11–13
 selecting single, 9–10, 11
 source, definition of, 71
 tracing dependent, 154–55
 values, self-actualizing, 3–4
CELL(), 139
Cell Note dialog box, 145, 156
Center Across Columns button, 34
Change Links dialog, 277
Change Source button, 277–78
character formatting, 68–74
chart(s), 171–201, 285, 286
 3-D, 189–90
 adding data to, 182–83
 area, 189–90
 creating, 178–90
 cross-hatchings on, 189
 data series in, 190
 displaying, 180
 donut-like, 189–90
 dynamic, 183–85
 embedded, 180–81, 183, 185–86, 256, 258
 in-sheet editing and, 180–81
 the "keep it simple" rule and, 187–88
 problems with, 186–90

radar, 190
 resizing, 181
 scale settings and, 186–87
 see-through, 187
 sheets, 52, 59, 251
CHART.XLT, 242
ChartWizard, 32–33, 59, 179–80
ChartWizard button, 32–33, 179–80
circle tool, 255–56
circular references, definition of, 140–41
CIS (CompuServe Information Service), 248, 312–13
Clark, Mark, 164
Clarke, Arthur C., 287
Clear Contents, 87
clip art, 188–89
clipboard, 89–90, 133
Close button, 27, 210
Color button, 45
column(s)
 cell addresses and, 110–12
 changing, 55–56
 clip art, 188–89
 the differences options and, 169–70
 frozen, 197
 hidden, 56, 170, 198, 212
 labels, 98, 206–7, 210, 219
 moving up or down by, 79
 multiselecting, 55
 naming, 94, 97
 numbers, 110–11
 printing, 107
 resizing, 56
 width, 56, 74–75, 193
COLUMNS(), 139
commas, 34–35, 131
Comma Style button, 34–35
comments, 253–54
comparison operators, 130, 131
COMPOUND.DOC, 274
CompuServe
 Information Service (CIS), 248, 312– 13
 MSEXCEL forum, 126, 290, 313, 315
concatenation operators, 61–62, 66
Consolidate_Area range name, 108
constants, definition of, 106
Constants button, 167, 168
CONTAINR.XLS, 276
Control key, 7, 81, 90–91, 254, 271. *See also* Control
 key combinations
Control key combinations
 CTRL+' (back apostrophe), 49–50, 65, 157
 CTRL+AutoFill, 82–83
 CTRL+C, 92
 CTRL+click, 11, 101, 261
 CTRL+DOWN ARROW, 9
 CTRL+drag, 91, 132–33
 CTRL+END, 9, 147, 157–58, 160, 167
 CTRL+ENTER, 81, 127
 CTRL+ESC, 121
 CTRL+HOME, 9
 CTRL+INSERT, 92
 CTRL+key, 9
 CTRL+key zap, 9
 CTRL+PAGE DOWN, 9

CTRL+PAGE UP, 9
CTRL+RIGHT ARROW, 9
CTRL+SHIFT+arrow, 11, 87–88
CTRL+SHIFT+ENTER, 136
CTRL+V, 92
CTRL+X, 92
Control menu box, 121
conversion
    of dialogs, 210
    of embedded data, 268
    of formulas to values, 132–33
Convert, 268
Coolidge, Calvin, 151
copying
    range names, 102–3
    shortcut key for, 92
    with TipWizard, 45
    worksheets, 7
Copy to Another Location radio button, 223
COUNT(), 184
COUNTA(), 184
COUNTBLANKS(), 76
COUNTIF(), 225
criteria
    computed, 223
    ranges, 108, 222–23
Crystal, Billy, 18
curly braces, 136–38
Currency button, 34–35
current region, 169
Customize dialog box, 27–30, 36, 37
Custom lists, 83–84
Custom palette, 26
cut and paste, 29, 89–90. *See also* paste operations
    range names and, 102–3
    shortcut key for, 92
Cut button, 29

Data analysis, 203, 227–34
Database range name, 107–8
databases, definition of, 204–5
data entry, 77–86, 88
    in-cell editing and, 77–78
    using AutoFill, 83–84
    using the fill handle, 81–83, 84–86
Data Filter, 219
data forms, 108, 209–11
Data menu, 180
Data Series, 80
date
    of last update, documenting, 144
    of origin, documenting, 144
    values, serial, 65–66
Davies, Robertson, 44
DDE (Dynamic Data Exchange), 257, 273,277, 287, 288
debugging, VBA tools for, 298. *See also* auditing;
    error(s); error messages
Decrease Decimal button, 34–35
Default File Location, 42
Define Name, 95–97, 101, 102, 113, 115
DefSheets= setting, 246
DELETE, 87

deleting, 96
    buttons, 27
    vs. clearing, 86–87
    records in lists, 205, 209
    worksheets, 7
Detroit, Nathan, 51
Dialog Sheet, 52, 60
DIALOG.XLT, 240–41
directories
    Alternate Startup File Location, 42, 237, 238, 246
    \EXCEL, 289
    startup switches and, 243
    XLSTART, 42, 237, 238, 246
Directory of Microsoft Solution Providers, 312
displaying
    arrays, 137
    the auditing toolbar, 151
    charts, 180
    display option summaries, 20
    margins, 193
    syntax errors, 291
    VBA modules, 294–95
Disraeli, Benjamin, 85
DLLs (dynamic link libraries), 217, 272, 282, 283
DOC1.DOC, 53
documenting models, 144–45
documents, compound, 258, 259
dollar sign, 113, 114, 130, 175, 176
Dowd, Elwood P., 238
drag-and-plot, 182–85
dragging, 7, 11, 88–91, 133, 294
    boxes, 254–55
    OLE objects, 269, 270–71
Drawing button, 32–33
Drop Shadow button, 35–36, 255

Edit, 268
Edit Clear Notes, 166
Edit Copy, 18
Edit Cut, 18, 90
Edit Fill, 80
Edit Go To Special, 164–70
Edit Go To Special Blanks, 76
Edit Go To Special Formulas Errors, 76
Edit Go To Special Formulas Logicals, 76
editing
    in-cell, 77–78
    in-place, 265–70, 280, 282, 285
Edit menu, 80, 87, 164, 185, 261, 268
Edit Object option, 261
Edit Paste Special, 132, 133
Edit Paste Special Formats, 73
EDK (Excel Developer's Kit), 245–46
Einstein, Albert, 259
Eliot, Thomas S., 291
ENTER key, 78–79, 121, 123, 157–58, 160, 176
    the auditing toolbar and, 151
    building formulas and, 127
    the Paste Special operation and, 132, 133
    troubleshooting formulas and, 163
    using AutoSum and, 128
equal signs, 66, 125, 130

error(s), 137, 186, 301. *See also* auditing; error
        messages; GPFs (General Protection Faults)
    building formulas and, 118–20, 122, 123
    -checking crossfoot formula, 159
    circular references and, 141
    default sort order rules for, 213
    OLE and, 282, 286
    pivot tables and, 230
    tracing, 76, 155–56
    trapping, 121, 148–51, 291
    untrappable, 121
    using the Name Box and, 95
    values, arguments and, 126
    the View Manager and, 198
error messages
    "Cannot access directory `d:\badpath`," 42
    "Cannot start the source application for this
        object," 261
    "Error in parse line," 221
    "Microsoft Excel…Cannot quit Microsoft Excel,"
        121, 122
    "#NAME?," 103
    "#NUM!," 163
    "Out of Memory," 5
    "#REF," 260, 276
    "That name is not valid," 96
    "#VALUE!," 135
ESC key, 121, 132–33, 163, 286
Euripides, 97
EXCEL5.INI, 243–46
EXCEL5.XLB, 37, 84
EXCELDE.EXE, 60
exclamation point, 99
exiting Excel, 121–22, 283
Extract range name, 108

F3 feature, 185
F5 feature, 297
F9 feature, 132, 139, 163
fields, 215, 217
    in data forms, maximum number of, 209
    OLE and, 259–64
file(s). *See also* file extensions
    binary, 258, 259
    MRU (most recently used) list of, 29, 238
    read-only, 248, 249
FileClose button, 24, 25, 26, 27, 159
File Exit, 121
file extensions
    .CSV, 227
    .INI, 243, 246
    .TXT, 227
    .XLC, 5
    .XLM, 5
    .XLS, 4, 5, 100
    .XLT, 237, 240–42
File Manager, 37
File menu, 28, 192, 265
File New, 239
File Not Found dialog box, 100
File Open, 100, 249, 277
File Save As, 248

filling, 80–86, 212, 292. *See also* AutoFill
filtering, 204–7, 211, 217–26, 234. *See also* AutoFilter
    activating, 219
    column labels and, 207
    naming lists and, 208
    PivotTable vs., 232–33
    turning off, 219
Find File Search dialog box, 40
Find Next, 209–10
Find Prev, 209–10
Finish button, 59
fIsValidToolbarName(), 303–5
flipping worksheets, 157–59, 161, 167
Fly method, 292
font(s), 35–36, 69, 70, 72–73, 207
    Arial, 32
    ATM, 187
    Bitstream, 187
    Normal style, 56
    printing charts and, 187
    setting standard, 42
Font Color button, 35–36
Forgy, Howell M., 164
Format menu, 56, 240, 270
Format Object, 256, 205
Format Painter, 29, 74
formatting
    currency formats, 175
    custom indents, 177
    custom rounding, 177
    floating palettes and, 177–78
    the "hard way," 171–72
    one click, 172–73
    output, 171–201
    styles and, 174–77
formula(s), 93, 110–42. *See also* formula bar
    advanced concepts for, 130–38
    array, 136–38
    building, 115–25, 127–28, 133–35
    converted to values, 132–33
    definition of, 66
    error-checking crossfoot, 159
    in names, 105–6
    names in, 103–4
    that return errors, 155–56
    trapping errors with, 148–51
    troubleshooting, 162–64
formula bar, 77–78, 157. *See also* formula(s)
    building formulas and, 121, 122
    exiting Excel and, 121
    getting help for, 19
    selecting a range address while in, 122–23
Formula Flipper button, 157–59, 161
Formulas button, 167, 168
Formulas cell content type, 60, 66–76
Formulas check box, 39
Franklin, Benjamin, 4, 274
freeze pane settings, 196–97
Full Screen button, 36, 147
function(s), 93, 110–42. *See also* Function Wizard;
        specific functions
    definition of, 5, 125
    mechanics, 125–27

names, 125
  OLE and, 259–64
  volatile class of, 139
Function Wizard, 30, 115, 123–27

Gandhi, Mahatma, 47
Gates, Bill, 257
General filecard, 39–42
Get External Data, 216, 217–18
Gilbert, William S., 228, 298
Goodman, John, 209
Gordon, J. J., 93
Go To, 9–13, 95, 101–3, 106, 155–56
GPFs (General Protection Faults), 282, 283
Graphic object grabbers, 18
Graphics buttons, 32–33
Graves, Robert, 13
gridlines, 39, 188

Haldeman, H. R., 247
Header/Footer settings, 193, 195
Heller, Joseph, 154, 250
help, 18–20, 126, 198. *See also* Help
button
  AutoFilter and, 221
  building formulas and, 118–20, 124
  "real-time," 311–14
Help button, 33, 297
  building formulas and, 118–19, 120
  using the Name Box and, 95
Henri, Robert, 204
Herbert, George, 123
Hesiod, 80
hidden data
  cells, 252
  columns, 56, 170, 198, 212
  rows, 56, 170, 198, 215
  windows, 260, 263
Holmes, Oliver Wendell, Jr., 115, 118
Home key, 9
Hope, Bob, 127

IF, 149, 150–51
=IF, 159
IFCIF rule, 71–72
Ignore Other Applications box, 39
Increase Decimal button, 34–35
indents, 152, 177
INDEX(), 139
INDIRECT(), 139
Info Window settings, 156–57
Insert menu, 98
Insert Name Create, 101
Insert Worksheet, 241
intersection
  implicit and implied, 135
  operators, 132–35, 168
Italic button, 34
iteration settings, 141

Johnson, Lyndon B., 203
Jonson, Ben, 33
Joyce, James, 281

Kafka, Franz, 118
Kahlil Gibran, 235
Kennedy, John F., 172
keystroke combinations
  ALT+ENTER, 64
  ALT+PAGE DOWN, 9
  ALT+PAGE UP, 9
  ALT+R, 114
  ALT+TAB, 121
  CTRL+' (back apostrophe), 49–50, 65, 157
  CTRL+C, 92
  CTRL+click, 11, 101, 261
  CTRL+AutoFill, 82–83
  CTRL+DOWN ARROW, 9
  CTRL+drag, 91, 132–33
  CTRL+END, 9, 147, 157–58, 160, 167
  CTRL+ENTER, 81, 127
  CTRL+ESC, 121
  CTRL+HOME, 9
  CTRL+INSERT, 92
  CTRL+key zap, 9
  CTRL+PAGE DOWN, 9
  CTRL+PAGE UP, 9
  CTRL+RIGHT ARROW, 9
  CTRL+SHIFT+arrow, 11, 87–88
  CTRL+SHIFT+ENTER, 136
  CTRL+V, 92
  CTRL+X, 92
  SHIFT+click, 7, 11, 261
  SHIFT+CTRL+HOME, 147
  SHIFT+drag-and-drop, 91
  SHIFT+ENTER, 64, 78, 79
  SHIFT+F2, 145, 156
  SHIFT+F9, 139
  SHIFT+TAB, 78, 79

Labels, 61, 98, 206–7, 210, 219
Lao-tzu, 130
Laplace, Pierre Simon de, 227
Lattimer, Dean, 113
Leonhard, Woody, 26, 70
LIFO inventory rule, 69
Light Shade button, 36
Light Shading button, 255
line feeds, 64
Links dialog, 262, 264, 277, 286
list(s), 203–26
  AutoFilter and, 206, 208, 211, 217–26, 234
  automatic outlining of, 225
  custom AutoFill, 83–84
  data forms used in, 205, 208–11
  definition of, 204
  deleting records in, 205, 209
  extremities, 206
  management features, 205
  MRU (most recently used) file list, 29, 238

multiple, in worksheets, 206
naming, 208
rules for, 205
size of, 206
sorting data in, 205–7, 211–16
subtotaling, 224–26
as "tactical weapons," 203
List Entries box, 83
loading
Add-ins, 246
on-demand, 196
Locked attribute, 252
logic testing, 150–51
Lotus, 2, 8, 119, 130, 168
Lowell, James R., 298
Lyly, John, 88

MacArthur, Douglas, 113
MacNeice, Louis, 116
MACROFUN.HLP, 289
macros, 52, 108–9, 251, 277, 289–90
creating, 22–26
dialog boxes and, 60, 305–9
editing, 294–95
recording, 293–94
running, 297–98
MACRO.XLT, 240–41
MAINXL.HLP, 290
Mann, Thomas, 211
MANUCALC.XLS, 140
margins, setting, 193, 195
marquees, 18, 123
Marx, Groucho, 106
=MAX(), 63
Maximize button, 182
Medawar, Peter Brian, 243
Melville, Herman, 257
memory, 45, 206, 223, 292
"Out of Memory" message, 5
random-access (RAM), 272–73, 282
section limitations and, 201
spreadsheet models and, 57
Menu Bar, getting help for, 19
Merge command button, 240
microprograms, 4
Milton, John, 284
=MIN(), 63
Minimize button, 121
"modeless behavior," 122–23
MODULE.XLT, 242
molecular programming, 3–4
Morley, Christopher, 216
mouse pointers, 13–18
Bi-directional Split Bar Grabber™, 14, 17
Drag-Copy Pointer™, 16, 18
Fill Handle Grabber™, 14, 16, 81, 179
Help Button Pointer™, 14, 17
Horizontal Sizing Grabber™, 14, 16–17, 56
Horizontal Split Bar Grabber™, 14, 16–17
I-Beam™, 14, 15, 88
Insertion Point™, 14, 15
No-Drop Zone Pointer™, 16, 18

Pointing Index Finger™, 14, 17
Selection Crosshair™, 14, 15, 87, 89
Sizing Grabber™, 55
Split Bar Grabber™, 56
Traditional Northwest Mouse Pointer™, 14, 15, 27, 87–89
Vertical Sizing Grabber™, 14, 16–17
Vertical Split Bar Grabber™, 14, 16–17
Zoom Pointer™, 16, 17
MRU (most recently used) file list, 29, 238
MSEXCEL forum, 290, 313, 315
multidimensional models, 46–47

Nagyrapolt, Albert von, 206
Name Box, 10, 12, 103, 94–95, 99, 100, 103, 106–7, 148
name(s), 93–109
3-D, 101–2
absolute range, 113–14
applying, 104–5
book-level, 99, 100, 101
built-in, 107
cell, 12, 94
classification, 146
column, 94, 97
creating, 94–95
default, 53
defining, 94–97
file, in the MRU list, 39
formulas in, 105–6
in formulas, 103–4
function, 125
jumping to named objects and, 95
list, 208
OLE object class, 276
and the 100-name limitation, 94
range, 12, 93–109, 113–14, 141, 192, 301–3
row, 94, 97
sheet-level, 99–101, 102
style, 175–76
using unique, 53
NameSetter() macro, 159, 161
Napier, Jack, 193
Nash, Ogden, 13
Natwick, Mildred, 169
navigating, 6–9, 10, 79, 296–97
New button, 21–23, 210
Nilsson, Harry, 162
Nixon, Richard M., 224
notes, 145–46, 156–57, 166–67
Now(), 126, 139
number(s)
cell content type, 60, 64–66
default sort order rules for, 213
displayed as text, 63–64
formats, custom, 177
settings, cell-level formatting and, 69, 70

Object Browser, 295, 296–97
Object option, 261, 268
objects, definition of, 264, 278, 292
Objects button, 167

ODBC (open database connectivity), 216–17, 218–19, 233, 290
OFFSET(), 139, 184
OLE (Object Linking and Embedding), 92, 257–85, 290. *See also* OLEAuto (OLE Automation)
  compound documents and, 258, 259
  converting embedded data and, 268
  dynamic link management feature, 277
  fields and, 259–64
  formatting objects and, 269–70
  functions and, 259–64
  handling broken links and, 277
  improved user interface of, 274–75
  in-place activation and, 265–70, 280, 282, 285
  intraaplication issues and, 270–71
  locking links and, 262
  managing links and, 261–62
  manual links and, 264
  nested embedding and, 278–81
  nested links and, 284–85
  object class names, syntax for, 276
  RAM and, 272–73, 282
  roving links and, 276–77
  scaling objects and, 269–70
  simple cell links and, 259–60
  sizing objects and, 269–70
  tips for, 286
  updating links and, 262–64
  video drivers and, 273
OLEAuto (OLE Automation), 287–88, 292–93, 296, 299–300, 309–10
On Error statements, 166
OnSheetActivate, 109
OnSheetDeactivate, 109
Open, 268
Open button, 21–22
operator(s)
  arithmetic, 130
  comparison, 130, 131
  intersection, 132–34, 168
  intersection reference, 131
  precedence rules, 117
  range, 131
  reference, 131
  symbols representing, 66
  text, 130
Options5= setting, 246
Options button, 173, 248
Options menu, 28, 194

Page setup, 28, 107, 193–97
  header and footer settings, 193, 195
  page breaks, 38
  page numbers, 201
palettes, floating, 177–78
parentheses, 116–18, 123, 125–26, 130, 131
parsing, intelligent text/data file, 227–28
passwords. *See also* security
  breaking, 253
  as optional, 250
  Protection Password, 247, 248, 249
  setting, 248–49

  syntax of, 248
  Write Reservation Password, 247–48, 249–50
Paste button, 29
Paste List button, 105
Paste Names, 30, 103–4, 106–7, 115, 194
paste operations, 29–30, 89–92, 132–33. *See also* cut and paste; Paste Names; Paste Special
Paste Special, 72–74, 132, 163, 261, 271
Pattern attributes, 207
Patterns settings, 69, 71
Percent button, 34–35
percentages
  scaling, 196
  using formulas in names and, 106
  zoom, 147–48, 197
period, 94, 96, 99
Person, Ron, 60
PERSONAL.XLS, 152, 157–58, 159, 160, 237, 238, 296
Petrarch, 273
pivot table, 107, 205–7, 226, 228–34
PivotTable, 226
PivotTable File button, 230
PivotTable Wizard, 207
Plato, 278
Plautus, 144
Play, 268
plus sign, 66, 130
pointers. *See* mouse pointers
point size, setting standard, 42
Pope, Alexander, 114
Portage button, 29
pound sign, 196
PowerPoint, 258
precedents, 152–53, 170
Precision as Displayed, 65
PRIME Consulting Group, 312, 315–16
Print_Area, 106, 107
Print_Area range name, 192, 193–94
Print Area text box, 107
Print button, 28–29, 191
printing, 171, 190–201, 256
  charts, 187
  display attributes and, 196–97
  freeze pane settings and, 196–97
  laser printers and, 187
  page numbers, 201
  print attributes and, 197
  previewing before, 28, 180, 192–93, 196
  range names and, 106–7
  rows and columns, 56, 107
  section limitations and, 201
  specified page ranges, 191, 192
Print Manager, 199, 200
print preview, 28, 180, 192–93, 196
Print Report, 199–200
Print_Titles, 107, 193, 194–95
Print What group box, 192
ProgMan Item Properties dialog box, 242–43
Program Manager, 19, 42, 242–43, 263, 286
Prompt for Summary Info box, 39
Protection settings, 69, 71

Quattro Pro, 6
Query, 216–19, 233
question mark, 6, 94, 96
quiting Excel, 121–22, 283
Quit method, 292

R1C1 notation style, 93, 111, 112–14, 160–62, 167, 170
RAND(), 139
range(s)
    criteria, 222–23
    filling data into, 80
    names, 12, 93–109, 113–14, 141, 192, 301–3
Read Only, 249
recap sheets, 46–47
Recently Used File List, 39
Recorder range name, 109
Remove All Arrows button, 155, 156
Remove Dependent Arrows button, 155
Remove Precedent Arrows button, 153, 155
Repeat button, 29
Report Manager, 199–201
Require Variable Declaration, 291
Reset TipWizard check box, 40
results
    converting cell contents to, 67
    definition of, 5
Right Mouse button, 85–86, 91
Rogers, Rutherford D., 203
Roosevelt, Theodore, 272
row(s)
    changing, 55–56
    the differences options and, 169–70
    formatting, 74–75
    frozen, 197
    header, 220–21
    height, 56, 75
    hidden, 56, 170, 198, 215
    labels, 98
    moving across by, 79
    naming, 94, 97
    printing, 107
ROWS(), 139
RptLines style, 177
Run Macro button, 297
Run Start, 297

SAMPLES.XLS, 289, 291
Sandburg, Carl, 293
Save As, 275
Save button, 21–22, 26, 52–53
Save Copy As, 274
saving
    calculating options, 139–40
    changes in lists, 210
    data files in binary file format, 258
    files to disk, 21–22
    new macros and buttons, 26–27
    OLE objects, 274–75, 286
    recalculating before, 139
    workbooks, 39–40, 51, 52–53, 121
    write-access files, 248

Scaling option, 196
Scenario drop-down list, 200–201
scroll bars
    expanded formula bars and, 78
    navigating and, 7
searching
    criteria, 210, 222–23
    for records in lists, 209–10, 221–23
security, 235, 246–53
    book-level protection, 250–51
    bypassing password protection, 253
    cell-level protection, 251–52
    controlling access to files, 247–48
    setting passwords, 248–49
    sheet-level protection, 251
semicolon, 6, 131
Sendak, Maurice, 237
serial date values, 65–66
Series, 80, 85
=SERIES(), 184–85
Serling, Rod, 185
Set Print Area button, 28–29, 106, 192–93
Sextus Propertius, 72
Shakespeare, William, 30, 61, 65, 258, 276
Shape palette, 255
Shape button, 32–33, 255
Shaw, George Bernard, 262
Sheet drop-down list, 200–201
Sheet filecard, 193
Sheets in New Workbook, 40
Sheet_Title range name, 108
sheet types, 52
SHEET.XLT, 240–41
Shelley, Percy Bysshe, 137
SHIFT+CTRL+HOME, 147
SHIFT+click, 7, 11, 261
SHIFT+drag-and-drop, 91
SHIFT+ENTER, 64, 78, 79
SHIFT+F2, 145, 156
SHIFT+F9, 139
Shift key, 11, 83, 87–88, 90, 238, 254–56
SHIFT+TAB, 78, 79
Show Info Window button, 156–57, 159
Simple Table Format, 173
Sort buttons, 30–32
Sort dialog, 207, 211, 215
sorting
    capitalization and, 206, 207
    column labels and, 206–7
    data in lists, 205–7, 211–16
    default order rules for, 213–14
    range names and, 102–3
    tips, 214–15
    tailer-made orders for, 215–16
SOURCE.DOC, 276
Spell button, 28–29
Split Bar, getting help for, 19
starting Excel, 42, 151, 242–46
Status Bar
    getting help for, 19
    turning off, 38
Stockman, David, 2
Stop Recording button, 22

strings
    joining, 61–62
    text, definition of, 61
    wrapping, 64
Structure option, 251
styles, 33–34, 69–70, 161, 176, 240
SUM, 131, 229
=SUM, 159, 162
=SUM(), 63
SUMIF(), 225
summary information, 39–41, 231
SuperAutoEntry™, 79, 88
symbols
    & (ampersand), 61–62
    ' (apostrophe), 6, 120, 214
    * (asterisk), 6, 66, 130, 249
    @ (at symbol), 177
    \ (backslash), 6, 94, 96
    ^ (caret), 130
    , (comma), 131
    {} (curly braces), 136–38
    $ (dollar sign), 113, 114, 130, 175, 176
    = (equal sign), 66, 125, 130
    ! (exclamation point), 99
    () (parentheses), 116–17, 118, 123, 125–26, 130, 131
    . (period), 94, 96, 99
    + (plus sign), 66, 130
    # (pound sign), 196
    ? (question mark), 6, 94, 96
    : (semicolon), 6, 131
    _ (underscore character), 94, 95, 98, 177
system modal, definition of, 122

Tab key, 6–7, 79, 152, 167, 252
Table Formats, 173–74
Tarkington, Booth, 273
template(s), 235–42
    creating, 236–37
    definition of, 236
    managing styles in, 240
    multiple, 238–42
    password-protected, 249
    precedence, 237
Tennyson, Alfred Lord, 146, 253, 289
test computers, 282
TEXT(), 214
text boxes, 32–33
    creating, 254
    number of characters contained in, 96–97
Text cell content type, 60, 61–64
Text Note edit box, 146
text operators, 130
text strings, definition of, 61
TextWizard, 227–28
Thurber, James, 178
TipWizard, 40, 44–46
Title Bar, getting help for, 19
TODAY(), 139
Toggle Grid button, 36, 39
toolbar(s)
    Auditing, 47–50, 151–57, 166
    AutoFill settings, 37

Chart, 180
    default options for, 37–42
    displaying all, 20
    floating palettes and, 177–78
    Formatting, 21, 33–37, 255–56
    getting help for, 20
    mini-, 177–78, 255
    Pivot, 230
    Query, 230
    settings, storing, 37
    Standard, 20–37, 43, 103, 106, 191, 192, 238–39
    TipWizard, 21, 44–46
    turning on and off, 21
    Visual Basic, 293
Tools Macro, 298
Tools Macro Run, 297
Tools menu, 26, 38
Tools Options, 138–39
Tools Options Calculation, 65, 67, 141
Tools Options Custom Lists, 215
Tools Options Edit, 77, 78, 262
Tools Options General, 45
Tools/Options/General dialog box, 40
Tools Options Transition, 298–99
Tools Options View, 156, 196–97
Tools Protection Protect Sheet, 251–52
Tools Protection Protect Workbook, 250
Tools Protection Unprotect Workbook, 251
Tools Record Macro, 109
Trace Dependents button, 154, 170
Trace Errors button, 155–56
Trace Precedents button, 48–49, 152–53, 170
Transition Navigation Keys, 298–99
true and false values, 76, 126, 130–31
Tufte, Edward R., 59, 178–79
Twain, Mark, 169

Underline button, 34
underscore character, 34, 94, 95, 98, 117
Undo button, 29
updating, 286
    documenting, 144
    OLE and, 262–64, 283
    views, 198
Updike, John, 270
User Name box, 42
User= setting, 246

Valéry, Paul, 222
"vanishing formula" syndrome, 49–50
VBA (Visual Basic for Applications), 59, 125, 140,
    142, 287–310
    adding range names and, 301–3
    the Auditing toolbar and, 151–52
    checking Module Settings for, 291–92
    data typing conventions and, 291
    debugging tools, 298
    explicit declaration and, 292
    the Go To Special dialog box and, 165–66
    "If...Then...Else" construct, 166
    lists and, 210, 216

navigating in, 296–97
object.method form, 292, 300
object.property form, 300
OLEAuto (OLE Automation) and, 287–88, 292–93,
    296, 299–300, 309–10
range names and, 108–9
splitting panes and, 294–95
toolkit, 290
Tools Options Transition filecard, 298–99
Transition Navigation Keys check box, 298–99
Underground Toolbar Lister example, 298, 305–9
user-defined functions and, 303–5
WordBasic portability, 305–6
XLM and, 289, 290
Vernon, William, 236
video drivers, 273
View drop-down list, 200–201
View filecard, 38–39
View Manager, 196, 196, 197–99
View menu, 21, 43, 197
View Next button, 209
View Previous button, 209
Virchow, Rudolf, 94
Visible Cells Only option, 170
Visual Basic for Applications (VBA). *See* VBA
    (Visual Basic for Applications)
Visual Basic Module, 52, 59–60
volatile functions, 139

Wells, Eric, 313
Whitman, Walt, 296
wildcard characters, 221, 223
Wilson, Edward O., 312
WIN.INI, 243
Window menu, 24–25, 156
windows, hidden, 260, 263
Windows option, 251
WinWord, 2, 22, 24–27, 34, 309–10
  auditing and, 166
  bookmark feature, 93
  breaking passwords in, 253
  clipboard, 90
  compound documents and, 258
  DDE and, 287
  default document names and, 53
  drag-and-drop in, 90
  multilevel undo's and, 29
  OLE and, 259–60, 262–63, 266–67, 269–72, 274, 276–77,
      279–81, 283–85
  printing and, 191
  templates and, 235

VBA and, 288
zooming and, 43, 44
Woolf, Virginia, 59
WordArt, 266–67, 269, 279–81
WordBasic, 305–6
workbook(s)
  calculating, 138–42
  creating, 21–22
  default, 239, 241
  definition of, 5, 51–60
  empty, 41
  number of bytes consumed by, 41
  opening existing, 21–22
  saving, 39–40, 51, 52–53
  storage of, 51
  templates and, moving styles between, 240
  viewing a list of all sheets in, 6
worksheet(s), 53–60
  building, 55–58
  copying, 7
  default, 241, 246
  definition of, 52
  deleting, 7
  drag-and-drop within, 89, 91–92
  empty, 3, 4–5
  flipping, 157–59, 161, 167
  functions, three parts of, 125–26
  inserting, 53–54
  making templates as models for inserted, 240–41
  printing, 190–201
  recalculating current, 139
  size of, 3, 5
  spreadsheet modeling on, 57–58
  toggled between A1 and R1C1, 160–62
Wrap Text property, 75
write-access, 248, 250
Wurman, Richard Saul, 187

XL5TOP.EXE, 290
XLM macro programming language, 60, 108–9,
    289, 290
XLOBJ.DOC, 290
XLSTART, 42, 237, 238, 246

Zap technique, 8–9
Zoom Control, 33, 43–44
zooming, 33, 42–44, 168
  displaying charts and, 180
  percentages, 147–48, 197
  printing and, 197

Also available from Addison-Wesley in The Underground Series

THE UNDERGROUND GUIDE TO WORD FOR WINDOWS™
Slightly Askew Advice from a WinWord Wizard

— Woody Leonhard —

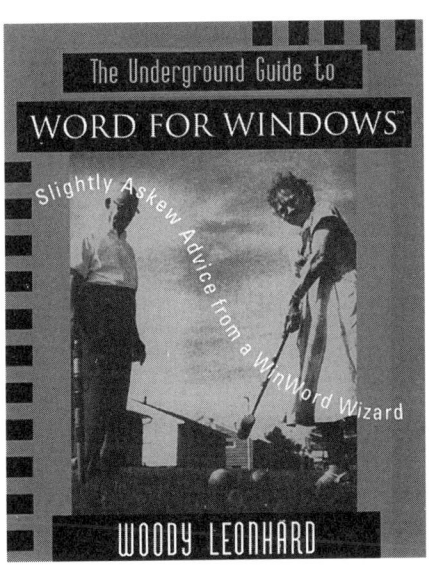

*T*he *Underground Guide to Word for Windows*™ is the story the official books dare not tell. In his famous, irreverent, off-the-wall style, Woody Leonhard takes you on a guided tour of WinWord's dark underside, telling you what works, what doesn't, and how to get the most out of WinWord. You'll learn how to customize WinWord's appearance to turn it into a lean, mean, word-processing machine, recognize and avoid the most common species of WinWord bugs, and much more. Every page is packed with immediately useful information, advice, warnings, tips, and workarounds for everyone who loves to use and abuse WinWord.

$19.95, paperback, 336 pages
ISBN 0-201-40650-0

ORDER INFORMATION

Available wherever computer books are sold or call Addison-Wesley at 1-800-358-4566 in the United States. Outside of the U.S. call your local Addison-Wesley office.

Addison-Wesley books are available at special discounts for bulk purchases by corporations, institutions, and other organizations. For more information, please contact our Corporate, Government, and Special Sales Department at 1-800-238-9682.

PRIME 5 for Excel

SPECIAL $5 DISCOUNT FOR
UNDERGROUND GUIDE READERS

As you read through this tome, perhaps you took mental inventory of the bug graphics in the margins and wondered, "Gee, is there a solution to any of the problems posed by these pesky varmints?" Indeed there is, and its name is *PRIME 5 for Excel*.

Throughout our Underground tour we offered you our best tips, we pointed out the most offensive and time-wasting bugs, and now we're offering you a panacea. Well, maybe not a complete panacea, but certainly a shareware add-in that addresses many of Excel's, er, uhm, shortcomings, and that takes many of Excel's good features and makes 'em even better! We're offering utilities like *View Manager Assistant* to track the current view. *Window Manager* for one-stop window management. *Toolbar Lister* for inspecting toolbar contents. *Zoomer, Macro Manager, Note Manager, Locked Cell Flipper, ProgMan Icon Generator, custom VBA subroutines and functions*, et cetera.

All this from your Underground tour guides. If you place an order and mention that you're an Underground Guide reader you'll get $5.00 off the list price of $39.95 (plus $4.50 shipping and handling in the USA and Canada; $9.50, all other countries). In keeping with a standard set by Woody Leonhard and the folks at Pinecliffe International, all our shareware add-in products—including *PRIME 5 for Excel for Windows* and *PRIME 6 for Word for Windows*—come with an unlimited, lifetime, no-questions-asked, 100% money-back guarantee. You absolutely can't go wrong. If you don't like *PRIME 5*, send it back, tell us what you paid for it, and we'll rush you a full refund. We promise. Hacker's honor.

PRIME Consulting Group, Inc.
c/o Advanced Support Group, Inc.
11900 Grant Place
Des Peres, Missouri USA 63131

Voice: 800-788-0787, (314-965-5630 outside North America)
Fax: 314-966-1833
CompuServe: 70304,3642 or GO WOPR